Balanced
Budgets
& American
Politics

Balanced Budgets & American Politics

JAMES D. SAVAGE

Cornell University Press

Ithaca and London

CORNELL UNIVERSITY PRESS GRATEFULLY ACKNOWLEDGES
A GRANT FROM THE ANDREW W. MELLON FOUNDATION
THAT AIDED IN BRINGING THIS BOOK TO PUBLICATION.

First published 1988 by Cornell University Press.
First published, Cornell Paperbacks, 1990.

International Standard Book Number 0-8014-2047-4 (cloth)
International Standard Book Number 0-8014-9775-2 (paper)
Library of Congress Catalog Card Number 87-25061

Printed in the United States of America.

*Librarians: Library of Congress cataloging information
appears on the last page of the book.*

⊛ The paper in this book meets the minimum requirements
of the American National Standard for Information Sciences
—Permanence of Paper for Printed Library Materials, ANSI
Z39.48-1984.

For Celia
and
My Mother, Naomi

Contents

List of Tables
and Figures

Figures

Preface

This book attempts to identify the source of the concern for balancing budgets in American political history, to outline its development from 1690 to 1984, and, above all, to examine how the idea of balancing the federal budget influenced American politics, public policy, and the evolution of relevant political and economic institutions.

This research began at the University of California, Berkeley, in 1980. At the time the principal domestic political issue was the nation's accelerating inflation rate that was brutalizing the economy. Both Jimmy Carter and Ronald Reagan, as well as countless other politicians, traced the cause of this inflation to the budget deficits of the federal government. Although their programs for achieving the result differed significantly, Carter and Reagan agreed that balancing the budget was the first and most important step in aiding the economy. Yet the empirical economic literature, produced by economists of both conservative and liberal orientation, convinced me that only a tenuous link existed, if there was any at all, between these deficits and inflation. If this was indeed the case, how did the subject of balancing the budget become perhaps the preeminent issue in American politics?

To answer this question I initially narrowed the scope of my study to examine how Ronald Reagan, the newly elected president, employed the balanced budget issue as a rhetorical device and as a guide to his controversial budget policies. In addition to considering the economics of deficit spending, I intended to precede this rather straightforward political science analysis with a very brief historical statement on the role the balanced budget issue played in previous elections and presidencies, by drawing on the standard works in the field by such researchers as Herbert Stein and Lewis Kimmel. Summarizing Kimmel, for example, whose work traced federal budget policy back to 1789, I thought would be sufficient for my purposes. But even Kimmel's useful study left me unsatisfied. Despite its many virtues, it had not revealed the circumstance that accounted for the special place of the balanced budget issue in American political life.

To satisfy my curiosity, I resolved to dig deeper into the nation's past to identify the source of this enduring concern for balancing the budget. As a result, my research focused less on Ronald Reagan and more on the events that preceded him. By examining the conditions that generated and led to the persistence of the balanced budget issue, we may better understand not only the Reagan presidency but a subject that is seemingly eternal to American politics and political thought.

I am deeply indebted to many people for their assistance and encouragement during the years it took to complete this work. I benefited greatly from the wisdom and guidance of Nelson W. Polsby, Allan P. Sindler, Aaron B. Wildavsky, and James L. Pierce. I have learned much about American politics and political economy from these gentlemen. William K. Muir, Jr., and Charles Sellers provided me with valuable comments on the early American history chapters. Henry Brady contributed a careful reading of my research design. Eugene C. Lee and the Institute of Governmental Studies granted me a much-needed fellowship and travel budget. Joanne Hurley allowed me access to her personal notes and assisted me in obtaining several important interviews. Gregory Grossman taught the inspiring economics course that precipitated this study.

Victor Magagna, who knew as much about my research as I did, patiently listened and made invaluable suggestions while I outlined my research strategy. John Gilmour, Mark Westlye, and Joseph White were always ready to talk about budgets and read sections of my manuscript.

Charles Stewart III generously read the complete manuscript, and through his helpful comments he provided me with a better understanding of Gilded Age budgeting.

Thomas J. Cohagan, in conversations too numerous to count, forced me to clarify my thoughts on the role of the state in society.

Without the goodwill of my colleagues in the Office of the President, University of California systemwide administration, who tolerated my strange academic hours, this study would have become an intolerable burden. William Baker, Carl Bovell, Belle Cole, Joanne Hurley, Jesse Shaw, Susan Spitz, David Wilson, and Judith Woodard made this task an easier one.

I received encouragement and intellectual stimulation from a number of close friends: Carlos Bolanos, Linda and Leigh Barker, Lee Berrigan, Linda Cohagan, Dennis Frieda, Robert John Hodge, Randy Lert, Stephen McDougal, George Putris, Rick Robins, Jeffrey and Susan Shaffer, Nancy Schneider, Allan Schwartz, and William Work III.

Peter Agree of Cornell University Press reviewed and processed this manuscript in a most timely and efficient manner. Adrienne Mayor strengthened the manuscript through her careful editing.

Jacqueline Cisneros, my friend and confidante, dutifully typed the manuscript after long days at work at her regular job.

In addition to being a loving friend, my mother, Naomi, helped introduce me to politics when I was at a young and tender age.

Finally, this book is in part dedicated to Celia Politeo, who engaged me with her interest in nineteenth-century American thought and who, more importantly, gave me her love and companionship during the years it took to write this book. I am most grateful.

JAMES D. SAVAGE

Berkeley, California

Balanced Budgets & American Politics

1

Balanced Budgets and Symbolic Politics

> The victories and defeats, the compromises and the bargains, the realms of agreement and the spheres of conflict in regard to the role of national government in our society all appear in the budget.
>
> AARON WILDAVSKY, 1979

From the earliest days of the republic the idea of balancing the federal government's budgets has played a central role in American political life. In the name of balanced budgets, early American history was marked by deep political divisions that distinguished friend from foe on such issues as banking, economic development, taxation, currency, and states' rights. Since the Great Depression, the nation's two major political parties remain embattled over the issue of deficit spending, as they argue about how the presence of balanced or unbalanced budgets influences the economy or determines spending priorities. Yet this modern concern for the economics of deficit spending or the outcome of a given year's budget battle often obscures how the idea of balanced budgets acts as a standard and reflects political values that extend beyond, say, an accounting interpretation of such a matter. The subject of balanced budgets refers not only to whether the central government's ledger should be balanced, but to broader issues such as the makeup of federal spending, the direction of fiscal policy, the legitimacy and extent of the federal government's intervention in the economy, and to the central question of what role the national government should play in American life. In this fashion, the balanced budget idea serves as an organizing principle that guides public policy and public discourse and acts as a symbol for competing visions of government and society in a manner unique to American politics.

At first glance, the federal budget's instrumental and economic effects presumably account for the historically compelling nature of the bal-

1

anced budget idea. The federal government's budget allocates scarce public resources to large numbers of citizens, and related tax policies determine just who shall provide those resources. By distributing goods and services, budgets fundamentally determine political winners and losers. Interested groups and politicians consequently pay great attention to budgetary deliberations and to rules altering the budgetary process. In addition, the federal budget is considered to have a significant influence on the economy. During the 1970s, for instance, numerous political leaders, Wall Street executives, and news media commentators regularly proclaimed that, depending on the economic malady suffered by the nation at the time, federal deficit spending brought havoc to the economy by producing various combinations of double-digit inflation, high interest rates, and the crowding out of private investment. This anxiety about the economic consequences of large and persistent federal deficits reflected disenchantment with the Keynesian and neo-Keynesian economic theories that justified large-scale peacetime deficit spending. Within their conceptual frameworks, these theories seemed unable to explain the workings of stagflation, with its combination of high inflation and unemployment, or to provide the country with a remedy for its economic afflictions. Taken by themselves, however, these instrumental and economic interpretations of the federal budget fail to explain the persistence of the balanced budget principle as a singularly American institutional value.

Governments of all nations allocate material benefits, but the United States historically has been influenced by a normative concern for balanced national budgets that is truly distinct, one that is grounded in political philosophy and political economy, rather than in some fiscal or purely financial interest. This fact becomes evident when the economic argument against deficit spending is considered. Although the defenders of Keynesian and neo-Keynesian economics were perplexed by the stagflated economy of the 1970s, the best empirically based research available indicates that deficit spending had at most a minor effect on the crowding out of private investment and little or no influence on interest rates or inflation. Indeed, as will be shown, even Ronald Reagan's massive deficits incurred from fiscal year (FY) 1982 through FY 1984 proved to help rather than hinder the economy. Moreover, while the political debate in the United States during the 1970s and early 1980s focused on deficit spending, Japan and most Western European nations frequently ran deficits larger than America's, measured as a proportion of their Gross National Product (GNP).[1] At the same time, these economies appeared to be free from stagflation. In the case of Japan, that country ran significantly larger deficits but experienced higher levels of productivity and economic growth than the United States. More important, in these countries the subject of balanced and unbalanced budgets did not reach the center stage of daily political discussion.[2]

The American fascination with the idea of balancing the central government's budget is deeply rooted and reflects more than a contemporary concern about interest rates, inflation, or even the outcome of some recent budget battle. Economist Herbert Stein intimated as much, when he wrote in his book, *The Fiscal Revolution in America*, "The idea that government budgets should be balanced had a great deal of force in popular thinking and in the thinking of leaders of government, business, and finance. . . . The budget balancing principle left considerable room for maneuvering, but that it was inhibition to some degree is undeniable."[3] Stein was referring to the politics and policies of Herbert Hoover's administration, but what he had to say applies equally well to any period of American history. Whether called a balanced budget "principal" or "idea," since the early nineteenth century public policy in the United States has been influenced by a budget balancing tradition that originally incorporated rather than supplemented daily instrumental and economic considerations.

The source of this budget balancing principle has often been suggested to be a combination of concerns or themes, which through their cumulative influence produced a budget balancing tradition that encouraged, or coerced, federal officials into balancing the budget. Among these concerns is the common notion that people somehow consider the federal budget as similar to their own finances, so that deficit spending is regarded as an overdrawn checking account or a defaulted personal line of credit. Other explanations include the notion that citizens see deficit spending as synonymous with administrative inefficiency, or they believe public debt to be an immoral "burden" resting on the backs of future generations. In each case the public is said to demand a balanced budget to promote, say, bureaucratic efficiency or to prevent the intergenerational burden. More ambitious efforts at tracing the source of the budget balancing principle have located its origins in the Enlightenment; the influence of Newtonian physics with its emphasis on balance and harmony is suggested as a factor in the design of eighteenth- and nineteenth-century budgets.[4] webber

These assorted reasons for balancing the budget provide at best a partial explanation of the popularity for the budget balancing principle or tradition to which Stein and others refer. If indeed notions, for instance, of budgets-as-personal-finance or Newtonian balance played an important if not decisive role in creating the balanced budget principle, then some degree of uniformity should appear in cross-national budgetary and debt management policies. Instead, by the time of the American Civil War every major European power, particularly those influenced by the Enlightenment, had incurred debt loads ranging from three to eleven times the magnitude of the combined American federal and state debts.[5] Furthermore, the desire to keep the federal debt in check stemmed largely from the repugnance with which most Americans regarded the foreign debt. In a more current setting, despite the fact that Japan ran deficits in 1979 and 1980 that were larger as a proportion of GNP than even Ronald Reagan's FY 1983 $195 billion deficit, other nations still requested that Japan increase the size of its deficit spending.[6] The balanced budget principle that influenced American politics and developed into a "tradition" was uniquely an American concern, one that emerged from a strikingly coherent interpretation of political economy which had little to do with views that budgets corresponded to personal finance or that all public sector deficits and debts were inherently evil.

This book traces the source of the budget balancing principle in American political history, outlines its evolution over time, and examines how the idea of balancing the federal budget influenced American politics, public policy, and the development of relevant political and economic institutions.

This principle was first applied to the federal government's budgets during the political conflict that took place between Thomas Jefferson and Alexander Hamilton in the period shortly after the Constitution's ratification. The balanced budget idea, embodied in the concept of "corruption," guided public policy not only on budgetary matters but also on such related issues as administrative growth, "internal improvements," the nature of currency, banking, tariffs, national defense, and especially federal-state relations. Borrowed from classical and English political thought, the concept of corruption became uniquely American through its particular understanding of federalism, which objected to unbalanced federal budgets but tolerated those occurring at the state level. By balancing the federal budget the Jeffersonian Republicans, and later the Jacksonian Democrats, believed they were saving the young republic's agrarian democracy from the "corruption" that a national debt and unbalanced budgets would promote. Meanwhile, state debt was accepted, even encouraged. This concept of corruption and the budget balancing ideas that followed, such as the Progressives' understanding of balanced budgets and administrative efficiency, the neo-Keynesian full-employment budget, and Ronald Reagan's notion of structural deficits, played a central role in American state building and economic development.

The span of American history examined here extends further into the past than Jefferson's feud with Hamilton. The first deficit spending by a major unit of government in the New World occurred in 1690, and the colonies' ongoing experience with public debt served as a factor in their drive for independence. Moreover, in reaction to the long-term use of deficit spending, the Constitutional Convention debated and adopted provisions in the governing document which prohibited deficit spending, as it was known at the time, by specified levels of government. Consequently, the belief that deficit spending was essentially unknown to the American people prior to the Great Depression, and the opinion that a consitutional amendment requiring balanced federal budgets "would undermine the fundamental understanding of our Founding Fathers that precise economic and fiscal rules would not be incorporated into the Constitution," are false.[7] Accordingly, the period of American political economy reviewed here covers the years 1690 through 1984.

Budgets have symbolic as well as instrumental or economic properties, and the idea of a balanced budget is far from being a neutral symbol. Thomas Anton has pointed out that during budgetary deliberations political leaders ascribed to their budgeting activities certain qualities, such that "the budget, as document and process, creates symbolic satisfaction built upon the idea that affairs of state are being dealt with, that responsibility is being exercised, and that rationality prevails."[8] Budget reductions, Anton said, symbolized "a popular check on government excess," whereas balanced budgets signified "prudent management" and increased expenditures suggested the government's improved "service" to the public.[9] According to Anton, political actors employed budgetary symbolism, regardless of its true instrumental or tangible relation to government programs and services, in order to justify political decisions, to enhance the politician's role and standing as a lawmaker, and to communicate policy to constituents. Politicians do indeed refer to budgets in the manner Anton described. Yet the balanced budget principle possesses symbolic meaning of broader proportions than either simple "prudent management" or what might be called an accountant's interpretation of budgetary balance.

Throughout American history, balanced and unbalanced federal budgets have served as powerful and politically evocative symbols of competing visions of government and society. Used in this manner, a symbol by definition stands for, represents, or denotes a material or abstract object as being an idea, quality, or condition.[10] In the American context, balanced budgets originally assumed their symbolic characteristics in the years of Jeffersonian and Jacksonian democracy. A balanced national budget signified a popular willingness and ability to limit the purpose and size of the federal government, to restrain its influence in the economy, to protect states' rights, to maintain the Constitution's balance of powers, and to promote republican virtue. The absence of deficits, unnecessary surpluses, and debt implied that the forces of "corruption" which sought to strengthen the federal government's authority were restrained, whereas the Jeffersonian and Jacksonian vision of a political economy of small agrarian producers prospered. A balanced budget symbolized the preservation of republican government in a postrevolutionary world, not merely a distribution of resources or simple administrative efficiency.

The budgetary symbolism invoked in the early nineteenth century continued to have effect well into modern American political life. After Jefferson and Jackson, no politician could consider federal budgets to be dispassionate instrumental or economic concerns. Balanced and unbalanced federal budgets became symbolically meaningful in a uniquely American fashion, and the public desire for balanced budgets was sufficiently powerful to constrain political action. If, for example, the Jeffersonians and Jacksonians sought to restrain the national government, the Gilded Age Republicans acted to expand its powers, but they were forced to do so while operating within the confines of the balanced budget principle. How the Republican party of the late nineteenth and early twentieth centuries achieved its vision of a greatly strengthened national government while proclaiming the virtues of a balanced federal budget is a fascinating and crucial chapter in American nation and state building. These Republicans preserved a semblance of the balanced budget idea, eventually substituting the Jeffersonian and Jacksonian interpretation with the Progressives' symbolic inference that balanced budgets enabled the federal government's authority to grow in an orderly, bureaucratically efficient, but limited manner. It was this symbolic and historic legacy that Franklin Roosevelt had to overcome in order to set aside the target of balancing the budget during the Depression, and that later the New Frontier and Great Society Democrats struggled against when they introduced the idea of the full-employment budget.

For Ronald Reagan, balancing the federal budget symbolized the "renewal" of "constitutional government," which would restrict the federal government's authority by decentralizing the national government's powers and constraining its ability to increase domestic expenditures. Drawing its strength from the nation's distinctive political culture, which Aaron Wildavsky described as the public's "shared values and special practices," Reagan's budgetary symbolism provided the Republican party with a rallying cry for the mobilization of popular support for the president's unusual brand of fiscal policy.[11] Considered from this perspective, Ronald Reagan's symbolism may be better understood as a guide to his public policy and political ideology, rather than as a "nonrational" device to "boost self-esteem," as some analysis has suggested.[12]

The balanced budget's symbolism exhibits a remarkable degree of continuity in the "visions" that have guided American politics. Historians and political scientists as diverse as Louis Hartz, Charles and Mary Beard, Arthur Schlesinger, Jr., Bruce Palmer, R. Jeffrey Lustig, and Leonard D. White have made the distinction between what is called Jeffersonian and Hamiltonian government.[13] Briefly, Jeffersonian government refers to restrained federal authority, decentralized political power favoring the states and local governments, and limited federal intervention in the economy. Hamiltonian government describes an enhanced federal authority, reduced state and local powers, and federal promotion of the economy. At the same time, Jeffersonian government strives to achieve a form of social equality that allows a "natural aristocracy" to emerge, whereas Hamiltonian government seeks to aid the forces of social hierarchy. As Leslie Lipson observed, variations of the Jeffersonian and Hamiltonian notions of government permeate the American scene: "It is remarkable that the dialectic between these opposites evolved so early in American history. For much of the subsequent politics of the United States can be interpreted in terms of the conflict between these outlooks and the attempts to synthesize them."[14] The balanced budget principle arose from the conflict separating these two visions of government, and it continues to distinguish between them, and attempts at synthesis, in the world of contemporary politics.

Chapter 2 of this study of balanced budgets and American politics asks the question "What has been the effect of federal deficit spending on the economy during approxiamtely the last two decades?" Relying upon various empirical economic studies and the observations of prominent economists, the chapter concludes that the harmful consequences attributed to deficits have been overstated, and that a strictly economic interpretation of deficit spending fails to account for the nation's preoccupation with the balanced budget issue. The remaining chapters seek to provide a more complete explanation.

Chapter 3 examines the period from 1690 through the creation of the Constitution, indicating the extensive role deficits and debt played in colonial finance and in the deliberations that shaped the Constitution. Chapter 4 describes how the concept of corruption and balanced budgets divided Jeffersonians from the Hamiltonians, and later the Jacksonians from the Whigs.[15] This crucial period in American history, extending to the Civil War, forever sensitized the nation to the balanced budget principle. Chapter 5 demonstrates how the balanced budget principle, diverted from its Jeffersonian and Jacksonian intent, enabled the Republican party in the post–Civil War, pre–Great Depression years to enhance federal powers far beyond what the original Republican and Democratic parties considered permissible. Contrary to the argument often made that serious nation and state building began during the New Deal and that there existed a mythic "nineteenth-century ideal" of an undifferentiated and limited federal authority, this chapter suggests that the post–Civil War period was an equally if not more important transition phase.[16]

Chapter 6 enters the more recent period of the New Deal, New Frontier, and Great Society years, in which the Democrats attempted to replace the older balanced budget tradition with a new symbolic understanding of balance offered by the idea of the full-employment budget. The Carter administration's retreat from this effort left the Democratic party in search of a vision to guide it into the future. Chapter 7 traces the role balanced budget symbolism has played during the Reagan presidency, showing how the politics of the balanced budget can help explain the victories and failures of both the Reagan administration and the Democratic party. The great paradox of the Reagan years is how the president employed the largest deficits in the nation's history to further his particular vision of government and society. Appendix 1 outlines the development of state debts and off-budget spending from the Civil War years to 1984. Appendix 2 provides a detailed summary of the budget battles that took place during Reagan's first term. Appendix 3 lists federal expenditures, revenues, and debt from 1789 through 1984.

2

The Economics of Deficit Spending

As a strong supporter of a constitutional amendment
requiring the federal government to balance its budget and
limit spending, I clearly share the aversion to deficits that
politicians of all shades of opinion have been expressing so
loudly. But my reasons are quite different from theirs. In my
view, the key question to deficits is political, not economic.
The economic harm attributed to deficits—whether high
interest rates, inflation or economic stagnation—comes not
from the deficits but from the high level of government
spending that those deficits help to finance.

MILTON FRIEDMAN, 1984

The matter of the federal government's deficit spending has been discussed almost exclusively in terms of what effect the deficits might have
on the American economy. Certainly since the last year of the Carter
administration, the nation's news media, its political leaders, and corporate executives speculated on a daily basis about how interest rates,
inflation, and private investment activities would be influenced by the
latest forecast on the size of the deficit. These speculative efforts proved
to be quite remarkable for their never-ending inaccuracy. Time and again
the government's deficits took the blame for the economic consequences
of the Federal Reserve's attempt to stimulate the economy and then
control the country's inflationary tendencies. These various observers
first claimed deficit spending created the double-digit inflation of 1979
and 1980. Yet when the inflation diminished, the deficits were said to be
responsible for the very same high interest rates that cut the inflation rate
in half. Then the speculators declared that the government's growing
deficits would prevent economic recovery. Instead, the deficits not only
lessened the effects of recession during 1982, they also stimulated the
economy's recovery in 1983. By the end of Ronald Reagan's first term as

9

president, most empirically based economists agreed that federal deficit spending during the preceding half-century produced primarily a salutary, or at worst a benign, effect in the economy.

As a result of this inaccurate, panic-induced, and often self-serving speculation, the public has been left confused, uninformed, and largely unable to distinguish between economically harmful and beneficial deficit spending. Moreover, because of this overwhelmingly economic interpretation of deficit spending, the political aspects of the federal government's balanced and unbalanced budgets have been relegated to studies of the machinations inherent in the budgetary process, or to more speculation about which political party possesses the "will" to reduce the federal deficit. In order to establish the broader, political importance of balanced and unbalanced federal budgets, a review of the economics of deficit spending is needed to separate economic fact from fiction.

Did the federal government's deficit spending produce inflation during the years 1965 through 1984? Did these deficits cause interest rates to rise, and did they limit private investment? How justified were the fears many Americans expressed about the supposed economically unsettling effects of the government's deficits? This chapter reviews the economic effects of the federal government's deficit spending from 1965 to 1984. By surveying the most authoritative empirical research and by examining the statements made by the nation's foremost economists, we may reach a summary judgment about the five most common and important objections offered against employing deficits as economic policy instruments. The argument presented here suggests that regardless of whatever economic consequences the Reagan deficits produce in the budgetary "out-years" of FY 1990 and beyond, the government's deficit spending through FY 1984 acted as a valuable tool in the nation's economic stabilization efforts. Once the economic effects of deficit spending are evaluated, the issue of the federal government's balanced and unbalanced budgets may be examined for its meaning in terms of political economy.

Deficits and the Economy

Regardless of their school of thought, most leading economists expressed their doubt or outright rejection of the position that prior to 1984 the government's deficits produced the harmful effects in the economy, as so often claimed by various political leaders. Particularly before President Reagan took office, many economists considered deficit spending to be "symbolic" or that deficits represented a lack of administrative efficiency in the bureaucracy. But balanced budgets by themselves were not thought to cure inflation, nor would unbalanced budgets cause inflation. For instance, in December 1980 four American Nobel Prize winners in economics expressed their views on the need to balance the federal budget:

"When it comes to the U.S. budget," said Paul Samuelson, "the issue of whether the budget is one pfennig out of balance or two pfennigs in balance is an ideological and symbolic one." Added Lawrence Klein, "Forcing the federal government to have a balanced budget is good discipline. It's a way to enforce efficiency in the operation of the bureaucracy, so we should aim for it as a goal. But a balanced budget is not particularly useful as a symbol of the fight against inflation or as a guide for whether we're operating the macroeconomy appropriately." "On the budget, it is not essential to balance it. It's much more important that government spending be lowered as a share of national income," claimed Milton Friedman. "There is no good theory showing that budget deficits are a problem as far as inflation is concerned," Kenneth Arrow declared, "and certainly not deficits of the size we have now. They really are modest in the overall economy."[1] To understand why these economists disagreed with the view widely held in 1980 that deficits were the principal cause of inflation, and how economists continued to regard deficit spending, it is necessary to explore Arrow's point about how deficits are relative to the entire economy, and how often and why they occur.

By 1932 a third of all federal budgets contained deficits, despite the moral, ideological, and pragmatic pressures faced by the nation's political leaders to balance the budget before the rise of the welfare state. Since 1932, of course, the record is much different; only eight of the subsequent fifty-two budgets were balanced. At least fifteen of these contemporary deficits were primarily the result of America's involvement in World War II, Korea, and Vietnam, specifically the deficits for the fiscal years 1942–46, 1952–53, 1966–68, and 1970–75. Though surpluses were recorded in the fiscal years 1960, 1961, and 1969, deficit spending since 1970 has become chronic.[2] These "chronic" deficits remain unrelieved by surpluses and they tend to be at least "double-digit" and then "triple-digit" in magnitude.

Although this record of deficit spending may not be considered enviable, one of the more interesting facts about these deficits is that while they grew in size and increased in frequency, until the large FY 1983 deficit the overall economy grew at least as fast as the deficits. In other words, deficit spending as a proportion of the GNP remained at a somewhat constant level during most of the last twenty years (see Table 1). Between FY 1965 and FY 1982 deficit spending averaged only 2 percent of GNP. Deficits grew larger in the last fourteen years indicated in Table 1, yet they still averaged just 2.3 percent from FY 1965 through FY 1984. The deficits actually decreased in size between FY 1976 and FY 1981 if the combined deficits of the Ford and Carter administrations are compared. President Gerald Ford's two-year cumulative deficit of $111.6 billion accounted for an average of 3.5 percent of GNP at that time, whereas President Carter's $194 billion cumulative deficit averaged 2.2 percent of GNP. These fig-

Table 1. Unified budget deficit and GNP

Fiscal year	Unified budget deficit*	GNP*	% deficit of GNP
1965	−1.6	695.5	0.2
1966	−3.8	724.1	0.5
1967	−8.7	777.3	1.1
1968	−25.2	831.3	3.0
1969	+3.2	910.6	—
1970	−2.8	968.8	0.3
1971	−23.0	1,031.5	2.2
1972	−23.4	1,128.8	2.1
1973	−14.8	1,252.0	1.9
1974	−4.7	1,379.4	0.3
1975	−45.1	1,479.9	3.0
1976	−66.4	1,640.1	4.0
1977**	−57.9	1,951.7**	3.0
1978	−48.6	2,091.3	2.3
1979	−27.7	2,357.7	1.2
1980	−59.6	2,575.8	2.3
1981	−57.9	2,885.9	2.0
1982	−110.6	3,069.3	3.6
1983	−195.4	3,401.6	5.7
1984	−175.3	3,774.7	4.6

Sources: *Budget of the United States Government, FY 1986;* Department of Commerce, *Survey of Current Business.*
*In billions of dollars.
**Beginning with the 1977 fiscal year, the budget shifted from a June through July to an October through September fiscal calendar. During the shift, a "spare" quarter appeared, attached to neither FY 1976 or FY 1977, which is commonly called the "transition quarter." The deficit incurred in the transition quarter was $12.9 billion, and for ease of calculation the "TQ" deficit is added to the FY 1977 deficit throughout these tables. The GNP figure has been adjusted to reflect the transition quarter.

ures suggest that those individuals who in recent years claimed deficits individually or collectively produced a significantly negative effect in the economy needed to demonstrate, for example, that a deficit comprising only 2 percent of GNP in FY 1981 could create double-digit inflation in America's $2.8 trillion economy.

In addition to comparing the size of deficits to the GNP, some indication of their magnitude and potency may be inferred by observing how large the deficits are when adjusted for inflation. Richard Nixon's largest deficit of $23.4 billion occurred in FY 1972. Jimmy Carter's largest deficit of nearly $60 billion was incurred in FY 1980. Yet when the Carter deficit is adjusted for inflation by setting it in 1972 constant dollars, that $59.6 billion reduced to $33.5 billion. Thus, the real growth in the deficit between those two years was just $10.1 billion. Even Ronald Reagan's monster FY 1983 deficit falls by more than 50 percent when set in 1972

Table 2. Unified budget deficits adjusted for inflation (1972 dollars)

Fiscal year	Unified budget deficit* (current dollars)	Unified budget deficit* (1972 constant dollars)
1965	−1.6	−2.1
1966	−3.8	−4.9
1967	−8.7	−11.0
1968	−25.2	−30.6
1969	+3.2	+3.7
1970	−2.8	−3.1
1971	−23.0	−24.0
1972	−23.4	−23.4
1973	−14.8	−14.2
1974	−4.7	−4.2
1975	−45.1	−36.3
1976	−66.4	−50.3
1977**	−57.9	−41.1
1978	−48.6	−32.3
1979	−27.7	−16.9
1980	−59.6	−33.5
1981	−57.9	−29.6
1982	−110.6	−52.8
1983	−195.4	−89.8
1984	−175.3	−77.6

Sources: *Budget of the United States Government, FY 1986*; National Science Foundation—Division of Science Resource Studies, Implicit GNP Price Deflator.
*In billions of dollars.
**Includes transition quarter deficit.

dollars, as indicated in Table 2. When the deficits from FY 1965 through FY 1984 are adjusted for inflation, then it may be seen that much of the current dollar increase in deficit spending was less substantial than the unadjusted figures suggest. Inflation distorts the growth of deficit spending to such an extent that even deficits in the $263 billion dollar range once projected for FY 1989 by the Congressional Budget Office in mid-1984 would largely be the consequence of inflation and not constant dollar growth in the deficit, for in FY 1989 a deficit of that size would be approximately $100 billion in FY 1972 dollars.

The contemporary debate over deficit spending rarely tries to put the government's unbalanced budgets into perspective; deficits when considered individually appear to be huge, but when placed against the backdrop of the entire economy they have been actually rather small in magnitude. Perhaps because of their size relative to the economy's, or because they appear and grow during peacetime while the economy is in recession or depression, the federal government's deficit spending

through FY 1984 has not proved to be responsible for the nation's inflation or high interest rates. Before this claim is examined further, there is
some value in reviewing the reasons why deficits occur, to see why deficit
spending through this period was more a response to economic conditions rather than their cause.

Causes of Deficit Spending

Simply stated, budget deficits occur when expenditures exceed revenues.
Many political and economic theories attempt to explain why these gaps
in revenue and spending exist, but three reasons deserve special mention
because they illustrate the point that deficits can be intended or unintended, and that most deficit spending through FY 1984 was chiefly the
result of a weak economy or events that forced the federal government
into situations where deficit spending was unavoidable.[3]

First, the federal government may run planned deficits in order to
stimulate the economy if economic resources are significantly under-
utilized and when unemployment rates are high. When government
spending increases and additional money is distributed to the public by
way of transfer payments, public works projects, defense spending, or
through other expenditures, aggregate consumer demand for goods and
services theoretically grows due to this added income circulating in the
economy. Encouraged by this new demand, entrepreneurs will increase
their capital investments, hire new workers, and return production to
prerecession levels. Most notably, Franklin Roosevelt's administration
employed this policy of planned deficit spending during the last years of
the Great Depression. Since Roosevelt, deficit spending has been a generally accepted weapon of countercyclical policy among economists and,
somewhat grudgingly so, by both Republican and Democratic presidents.
A program of this sort, which fights depression and recession through
federal spending and deficits to stimulate demand, is labeled by some
observers as "demand-side" management.

Deficit spending may also occur as a result of the "automatic stabilizers" built into government tax and spending programs. During a
recession when unemployment rates are growing, government tax revenues fall while expenditures for unemployment compensation and other
benefits climb. These benefits are the consequence of political decisions
made over the years primarily by the Democratic party, in particular
during the years of Lyndon Johnson's Great Society. Many of these programs, including most entitlement programs, contain cost-of-living provisions that adjust benefits to changes in the inflation rate. The size of the
deficit, therefore, grows if the inflation rate requires expenditures that are
not met with a similar increase in revenues during a period of stagflation.
When the economy is expanding while the inflation rate remains low,

however, federal revenues should increase and federal expenditures for unemployment benefits decline. Thus, when the economy is in recession the budget tends to be unbalanced and deficits will grow; if the economy is healthy and expanding, the size of the existing deficits should decrease.

Third, the federal government may run deficits if its budget lacks sufficient contingency funds to meet unforeseen emergencies that require substantial and unexpected outlays, or if the government fails to predict accurately the future of the economy in coming years. In other words, for the government to realize a budget surplus it must correctly plan for the uncertain and the unexpected. Revenues may be overstated and expenditures underestimated if, for example, major natural disasters, regional economic disruptions, unplanned military activities, or other costs exceed planned allocations.

The FY 1980 budget was afflicted with emergency expenditures stemming from the Mount Saint Helens volcano eruption in Washington, the infusion of Cuban refugees into Florida, the additional expenses incurred by military operations in the Persian Gulf as a consequence of the Iranian hostage crisis, and an unpredicted decline in the economy. The volcano's explosions and the influx of refugees raised spending by an estimated $1.2 billion in FY 1980 and $4.2 billion in FY 1981. The hostage crisis added $1.6 billion in military spending to the FY 1980 budget and $6.9 billion in FY 1981. Furthermore, the Carter administration reported in 1980 that the nation's unemployment rate would exceed the level it initially projected. Unemployment benefits rose and tax revenues from individuals and corporations fell, causing unemployment benefits to grow by $3.3 billion in FY 1980 and $9 billion in FY 1981, while the collection of tax revenues dropped by $17.7 billion and then $29.5 billion in FY 1980 and FY 1981, respectively.[4] When the Carter administration designed the FY 1980 budget neither these emergency expenditures nor the reduction in revenue were calculated into the budget, and these events helped to raise that year's deficit from an original estimate of $36.5 billion to $59.6 billion.

The extensive stagflation, recession, and high levels of unemployment, which characterized the American economy of the 1970s and early 1980s, all forced the federal government's budget deficits and the national debt to expand accordingly. Table 3, for instance, shows the parallel relationship between unemployment and deficit spending. Deficits are invariably linked to a weak economy, for a 1 percent increase in unemployment equals approximately one million jobless people and adds an estimated $30 billion to the deficit.[5] Because the government's deficits of the 1970s and early 1980s originated under these circumstances, and thus assisted rather than hindered the economy according to macroeconomic theory, the often-made charge that this deficit spending harmed the economy has been misplaced. "The chief problem . . . has been the failure to dis-

Table 3. Unified budget deficit and unemployment rates

Fiscal year	Unified budget deficit*	Unemployment rate (%)
1965	−1.6	4.5
1966	−3.8	3.8
1967	−8.7	3.8
1968	−25.2	3.6
1969	+3.2	3.5
1970	−2.8	4.9
1971	−23.0	5.9
1972	−23.4	5.6
1973	−14.8	4.9
1974	−4.7	5.6
1975	−45.1	8.5
1976	−66.4	7.7
1977**	−57.9	7.0
1978	−48.6	6.0
1979	−27.7	5.8
1980	−59.6	7.1
1981	−57.9	7.6
1982	−110.6	9.7
1983	−195.4	9.6
1984	−175.3	7.5

Sources: *Budget of the United States Government, FY 1986*; Department of Commerce, *Survey of Current Business*.
*In billions of dollars.
**Includes transition quarter deficit.

tinguish clearly between passive deficits that emerge as a result of depressed levels of economic activity," Harvard economist Benjamin Friedman noted in testimony before the Senate in December 1983, "and fundamental deficits that persist even when the economy's labor and capital resources are fully employed. Many of the most frequently expressed criticisms of the U.S. Government's deficit during fiscal years 1981–83, when economic weakness accounted for much of the deficit that the government then ran, were either largely or wholly misguided."[6]

At the same Senate hearings, Carnegie-Mellon economist Allan Meltzer was a bit more caustic in his opinion of the deficit speculators:

A year ago [1982], the dominant view of Wall Street economists, the media and prominent politicians was that deficits would produce rising inflation, slow growth and a hesitant recovery in 1983. Interest rates could not decline, we were told, in the face of projected Treasury borrowing. Virtually every blip in interest rates was attributed by commentators to changing views about the possibility of financing a $200 billion deficit. A member of the Council of Economic Advisors [William Niskanen] who suggested, at one point, that there was no accurate or reliable evidence relating deficits to interest rates was made humble for his apostasy. Now that many of these forecasts have been shown to be wrong the rhetoric has changed. Tub-thumping about the deficit continues, but most financial market forecasters do not predict a prompt return to high inflation, recession, stagnation or a rise in interest rates to the levels of 1981. The locus of concern about deficits and their effect on interest rates and inflation has changed markedly.[7]

What these criticisms were, why they were inaccurate, and when indeed deficits may pose a threat to the economy require some explanation.

The Negative Effects of Deficit Spending

Though the economic pressures that produce passive deficits are readily identifiable, other questions raised in recent years concern the possible negative effects the government's deficits have on the economy. These deficits are often said to be harmful for five major reasons. First, particularly during the 1980 national elections, Republicans and Democrats alike proclaimed that deficits were the primary, if not the single source of inflation. Second, deficits were said to be inflationary because they produced high interest rates which raised the price for goods and services. When the government entered the credit markets to borrow money to finance the deficit, the supposed effect of this borrowing was an increase in interest rates as the government was forced to make its bonds and securities competitive with other public and private financial instruments. Third, deficit financing reportedly "crowded out" the investment funds normally available to the private sector. As government securities were made attractive by offering competitive interest rates, they attracted funds that otherwise would have been invested in entrepreneurial activities, or interest rates supposedly rose so high they simply prevented private borrowing by those borrowers unable to afford the steep increase in rates. Fourth, deficits are incremental additions to the nation's overall public debt. Opponents of deficit spending claimed the public debt was a "burden" carried on the backs of all Americans, and one that will be passed on to future generations. Financing the debt reportedly was inflationary for the same reasons that deficit financing produced inflation. Fifth, the existence of deficits, whether or not they directly harm the economy by themselves, was said to create or reinforce expectations that inflation will continue at present levels or will become worse. Macroeconomic theory does state that public expectations about inflation play a central role in the behavior of consumers and wage earners. Each of these claims is evaluated separately.

Deficits and Inflation

On February 18, 1981, President Ronald Reagan presented to Congress his "Program for Economic Recovery," designed by the administration to relieve the nation of its inflation and other economic difficulties. A vital component of Reagan's program was its plan for achieving a balanced budget to fight inflation: "In the past, excessive deficit spending has been a major contributor to the initiation and persistence of inflation. . . . With the plans for controlling government spending, the Federal budget will become a weapon against inflation, rather than one of its major causes."[8] As the program outlined the president's intentions, federal spending would be reduced and government programs curtailed, "resulting in a balanced budget in 1984 and modest surpluses thereafter."[9]

Have deficits been a major source of the country's inflation, as President Reagan claimed in his program, while he campaigned for the presidency in 1980, and in the televised statements he made to the American people to gain support for his FY 1982 budget proposal? The economic evidence certainly provides few historical data to substantiate such an argument. On the other hand, Reagan was correct in stating that during the 1970s the economy experienced a chronic run of deficit spending mixed with inflation rates that remain among the highest in the nation's history. On the other hand, the pattern of deficits and inflation rates suggests there has been only a very uneven relationship between the two, as Walter Wriston, former chairman of Citicorp-Citibank and an economic adviser to President Reagan, pointed out in 1981: "Inflation is not caused solely by a budget deficit. So I am somewhat more sanguine than people who believe the other way around . . . it is hard in the face of the evidence to say that a large budget deficit creates inflation. We have had a balanced budget on occasion in this country and high inflation, and we have had a high deficit and low inflation."[10]

Table 4 lists the inflation rates (based on the Consumer Price Index, CPI) and the unified budget deficits incurred since FY 1965, and Figure 1 graphically indicates the relationship Wriston noted. There is a fluctuating, unsteady pattern here of deficits and inflation rather than a sure correspondence between the two; this is easily seen in the latter half of 1960s and continues through FY 1984. In the late 1960s, for example, contrary to what some might expect, Lyndon Johnson's administration was not plagued with high deficit spending. From FY 1965 through FY 1969 only one deficit reached the double-digit level, a mark often passed during the following years. Yet, as measured by the Consumer Price Index, the growth in the inflation rate increased from 1.9 percent to 6.1 percent in this period, despite a budget surplus in FY 1969. In FY 1966 the deficit stood at $3.8 billion as the inflation rate grew at a rate of 3.4 percent, but the FY 1967 deficit rose to $8.7 billion while the inflation rate fell to 3 percent. Although the budget was usually unbalanced in the 1960s, deficits during this decade were relatively small, and the larger ones stemmed primarily from the Vietnam War. The deficits of the 1970s and early 1980s, however, were substantially larger, and they may offer

Table 4. Unified budget deficit and inflation (CPI)

Fiscal year	Unified budget deficit*	% Change CPI
1965	−1.6	1.9
1966	−3.8	3.4
1967	−8.7	3.0
1968	−25.2	4.7
1969	+3.2	6.1
1970	−2.8	5.5
1971	−23.0	3.4
1972	−23.4	3.4
1973	−14.8	8.8
1974	−4.7	12.2
1975	−45.1	7.0
1976	−66.4	4.8
1977**	−57.9	6.8
1978	−48.6	9.0
1979	−27.7	13.3
1980	−59.6	12.4
1981	−57.9	8.9
1982	−110.6	3.9
1983	−195.4	3.8
1984	−175.3	4.0

Sources: *Budget of the United States Government, FY 1986*; Department of Commerce, *Survey of Current Business.*
*In billions of dollars.
**Includes transition quarter deficit.

more conclusive evidence about the relationship between deficits and inflation.

As stated earlier, the 1970s experienced chronic federal deficits that almost always reached double-digit levels and were uninterrupted by budget surpluses. America's largest deficit recorded at that time came in FY 1976, and by the end of the decade inflation grew at a rate faster than 10 percent a year. Despite this apparent correspondence between deficits and inflation, the pattern of deficits throughout this period indicates a much weaker association between the two. In FY 1973 the deficit was $14.8 billion and the inflation rate was 8.8 percent. In the following year the deficit fell to only $4.7 billion, but inflation continued to rise to 12.2 percent. Even more interesting, the deficit jumped dramatically from $4.7 billion in FY 1974 to $45.2 billion in FY 1975, and the inflation rate actually dropped to 7 percent.

Although deficits failed to correspond in the one-to-one pattern public discourse often suggested, this simple graphic relationship should not obscure the possibility that the deficits perhaps produced some, though

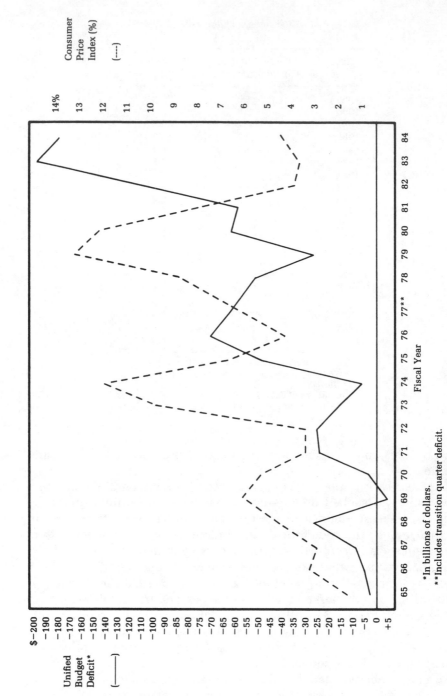

Figure 1. Unified budget deficit and inflation (CPI)

20

relatively small, amounts of inflation. Economists have employed large-scale econometric models to recreate slices of history to determine how the inflation rate would be influenced by budgets in balance rather than in deficit. In one example, economists Otto Eckstein and Christopher Probyn of Data Resources Incorporated (DRI), the well-known private econometrics firm, attempted to model the economy from 1966 to 1980 to analyze the effects of a balanced budget. "The benefits of budget balancing are important," Eckstein and Probyn concluded. The benefits "include better economic performance both in terms of real growth and inflation. . . . However, balancing the budget would not have cured all the economic ills; the general pattern of economic performance would still have shown gradual deterioration, with worsening core inflation and slowing productivity. For example, the core inflation rate, which was 10.1% in 1980, would have been 9.4% with balanced budgets."[11] To realize this 0.7 percent improvement in the inflation rate, however, the economy would have lost the deficit's stimulative effects, causing unemployment rates to be higher than they were.

In another study, Stephen Brooks employed the DRI macroeconometric model to examine the years 1972 through 1978. As in the Eckstein and Probyn findings, Brooks observed that if the budget had been balanced during his sample years inflation would have fallen "modestly before the onset of the recession. During and after the recession the inflation rates are also lower than the historical period, though by 1978 the spread is sharply narrowing."[12] Brooks also found a policy of continued balanced budgets could have proved economically unsettling: "The results show that the economy would have had a much rougher time handling the shocks of this seven-year period and would have been, throughout, much weaker than it actually was. . . . The swings in aggregate demand would have been considerably more severe. The drop in output during the 1974–1975 recession would have been 11.8%, over twice the 5.7% recorded decline. Unemployment in excess of 11% would have been recorded for two straight years. The costs in lost output would have achieved inflation gains averaging over 2% in the period 1976 through 1978."[13] As Brooks noted, a reduction of 2 percent in the inflation rate would have been coupled with an unemployment rate approximately 4 percent higher than it was during those years of recession and recovery, a standard trade-off between inflation and unemployment.

In a study published in 1984, researchers George Guess and Kenneth Koford examined the relationship between deficits and the economies of seventeen countries. In their empirically based evaluation of data for the United States and sixteen other economically developed countries, Guess and Koford tested the effect deficits had on inflation, GNP, and private investment for the years 1949–81. They concluded: "Deficits are never a statistically significant determination of inflation for the United States. But deficits *increase* GNP ... supporting the Keynesian position.... Possibly Keynesian policies work better in the United States than elsewhere. Similarly, deficits *increase* investment ... implying that crowding-in may occur in the United States."[14] The Guess and Koford data extended to 1981, but it is worth noting that since then, from 1981 through 1984, the federal deficit grew enormously while the growth in the inflation rate was greatly reduced.

The budget deficit employed throughout this chapter's analysis up to this point is the unified budget deficit, which includes only the so-called on-budget expenditures. In addition to the unified budget spending there is another set of federal expenditures known as "off-budget" items, recorded in this fashion since FY 1973. Programs funded in the off-budget fashion are the Rural Electrification and Telephone revolving fund, the Synthetic Fuels Corporation, and a program of the U.S. Railway Association. In FY 1984 the off-budget deficit was $10 billion, or $4.2 billion less than in FY 1980. These off- and on-budget deficits are combined in Table 5. To get some sense of the relative effect of the on-budget versus the off-budget deficit on inflation, simple correlation coefficients are employed to illustrate the association between inflation and these deficits. The correlation between inflation and the on-budget deficit is −.74 for the fiscal years 1973–84, indicating a strong inverse relationship, whereas the combined on- and off-budget correlation with inflation is −.73. In both instances deficits associate negatively with inflation, thereby indicating

Table 5. On- and off-budget deficit and inflation (CPI)

Fiscal year	Unified budget deficit*	Off-budget deficit*	Total on- and off-budget deficit*	% Change CPI
1973	−14.8	−0.1	−14.9	8.8
1974	−4.7	−1.4	−6.1	12.2
1975	−45.1	−8.1	−53.2	7.0
1976	−66.4	−7.3	−73.7	4.8
1977**	−57.9	−10.4	−68.3	6.8
1978	−48.6	−10.4	−59.0	9.0
1979	−27.7	−12.5	−40.2	13.3
1980	−59.6	−14.2	−73.8	12.4
1981	−57.9	−21.0	−78.9	8.9
1982	−110.6	−17.3	−127.9	3.9
1983	−195.4	−12.4	−207.8	3.8
1984	−175.3	−10.0	−185.3	4.0

Sources: *Budget of the United States Government, FY 1986;* Department of Commerce, *Survey of Current Business.*
*In billions of dollars.
**Includes transition quarter deficit.
Note: The off-budget was first calculated for FY 1973.

that deficits are generally larger when inflation is low, as should be expected considering the passive role deficits are intended to play: deficits "automatically" grow larger when the economy is weak and unemployment is high, and when unemployment rates are high the inflation rates tend to diminish. Thus, the correlations imply that off-budget deficits produce only a small marginal effect on inflation beyond that of the on-budget deficits.

The evidence presented so far takes into account only the federal government's deficit spending. But a substantial amount of federal revenue has been distributed to the states, for example, in the form of revenue sharing and block grants. In many fiscal years the federal budget could have been balanced merely by eliminating these state benefits, and by applying this money exclusively to federal programs. Such a strategy would leave the states with the decision to either raise taxes to cover the lost federal funds or reduce those programs previously financed by the federal government. The infusion of billions of federal dollars has enabled many states to accumulate budget surpluses at the same time the federal government incurs deficits. When these state and local government surpluses are added to the federal on- and off-budget deficits, as in Table 6, an important fact is revealed: evaluated as a whole, the public sector in the economy ran deficits above $20 billion just four times

Table 6. Public sector deficits and inflation (CPI)

Fiscal year	Federal on- and off-budget deficit*	State & local goverment budget surplus or deficit*	Net deficit or surplus*	% Change CPI
1969	+3.2	+0.1†	+3.3	6.1
1970	−2.8	−12.9	−15.7	5.5
1971	−23.0	+4.0	−19.0	3.4
1972	−23.4	+12.3	−11.1	3.4
1973	−14.9	+9.2	−5.7	8.8
1974	−6.1	+7.3	+1.2	12.2
1975	−53.2	+5.9	−47.4	7.0
1976	−73.7	+20.7	−53.0	4.8
1977**	−68.3	+26.8	−41.5	6.8
1978	−59.0	+29.0	−30.0	9.0
1979	−40.2	+23.9	−16.3	13.3
1980	−73.8	+28.2	−45.6	12.4
1981	−78.9	+31.7	−47.2	8.9
1982	−127.9	+32.9	−95.0	3.9
1983	−207.8	+48.6	−159.2	3.8
1984	−185.3	+64.4	−120.9	4.0

Sources: *Budget of the United States Government, FY 1986*; Department of Commerce, *Survey of Current Business.*
*In billions of dollars.
**Includes transition quarter deficit.
†National income products account budget base.

between FY 1970 and FY 1979. Moreover, the public sector deficit in FY 1983 is reduced by a fifth when the state and local government's huge surplus is considered. This state and local surplus is growing to its highest level in American history, and in the absence of significant changes in policy by these governments this surplus is projected to continue growing.[15] Consequently, because the net public sector deficit is smaller due to these surpluses, its ability to create inflation is therefore lessened by this amount.

Deficits, Interest Rates, and the Money Supply

The role federal deficits play in the nation's credit markets gets to the heart of the issue of how much effect deficits have on the economy. Earlier, the federal government's deficits were found to be relatively small when compared to the GNP. Though a comparison of this sort is legitimate and commonly made, it still begs the question of how deficits are financed in the economy. Lester Thurow noted in *The Zero Sum Society,* "The only thing that affects the economy is the balance between what governments collect in taxes and what governments spend."[16] When state and local surpluses are added to federal deficits, as in Table 6, Thurow declared, "it is simply a matter of accounting where the government surplus appears."[17] Unfortunately, "balance" and "accounting" are not abstractions, for to achieve this balance the federal government borrows billions of private dollars from the nation's credit markets. If the federal government restrained itself from transferring billions of dollars to the states, the Treasury Department would borrow substantially fewer dollars from these credit markets. Federal borrowing to finance the deficit absorbs a huge portion of the funds made available in the credit markets by private investors. In FY 1983, for example, investors raised $501.8 billion they were willing to risk in those markets. At the same time the federal government required approximately 42.3 percent of those funds to finance its on- and off-budget related deficits, as shown in Table 7.

When the federal government runs a deficit it must find money to cover the gap between revenues and expenditures. Deficits may be financed by printing new money to meet cash-flow needs, by drawing on assets directly available to the government, or by borrowing from the public. A common misconception is that the federal government simply prints any amount of money it requires to finance a deficit, thereby adding money to the economy and increasing the rate of inflation. The responsibility for guiding the money supply lies with the independent Federal Reserve (the Fed). The Federal Reserve attempts to increase or decrease the money supply through its discount and reserve requirements, and by buying or selling federal securities offered by the Treasury Department in the credit markets. When the Federal Reserve purchases these securities and adds to the money supply, it "monetizes" a portion of the debt. The deficits

Table 7. On- and off-budget deficits financed in the nation's credit markets

Fiscal year	On- and off-budget related deficits publicly financed*	Funds loaned in U.S. credit markets*	% Federal participation	% Prime interest rate
1970	−3.8	93.6	4.0	7.91
1971	−19.4	125.7	15.4	5.72
1972	−19.4	151.9	12.8	5.25
1973	−19.3	198.5	9.7	8.02
1974	−3.0	187.5	1.6	10.80
1975	−50.9	178.0	28.6	7.86
1976	−82.9	243.3	34.0	6.84
1977**	−71.5	374.7	19.1	6.82
1978	−59.1	385.7	15.3	9.06
1979	−33.6	423.5	7.9	12.67
1980	−70.5	357.6	19.7	15.26
1981	−79.3	417.2	19.0	18.87
1982	−135.0	401.8	33.6	14.86
1983	−212.3	501.8	42.3	10.79
1984	−170.8	672.6	25.4	12.04

Sources: *Budget of the United States Government, FY 1986*; Department of Commerce, *Survey of Current Business*.
*In billions of dollars.
**Includes transition quarter deficit.

incurred during the 1970s and 1980s were almost completely financed through public borrowing or by drawing upon other sources of revenue. These other sources include seignorage from coins—the difference realized from the face value of newly issued coins less the actual cost of production; cash balances and other monetary reserves held by the Treasury; the option of increasing deposit fund balances collected by the federal government for other levels of government; the option of increasing monetary penalties incurred by debtors; and the leasing and selling of federal land. The total on- and off-budget deficit in FY 1984 was $185.3 billion, but $170.8 billion was financed through borrowing, as the government financed the remainder primarily by drawing on its own cash balances.[18]

Not all money borrowed from the public comes from domestic sources. Though there are real economic costs to transferring economic resources abroad, some 15.4 percent of all federal deficits sustained from FY 1965 through FY 1984 were financed by foreign lenders who invested in U.S. credit markets. Through mid-FY 1984, foreign lenders held $175.5 billion worth of federal securities, thus reducing pressure on domestic credit markets and interest rates. Although this is a large sum, there are many misconceptions concerning its source and rate of growth.[19] As shown in Table 8, $163.7 billion of the debt was contracted after FY 1965 with the balance accumulated beforehand. Of the $163.7 billion, the Reagan ad-

Table 8. On- and off-budget related deficits financed through foreign borrowing

Fiscal year	On- and off-budget related deficits publicly financed*	Foreign borrowing to finance the on- and off-budget deficits*	Net U.S. financed*	% Foreign borrowing
1965	−4.1	−0.3	−3.8	7.3
1966	−3.1	+0.7†	−3.1	0
1967	−2.8	+0.2	−2.8	0
1968	−23.1	+0.7	−23.1	0
1969	+1.0	+0.4	0	0
1970	−3.8	−3.8	0	100.0
1971	−19.4	−17.8	−1.6	91.7
1972	−19.4	−17.3	−2.1	89.2
1973	−19.3	−10.3	−9.0	53.4
1974	−3.0	+2.6	−3.0	0
1975	−50.9	−9.2	−41.7	18.1
1976	−82.9	−3.8	−79.1	4.6
1977**	−71.5	−25.8	−45.7	36.9
1978	−59.1	−25.5	−33.7	43.0
1979	−33.6	+0.7	−33.6	0
1980	−70.5	−1.4	−69.1	2.0
1981	−79.3	−9.0	−70.3	11.3
1982	−135.0	−9.9	−125.1	7.3
1983	−212.3	−19.5	−192.8	9.2
1984	−170.8	−15.4	−155.4	9.0
	$−1,062.9	$−163.7	$−910.6	14.9

Sources: *Budget of the United States Government, FY 1986*; Department of Commerce, *Survey of Current Business.*
*In billions of dollars.
**Includes transition quarter deficit.
†In some years domestic and foreign lenders sold rather than purchased U.S. securities. These years, 1966–69 and 1974, are signified by a positive rather than a negative sign.

ministration incurred $53.8 billion through FY 1984, but this total is less in constant dollars than the foreign debt gathered by either the Carter or the Nixon administration. Measured in current dollars, Reagan's foreign borrowing is within $2 billion of Carter and $8 billion within Nixon's borrowing. Thus, despite claims that the United States is becoming a "debtor state" because of the deficit, the rate of growth in foreign debt holding stemming from the government's deficits declined as a constant dollar accumulated total between the Carter and Reagan administrations through FY 1984.

Are deficits responsible for the high interest rates that have been found in the credit markets in the last decade? At first glance it may appear deficits are indeed the cause of high interest rates, as these rates did climb during the same period that deficits grew to be chronic. As Walter Wriston observed, however, the pattern of deficits and interest rates suggests this relationship is often tenuous. "We've reviewed the past 30 years," said the former chairman of the nation's largest bank, "and I don't see any direct correlation between the size of the deficit and interest rates. In 1973–74, for example, the deficit was much larger as a percent of the total national product than it is today [in 1981], and interest rates fell like a stone."[20] Table 7 and Figure 2 illustrate Wriston's comment, showing how deficits and interest rates fluctuated in these years. The two important variables are the total on- and off-budget deficit related debt financed in the credit markets and the prime interest rate. If this borrowing greatly raises interest rates there should be a strong degree of correspondence between the two, but as Wriston pointed out the relationship is a weak one.

Many economists are aware of the questionable association between deficits and interest rates. In September 1981, Milton Friedman analyzed the pattern of deficits and interest rates, which at the time were close to 20 percent, and stated:

> Here again, the reality is very different from the talk. The current deficit is not as large as in many past years, if it is measured, as it should be, not in dollars but as a fraction of the national income or gross national product. The deficit (including off-budget items) for the current fiscal year ending Sept. 30, 1981, is expected to be less than 3 percent of GNP. The corresponding percentages were 3.6, 4.5, 2.9, and 2.8 for fiscal years 1975, 1976, 1977, and 1978. Those earlier deficits were associated with T-bill [Treasury bill] rates of less than 8 percent, and with negative real rates. *Why should a similar or smaller deficit now lead to T-bill rates of 15 percent and positive real rates of 5 to 9 percent?* . . . Well, it is said, maybe the current deficit isn't so frightening, but what about future ones? Don't tax cuts plus increased military spending mean even bigger future deficits? Whether these fears are justified or not, they cannot explain current interest rates. Higher future deficits and higher future inflation would lead investors to expect high interest rates in future years. That should make long-term interest rates higher than short-term, yet the opposite is true. In the jargon of Wall Street, the yield curve is negatively sloping, yet this explanation requires it to be positively sloping. So this explanation, too, can be rejected out of hand [emphasis added].[21]

Friedman therefore found that neither the pattern of past deficits nor the expectations of future deficits could explain the high levels of interest rates then in effect.

Earlier, in 1975, James Pierce, a staff member of the Board of Governors of the Federal Reserve and later an economics professor at the University of California, Berkeley, attempted to predict what effect the large deficits of FY 1975 and FY 1976 would have on interest rates. Pierce reviewed the historical relationship of deficits and interest rates from FY 1952 through FY 1975. As the record later indicated, Pierce correctly predicted that the large deficits of that period would have little effect on the rate of interest: "There is no reason to believe that deficits resulting from recession-

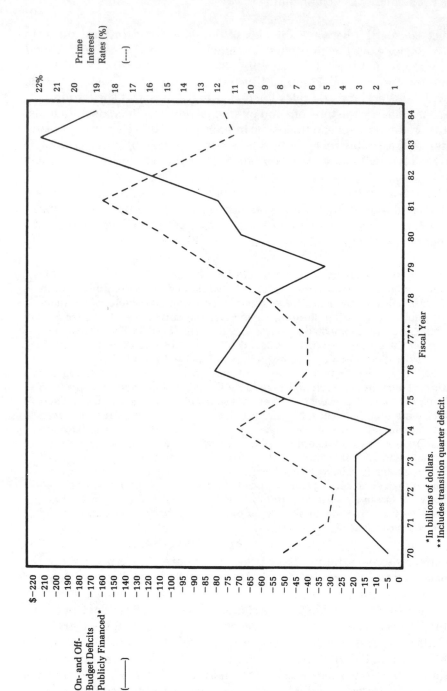

Figure 2. On- and off-budget related deficits publicly financed and interest rates

*In billions of dollars.

**Includes transition quarter deficit.

On- and Off-
Budget Deficits
Publicly Financed*

Prime
Interest
Rates (%)

(----)

28

induced declines in tax revenues will spur increases in interest rates. . . . Thus, the basic determinant of interest rates is the growth of the money supply relative to current and lagged income, not the volume or relative supply of debt."[22] Pierce reported that deficits produced by recessions would not raise interest rates, and, as noted earlier, nearly all peacetime deficits occurred in times of high unemployment and recession.

Pierce raised another issue by pointing out the relationship between interest rates and monetary policy. Certainly the years 1978 to 1984 demonstrated repeatedly the Federal Reserve's dominant role in setting interest rates through monetary policy. In 1980, for example, the Federal Reserve exercised increasingly tighter restraint over the growth in the money supply to control inflation.[23] Reducing the country's double-digit inflation clearly was the Fed's top priority, as Chairman Paul Volcker often noted in the years preceding the 1982 recession: "Our main problem and objective has been [lowering] inflation . . . the basic ill in the economy is inflation." Through its powers, said Volcker, the Federal Reserve practiced "a policy of restraining growth in money and credit."[24]

The Federal Reserve acted to keep the money supply in check because other controls either proposed or implemented were rejected or failed over time. In the early 1970s the Nixon administration initiated a three-phased plan of wage and price controls that temporarily restrained inflationary growth. The controls were removed because although they were effective in the short run, they suffered a loss in efficiency due to the need for some sectors in the economy, such as agriculture, to be left free from restraint; because interest groups became increasingly vocal and uncooperative about inequities frozen into the economy by the controls; and because the wage and price guidelines were difficult to administer in an unplanned capitalist economy, particularly without the morally induced public compliance that existed when the nation was at war.

Later, President Carter proposed to Congress that extensive credit controls be employed to curb the tremendous expansion of consumer credit in the private sector. Congress rejected Carter's credit controls, in part, because they would have created an economic outcome similar to the effect of a tight monetary policy: money and credit would have become more expensive to obtain, the rate of economic growth would decline, and deficits would grow larger as unemployment increased. Economic hardship would be the trade-off paid for a lower rate of inflation, but by passing credit controls Congress would be directly responsible for such a strategy. On the other hand, if the Federal Reserve's Board of Governors maintained high interest rates, no elected official needed to face the public on election day carrying the political burden of these high rates. Moreover, particularly during 1981 and 1982, members of Congress and individuals in the Reagan administration found that attacking the Federal Reserve for its policy could be politically advantageous. In the absence of

congressional action, a restrictive monetary policy that produces economically constraining high interest rates, and thus high rates of unemployment and therefore high deficits, remains the nation's single most
powerful weapon against inflation.

A related issue is that of the influence the government's deficit spending has on monetary policy, which in turn affects interest rates. One fear
many investors have expressed repeatedly is that an abnormal expansion
of the money supply would force the Federal Reserve to take action to
counter the potentially inflationary effect this expansion might produce.
Deficit spending could lead to such a monetary expansion if the Federal
Reserve determines it must purchase federal securities in the open market, thus adding money to the economy by monetizing the deficit. The
money supply did grow rapidly from 1971 through much of 1984: M_{1A}
and later M_1, the narrow measures of the money supply, grew by 139.6
percent, and the broader measure of money M_2 increased 239.4 percent
(see Table 9). Most of this growth was due to the normal expansion of the
economy. Still, the rate of monetary expansion was greater by 2 or 3
percent in the years prior to 1981 when deficits were unusually high.[25]
The matter at hand is to assess the reasons why the Federal Reserve added
to the money stock in the economy.

Table 9 presents a snapshot of some key economic indicators for FY
1971 through FY 1984. The money supply grew most rapidly in FY 1972,
from FY 1975 to FY 1977, and in FY 1983. In FY 1972 the Nixon administration supported the Federal Reserve's policy to increase the money
supply to stimulate the economy even as wages and prices were controlled. Robert Aaron Gordon, the late Berkeley economist, studied this
policy and concluded that "after the temporary solution of the balance-
of-payments crisis in the closing months of 1971, and with the rate of
inflation restrained by wage and price controls, the Fed could concentrate
on expediting the business recovery during 1972. The money supply
grew at a rate of more than 8 percent during the year."[26] At the time, only
$1.6 billion of the on- and off-budget deficit was domestically financed,
with the bulk of the deficit financed by selling securities to foreign lenders. Later, in 1975 through 1977, the money supply again expanded
substantially, but then in the presence of exceptionally large deficits.
Nevertheless, Table 9 reveals that the CPI actually fell during this period,
as did the prime interest rate.[27]

There is a reason for the turn of events during FY 1975–77 when the
money supply grew dramatically, yet the negative effects of this growth
were limited, certainly in the short term. These years witnessed high rates
of unemployment, and the Federal Reserve responded by expanding the
money supply to assist the economy's recovery. Because the money
supply grew principally to aid the economy in a time of recession rather
than to monetize the federal deficit, the inflationary side effects of the

Table 9. On- and off-budget deficits publicly financed and money supply growth

Fiscal year	On- and off-budget deficit* publicly financed	Prime interest rate	% Change CPI	M_{1A}/M_1*	% Growth M_{1A}/M_1	M_2*	% Growth M_2
1971	−19.4	5.72	3.4	228.5	6.6	673.6	12.1
1972	−19.4	5.25	3.4	248.0	8.5	757.8	12.5
1973	−19.3	8.02	8.8	262.1	5.7	835.2	10.2
1974	−3.0	10.80	12.2	274.3	4.6	886.9	6.2
1975	−50.9	7.86	7.0	287.2	4.7	971.3	9.5
1976	−82.9	6.84	4.8	303.2	5.5	1,099.2	13.1
1977**	−71.5	6.82	6.8	326.3	7.7	1,241.2	12.9
1978	−59.1	9.06	9.0	350.5	7.4	1,351.4	8.9
1979	−33.6	12.67	13.3	364.4	4.0	1,473.0	9.0
1980	−70.5	15.26	12.4	401.4	10.1	1,591.7	8.1
1981	−79.3	18.87	8.9	429.6	7.0	1,747.1	9.8
1982	−135.0	14.86	3.9	458.0	6.1	1,878.3	7.5
1983	−212.3	10.79	3.8	509.8	11.1	2,110.2	12.3
1984	−170.8	12.04	4.0	545.0	6.9	2,277.5	7.9

Sources: *Budget of the United States Government, FY 1986*; Department of Commerce, *Survey of Current Business*.
*In billions of dollars.
**Includes transition quarter deficit.

monetization that did occur were quite limited. Economist Alan S. Blinder examined the consequences of monetization from 1961 through 1981 and concluded: "If deficits are mainly inflationary to the extent that they are monetized, then budget deficits should kindle little in the way of inflationary fears."[28]

Subsequently, of course, the Federal Reserve undertook a policy of monetary contraction to combat the double-digit inflation of 1979 and 1980.[29] The money supply, as measured by M_2, fell from a growth rate of 9.8 percent in 1981 to 7.5 percent in 1982, thereby keeping interest rates high while unemployment rose. The recession deepened, the deficit grew, and the Federal Reserve came under tremendous congressional pressure to ease its restrictive monetary policy and bring some relief to the economy. Chairman Volcker, in turn, blamed these high interest rates primarily on the government's deficits. Many observers, including 1981 Nobel Prize winner James Tobin, found the cause of the high interest rates to be the Fed's policies rather than the federal deficit. Said Tobin soon after he was awarded the prize:

> Monetary policy brought the high interest rates. Those rates crowded out investment and all kinds of interest-sensitive demand for goods and services. This collapse produced the recession, and the recession ballooned the deficit for this fiscal year. *The only sense in which this year's fiscal policy, including the first two installments of tax reduction, is responsible for today's interest rates is that by keeping the economy from being even weaker, it prevents interest rates from going a bit lower.* In short, it is not that monetary policy is colliding with fiscal policy—it is colliding with the economy. Monetary policy would block full recovery whether the demand fuel for recovery were government spending for defense, private spending of tax cuts or entitlements, or spontaneously buoyant private investment or consumption [emphasis added].[30]

For Tobin, monetary policy, not fiscal policy and deficits, ruined the economy.

Without describing the Federal Reserve's monetary policy in excessive detail, it is worth noting that the Fed engineered the 1983 recovery by rapidly increasing the money supply 5.1 percent above the M_2 level in 1982, thereby enabling interest rates to fall by some 4 percent. To prevent the recovery from producing what the Fed regarded as excessive inflation, that is, an inflation rate increasing more than 4.5 to 5 percent a year, the rate of monetary expansion once again slowed in 1984.[31] By August, M_2 had grown only 8 percent over 1983, a level similar to that of 1982. At the same time, the prime interest rate slowly climbed, thus reducing the economy to what was called a "growth recession." By May 1984 even the vice-chairman of the Federal Reserve attacked the Board of Governors' monetary policy, declaring that there was "undue pessimism with regard to a return of inflation." "I want to disassociate growth from inflation in this expansion," said Preston Martin. "As long as inflation is not increasing very much . . . we should be more concerned with growth than with inflation."[32] Through November 1984, reported the *Wall Street Journal*, "M_1, the Fed's narrowest money measure, has barely increased in the past few months. The money measure currently is near the bottom of the Fed's target range of 4% to 8% growth for 1984."[33]

The high interest rates present in the economy during much of the late 1970s and the early 1980s, according to economists who have examined the empirical data on the relation between interest rates and deficits, stem from the country's monetary policy rather than from the federal government's deficit spending. "There is no reliable evidence that the size of the budget deficit has any effect on interest rates," declared economist Allan Meltzer, "and there is no reason to expect to find evidence of an effect."[34] Instead, monetary policy appears to be the single most important source of interest rates, real or otherwise, as recently noted by the Federal Reserve Bank of San Francisco. Brian Motley, a senior economist at the bank, examined the pattern of deficits, Treasury bill rates, monetary policy, and inflation, and concluded:

> At least over the sample period examined in this study [1953–82], high real rates appear to have been more closely linked to monetary policy—and to expectations of policy—than to fiscal policies that have produced federal deficits. . . . The empirical results do not support the proposition that there is any simple direct causal link between the recent sharp increase in the federal deficit and high real rates. In the equation estimated for the period between April 1970 and January 1982, for example, the estimated coefficient on the federal borrowing variable is small and not statistically significant.[35]

Thus, monetary policy influences the direction of interest rates and the growth of the federal deficit, but this situation is not necessarily reversed. If the Federal Reserve does constrain the money supply and therefore economic expansion due to its concern for inflation, one consequence is that deficit reduction by way of economic growth becomes a much more difficult goal to realize.

Deficits and "Crowding Out"

America's financial and business community is concerned about deficit spending because investors commonly believe deficits raise interest rates and "crowd out" private investment. This view was stated, for example, by David Jones, vice-president and chief economist for the Wall Street firm of Aubrey G. Lanston Company, in 1981: when "the government has to borrow more under the current circumstances. . . . It tends to push interest rates higher, make credit tighter, and most importantly for private borrowers, we find the money less available. It's harder to come by for both business borrowers, who need the money for long-term plant and equipment—part of the program the administration is trying to encourage—and for the mortgage borrowers who again are virtually shut out of the markets."[36] As suggested in the preceding section, monetary policy rather than deficits is widely regarded by economists to be the principal cause of high interest rates, but Jones also argued that federal participation in the credit markets attracts funds that otherwise would go to private borrowers. These private borrowers, presumably, would then use this capital for investment purposes, to hire new workers, to finance research and development opportunities, and to engage in other forms of economic activity. The validity of Jones's charge concerning this particular effect of deficit spending on the credit markets and private investment is considered next.

The decrease in investment spending due to public borrowing is called the "crowding out" effect, which takes two forms: transactions crowding out and portfolio crowding out. Macroeconomists assume for analytical purposes that a fixed supply of money is present at any one time in the economy. When the government borrows from the credit markets and increases transfer payments, government purchases, and the like, private income and aggregate demand for goods and services increase. Income exceeds the initial rate created by government spending because of the multiplier effect operating in the economy. As income and demand grow, more money is required to conduct economic transactions—the selling and buying of goods and services. To keep the fixed money supply equal to the demand for money, interest rates rise to reduce that demand. The higher the interest rate, the more expensive money becomes to borrow from the credit markets, and thus investment spending is reduced. This situation is called transactions crowding out, and it describes the situation in which high interest rates, created by government borrowing to finance deficits, limit individuals and firms from borrowing money from the credit markets to conduct economic transactions.

Portfolio crowding out takes place when some private firms find their securities are unable to compete with high-interest-yielding federal securities. Those investors who buy securities in the credit markets either sell their portfolio holdings of private securities for federal securities or for money. Money is held by investors because as the size of the credit market financed deficit grows larger, money becomes increasingly scarce and expensive to borrow and therefore is a more valuable asset to hold. One economist observed, "Due to the additional role money could play as an asset in the investors' portfolios, the bond-financed deficit also increases the demand for money . . . such wealth-induced increases cause the interest rate to rise as investors attempt to sell bonds to increase their money holdings."[37] As interest rates rise, borrowers must either offer their securities at these high interest rates to attract investors or curtail private investment projects. Some firms may simply withdraw their securities from the market as they are unable to offer the high rates of return made by the Treasury's securities. The combined effects of portfolio and transactions crowding out resulting from federal borrowing are steeper interest rates and less money in the economy for transactions and investment activities.

Before the crowding out effect is examined further, some mention needs to be made about the "crowding in" effect. Crowding out refers to a decline in private investment as a consequence of public borrowing. Crowding in describes the situation in which government borrowing actually stimulates private investment. When economic "resources are unemployed . . . government spending can stimulate investments in productive capacity and thereby increase real private spending. . . . Such increases can follow, for example, from the response of the demand for capital stock to the observed or expected demand for final product."[38] This crowding in is a consequence of "demand-side" management of the economy, where government spending partially financed through the private credit markets encourages higher demand in the economy. This increased demand stimulates capital investment to produce the goods and services necessary to meet that consumer demand.

Where does the money come from to finance private investment if the government is borrowing heavily in the credit markets and when interest rates are high? Recall the reasons why deficits occur and borrowing becomes necessary: deficits take place most frequently and reach their highest levels during wartime or in periods of recession and high rates of unemployment. Private investors are very cautious about borrowing money to invest during a recession. Consequently, the credit markets retain enough funds to loan to the government without producing a negative effect on the limited amount of private borrowing taking place. Moreover, because the demand for money is more easily accommodated when the economy is weak, interest rates remain stable. The U.S. economy experienced just this situation in 1975 and 1976, when the deficit grew to proportions then considered enormous without raising interest rates. Through 1984, historical experience shows that when the government does borrow, private investors are able to find funds available at reasonable interest rates for investment purposes to rebuild the economy following a recession.

If crowding out and crowding in are both possible, which effect is present in the economy? Economic research examining the crowding out effect fell off somewhat during the middle 1970s, as the absence of high interest rates in the face of the FY 1975 and FY 1976 deficits eliminated a crucial theoretical component of the crowding out effect.[39] In the late 1970s and early 1980s, however, two important pieces of research were

conducted by Harvard economist Benjamin Friedman and V. Vance
Roley, a former student of Friedman's and later assistant vice-president of
the Federal Reserve Bank of Kansas City. Their studies produced three
primary findings: (1) crowding out is not an automatic economic reaction
to large deficits and public borrowing; (2) a substantial amount of crowding in exists in the economy, limiting the effect of any crowding out; and
(3) although some crowding out does occur, it may be reduced by specific
debt-management policies practiced by the Treasury Department.

When approaching the question of whether the economy is in a condition of crowding in or crowding out, economists answer the question in
terms of the success of fiscal policy's ability to stimulate aggregate demand. Simply stated, if fiscal policy does stimulate demand and consumption despite a large deficit and extensive borrowing, then crowding
in is more likely to be present than is crowding out. In 1978 Benjamin
Friedman reported, "Transactions crowding out offsets only a small part
of the expansionary effect of government spending, particularly in the
short run. . . . In the long run, transactions crowding out is more powerful, but even then one-half or more of the expansionary effect remains."[40]
Therefore, "the consequences of bond financing (and of transactions
crowding out) do not appear as damaging for expansionary fiscal policy
as previous analysis has indicated. . . . If fiscal policy is necessarily inef-
fective in a given situation, it is likely to be so because of those effects in
the goods market and not because of problems caused in the financial
markets by an excess supply of bonds."[41]

Friedman also found the crowding in or crowding out effect could be
controlled somewhat by the debt-management policies implemented by
the Treasury, as bonds with a short-term maturity were less likely to
cause crowding out. Friedman did report that portfolio crowding out is
possible if debt-managers fail to consider the outcome of issuing long-
over short-term bonds; moreover, "the change in U.S. debt-management
policy that began after 1975 [toward long-term bonds] has been counterproductive from the standpoint of promoting capital formation."[42]
Nevertheless, as Friedman indicated, the vast bulk of outstanding federal
securities was in the form of short-term maturing instruments. Friedman
concluded with the reminder that "debt-management policy can determine which effect—portfolio crowding out or crowding in—results from
financing deficits, and how much."[43]

V. Vance Roley, like Friedman, employed an econometric model to test
for crowding in or crowding out in the economy. Roley's 1981 study
focused on portfolio effects, as Friedman demonstrated that portfolio
crowding out was a greater problem for private investment than transactions crowding out. Roley found that his own "empirical estimates indicate that the total crowding-out effect may in fact be relatively small,
implying that stimulative fiscal policy actions will increase aggregate

demand in the economy."[44] Portfolio crowding in was evident despite rising interest rates on long- and short-term Treasury bonds. Roley reasoned that those high interest rates were "sufficient to reduce the demand for money more than the increase in wealth increases the demand for money."[45] The higher interest rates lowered the demand for money, thereby making the portfolio holding of money by investors a less lucrative proposition. This reduced demand for money in the presence of high interest rates, however, describes transactions crowding out, and the consequence of reducing portfolio crowding out in this fashion is indeed higher levels of transactions crowding out. Still, the total effect is less crowding out in the economy because the reduced portfolio crowding out more than compensates for the increase in transactions crowding out. So, "in the short run the magnitude of transactions crowding out overstates the actual amount of total crowding out."[46] Roley concluded, "either an increase in federal spending or a reduction in federal taxes will increase aggregate demand in the economy."[47]

What has been the effect of more recent deficits on crowding out in the economy? "At present federal budget deficits are not crowding out anything. What is there to crowd out?" James Tobin wrote in early 1984. "Investment demand has already been crowded out by high interest rates generated not by fiscal policy but by monetary policies adopted long before the present Administration's tax and spending initiatives."[48] Commenting on the relationship between the deficits of FY 1981 through FY 1983 and capital formation, Benjamin Friedman told the Senate Finance Committee in December 1983:

> This problem will bear little resemblance to the decline in U.S. capital formation experienced during 1981–83. With ample unemployed resources available throughout the economy, and the budget nearly balanced on a full employment basis, it is implausible to suppose that the federal deficit was responsible for the low rate of capital formation during these years. . . . Even larger deficits, representing an active fiscal response to the 1981–82 recession, would probably have led to more capital formation rather than less in the preponderance of industries in which inadequate product demand constituted the chief impediment to investment.[49]

These deficits, therefore, crowded in rather than crowded out private investment, and according to Friedman larger deficits would have produced even greater amounts of private investment. Lawrence Klein agreed with Tobin and Friedman, also reporting to the Senate in 1983: "It is more than one year since the recovery began, and private investment has not been crowded out, it is still recovering briskly and expected to continue; therefore we lack concrete evidence that the existence of the large imbalances does indeed crowd out private investment [or] threaten the choking off of the present recovery."[50]

After reviewing the country's economic experience during the 1974–75 and 1981–82 recessions and examining the Friedman and Roley studies, it is possible to say that some crowding out has existed in the economy, but its total effect was far less than suggested by public discourse. During the 1970s and early 1980s this crowding out was not strong enough to prevent the effective use of fiscal policy, and when it does exist crowding out may be limited by a combination of debt managment and monetary policy. Moreover, crowding in has also been at work in the economy, curbing the crowding out effect. Most important, crowding out does not appear to be a significant factor in the credit markets when the economy is in recession, as during 1974–75 and 1981–82, when both consumer and investor demands for money decline. As for the high interest rates associated with the crowding out effect, they are more than likely due to Federal Reserve policy, as James Tobin suggested, than to deficit spending. Finally, crowding out, when it exists, is a consequence of debt-financed and not money-financed deficits. To the extent the Federal Reserve monetizes deficits, more credit market funds are left available for investment purposes.

Deficits and the National Debt

In anticipation of the national debt passing the one trillion dollar mark, which occurred on October 22, 1981, President Reagan declared, "One trillion dollars of debt—if we as a nation needed a warning, let that be it."[51] Yet there was no great public outcry bemoaning the trillion dollar debt, and the news media paid the event its obligatory, historical due, then passed over the issue in a few days. Perhaps the public remained so quiet about the matter because President Reagan had recently cut the growth rate in the FY 1982 budget, or because the political and economic debate conducted during the 1976 and 1980 elections focused on deficits rather than the public debt. Each reason considered separately may explain the public's relative silence. Still, it would not be dishonest to say the national debt is regarded by the public at best a necessary evil, and that deficits are considered harmful in part because they add to the debt. Individual deficits do add to the total national debt—which by the end of FY 1984 had grown by another $576 billion—however, the important question here is what effect a large debt has on the economy.

From the earliest days of the republic, hundreds of economic studies have attempted to determine just what effect the debt does have on the economy. One reason so many studies were conducted is because the United States has always been in debt. From the Continental Congress through modern times, every national budget was created in the presence of the debt. The closest the nation came to retiring the debt was in 1834 and 1835, when it fell to approximately $38,000. Since 1944 the debt has never fallen below $200 billion, and the prospect for future growth in the debt appears unlimited. So the American people are indeed familiar with the debt, and perhaps have become rather nonchalant about its size and continuing expansion.

Much of the economic debate over the public debt is philosophical in nature rather than economic, which partially explains why the debate continues. What right, economists ask, does one generation have to borrow money that must be repaid by future generations, without the permission of those future generations? The "burden" of the debt must then be borne by those yet-to-be citizens, as they may be required to pay both the debt's interest and principal. Nevertheless, these same generations receive the benefits of expenditures made in the present, which aid the economy and protect the nation, thereby making future living conditions theoretically safer, more pleasant, and economically well-off. "In short, to the extent that public borrowings do not displace private needs," economists David and Attiat Ott noted, "deficit financing and increases in the national debt do not impose a burden on future generations. In fact, running deficits to promote full employment leaves future generations better off in increased real output and investment. In this setting at least, intergenerational equity is not violated."[52]

To make matters more complicated, political factors rather than economic ones may be more important in determining the proper mix of expenditures that add to the debt. For example, defense spending is commonly considered by economists to constitute expenditures for short-term consumption rather than long-term spending for investment, such as spending for roads and bridges, and thus is a necessary but often less efficient use of resources. Moreover, the benefits stemming from military spending are often difficult to measure (for example, "peace"), while appearing to be intractably wasteful and overpriced. Thus, this debate over the debt partially rests upon notions of public intergenerational rights, and the nearly unmeasurable moral and economic cost-benefit ratio future generations would have to make when deciding whether the debt established in the past was favorable and justified.

Aside from this philosophical contest, some empirical observations can be made about the national debt. First, since the end of World War II, publicly held debt fell as a percent of the GNP through the 1960s and into the early 1970s, only to climb again during the recessions of 1974–75 and 1981–82, as indicated in Table 10. Nevertheless, the size of the debt as a proportion of GNP is still smaller than it was during the early 1960s, which suggests the debt's existence has not been so economically harmful as to prohibit the country's economic growth. In addition, the government's debt accounts for only one side of the ledger. A study published in 1984 by economists Robert Eisner and Paul J. Pieper examined all forms of the federal government's assets and liabilities during the period 1946 through 1980. They found that by 1980 the government's net worth was

Table 10. Federal debt and GNP

Fiscal year	Gross federal debt*	Debt outstanding, held by the public*	GNP*	Publicly held debt as % of GNP
1965	323.2	261.6	659.5	39.7
1966	329.5	264.7	724.1	36.6
1967	341.3	267.5	777.3	34.4
1968	369.8	290.6	831.3	35.0
1969	361.7	279.5	910.6	30.7
1970	382.6	284.9	968.8	29.4
1971	409.5	304.3	1,031.5	29.5
1972	437.3	323.8	1,128.8	28.7
1973	468.4	343.0	1,252.0	27.4
1974	486.2	346.1	1,379.4	25.1
1975	544.1	396.9	1,479.9	26.8
1976	631.9	480.3	1,640.1	29.3
1977**	709.1	551.8	1,951.7**	28.3
1978	780.4	610.9	2,091.3	29.2
1979	833.8	644.6	2,357.7	27.3
1980	914.3	715.1	2,575.8	27.8
1981	1,003.9	794.4	2,885.9	27.5
1982	1,147.0	929.4	3,069.3	30.3
1983	1,381.9	1,141.8	3,401.6	33.6
1984	1,576.7	1,312.6	3,774.7	34.8

Sources: *Budget of the United States Government, FY 1985*; Department of Commerce, *Survey of Current Business.*
*In billions of dollars.
**Includes transition quarter data.

$279.4 billion, as compared to a negative net worth of $55.9 billion in 1946 and a negative $84 billion in 1950. In 1960 assets approximately equaled liabilities, and by 1970 the federal net worth had grown to $48.3 billion. Based on their calculations, Eisner and Pieper reported:

> Adjustments for the changing relations between the par and market value of government financial assets and liabilities and further adjustments for the effects of inflation on the real value of net debt reveal a very great secular *decline* since the end of World War II in the explicit net claims (excluding Social Security and other future retirement benefits) of the private sector on the federal government. This suggests that by relevant economic measures, consistent with changes in the real value of the debt, the federal budget may properly be viewed as more frequently in surplus than in deficit.[53]

Although the debt has grown, so too have the government's financial assets.

Second, approximately 17 percent of the debt is held by the Federal Reserve system or in other U.S. government accounts. Consequently, Brookings economist Robert Hartman observed in 1981: "One trillion dollars is really an exaggeration of what the Government owes non-

Government bodies. Interest payments on the part of the debt held by the Government are really paper transactions. The Government is both making interest payments and receiving those same interest payments."[54] At the time Hartman wrote, the federal government and related agencies held 21 percent of the debt, and therefore even with the debt's rapid expansion the government continues to hold a sizable share of the debt.

Third, although the federal debt grew dramatically over the last few years, private debt grew much faster, which implies the national debt did not prevent private borrowers from obtaining credit. "The regularly yearly increases in consumer borrowing—installment plus mortgage— are running at $150 billion," William Cates, former deputy assistant treasury secretary in the Nixon administration, pointed out prior to the 1981–83 recession.[55] Continued Cates: "It is an old cliché that every family has to balance its budget, and therefore the government should do the same. What is going on today would suggest that this cliché is passé. American families are as a whole not balancing their budgets, and the American banking system seems only too happy to accommodate these family budget deficits."[56] Consumer debt is similar to federal debt in that both forms of borrowing from the credit markets are capable of depriving business firms of investment funds. But they are also similar in their ability to sitmulate the economy and provide an incentive for firms to invest and expand production.

Perhaps the single greatest difficulty posed by the growing debt is political rather than economic in nature. As the debt expands the amount of interest the federal government is required to pay also swells. Under President Reagan's initial FY 1985 budget proposal, the government would spend $116.1 billion on interest payments, $47.4 billion more than in FY 1981. The difference in interest payments eliminated the budget savings Reagan achieved in his earlier budget victories, as the Congressional Budget Office (CBO) estimated these savings from social programs would be approximately $39.6 billion in FY 1985.[57] Furthermore, the CBO projected that each fiscal year deficit in the $200 billion range "permanently" added $20 billion in interest costs, which could tend to "crowd out" other forms of expenditures. In one sense, whether the mix of federal expenditures includes more defense, social, or interest outlays is a political decision, even though interest payments reduce budget flexibility. In another sense, the increase in interest payments is an economic consideration, for these payments are simple transfers in wealth, often to upper-income earners who can afford a $10,000 Treasury bill, the smallest denomination sold by the government. Finally, as interest rates fluctuate, the government may at some point find it difficult to predict the amount of budgeted funds needed to accommodate all interest payments. If the difference between the earmarked outlays for interest payments and the costs associated with unexpected increases in payments due to higher interest rates are not made up by reducing other expenditures or by increasing revenues, the budget deficit itself will heighten and then new funds must be obtained through the credit markets.

Deficits and Inflationary Expectations

Deficit spending may or not be a primary cause of inflation, but if chronic deficits lead people to expect inflation will continue to advance at increasingly higher levels, and then people act on this belief in ways which promote inflation, should not deficits be eliminated to end inflationary expectations? This line of argument has often been expressed, and it served as the basis for much of President Reagan's Program for Economic Recovery in 1981: "Central to the new policy is the view that expectations play an important role in determining economic activity, inflation, and interest rates. . . . Not only have Federal budget deficits at times of expanding private sector activity fueled inflationary pressures, but government's tendency to stop inflation with the first signs of a slackening economy has persuaded firms and workers that they need not fear pricing themselves out of business with inflationary wage and price increases."[58] The Reagan program aimed to "break that cycle of negative expectations . . . [so] we can regain our faith in the future.[59]

The notion that deficits are tied to inflationary expectations is based on a variation of economic theory that claims people have "adaptive expectations" about economic activity, that workers compare their earnings to past inflation rates and then will adjust their wage and salary demands accordingly.[60] As wages rise, prices rise to cover the employer's additional salary costs, thus "fueling inflationary pressures" by forming a wage-price spiral. The necessary extrapolation from this theory of wage-price spirals calls for labor unions and workers to examine "rationally" present and future government economic policy and federal deficits with as much vigor as they do the inflation rate; deficits or surpluses would then be used as a basis for salary negotiations with management. This variation of the "adaptive expectations" model is commonly labeled "rational expectations," and for it to have some economic validity an incentive must exist for workers to employ federal deficits as their guide for expecting inflation rates to rise or fall. More important, if the relationship between deficits and expectations of inflation is valid, a believable new "regime" of government policy is needed to break that relationship.

The ideological and economic arguments supporting the rational expectations model deserve some mention. What is known as "classical" or pre-Keynesian economics assumes that individuals maximize their economic activities, that people make rational decisions using their economic resources—labor, leisure, income, and so on—to the best advantage in the marketplace. "In other words, the model's economic agents—

both firms and individuals—seek maximum expected profits or maximum expected utility, within the limitations of their incomes and tech-
nologies."[61] Derived primarily from Adam Smith and nineteenth-century
liberal political and economic thought, the foundation of economics was
the rational individual, and the study of economics truly was "micro"
economic analysis.

The Keynesian economic revolution changed this emphasis on the
individual actor and substituted "aggregate" analysis in its place. Macroeconomics is the study of aggregate supply and aggregate demand, of
the economy as a "whole," rather than the study of the individual or
single firm. By working with aggregates, John Maynard Keynes was able
to explain the persistence of involuntary unemployment in the economy
during a depression. Instead of the labor market "clearing," as assumed
by classical economics, in which rational maximizing firms would lower
wages instead of laying off workers, wages were "sticky," meaning that
"when business is bad employers lay off workers rather than cut wages,
and aggregate demand falls."[62] Individual behavior simply could not
explain what Keynes could with aggregate analysis.

In recent years, however, a conservative or neoconservative "counterrevolution" to Keynesian economics and the welfare state reemphasized
individual optimization and rational decision making in economic theory. Keynesian economics presumably failed because it could not explain
stagflation, the presence of high inflation existing simultaneously in an
economy with high unemployment rates. The rationalists claim the "expectations school has demonstrated that all existing macroeconomic
models are useless for policy evaluation."[63] This school endorses a sort of
radical expectations model, which differs from Keynesian models employing a more passive "adaptive" expectations effect.

Keynesian economists did not ignore the role individuals play in the
economy; they incorporated the notion of adaptive expectations to construct the wage-price spiral. Workers are said to base their expectations of
inflation or higher prices on an averaging of past prices, or prices registered in the immediately preceding period. Expectations adapt after the
inflation rates change, and wage demands slowly follow inflation. Adaptive expectations are passive, and workers' income never quite maintains
pace with an ever-changing, ever-increasing inflation rate. A more important consequence of this model for the rationalists is that "according to
this theory, the only way to eliminate inflation through conventional
monetary and fiscal restraint is by moving along the 'short-run' Phillips
curve [where higher unemployment is traded for lower rates of inflation,
or lower unemployment for higher inflation] and suffering a period of
high unemployment that is long enough to break the slowly moving
inflationary expectations. . . . Reductions in inflation are costly because it
takes agents a long time to understand that they are in a less inflationary

environment. If they learned faster, reducing inflation would be less costly."[64]

The rationalists view people as dynamic optimizers who are faster learners than in traditional neo-Keynesianism. Consequently, "In a rational expectations model of the economy, agents change their decisions to take full advantage of whatever opportunities are produced by a new [economic] policy. . . . Keynesian models, in fact, are the ones limited to constant policies because they do not recognize that people react to a new policy—that if people are faced with a new policy, their decision rules will change."[65] New and decisive policies are both possible and necessary to redirect a stagnant inflationary economy, the rationalists argue, and the influence of the rational expectations school on the Reagan Program for Economic Recovery was pervasive. The program was to be a "plan for national recovery [that] represents a substantial break with past policy. . . . Decisions to work, save, spend, and invest depend crucially on expectations regarding future government policies. Establishing an environment which ensures efficient and stable incentives for work, saving, and investment now and in the future is the cornerstone of the recovery plan."[66] Just as the rationalist school argues against Keynesian economics and believes "activist macroeconomic policies—those designed to stimulate economic growth by cutting taxes, increasing government spending, increasing the money supply, or increasing the federal deficit—must be curbed," the Reagan administration sought "to nurture the strength and vitality of the American people by reducing the burdensome, instrusive role of the Federal Government."[67]

The rationalists oppose activist policies both because these policies create an unstable decision-making environment for the rational actor, and because rationalists claim historical experience demonstrates activist policies spell inflationary disaster. Thomas Sargent, professor of economics at the University of Minnesota and an economist for the Federal Reserve Bank of Minneapolis, marshaled historical data suggesting that the hyperinflation suffered by Austria, Hungary, Poland, and Germany (as well as France's moderate inflation) between the world wars was substantially curtailed by a rapid implementation of conservative policies that drastically reduced their money supplies, restored the gold standard, and balanced their national budgets. Sargent found it significant that each country's national budget was severely unbalanced; in the case of Austria, yearly deficits often totaled more than 50 percent of all government expenditures. Government deficits were usually financed by an expansion of central bank notes, rather than "backed" by gold or by a solid credit mechanism. Consequently, a rapidly expanding money supply multiplied 288 times in three years; a similar pattern of expansion was found in Poland and Germany, where the wholesale price index rose by a factor of 1,397 and 2,038, respectively.

Sargent argued that the proper mix of conservative fiscal and monetary policies created the "extensive preconditions" needed for a rapid recovery from the existing inflation.[68] Presented as a package instead of bit by bit, these policies constituted a new economic "regime" in which the change from past policies was "widely understood, uncontroversial and unlikely to be reversed."[69] The new policies had a shock effect; the rational actor could form expectations of an economy free from inflation and then act accordingly. Sargent contended that the persistence of large deficits prevented the rational actor from accepting government pronouncements that deficits and the inflated currency would eventually be brought under control: "Inflation only *seems* to have momentum of its own, while it is actually the long-run government policy of persistently running large deficits and creating money at high rates which imparts the momentum to the inflation rate." Eradicating inflation requires "an abrupt change in the continuing government *policy* or *strategy* for setting deficits now and in the future that is sufficiently binding as to be widely believed."[70]

Returning to contemporary America, it is difficult to translate Sargent's prescriptions into current policy. The problem is not only that Poland, Hungary, and the others suffered from hyperinflation, as compared to the relatively mild inflation in the United States. Rather the problem lies in how federal deficits are financed. In each case Sargent cited, deficits were easily monetized as the governments in question had direct control over the central bank and monetary policy. Rational actors in Sargent's countries had reason to be attuned to those deficits, and the quick-fix return to the gold standard and related currency reforms, initiated by the economic "regimes" of post–World War I Europe did directly influence the size of future deficits and government expenditures by preventing governments from increasing their money supplies at will. American deficits are also monetized to some extent, as suggested by the historical increase in the money supply during periods of large deficit spending. Since 1979 Federal Reserve policy has produced a largely restrictive money supply, however, and this tight money supply is the primary reason for the nation's high interest rates. If the money supply did expand to meet completely the financing of contemporary deficits, the Treasury would find it unnecessary to borrow from private investors, and theoretically no crowding out would occur. The Federal Reserve remains unwilling to accommodate what could be an inflationary money supply increase, and therefore the federal government's deficits continue to be principally debt-financed rather than monetized.

Debt-financed deficits are dependent for their financing on the confidence and willingness of private investors to purchase government securities. As Sargent points out, the Europeans knew that the deficits were "unbacked," and in the years following the conclusion of World War I few people could be certain their shaky governments were capable of paying off the deficits; Hungary and Austria, for example, were newly created states without any credit history. The U.S. government, in contrast, proved itself over time to be a reliable and sound credit risk, which is one reason federal securities are so attractive to private investors in the credit market.[71] Balancing the federal budget would not have the same effect in the United States as in Europe, because the historical, institutional, and economic contexts are so dissimilar. Sargent can generalize among his selected countries, but their experiences are of questionable application to the United States.

Even if the rational expectations school's assumptions about human nature are correct, there must be some rational reason for unions and workers to expect that reductions in the federal deficit would lower inflation, thus inducing workers to lower wage demands and act in other ways that might reduce inflation. Unfortunately, there is no empirical evidence to substantiate such a claim. No evidence exists that shows workers make their wage demands based on the size of the deficit. Indeed, there is no "rational" reason for them to do so. Deficits and inflation historically and statistically are negatively correlated, and labor unions and workers basing their salary claims on the deficit would simply short-change themselves. As Figure 1 indicates, the pattern of deficits and the Consumer Price Index measuring the inflation rate fluctuates greatly. The rate of change and the growth of deficits sometimes surpasses the inflation rate, and sometimes the opposite occurs. Workers using the deficit level instead of the CPI as a basis for their wage demands would soon find their income levels highly unstable relative to the inflation rate, and thus irrational. Because this uncertain relation between deficits and inflation exists, labor unions negotiate with management on the basis of the CPI itself, just as government contracts, private business agreements, and federal entitlement benefits are influenced by changes in the CPI and not the deficit. The dependence that unions and other interested groups have on the CPI is evident in the concern they expressed in 1981 when the Reagan administration proposed that changes be made in the CPI to better reflect the inflation rate. Even if the public *believes* deficits are inflationary, their *actions* as demonstrated in their wage demands have more to do with the growth of inflation.

In the Reagan Program for Economic Recovery, unions and workers were said to make wage demands based upon their expectations of future government policies and the size of the federal deficit, which supposedly caused inflation and was a guide to the rate and persistence of inflation. But there is another, more compelling reason why workers and unions ignore deficits when they negotiate their salaries. High deficits are symptomatic of a weak economy and high unemployment (see Table 3). Workers who demand high wages when the economy is in recession would quickly price themselves out of the labor market. Instead, as in the United Auto Workers' wage concessions to Chrysler Corporation, many of America's major unions lowered their wage and compensation demands at the same time federal deficits grew larger during the 1981–82 recession.

The rational expectations school claims deficits and inflationary expectations are inevitably linked, yet the rationalists fail to answer empirically these questions: How are the public's attitudes about deficits associated with their economic actions? If the public believed a new policy "regime" could balance budgets, how would these presumably inflationary producing actions change? What is the instrumental relationship between deficits and a worker's or a firm's material interests? If workers' wage demands have little to do with deficits, what is the "rational" reason for their worrying about a deficit's size? The notion that people will make substantial alterations in their behavior if they expect balanced budgets—alterations leading to the elimination of inflation—is based on theoretical constructions about economic activity lacking empirical validation. Sargent's research, for example, fails to include a single public opinion survey identifying elite or mass attitudes about deficits before or after policy changes were made or budgets were balanced; no evidence is offered to show how behaviors changed following an alteration in expectations. One of the most complex areas of study in the social sciences is identifying how people process and analyze selected bits of information to create attitudes or belief systems and, where possible, tying these attitudes to behavior. The research of many respected social scientists raises serious questions about the expectations school's hypothesis regarding deficits and rational inflationary expectations.[72]

Deficits, Recession, and Recovery

Despite the ever-present drumbeat about the evils of deficit spending, most responsible economists point out that the deficits incurred during Ronald Reagan's first term in office, certainly FY 1982 through FY 1984, helped stimulate the economy and lessened the effects of recession. As the recession grew deeper, economists recognized the deficits posed little threat to the economy, at least in the short run. Economist Isabel Sawhill, for example, observed in 1982: "The message is clear: the current deficit (for 1982) is not a problem. Even the $68 billion increase in the high-employment deficit that would occur between 1982 and 1983 in the absence of congressional action would not necessarily be inappropriate—given the depressed state of the economy."[73] During 1983, in testimony before the House of Representatives, Sawhill again found the effects of current deficits to be beneficial for the economy: "Fiscal policy is currently projected to provide $46 billion in new stimulus for the economy between FY 1982 and FY 1983 and an additional $22 billion between FY 1983 and FY 1984. I estimate that the shortfall between potential and actual GNP will be about $300 billion during 1983 and $270 billion during 1984. With this amount of slack, *current* deficits can be enlarged without significant risk of accelerating inflation or driving up interest rates."[74]

Once again, in 1984, Sawhill and Charles Stone reported on the salutary consequences of the government's deficits: "On balance, . . . the Reagan deficits have thus far been good for the economy. They moderated the recession a little, they hastened the recovery, and they strengthened business investment, albeit at the expense of housing and exports. Unfortunately, the effect of the recession on the deficits was not similarly salutary since revenues automatically fall and some types of expenditures (e.g., unemployment insurance) automatically rise when incomes are depressed."[75]

Though frighteningly large, the federal deficits grew primarily in response to the nation's severe recession, as the automatic stabilizers long-ago embedded into the government's fiscal policy dictated they should. Moreover, as the Urban Institute's Sawhill suggested, the deficits assisted rather than harmed the economy. On the other hand, had the budget been balanced the recession would have been significantly worse. According to a study completed in mid-1982 by the Wharton Econometric Forecasting Associates, if the government had found some way to balance the budget in line with President Reagan's tax and spending programs passed in July 1981, the combined unemployment rate for 1982 and 1983 would have been 4.26 percentage points higher, and the nominal GNP for the two years reduced by $989 billion.[76] Thus, the recent history of federal deficit spending lends little support to those who argue that these deficits, including Ronald Reagan's, have been disastrous for the economy.

The Reagan deficits, in fact, have behaved in an economic fashion quite similar to those incurred in earlier recessions. Although the 1981–82 recession was government-induced, the product of high interest rates and tight monetary policy, and the 1974–75 recession resulted primarily from huge international trade imbalances and oil price supply shocks, we are still left with the familiar description of a troubled economy. The 1974–75 recession drove unemployment to 8.5 percent, a figure nearly equal to the unemployment rate of 1981. The on- and off-budget deficit stood at $50.9 billion in FY 1975, and then FY 1976 registered a record $82.9 billion deficit, both figures substantially above the $3 billion FY 1974 deficit. The recession took its toll in other forms as well, as gross private investment fell 12 percent in 1975 from the 1974 rate, reflecting the standstill in consumer expenditures. While the deficits grew, however, the inflation rate fell sharply from 12.2 percent in 1974, to 7 percent in

1975 and 4.8 percent in 1976. After the recession, the prime interest rate actually dropped below the 1974 level of 10.8 percent in the face of the government's deficits, never to rise above 10 percent until the Federal Reserve implemented its restrictive monetary policy in 1979. Moreover, despite the presence of the government's growing deficits, private spending for gross domestic investment rose 28.5 percent in 1976, 24.8 percent in 1977, and 23.7 percent in 1978.

The Reagan deficits recorded through FY 1984 emerged in similar circumstances. Surveying the economy in January 1982, supply-side economist Arthur Laffer found it "sicker than a dog." Laffer's reasoning was not difficult to understand.[77] By the end of 1981 the nation's unemployment rate hovered near 9 percent, later reaching 10.5 percent by the end of 1982. Reflecting the automatic stabilizers present in the nation's spending and tax programs, the government's deficits grew passively, as the government refrained from initiating activist fiscal measures, such as a large-scale, New Deal-type jobs program, while the first phase of the Reagan tax cuts did not take effect until July 1982, only four months before the recession "bottomed out" in November. As in the 1974–75 recession, the deficits climbed while inflation and interest rates declined and unemployment increased, thereby providing at least short-term evidence for the existence of the Phillips Curve trade-off between inflation and unemployment.

In addition, although the publicly financed on- and off-budget deficit registered $212.3 billion in FY 1983, gross domestic investment expanded by 21.0 percent in 1983, and then by 34.3 percent in 1984 (see Table 11). Not surprisingly, recent economic history suggests that recessions rather than deficits limit private investment. Investment spending takes place when consumer demand increases, when unemployment levels signal a generally healthy economy, and not during the depths of recession, as in 1974–75 and 1981–82. Large deficits, if they have any effect on investment decisions during a recession, may actually stimulate and crowd in investment by placing money in the hands of the public, thereby boosting consumer demand.

As passive as the early Reagan deficits were in response to the recession, the great fear of nearly every economist cited thus far is that the government's "active" deficits, produced by a dramatic increase in defense expenditures and tax reductions, will inhibit the country's economic recovery and long-term prosperity. In just one of many examples, Benjamin Friedman informed the Senate in 1983: "The issue now facing U.S. fiscal policy is not the familiar one of the role of automatic stabilizers, or even the desirability (or lack thereof) of temporary active deficits as discretionary stabilizers, but rather the effects of sustained deficits at full employment as a permanent feature of the economy's ongoing development. Among the most important of those effects is the

Table 11. Deficits and private investment

Fiscal year	On- and off- budget deficit publicly financed*	Private investment in new plant and equipment*[1]	Annual % change	Gross private domestic investment*[2]	Annual % change
1966	−3.1	82.22	+16.9	120.8	+12.5
1967	−2.8	83.42	+1.5	116.0	−4.0
1968	−23.1	88.45	+6.0	126.5	+9.0
1969	+1.0	99.52	+12.5	137.8	+8.9
1970	−3.8	105.61	+6.1	137.1	−0.5
1971	−19.4	108.53	+2.8	153.2	+11.7
1972	−19.4	120.25	+10.8	179.3	+17.0
1973	−19.3	137.70	+14.5	209.4	+16.8
1974	−3.0	156.98	+14.0	215.0	+2.7
1975	−50.9	157.71	+0.5	189.1	−12.0
1976	−82.9	171.45	+8.7	243.0	+28.5
1977**	−71.5	198.08	+15.5	303.3	+24.8
1978	−59.1	231.24	+16.8	375.3	+23.7
1979	−33.6	270.46	+16.7	415.8	+10.8
1980	−70.5	295.6	+9.3	395.3	−4.7
1981	−79.3	321.49	+8.7	474.9	+20.1
1982	−135.0	316.43	−1.6	414.9	−12.6
1983	−212.3	343.35	+8.5	501.9	+21.0
1984	−170.8	398.99	+16.2	674.0	+34.3

Sources: *Budget of the United States Government, FY 1986*; Department of Commerce, *Survey of Current Business.*
*In billions of dollars.
**Includes transition quarter deficit.
[1]Excludes agricultural plant and equipment.
[2]Includes agricultural and all forms of investment.

impediment that such deficits will place in the way of the economy's ability to undertake capital formation."[78] Friedman's concern echoes that of Isabel Sawhill, Charles Stone, and Allan Meltzer, who noted that interminably high federal deficits during recovery and periods of nearly full employment could crowd out private investment and produce high interest rates.[79] Although macroeconomic theory encourages deficit spending in times of recession, during recovery and full employment macroeconomists regularly urge that government take action to reduce the deficit. If good deficits stimulate the economy during recession to supplement a weakened private sector, bad deficits overstimulate the economy and infringe upon the private sector in a recovery.

Yet at least through 1984 the government's deficits did not pose a threat to recovery. Instead, during the first half of 1984 the economy absorbed a 20 percent increase in consumer credit demands, a 34.3 percent increase in gross domestic investment, and accommodated what by the year's end would be a $185 billion on- and off-budget deficit. At the same time, inflation remained nearly constant at 4 percent, as interest rates fell to

11.25 percent by the end of November. What emerged through the latter half of 1984 was that restrictive monetary policy rather than high deficits reduced GNP growth, as econometric estimates found that high deficits would not impede recovery.

"Concern that the deficit would abort recovery has faded," observed Herbert Stein, "as the recovery has actually begun and seems to be following a fairly typical path. The most common forecasts call for the recovery to continue with typical durability and strength. That is, these forecasts imply that the recovery will continue despite the deficits."[80] The Wharton Forecast provided one example of the projections Stein described. Lawrence Klein outlined the forecast for the Senate in December 1983:

> The crowding out scenario runs as follows: Large credit demands by the federal government for the purposes of deficit financing absorbs large amounts (some $200 billion) of funds from the money market. . . . high interest rates must be paid. This will drive up the cost of capital to investors, who will then retrench and send the economy into a relapse. The Wharton Forecast does not accept this scenario. It fully recognizes the huge borrowing requirements of the federal government . . . and projects a sources and uses statement of funds flows that permit the recovery to continue with only moderate increases in interest rates and a steady revival of capital spending.[81]

Furthermore, the September 1984 University of California, Los Angeles (UCLA) National Business Forecast estimated that during 1985 real business investment in producers' durable equipment would jump 21.2 percent, the largest gain since the end of World War II; real investment in nonresidential structures would grow 18 percent, a tie for the biggest gain since World War II; and that real consumer spending would rise 5.8 percent, the second strongest increase since World War II.[82] In September, when the UCLA Forecast was published, the prime interest rate ranged over 12 percent, but by November the Federal Reserve eased its restraint over the money supply by reducing its discount rate, and in response the nation's largest banks lowered their prime rate to 11.25 percent.

Deficit Spending and Public Policy

The economy's astonishing capacity to accommodate the federal government's deficit spending overwhelms the position that balanced budgets are required for a healthy economy. Instead, the economy continued to absorb the government's deficits without producing excessive inflation, the crowding out of investment, or high interest rates. Consequently, the pressure to reduce the deficits stems from the fear of what they may do to the economy in the yet-undetermined budgetary "out-years." Some economists have argued that less emphasis should be placed on cutting deficits and more on increasing economic growth through government stimulus. James Tobin noted in early 1984 that "there is no case for reducing fiscal stimulus for the next two fiscal years, while the economy is still slack."[83] Paradoxically, Keynesians like Tobin are joined by the supply-siders who oppose tax increases more than they fear deficits. "The mandate I heard was for economic recovery," Congressman Jack Kemp declared after the 1984 election, "and [OMB Director David] Stockman is still talking about reducing the size of government."[84] The Reagan administration, more than any other in the nation's history, has tested the economy's ability to endure high deficit spending, thus creating uncertainty about the boundaries of tolerable and intolerable deficits.

As the deficit grew during the 1981–82 recession, so too did the standard for what might be considered an acceptable deficit while the economy grows in a healthy fashion. In early 1983, for example, Albert T. Sommers, vice-president and chief economist for the Conference Board, the nonprofit, corporate-sponsored research organization, testified before the House Budget Committee that an $80 billion deficit in FY 1986 would be "an acceptable normal level of the deficit under conditions of moderately high resource use."[85] Paul McCracken, an economic adviser to Republican presidents, stated that a $100 billion deficit in FY 1988 "should not strain our capability to pursue a noninflationary policy."[86] As the possibility of achieving a balanced federal budget became increasingly distant, deficits of $80 to $100 billion—once considered unthinkable—soon took on the air of fiscal responsibility. These observations suggest that what has been lost during the Reagan years is the sense of economic innocence, or ignorance, which argued that balanced budgets would solve the nation's economic woes, as well as the moral restraint responsible for forcing the government to regard balanced budgets as an important goal. "The federal government has been running budget deficits for a long time," observed Herbert Stein, "but there has always been a certain amount of shame and guilt about that, which limited the size of the deficits. . . . We may be in the process of losing all inhibitions about deficits, especially since the most conservative administration of the past fifty years is engaged in defending the largest deficits in history."[87] Ironically, perhaps the only way the nation will regain the sense of shame and guilt about deficit spending Stein referred to is for the president and the Congress to approve and send to the states for ratification a constitutional amendment requiring balanced federal budgets, an amendment that numerous economists consider economically self-defeating.[88]

In another sense, however, whether at some point deficits do harm the economy in the budget's "out-years" is not the major question addressed here; that is a matter for analysis based on empirical economic evidence, not speculation. Rather, the purpose of this review is to suggest that before the end of Ronald Reagan's first term as president, deficit spending failed to produce the economic difficulties attributed to it between 1965 and 1984. If this is the case, or if at least a healthy skepticism exists concerning the supposedly economically harmful effects of deficit spending, then perhaps a more important task is to determine why balancing the federal budget has proved over time to be such an emotional and politically volatile issue, now that it is possible to set aside a strictly economic reason for being concerned about deficit spending. What is the source of the "guilt" and "shame" Herbert Stein mentioned? The uniquely American interest in balancing the national budget, the origins of this interest in American political thought, and its influence on politics, public policy, and the development of the nation's political and economic institutions, are examined in the following chapters.

3

Colonial Deficits, Constitutional Restrictions, and the Rise of Hamiltonian Government

Whether that which increaseth the stock of a nation be not a means of increasing its trade? And whether that which increaseth the current credit of a nation may not be said to increase its stock?

Whether the credit of the public funds be not a mine of gold to England? And whether any step that should lessen this credit ought not to be dreaded?

GEORGE BISHOP BERKELEY, on the value of
England's public debt, 1735

Contemporary economic evidence on deficit spending suggests that unbalanced federal budgets have not created the harmful effects often attributed to them in recent years. Instead, the federal government's deficits most probably helped rather than hurt the economy during the 1981–82 recession and played an important role in assisting the 1983–84 recovery. In addition, predictions about the government's future deficits are quite vague concerning their size and true influence on the nation's day-to-day economic affairs. If this is the case, then what makes the issue of balancing the federal budget such a powerful and emotional one, not only in recent years but throughout the history of American politics? This question may best be answered by exploring the nation's history, to determine just how the issue of balanced and unbalanced budgets shaped American politics and helped develop the republic's political and economic institutions.

As suggested in the preceding chapter, the most useful way to examine how the nation's political leaders and the general public regarded the idea of a balanced budget is to consider it as a symbol, standing for or representing a particular vision of government and society. How Americans symbolically interpreted the balanced budget did indeed greatly influence public policy in the broadest terms. Balanced budgets not only proved to be a potent symbol that defined the purpose and size of government, but the drive toward a balanced federal budget could either enhance or restrict the national government's powers and authority, especially in relation to those of the states. Furthermore, the use of balanced or unbalanced budgets as symbols originated, gathered strength, and found a place in political discourse because they were invoked in this manner and given credibility by "opinion leaders," who in turn employed the budget as a symbol because it was tied to some historical series of events or experiences commonly shared or known to the public. Balanced federal budgets in particular derived their initial legitimacy and utility as a symbol from historical events and ideas that took shape even before the Americans fought their Revolution.

Early Americans rarely considered deficit spending and public debt to be singularly economic matters, for they were instead discussed in terms of political economy. The debate over deficits and debt may be seen in a simplified fashion, at this point, as the clash between people holding moral, political, and economic values opposed to an expanding public credit, and those individuals who believed such expansion was necessary to alleviate political crises and improve the public's general welfare. The public was sharply divided over the matter of government credit, and it would be a mistake to assume that Americans were monolithically opposed to unbalanced budgets before the New Deal. People of goodwill, intelligence, and high standing in their communities argued vigorously over the existence and size of the public's credit since the earliest days of colonial America. Much of this debate focused not on "deficits" but on the debt, or "public credit," or the use of paper money, better known as "bills of credit." Under the Articles of Confederation and the new Constitution, for example, the young nation's year-to-year revenue difficulties paled beside the $77 million public debt. "Deficits" were harmful, because, among other reasons, they threatened the federal government's ability to retire the debt. In the proper context, employing paper money technically involved running budget deficits, and debate over bills of credit may be considered to represent more modern notions of deficit spending.

The balanced budget's symbolic content originally developed during two distinct periods in American history, the time before and after the

Civil War. This division is not arbitrarily drawn. Prior to the Civil War
the debate over deficit spending, in its various forms, was discussed
principally in terms of states' rights and popular control over a potentially "corrupt" federal government. Colonial and state governments frequently incurred deficits, and efforts by a centralized political authority,
be it Parliament or the Federalists at the Constitutional Convention, to
put a halt to such practices were regarded as an infringement upon the
autonomous rights of the decentralized colonies and states. While federal deficits and debt were subject to intense scrutiny, the states increased their debt levels even in the face of state constitutional restrictions. Deficits at the federal level were considered, particularly by the
Jeffersonians and Jacksonians, a reflection of the national government's
unwarranted attempt to gain power in a fashion harmful to the fragile
balance of powers established in the Constitution. Furthermore, the manipulation of federal finances by the "moneyed aristocracy" and the
imposition of revenue-producing tariffs that promoted a manufacturing
economy were believed to speed the demise of agrarian democracy. The
tone of the debate over deficits and debt was set by Alexander Hamilton
and Thomas Jefferson, the two dominant figures in post-Revolutionary
America, and their influence on public policy and political thought are
found throughout the first half-century of the new nation's political life.
It is this period, 1690 to 1860, that is the subject of the following two
chapters.

Colonial America and Paper Money

Colonial governments frequently faced the need to expand the public's
credit by issuing paper currencies to meet the financial demands of war,
economic recession, and ordinary commercial demands. England's numerous wars fought against the French and various Indian tribes, as well
as economic demands imposed upon the colonies through mercantile
arrangements with the mother country, produced severe hardship for the
colonials who found their supplies of gold and silver specie inadequate to
meet their financial needs. Designed to meet wartime exigencies and then
commercial requirements, the introduction of paper money by the colonies led to tense domestic and foreign relationships, which later helped
to spark the Revolutionary War. In the eighty years preceding the Revolution, "the privotal problem within and between the colonies and between
the colonies and the mother country remained the problem of the money
supply."[1]

When England fought France in the New World, the colonial economies were routinely stimulated and contracted. King William's War
(1689–97), Queen Anne's War (1702–13), King George's War (1744–48),
and the French and Indian War (1754–60) benefited those fortunate few

who could provide the supplies and weapons used by the British army and navy. During these times of international conflict the major trading cities of Boston, New York, and Philadelphia experienced temporary periods of rapid economic growth and well-being. The opportunities of war enabled bold and lucky merchant traders to make huge fortunes by exporting goods to Britain, through shipbuilding, and by supplying English troops stationed in America. These economic benefits, however, usually found their way to only a small minority of businessmen, while large numbers of poor lived in the great colonial cities. In New York, for example, during King William's War "the wealthiest 10 percent of the taxpayers owned 45 percent of the seaport's taxable assets, while the bottom half could claim only about 10 percent of the total wealth. By 1703 this concentration of wealth had become slightly more pronounced."[2]

inequable in the colonies.

Consequently, the colonial tax base devised to support these extended wars were often stretched quite thin in colonies like Massachusetts, which usually made the greatest effort to aid the British. Moreover, dependent for much of their economic success on exporting goods to England, the colonials found the sea lanes dangerously infested during wartime with enemy warships that disrupted normal shipping patterns. While foreign trade decreased, thus reducing revenues and access to specie, war taxes were levied and grew to be as much as twenty times their peacetime rate in Massachusetts.[3] As the financial burden of war overwhelmed the specie assets available to the government through taxation, paper money and therefore deficit spending became the remedy of last resort to cure colonial economic suffering:

> The heavy demands which war placed upon the provincial treasury could be met only by issuing paper money because taxes sufficient to subsidize military operations could never be extracted from property owners' pockets all at once. Thus, in the face of unpaid, mutinying troops in 1690, the legislature issued paper money for the first time in Massachusetts history. It was the initial experiment in deficit financing in the American colonies. In 1690–1691, £40,000 of paper bills were emitted and a decade later Governor [Joseph] Dudley found it impossible to undertake the war against the French without obtaining further issues of script.[4]

So, in response to its wartime emergency, Massachusetts in 1690 initiated the practice of deficit spending, and from 1702 to 1716 issued £405,000 in paper currency.

The "currency" issued by Massachusetts, and later by the other twelve colonies, consisted of "bills of credit." These government bonds employed as circulating currency became the cornerstone of colonial finance soon after their introduction in 1690; they were widely used by the states throughout the Revolution and during the immediate postwar period. Only the Constitution itself finally put an end to the states' distribution of bills of credit. These specie-poor governments issued interest-bearing securities called bills of credit that were sold to the public for gold and silver. In return for selling their specie to the government for bonds, investors redeemed their bills of credit for principal and interest payable in specie at some specified future date. Bills of credit, in turn, functioned as paper currency and could be used by the public to pay private debts and conduct economic transactions. These debt instruments made colonial deficit spending possible, but their worth depended upon public confidence in their governments' ability to make good their promise to redeem the bills of credit when they became due. The colonial legislators, therefore, realized the bills would maintain their face value only so long as they constituted a small portion of a colony's total money supply, and if their repayment was guaranteed by adequate taxation and made in specie.

In the case of Massachusetts, war and a weakened economy postponed this taxation, and the legislature was forced to issue large amounts of paper money while extending the life of old bills whose retirement was due. "It was a way of spreading out the costs of war over a number of years. But, unexpectedly, Massachusetts currency began to lose its value in 1705, the beginning of a depreciatory trend that was to last for two generations." The public lost faith in the colony's currency, and the gap between the currency's official and market value widened as Massachusetts suffered from inflation and a currency that depreciated 44 percent between 1715 and 1721. Later, the Massachusetts legislature again issued over £3 million to finance its expenses during King George's War (1744–48), and taxes were scheduled as far into the future as 1760 in order to retire the colony's notes. Consequently, Massachusetts currency fell in value "to about one-tenth of its English equivalent by 1747." While the colony struggled to pay the war debt, its economic condition was so seriously disrupted in this postwar period that by 1757 one of every fifteen people in Boston received public assistance by working in almshouses or through out-pensions.[5] For decades to come Massachusetts politics was largely directed at matters concerning the colony's public credit and debt. The experience of Massachusetts with paper money and inflation prior to the Revolution was the most severe of the colonies. Closer to the Canadian border where most conflict between England and France usually occurred, Massachusetts contributed more of its wealth and militia to Britain's cause than the other colonies. The economic benefits of war for the Commonwealth rarely matched their cost.

England's wars with France were not the only source of military-induced deficits. South Carolina fought the Tuscarora and Yamasee Indian tribes in wars lasting nearly a decade. The colony issued £90,000 by 1717, £120,000 by 1723, and £210,000 by 1736. "On a per capita basis this was more than even Massachusetts had emitted. Just as in the Puritan colony, paper money depreciated rapidly."[6]

Other colonies issued paper money, and not always in time of war. The colonies' boom and bust economic cycle took its toll when the wars' stimulus departed, leaving the port cities in particular to feel the pain of recession and depression. Following the Queen Anne's War, Pennsylvania experienced a serious depression in the early 1720s caused by a glut in the West Indian grain market, sending wheat prices tumbling. First farmers, and then artisans, merchants, and shippers were gravely afflicted by the depression. In response to the calamity, Pennsylvania emitted paper currency to assist the economy and aid the poor:

> The sting of the recession was relieved by the emission of £45,000 in paper bills in 1723 and 1724, to be lent at 5 percent interest and secured by mortgages on land and houses. These bills, according to the law, were "chiefly intended for the benefit of the poor, industrious sort of people," and although they could not improve the West Indian grain market, they at least kept debtors out of the clutches of the town's wealthiest merchant-money-lenders, who "exacted Bonds of every Body at 8 percent."[7]

This favorable experiment in public credit convinced the Pennsylvanians to issue more bills of credit in 1728, with similar positive results: "Paper money, issued in large amounts as a cure for fundamental economic problems in New England, had magnified the plight of Boston's wage earners. Issued in small amount in Pennsylvania to combat trade recession, it had proved Philadelphia's salvation."[8]

New York also distributed paper money to aid its economy. In 1724, William Burnet, governor of both New York and New Jersey, petitioned the English government for permission to issue paper money. England rarely reacted favorably to such requests, leaving Burnet convinced that the home government failed to appreciate the importance of "compulsive paper credit."[9] The colony added paper to its specie currency to ward off the ill effects of its eight-year trade depression in the early 1730s. New York printed £12,000 in 1734 and £48,350 in 1737 to remedy "the Decay of Trade & Other Difficulties which this Colony has the Misfortune to have Labored Under."[10] Another colony, Maryland, issued £90,000 in paper currency during 1733 "to enable the people to meet their taxes," and "a substantial share of the bills was allotted for a governor's house, repairs of the capital buildings, a prison in every county; but the bulk was to be a bounty to planters for destroying 'unmerchantable' tobacco."[11] To solve North Carolina's trade imbalance of the 1740s, colonial legislator William Borden " 'proved by arithmetick' that the remedy was £100,000 of non-interest-bearing loan bills of credit, or any sum for which there was a necessary demand."[12] The proposed expansion of the currency would act as a subsidy for North Carolina's merchants and planters to overcome their unfavorable economic circumstances.

The colonies emitted paper money not only to finance wars and fight recessions, but also to meet the demands of trading with England. Lacking adequate stores of gold and silver specie to conduct economic transactions, the colonies began distributing paper money to prevent what they called "oppression to debtors." The colonies were economically as well as politically subservient to England and the pattern of trade under the mercantile system drained the colonial merchants of specie. The intent and effect of trading under mercantilist measures was to benefit England at every turn. So the price of English goods bought by the colonists was often greater than that paid for colonial products in England and the trade imbalance made specie payments to the mother country increasingly difficult.[13] Many merchants and debtors were unable to pay their debts, as the colonies lacked sufficient circulating specie to meet transactions requirements. An alternative form of exchange was needed, at least to maintain trade within and between the colonies, and thus more bills were soon issued to meet this purpose.

Employing bills of credit in this fashion did not always make for easy relations between the colonies. For example, a colony plagued with unemployment and stagnated trading conditions could soon find itself distributing paper money of decreasing value, thereby leaving merchants from other colonies holding depreciated currency. On the other hand, if the currency held its value the economic outcome could benefit all parties concerned. The case of Rhode Island and Massachusetts exemplified the problem of colonial interchange:

> The advantage of such bills is seen from Rhode Island's great gains from paper. That colony used to purchase considerable European goods from Massachusetts. Thereby Massachusetts "gained the carriage, merchants' and often the wholesalers' profits." Massachusetts obtained not only gold and silver and other commodities for direct returns to the mother country, but also articles "capable of additional improvements" in Massachusetts, and at the enhanced value serving as returns to England in a more remote way.[14]

However, the gains from issuing paper money might also be unequal.

> But now the roles are reversed. Rhode Island will continue to gain if she continues to provide enough bills at low interest and reduces the term of issue so that the quantity can be varied as trade requires. Her great advantage of money at a low interest will eventually create a balance of debt against us, in her favor. This might be worse than the debt to the mother country, for after the payments of produce and treasure to her she will require our lands to make up the balance.[15]

Whatever difficulties paper money posed for economic transactions and political relations between the colonies, they were relatively minor when compared to the strain it exacted between the colonies and England.

England grudgingly tolerated the expansion of colonial public credit and debt by way of paper currency to accommodate war's economic necessities, but over time Parliament grew impatient with the practice. By 1764 England had adopted extensive restrictions on the distribution of paper bills in all colonial governments. Applied to New York and Pennsylvania, the Currency Act of 1764 was just one of several imperial policy statements aimed at controlling "the violent fluctuations in the Atlantic economy." England's tough enforcement of its custom laws, the 1765 Stamp Act, the 1767 Townshend Act, the 1774 Intolerable Act, as well as the Currency Act, were measures designed to gain revenues for the Crown and protect English sovereignty in the New World. By preventing colonial governments from issuing paper currency, the British intended to safeguard their overseas investments and economic arrangements from currences that were ever subject to rapid devaluation. The Currency Act's effects were immediately felt in New York and Pennsylvania: "Locally issued paper money thus provided the circulating medium of local trade. When it was disallowed, internal trade shriveled up, hurting merchant and artisan alike and obliging traders to concoct ingenious schemes for issuing fiat money that might gain legislative approval and escape royal notice."[16] Along with those other parliamentary actions that the colonists regarded as outrageous, the imposition of the Currency Act further strained colonial relations with England and eventually incited revolution.

As its widespread use suggests, these Americans accepted the distribution of paper money and the expansion of public credit as necessary colonial policy to finance their incessant wars and assist their all too often weak economies. The uneven rise and fall of the colonial economies, due to their dependence on England's wartime and mercantile interests, left large segments of the population in poverty and susceptible to politics that endorsed a prominent role for government in the marketplace. For instance, New York City's municipal elections of 1733 and 1734 found the Morrisite political faction calling for "the erection of a new almshouse and poorhouse [as] a campaign promise and worked for the emission of £12,000 in paper money, to be used primarily in construction of fortifications in the port." During Boston's 1719 local elections, the Boston Club, under the direction of Elisha Cooke, Jr., the creator of the country's first "urban political machine," won control over the city's public offices by supporting an expanded paper money supply. The club's "leaders assumed that the political interests of the artisans and laborers were well served by the same measures from which they hoped to benefit—an increase in the supply of paper money, a strict hedging of the governor's patronage and prerogatives, and the promotion of public works projects such as the construction of a bridge across the Charles River and a canal across Cape Cod. It was not against material gain that the popular leaders inveighed but privilege and narrowly concentrated power."[17]

Paper currency, in addition to poorhouses, workhouses, widow and veteran pensions, and public works, served as a device to help colonial artisans, lesser merchants, the poor, and those in debt. Many of these beneficiaries were respectable citizens whose economic condition stemmed from imperial economic and wartime policies, and they could be politically mobilized to oppose those politicians who sought to prevent the emission of bills of credit.

Considerable political discord did exist among colonials on the matter of paper currency and the expansion of the public credit. By 1747 in Massachusetts, "the long experience with paper money and the era of war had shattered all sense of community and commonweal."[18] Opposition to paper money arose for economic, moral, and political reasons, and the political divisions over the matter frequently reflected class antagonisms, as illustrated in the early Massachusetts experience with bills of credit. When the colony first issued paper currency dissent was initially weak and divided, and came from people like Judge Samuel Sewall. The judge argued that "the merchants unjustly complain of a scarcity of money, for they have exported and continue to export the real money."[19] A member of Boston's elite Puritan society, Sewall directed his comments at the poorer merchants and artisans who suffered from specie losses in the latest war. Later, in 1714, a group of small merchants led by Elisha Cooke, Jr., proposed that a private land bank be allowed to emit £300,000 in private paper money in lieu of the public bills. While the public bills were backed by the colony's projected tax revenues, the private land bank would be backed by subscribers mortgaging their property. Paul Dudley, the colony's attorney general and the governor's son, argued in his pamphlet *Objections to the Bank of Credit* that paper money was necessary to preserve the colony's economy in the short term. He laid the blame for the colony's specie-poor condition not on the recent wars, however, but on the "ordinary people" who he claimed were wasteful, profligate, and often drunk. Dudley "shared a class-biased view that it was the indulgence of the common people in buying imported European goods and falling into debt that contributed to the trade imbalance, drained the colony of specie, and thus necessitated issues of paper money, which in turn led to a depreciation of the currency."[20]

Dudley and his mercantilist allies defeated Cooke's proposal on the grounds that an emission of paper notes was best administered by the government, because only public institutions, such as the Bank of England, backed their paper money bills of credit with gold or silver specie. In 1739 Parliament prohibited similar schemes for a private manufacturing bank and a silver bank, at the request of Massachusetts governor Jonathan Belcher. Parliament eagerly limited the colony's paper currency supply, whether it was privately or publicly emitted.

Inflated prices and deflated currency plagued Massachusetts in particular, because of the Commonwealth's frequent and costly involvement in England's wars. Thus, Massachusetts rarely was in the position to retire its paper currency, which represented the colony's debt. In 1748, however, Parliament granted the Commonwealth £200,000 to compensate for the expenses it incurred in King George's War. How the colony would employ the sterling quickly became a matter of intense political debate, with Massachusetts governor William Shirley urging that the funds be used to reduce the government's volume of paper currency. Shirley and the colony's wealthier residents argued that the paper created inflation; the governor's opponents claimed the proposed currency contraction would disrupt trade and produce unemployment, thereby forcing the government to once again issue bills of credit to restore prosperity.[21] Moreover, the lower classes feared the English sterling would only find its way into the hands of the colony's wealthy merchants. The author of the currency redemption legislation in the Commonwealth's assembly, Thomas Hutchinson, observed this concern when he wrote that the common people believed the sterling would "fall to the share of men of wealth, and would either be exported or hoarded up, and no part of it would go to the labourer, or the lower class of people, who must take their pay in goods, or go without." The redemption bill passed the assembly, paper currency was redeemed, and Hutchinson and his fellow merchants were quickly voted out of office in the 1749 elections. Hutchinson's house was set ablaze, while "a crowd had gathered in the street, cursing the colony's most avid deflationist and shouting, 'Let it burn! Let it burn!' "[22]

During the 1720s the Pennsylvania legislature confronted the matter of how best to solve the colony's economic depression, which arose primarily from its trade imbalances with England. In 1721 a bill was introduced into the colonial legislature to permit the emission of paper money, but conservative merchants from Philadelphia defeated the plan. Most of these same Philadelphia representatives were turned out of office by angry voters in the next colonial election. The Quaker merchant Isaac Norris described the electorate's mood: "All Encouragement hath lately been given & all ways taken to Insult Creditors and render men of ability . . . obnoxious, in mobbish discourses & wretched argument." After observing the newly elected members of the legislature, Governor William Keith noted, "The clamor is universall for Paper Money." The legislature authorized the distribution of £15,000 in 1722 and £30,000 in

1723. Isaac Norris railed against "this Vile paper currency . . . our rotten paper money," for the currency was "the contrivance & refuge of Bankrupts & designers." James Logan, another wealthy Quaker, felt that "those who tried 'new politics' and invented 'new and extraordinary Measures' such as paper money misunderstood the roots of economic distress. The rich were rich because of their 'Sobriety, Industry and Frugality'; and the poor were poor because of their 'luxury, Idleness and Folly.'" In response, an unknown pamphleteer explained the positions of "Mr. Robert Rich," who opposed paper money, and its supporter "Roger Plowman." Said Plowman to Mr. Rich, "The principal Reason why you are angry with Papermoney [is] because People who are in your Debt can raise money to pay you, without surrendering up their Lands for one half of what they are worth."[23]

Finally, any review of colonial attitudes and policies on debt should mention the position taken by Benjamin Franklin on paper money. Franklin's career in Philadelphia politics began by his writing the 1724 pro-paper money pamphlet *A Modest Enquiry into the Nature and Necessity of a Paper Currency.* Franklin endorsed paper money's use to stimulate trade to benefit all parties involved, including England. Declared Franklin:

> Those who are Lovers of Trade, and delight to see Manufactures encouraged, will be for having a large Addition to our Currency. For they very well know, that People will have little Heart to advance Money in Trade, when what they can get is scarce sufficient to purchase Necessities, and supply their Families with Provision. . . . and allowing that the Crown is the more powerful for its Subjects increasing in Wealth and Number, I cannot think it is the Interest of England to oppose us in making as great a Sum of Paper Money here, as we, who are the best Judges of our own Necessities, find convenient.[24]

In another pamphlet, *The Administration of the British Colonies,* written in the early 1760s, Franklin said that paper money "lent upon interest to settlers, creates money," for it is the "true pactolian stream which converts all into gold that is washed by it." Nevertheless, though Franklin endorsed paper money, he continued to support the gathering of specie through industry and thrift, as "Poor Richard" encouraged, and he objected to the frivolous use of paper by other colonies.[25]

Franklin suffered his only electoral defeat in a matter related to paper money. In the colony's internal politics, Franklin opposed Pennsylvania's leader, Thomas Penn, and in 1764 Franklin and his allies endorsed a plan to obtain a royal governor for the colony to replace Penn. In 1764 Parliament prohibited Pennsylvania and New York from issuing paper currency, however, and this restriction, together with other impe-

rial policies that were considered unwarranted, made anyone associated
with the Crown highly unpopular. Through his plan to replace Penn with
a royal governor, Franklin was hopelessly linked with England and Parliament, and his subsequent electoral defeat, "given his immense popularity, [was] a reversal of public opinion almost unthinkable hereto-
fore."[26] Franklin soon informed his friends in England that a major
reason for America's hostility toward the mother country resulted from
Parliament's decision to restrict bills of credit.[27]

Before the Revolutionary War, every colonial government at one time
or another engaged in deficit spending by issuing interest-bearing securities that acted as circulating currency. Because this paper was redeemable in specie and paid interest it constituted an obligation on the
colonial governments' expected tax revenues, and thus it truly served as
deficit financing. Moreover, the distribution of paper currency was widespread and issued in large amounts. Between 1702 and 1750, for example,
Massachusetts emitted paper currency in all but three years. Following
the lead of Massachusetts, New Hampshire, Rhode Island, Connecticut,
New York, and New Jersey emitted paper currency before 1711. Then
South Carolina issued its bills of credit in 1712, Pennsylvania in 1723,
Maryland in 1734, Delaware in 1739, Virginia in 1755, and Georgia in
1760. By 1774, an estimated $12 million in paper currency circulated
throughout the colonies.[28]

Colonial America's experience with bills of credit had a decisive influence upon the way deficit spending and public debt would be regarded by
the nation until the late 1830s. First, based on the positive results drawn
from their colonial past, the emission of paper currency became the
primary financial device the states used to fund the Revolutionary War.
Colonial governments found paper money to be a valuable source of
revenue in past wars and in times of economic distress, "hence in the
crisis of the Revolution the colonists could hardly by expected to turn
away from paper currency."[29] Second, though an excessive emission of
bills of credit could stimulate inflationary tendencies in the economy and
depress the currency's value, colonial legislatures abstained from placing
statutory limits on the distribution of paper currency or what passed for
deficit spending. This tradition persisted when the colonies became
states, as no state adopted such a constitutional provision until after
1840. Third, this period before the Revolution came to be regarded as
something of a golden age of paper money. In 1785 a petition to the
Pennsylvania legislature that requested new paper emissions observed,
"From the earliest settlement of America most of our improvements have
been aided by medium of paper currency." David Ramsey, author of the
1793 book *History of the American Revolution*, claimed the successful
use of paper money during the Revolution's early stages "was in some
degree owing to a previous confidence, which had been begotten by

honesty and fidelity, in discharging the engagements of government." A New York newspaper correspondent wrote in 1786 that "before the commencement of the late war, when public faith was still in possession of vestal chastity, divers [or several] of the states, then provinces, had large sums in circulation . . . it circulated freely and at its full nominal value on a perfect equality with specie."[30] These expressions of faith in paper money and public credit, sometimes romantic and mythical, paved the way for future deficit spending by the state governments, despite restrictions placed on state-emitted bills of credit by the United States Constitution.

Revolution and Debt

When the American colonies initiated their war for independence they were economic "colonies" in the complete meaning of the word. Subjected to British economic control through the mercantile system, the colonies were in a terrible financial position to fight an extensive war against the world's most powerful economic and military power. Lacking adequate gold and silver specie to conduct even normal peacetime commercial transactions, thus requiring the frequent issue of paper currency, the former colonies faced the unpleasant prospect of financing a protacted war. To remedy this state of affairs the Continental Congress issued millions of dollars in paper currency, the famous "continental." The Congress also borrowed extensively from domestic and foreign lenders. When the war finally came to a victorious conclusion, the Congress found itself some $54 million in debt.[31]

The Continental Congress soon adopted a national paper currency after the war began, and then it emitted an initial $2 million in June 1775. "The issuance of paper money was the only way to finance the war—in any case, the habit of restoring the currency emissions was so ingrained in the colonists that nothing else was seriously considered."[32]

As the war progressed the Congress became increasingly desperate, and rapidly produced more paper currency as the country's domestic specie resources were simply unable to meet the cost of war. "The demands were so pressing that money had to be printed every month, then every fortnight. Congress stuffed the maw of the Revolution with paper money. By the spring of 1778, emissions were five and ten millions at a time and expenditures were about a million a week." Estimates vary, but the Continental Congress emitted over $200 million in paper currency during the war; one very reliable estimate is $226 million, and the several colonies issued independently a similar amount.[33]

The Congress borrowed liberally from foreign and domestic sources to supplement its meager income. Domestic borrowing was achieved principally by selling "loan-office certificates" to the public at interest rates varying between 4 and 6 percent, payable in specie after the war. The first issue of 4 percent certificates raised $5 million in October 1776. During the course of the war, Congress increased the interest rate to make the certificates more attractive to financiers. These rates, however, represented only the certificates' face value, for in real terms the rate of return was as high as 30 percent as repayment would be in specie, not paper currency.[34] Sold for no less than $200 or $300 each, these certificates were intended to act as long-term securities rather than circulating currency. Moreover, their high purchase price assured that the certificates were "purchased almost wholly by wealthy citizens," for these loan certificates "were the security of the moneyed investor."[35]

The rebelling colonies also found it necessary to seek financial assistance abroad, primarily from Holland, France, and Spain. Through the negotiations of its skillful agents in Europe, such as William Short, the war's fortunate battlefield turn of events which encouraged lenders, and the French king's desire to see Britain defeated, the Continental Congress obtained much-needed funds from other nations. Louis of France anxiously supported the Americans against England, making secret and outright grants and loans to Congress. During the years 1778 to 1783, France granted 6 million livres, and then loaned another 34 million livres, equal to $6.3 million. Holland, the other major lender, loaned the struggling Congress 23.5 million florines in eight separate loans, the equivalent of $9.4 million.[36] Thus, approximately a quarter of the war's debt was owed to foreign bankers and governments.

Foreign and domestic borrowing were crucial to the war effort, but the Revolution's financing depended foremost upon the distribution of paper currency. The Continental Congress originally expected its scrip to maintain face value, and for the war's first year and a half the currency's value held up well, "probably because cash payments replaced the credit transactions characteristic of the colonial period, and because the growing wartime economy created a need for an expansion of circulating medium."[37] As the war dragged on, however, the Congress issued larger amounts of currency, subjecting the scrip to devaluation and even speculation by government officials. "Speculation, peculation, engrossing, forestalling, with all concomitants, afford too many melancholy proofs of the decay of public virtue," declared an outraged George Washington.[38] How the Congress employed the paper currency was also a matter for concern. Benjamin Franklin angrily wrote in 1779: "The extravagant luxury of our country, in the midst of all its distresses, is to me amazing. When the difficulties are so great to find remittances to pay for the arms and ammunition necessary for our defense, I am astonished and vexed to find upon inquiry, that much the greatest part of the congress interest bills come to pay for tea, and a great part of the remainder is ordered to be laid out in gewgaws and superfluities."[39]

After a few years of combat the congressional currency was "not worth a continental." To control the country's high inflation rates and to rescue its deflated currency, a desperate Congress resolved on September 3, 1779, to end the future emission of paper currency when its total amount reached $200 million. Later, on March 18, 1780, the Congress drastically revalued the continental, setting one specie dollar equal to forty paper dollars, thereby reducing a portion of its debt from $200 million to $5 million.[40] Coinciding with the states' ratification of the Articles of Confederation in 1781, Congress took action to allow the states to assume a more prominent role in financing and administering the Revolutionary War.

One reason the Congress enlarged the states' control over the war effort was to raise public confidence in the national currency. Faith in the continental was so low that in 1778, for instance, the Reverend Charles Chauncy of Boston gave a lecture on the subject titled "The Accursed Thing be taken away from a People if they would reasonably hope to stand before their Enemies."[41] Congress authorized the states to tax the continental currency out of existence, and then issue new state and continental currency at the ratio of one new dollar for every twenty old continentals collected. Nevertheless, to a great extent the states were responsible for this fiscal mess. Because the states failed to tax themselves adequately to finance the War, Congress was left little choice except to print money, borrow heavily, and commit the nation to a course of deficit spending throughout the Revolution.[42] The political reality of the time called for prudence on the part of state governments that wished to impose heavy wartime taxation. After all, the Revolution itself was being fought, in part, to prevent British taxation, and the states had no desire to alienate their loyal citizens:

> Throughout the war the governments needed large sums of money. The people of Massachusetts shared the general reluctance to pay taxes, and at first many feared that taxes might create tories out of rebels. They therefore relied upon deficit financing, borrowing money, and issuing more paper than would have been necessary had heavier taxes been levied. Without adequate backing the paper depreciated more rapidly than was desirable. Laws making it legal tender only postponed the depreciation and defrauded creditors. A general fiscal reform became essential, and creditors of the state, private creditors, and everyone suffering from inflation joined forces to effect a reform. Their efforts produced a conflict within the legislature that foreshadowed the contest of the mid-eighties.[43]

The states generally failed to meet their financial obligations to the Congress. Some states were known, for example, to reduce their taxes and the size of their militia once British forces left the area.[44] "One head," Washington disgustedly wrote in 1780, was "gradually changing into

thirteen."[45] As late as 1782 when Congress requested $8 million from the
states to meet its expenses, the states provided only $400,000 of the
request. In July 1783, Robert Morris, the chief financial officer of Congress, wrote to the state governors that since 1781 the total state contributions to the national treasury added to less than $750,000. North Carolina,
Georgia, and Delaware failed completely to provide their assessed contributions. South Carolina was the only state to pay its quota; of the nine
other states Rhode Island paid "nearly" a quarter of its assessment, with
the rest paying less.[46] Only the fresh infusion of foreign loans, and the
competent direction and austerity measures offered by financier Morris,
provided the Congress with the necessary funds to bring the war to a
close.

Much of the difficulty in financing the war was due to the Articles of
Confederation, which undermined the nation's struggle for independence and hampered the retirement of the war's debt. The states argued
over the Articles of Confederation for four years before ratifying the
document, and the debate over ratification indicated that sectional concerns still outweighed national union.[47] Fearful of strong national authority, even during wartime, the states denied the central government the
right to raise revenue independently, or to control trade between the
United States and foreign countries. Article VIII of the Articles of Confederation treated the matter of taxation:

> All charges of war, and all other expences that shall be incurred for the
> common defense or general welfare, and allowed by the united states in
> congress assembled, shall be defrayed out of a common treasury, which
> shall be supplied by the several states in proportion to the value of all land
> within each state. . . . The taxes for paying that proportion shall be laid and
> levied by the authority and direction of the legislatures of the several states
> within the time agreed upon by the United States in Congress assembled.[48]

Article XII guaranteed the repayment of debts incurred:

> All bills of credit emitted, monies borrowed and debt contracted by, or
> under the authority of Congress, before the assembling of the united states,
> in pursuance of the present confederation, shall be deemed and considered
> as a charge against the united states, for payment and satisfaction whereof
> the said united states, and the public faith are hereby solemnly pledged.[49]

The Continental Congress could request funds from the states, but if a
state failed to comply and refused to make its payments to the national
treasury, the Congress had no leverage, outside of persuasion, to obtain
the state's obligations.

To paraphrase Karl Marx, in three important ways the Revolutionary
War's debt "weighed like a nightmare on the brain of the living." In the

first place, the debt's existence provided grist for the political mill at both the federal and state levels of government. How the debt would be financed, and who would benefit from its financing, deeply divided the public. Second, the war convinced a number of influential leaders that eventually the new nation would require a stronger central government than had operated under the Continental Congress. What particularly struck these men was the poor showing made by the states when they were requested to shoulder their share of the financial, as well as military burden. During the War of Independence, Alexander Hamilton noted in disgust that the "mode of supplying the army—by state purchases—is not one of the least considerable defects of our system." Hamilton's negative experience was reflected in his policy of debt management as secretary of the treasury, and in the statements made and actions taken by his fellow soldiers to strengthen the union of states.[50] The war created strong nationalists out of those who opposed the central authority of Parliament. Finally, the debt's financing at the national level after Yorktown was designed to give "rise to an economic motive for supporting the central government; its existence justified the demand for federal taxes. . . . The public debt was vital to the strategy of centralization."[51] "A national debt if it is not excessive," Hamilton claimed in 1781, "will be to us a national blessing; it will be a powerful cement of our union."[52] This strategy for centralization guided the policies of Robert Morris.

Robert Morris reluctantly accepted the position of superintendent of finance for the Continental Congress, but the appointment was hailed by all as a marvelous and necessary step. A wealthy merchant who distrusted centralized authority, Morris was the Revolutionary War's financial hero. Given ever-greater responsibilities, he not only managed congressional finances, but he in effect became Washington's quartermaster-general. Morris brought order to a chaotic treasury, and he forced the Congress and the states to accept the use of contracts for ordering supplies for the first time in the war. He brought trained clerks and managers to administer what was then the Treasury Board, centralized receipts and disbursements, and when necessary Morris used his own excellent credit, "which was always higher than that of the government," to supplement the funds of the Continental Congress.[53] Morris proposed the creation of a quasipublic Bank of North America to help provide credit and specie for the Congress and the states, and on May 26, 1781, the "national bank" received its charter, thus establishing the first commercial bank in the United States.

Appalled by the states' unwillingness and inability to assist the Congress, Morris, with the support of new members in the Congress who desired a stronger central government, began consolidating the public debt under congressional auspices, though such action ran counter to the Articles of Confederation:

The way in which Morris and the Nationalists proposed to deal with the public debt violated the letter and spirit of the Articles of Confederation. Under the Articles, the common charges of the war, including the expenses of the federal government, were to be paid by requisitions, and the same procedure applied to debts. It was expected that Congress would ascertain the amount of the debt and draw up a requisition assessing a certain proportion of it upon each state. As the states paid the requisition, Congress would discharge the debt.[54]

Morris and his colleagues claimed that the debt was the obligation of Congress, and the states' financial history did little to encourage the notion that on their own the states would repay the debt. Morris also proposed that Congress be allowed to adopt its own system of taxation. The states twice defeated this proposal in 1781 and 1783. Despite Morris's failure to gain approval for the national import duties needed to provide direct revenue for Congress, "the legacy which he and the Nationalist Congress bequeathed to the cause of national government was the appropriation of the Revolutionary debt for the federal government."[55] Left with a large visible and centralized debt, and inadequate financial support from the states, the financial pressures from domestic and foreign creditors on the nation were immense, and they were a major factor in the call for a constitutional convention.

Morris was correct in his assessment of the states' capability to pay their debts. The states had their own internal obligations to meet, which partially explains their inability to make their contributions to the national treasury. Each state had to consider how to retire its own debt, decide what sort of taxes should be levied and at what rate, and determine whose claim to the public revenues should be honored and in what order. The state legislatures found the debt's payment was "a problem that became one of the chief issues for more than a decade." As at the national level, state certificates and bills of credit "began to flow from the country to the towns and from the poorer citizens to the richer."[56] Like colonial bills of credit, the states' paper currency acted to relieve the financial burden of debtors by providing them with some sort of accepted money to pay their bills. Paper money almost always consisted of interest-bearing bonds that imposed future obligations on the states, however; thus the states engaged in deficit spending when they issued paper money. The notes were interest-bearing to make them acceptable to creditors and investors, and to maintain the value of paper currency relative to the worth of specie. These bills of credit tended to gravitate to the states' wealthy creditors who demanded payment in specie. To meet these demands for payment, the state governments taxed their own specie-poor public. Considerable animosity developed between creditors who generally opposed the distribution of paper money in favor of specie and debtors who favored paper currency to expand the money supply.

Historian Jackson Turner Main conducted an extensive analysis of seven legislatures' roll call votes taken between 1776 and 1787, and after reviewing the sociological backgrounds of the individual leaders in each state, Main concluded:

> The legislators with least property, localist experience, and humble origins usually tried to defer collection [of the debt]. . . . Thus during the war years the Localist group might be most anxious to pay expenses arising from the war. . . . Other things being equal, however, the Localists tried to restrict or reduce payment of these public debts. The reasons lay in the factors that led the Localists to oppose most such expenditures: the benefits flowed to men and to areas connected with the Cosmopolitans, while the money had to be raised by everyone.[57]

Serious divisions existed in the state legislatures over their public debt, and these divisions reflected class lines and financial interests. These legislatures faced tremendous financial problems, but they possessed few solutions. One alternative available to the states when further taxation was either politically unwise or economically impossible was to issue more paper currency. The distribution of additional paper "would not only enable private debtors to repay their obligations, thus satisfying creditors, but would permit governments to do the same even to the servicing of public debts.[58] By issuing this new currency the states essentially renegotiated their debts through deficit spending.[59]

Pressed by an uncooperative economy, the real needs of debtors and taxpayers to pay their obligations, the always depressing lack of specie, and the absence of bank and lending institutions in all but three states to provide credit, the states were forced to emit bills of credit and other forms of paper money. Creditors were displeased, speculators profited by the emissions, currency devaluated, and inflationary tendencies in the economy grew stronger. Until changes could be made in the nation's political and economic systems, however, the states had little choice except to follow the path the colonial and state governments had taken for the better part of the preceding century. These emissions, nevertheless, forced influential Americans to reconsider the Articles of Confederation's ability to provide for a healthy economy and an adequate national defense, and so in 1787 delegates from the several states met in Philadelphia to draft the Constitution.

Constitutional Limitations on Deficit Spending

The Revolutionary War left the states and the national government with a massive public debt, and the Articles of Confederation left the nation with an unworkable institutional arrangement for retiring that debt. Between 1781 and 1786 the Congress requested the states meet their as-

sessed financial obligations of $15.7 million, yet Congress received but
$2.4 million during those same years.[60] Clearly, some reorganization of
government finances was called for, and those who favored a stronger
central authority firmly believed they could ease the nation's financial
difficulties. Their thoughts on what this new institutional order should
resemble were best expressed by Alexander Hamilton and James Madison
in the *Federalist Papers.*

Hamilton began with the assumption that "money is, with propriety,
considered as the vital principle of the body politic; as that which sus-
tains its life and motion and enables it to perform its most essential
functions." Without proper financing, the nourishment of the body politic, "the government of the Union has gradually dwindled into a state of
decay, approaching nearly to annihilation." The problem was obvious to
all, even those citizens "least conversant in our public affairs."[61] The
method of financing established by the Articles of Confederation not only
had starved the central government, but it also placed a severe burden
upon the states, obligated as they were to share their revenue with Congress. Oppressed by their own debts, the states simply failed to respond to
the revenue quotas assigned to them by Congress and the Articles of
Confederation.

The state quotas, claimed Hamilton, were financially unproductive and
inherently unfair. Article VIII from the Articles of Confederation directed
that state contributions to Congress should be made "in proportion to the
value of all land within each state, granted to or surveyed for any Person,
as such land and the buildings and improvements thereon."[62] Hamilton
argued that "the wealth of nations depends upon an infinite variety of
causes," and thus, "there can be no common measure of national wealth,
and, of course, no general or stationary rule by which the ability of a state
to pay taxes can be determined." The result of imposing such a rule was
that a general inequality should exist among the states as to their ability
and willingness to meet their quotas and "this inequality would itself be
sufficient in America to work the eventual destruction of the Union." In
the presence of this inequitable method of raising revenue, with its disastrous long-term consequences, the national government was helpless to
secure revenue because it lacked power: "The United States as now
composed have no power to exact obedience, or punish disobedience to
their resolutions, either by pecuniary mulcts, by a suspension or divesti-
ture of privileges, or by any other constitutional means."[63] By appealing
to the need for reform and the states' vested interests, Hamilton thought
the solution was obvious: "What remedy can there by for this situation,
but in a change of the system which has produced it—in a change of the
fallacious and delusive system of quotas and requisitions? What substitute can there be imagined for this *ignis fatuus* in finance, but that of
permitting the national government to raise its own revenues by the

ordinary methods of taxation authorized in every well-ordered constitution of civil governments?"[64] # 30

If the national government was granted the power and authority to raise its own taxes, these revenues would be derived, primarily, from its control over import and export taxes, in other words, tariffs. Therefore, "the particular states, under the proposed Constitution, would have COEQUAL authority with the Union in the article of revenue, except as to duties on imports ... this leaves open to the states far the greatest part of the resources of the community." The states, however, would soon find their future need for revenue decreasing, "because in a short course of time the wants of the States will naturally reduce themselves within *a very narrow compass*; and in the interim, the United States will in all probability bid it convenient to abstain wholly from those objects to which the particular States would be inclined to resort."[65] As the national government assumed new and greater powers under the Constitution, particularly the centralized control over the nation's future war efforts, the states no longer would be forced to engage in deficit spending. Meanwhile, the states' expenses would be limited to maintaining their small administrative apparatus: "It is true that several of the States, separately, are encumbered with considerable debts, which are an excrescence of the late war. But this cannot happen again, if the proposed system be adopted; and when these debts are discharged, the only call for revenue of any consequence which the State governments will continue to experience will be for the mere support of their respective civil lists."[66]

As the states' wartime duties diminished, and with them the need to emit bills of credit, the Federalists believed the states would no longer need to issue paper currency. The states would be denied the authority to coin money, if for no other purpose, said Madison, than for reasons of economy, as "a right of coinage in the particular States could have no other effect than to multiply expensive mints and diversify the forms and weights of the circulating pieces."[67] Though simple economy might be the basis for prohibiting state mints, restrictions placed on bills of credit had moral overtones:

The extension of the prohibition to bills of credit must give pleasure to every citizen in proportion to his love of justice and his knowledge of the true springs of public prosperity. The loss which America has sustained since the peace, from the pestilent effects of paper money on the necessary confidence between man and man, on the necessary confidence in the public councils, on the industry and morals of the people, and on the character of republican government, constitutes an enormous debt against the States chargeable with this unadvised measure, which must long remain unsatisfied; or rather an accumulation of guilt, which can be expiated no otherwise than by a voluntary sacrifice on the altar of justice of the power which has been the instrument of it.[68] # 44

These suggested restraints on state power once allowed by the Articles of Confederation had the purpose of curbing the states' ability to engage in deficit spending and incur debt. Madison's concern for the "forms and weights or circulating purposes" extended further than saving the cost of minting coins. Several states, including Massachusetts and Connecticut, distributed copper coins to supplement their gold and silver specie and bills of credit. By ruling that only silver and gold could be used to pay debts the practice of emitting copper coins, except by the federal government, would be eliminated. Thus, the Federalists called for abolishing the traditional methods of deficit spending employed by colonial and then state governments during the preceding ninety-nine years.

Hamilton was quite clear that prohibitions applying to the state governments should not have the same effect on the national government, particularly in light of its new and enhanced responsibilities: "As the duties of superintending the national defense and of securing the public peace against foreign or domestic violence involves a provision for casualties and dangers to which no possible limits can be assigned, the power of making that provision ought to know no other bounds than the exigencies of the nation and the resources of the community."[69] Moreover, although the states were denied revenues that might arise from tariffs, the central government would have access to all revenue sources, as Hamilton argued there should be no distinction between "internal" and "external" revenue for the federal government.

> Who can pretend that commercial imposts are, or would be, alone equal to the present and future exigencies of the Union? Taking into the account the existing debt, foreign and domestic, upon any plan of extinguishment which a man moderately impressed with the importance of public justice and public credit could approve, in addition to the establishments which all parties will acknowledge to be necessary, we could not reasonably flatter ourselves that this resource alone, upon the most improved scale, would even suffice for its present necessitities.[70]

Hamilton reasoned there should be no restrictions on the national government's authority or power to tax, and thus to spend, "as revenue is the essential engine by which the means of answering the national exigencies must be procured, the power of procuring that article in its full extent must be necessary and comprehended in that of providing for those exigencies."[71]

To those who wished to limit the power of federal taxation, Hamilton replied that their "observations founded on the danger of usurpation [of the states' revenue sources] ought to be referred to the composition and structure of the government, not to the nature or extent of its powers." Hamilton rejected any overarching rule designed to prevent the central government's collection of revenue, even by way of issuing bills of credit.

Hamilton instead believed sufficient financial controls existed in the structure of the Constitution itself, in the legislative process, for "what is the power of laying and collecting taxes but a *legislative power*, or a power of *making laws* to lay and collect taxes?"[72] In any case, Hamilton predicted the national government would voluntarily curb its financial appetite:

> Although I am of opinion that there would be no real danger of the conse-
> quences which seem to be apprehended to the State governments from a
> power in the Union to control them in the levies of money, because I am
> persuaded that the sense of the people, the extreme hazard of provoking the
> resentments of the State governments, and a conviction of the utility and
> necessity of local administrations for local purposes, would be a complete
> barrier against the oppressive use of such a power.[73]

Hamilton did believe that if the federal government's excesses needed to be checked, the ultimate arbiter and authority rested in public opinion and political action: "If the federal government should overpass the just bounds of its authority and make a tyrannical use of its powers, the people, whose creature it is, must appeal to the standard they have formed, and take such measures to redress the injury done to the Consti-tution as the exigency may suggest and prudence justify."[74]

The Federalists and the Anti-Federalists debated the Constitution's worth in the journals and newspapers of the period, after the Constitution's adoption by the convention at Philadelphia. The proceedings at Philadelphia formed the basis for Hamilton and Madison's writings, and the argument over bills of credit reached a climax at the Constitutional Convention in August 1787. The Constitution had been through several drafts during the convention, which lasted from May until September, and these earlier drafts contained two provisions that differed signifi-cantly from the final copy distributed to the states for ratification. The draft of August 6 specified in Article VII, Section I, the legislative branch's powers, included the authority "to borrow money, and emit bills, on the credit of the United States."[75] This early draft reflected Hamilton's views, expressed later by Publius, that no constraints should be placed on federal deficit spending or in other words, the power to raise revenue and spend as necessary in times of emergency.

This section of the Constitution was altered somewhat in the motion made by Gouverneur Morris, delegate from Pennsylvania, on August 16, 1787. The subsequent debate was recorded by James Madison:

> Mr. Govr. Morris moved to strike out "and emit bills on the credit of the U.
> States"—If the United States had credit such bills would be unnecessary; if
> they had not, unjust & useless.
> Mr. Butler, 2ds. the motion.

Mr. Madison, will it not be sufficient to prohibit the making them a *tender?* This will remove the temptation to emit them with unjust views. And promissory notes in that shape may in some emergencies be best.

Mr. Govr. Morris, striking out the words will leave room still for notes of a *responsible* minister which will do all the good without the mischief. The Monied interest will oppose the plan of Government, if paper emissions be not prohibited.

Mr. Ghorum [Gorham] was for striking out, without inserting any prohibition, if the words stand they may suggest and lead to the measure.

Col. Mason had doubts on the subject. Congs. he thought would not have the power unless it were expressed. Though he had a mortal hatred to paper money, yet as he could not foresee all emergencies, he was unwilling to tie the hands of the Legislature. He observed that the late war could not have been carried on, had such a prohibition existed.

Mr. Ghorum. The power as far as it will be necessary or safe, is involved in that of borrowing.

Mr. Mercer was a friend to paper money, though in the present state & temper of America, he should neither propose nor approve of such a measure. He was consequently opposed to a prohibition of it altogether. It will stamp suspicion on the Government to deny it a discretion on this point. It was impolitic also to excite the opposition of all those who were friends to paper money. The people of property would be sure to be on the side of the plan, and it was impolitic to purchase their further attachment with the loss of the opposite class of Citizens.

Mr. Elseworth [Ellsworth] thought this a favorable moment to shut and bar the door against paper money. The mischiefs of the various experiments which had been made, were now fresh in the public mind and had excited the disgust of all the respectable part of America. By withholding the power from the new Governt, more friends of influence would be gained to it than by almost any thing else. Paper money can in no case be necessary. Give the Government credit, and other resources will offer. The power may do harm, never good.

Mr. Randolph, notwithstanding his antipathy to paper, could not agree to strike out the words, as he could not foresee all the occasions that might arise.

Mr. Wilson. It will have a most salutary influence on the credit of the U. States to remove the possibility of paper money. This expedient can never succeed whilst its mischiefs are remembered. And as long as it can be resorted to, it will be a bar to other resources.

Mr. Butler remarked that paper was a legal tender in no Country in Europe. He was urgent for disarming the Government of such a power.

Mr. Mason was still averse to tying the hands of the Legislature *altogether.* If there was no example in Europe as just remarked it might be observed on the other side, that there was none in which the Government was restrained on this head.

Mr. Read, thought the words, if not struck out, would be as alarming as the mark of the Beast in Revelations.

Mr. Langdon had rather reject the whole plan than retain the three words ("and emit bills").

On the motion for striking out

N.H. ay. Mass. ay. Ct. ay. N.J. no. Pa. ay. Del. ay.

Md. no. Va. ay.** N.C. ay. S.C. ay. Geo. ay.

The clause for borrowing money, agreed to nem. con.

Madison made the following footnote at the place of the double asterisk: "This vote in the affirmative by Virga. was occasioned by the acquiescence of Mr. Madison who became satisfied that striking out the words would not disable the Govt. from the use of public notes as far as they could be safe & proper; & would only cut off the pretext for a paper currency and particularly for making the bills a tender either for public or private debts."[76]

By a vote of 9 to 2 the convention deleted from the draft Constitution the federal government's specific authority to issue bills of credit, but the Constitution did not outlaw their use, as it would do at the state level. Nathaniel Gorham from Massachusetts emphasized this difference when he indicated the convention was "striking out" the authority to use bills of credit "without any prohibition." Furthermore, Gorham believed "the power [to issue bills] as far as it will be necessary or safe, is involved in that of borrowing." What the Constitutional Convention did was express its dissatisfaction with the traditional practice of allowing government securities to act as a circulating paper currency, which subjected government notes to speculation and devaluation. Furthermore, by striking out the federal government's express authority to distribute bills of credit, the opposition to the Constitution by influential men of money would be diluted. The convention did concur that the public use of noncirculating promissory notes was an acceptable method for incurring public debt for deficit spending. Gouveneur Morris agreed and stated that "striking out the words will leave room still for notes of responsible minister." Direct authority to engage in deficit spending was established by the Constitution, which granted Congress the power "to borrow money on the credit of the United States."

Madison's notes are quite clear on these points, and he appears to have played a decisive role in this debate. Madison claimed that by limiting the use of bills of credit as a tender, as a circulating currency, this action alone would sufficiently constrain their more harmful effects. Therefore, bills of credit could function as "promissory notes" to meet the nation's emergencies. Madison's fellow Virginia delegates, Edmund Randolph and George Mason, echoed Madison's concern that a complete suspension of the bills could harm the government's response to a national crisis. The Virginia delegation finally voted for Morris's motion, and, as indicated by Madison's crucial footnote, they felt reassured that the federal government's ability to incur debt and deficits was not prohibited. Madison wrote he "became satisfied that striking out the words would not disable the Govt. from the use of public notes . . . & would only cut off the pretext for a paper currency." Thus, Madison had skillfully transformed the issue of prohibiting bills of credit into the more pedestrian matter of constraining paper money's use as a circulating medium, and ensured the convention's support for the federal government's continued use of promissory notes and other debt instruments. In this fashion, Madison's interpretation of the Constitutional Convention served as a preface to the *Federalist Papers*, in which Hamilton stated that no constraints should be placed on the national government's ability to raise revenue.[77]

Gouverneur Morris and his supporters were no doubt pleased with this outcome, for now the new federal government's credit was guaranteed and moneylenders could make loans to the government without fear that their profits on the deal could be lessened by the fluctuating value of bills of credit. All the delegates, however, were aware of the financial and social consequences that might follow an act to suspend bills of credit. Morris feared the "monied interests," the nation's wealthy merchants and creditors, would oppose the Constitution altogether if the document validated bills of credit. Oliver Ellsworth from Connecticut believed that "men of influence" would be attracted to support the Constitution by such a prohibition. Meanwhile, James Mercer of Maryland thought it best to avoid the conflict that might occur between creditors and the "opposite class" of specie-poor debtors, small merchants, artisans, and farmers. Even if the delegates did not wish it, the Constitution would be intepreted by many to be a document favoring the wealthy elements in society. This interpretation did indeed exist after the convention prohibited bills of credit at the state level and required debts and taxes to be paid in specie.

Although the convention struck from the Constitution the provision authorizing the federal government's power to issue bills of credit, it did specifically prohibit the states from making such emissions. The August draft of the Constitution included this section in Article XIII: "No state, without the consent of the legislature of the United States, shall emit bills of credit, or make any thing but specie a tender in payment of debts."[78] Under this article the states could emit bills of credit if they gained congressional approval, but action taken by the convention on August 28 altered the language of this draft in a motion made by James Wilson of Pennsylvania and Roger Sherman of Connecticut:

> Mr. Wilson & Mr. Sherman moved to insert after the words "coin money" the words "nor emit bills of credit, nor make any thing but gold & silver coin a tender in payment of debts" making these prohibitions absolute, instead

of making the measures allowable (as in the XIII art:) *with the consent of the Legislature of the U.S.*

Mr. Ghorum thought the purpose would be as well secured by the provisions of art: XIII which makes the consent of the Gen. Legislature necessary, and that in that mode no opposition would be excited; whereas an absolute prohibition of paper money would rouse the most desperate opposition from its partizans.

Mr. Sherman thought this a favorable crisis for crushing paper money. If the consent of the Legislature could authorize emissions of it, the friends of paper money would make every exertion to get into the Legislature in order to license it.[79]

The convention passed the motion, with Virginia voting no, Maryland a split vote, and the eight other participating states voting for the measure.

Nathaniel Gorham was correct about the opposition the Constitution would "excite" if states' rights were violated by a prohibition on bills of credit. The Federalists and their supporters faced stiff opposition in their quest for a stronger national government, logically enough, from the Anti-Federalists, and the matter of paper money and debt was one of many issues that separated the two factions. Whereas the Federalists had their Publius, the pen name used by Madison, Hamilton, and John Jay to defend the Federalist point of view, the Anti-Federalist writers adopted the names of Brutus, Cato, Amicus, and Cincinnatus. Cincinnatus argued in the *New York Journal* during November and December 1787 that the suspension of state bills of credit only added to the pressure the states already experienced in paying their public debts. For the national government to force debt payments in gold and silver, as the proposed Constitution specified, dangerous new taxes, payable in specie, would produce new hardships for the people and deny economic reality:

> The state debts, independent of what each owes to the United States, amount to about 30,000,000 dollars; the annual interest of this is 1,000,000. It will be expected that the new government will provide for this also; and such expectation is founded, not only on the promise you hold forth, of its reviving and supporting public credit among us, but also on this unavoidable principle of justice—that is, the new government takes away the impost, and other substantial taxes, from the produce of which the several states paid the interest of their debts, or funded the paper with which they paid it. The new government must find ways and means of supplying that deficiency, . . . in hard money, for . . . paper . . . cannot [be used] without a violation of the principles it boasts. The sum then which it must annually raise in specie, after the first year, cannot be less than 4,800,000. At present there is not one half this sum in specie raised in all the states. And yet the complaints of intolerable taxes has produced one rebellion and will be mainly operative in the adoption of your constitution.[80]

The rebellion Cincinnatus refered to was Shays's Rebellion, which took place in Massachusetts and was but one of several such acts of violence occurring throughout the country, as specie-poor debtors found it increasingly difficult to pay their taxes and debts with hard money.

Disagreement over the Constitution's prohibition of state bills of credit surfaced elsewhere at the state ratifying conventions. At the North Carolina convention a Mr. Locke addressed the assembled delegates and reviewed the reasons that impelled the state to issue bills of credit:

> Great reflections are thrown on South Carolina [by the Federalists] for passing *pine-barren* and *instalment* laws, and on this state for making paper money. I wish those gentlemen who made those observations would consider the necessity which compelled us in a great measure to make such money. I never thought the law which authorized it a good law. If the evil could have been avoided, it would have been a very bad law; but necessity, sir, justified it in some degree. I believe I have gained as little by it as any in this house. If we are to judge of the future by what we have seen, we shall find as much or more injustice in Congress than in our legislature. Necessity compelled them to pass the law, in order to save vast numbers of people from ruin. I hope to be excused in observing that it would have been hard for our late Continental army to lay down their arms, with which they had valiantly and successfully fought for their country, without receiving or being promised and assured of some compensation for their past services. What a situation would this country have been in, if they had had the power over the *purse* and *sword!* If they had the powers given up by this Consitution, what a wretched situation would this country have been in! . . . This state could not pay her proportion in specie. To have laid a tax for that purpose would have been oppressive. What was to be done? The only expedient was to pass a law to make paper money, and make it a tender.[81]

In Virginia, Patrick Henry looked to the future and expressed his concern that some private speculators and state governments, particularly those in the North, had gathered up cheap, devalued paper currency and that then under the Constitution their repayment would necessarily be in specie at their nominal value. States like Virginia would be forced to make costly and unjust specie payments to speculators. Henry throughout this period refused to support the Constitution's ratification.

> Mr. Henry apologized for repeatedly troubling the committee with his fears. But he apprehended the most serious consequences from these restrictions on the states. As they could not emit bills of credit, make any thing but gold and silver coin a tender in payment of debts . . . though these restrictions were founded on good principles, yet he feared they would have this effect; that this state would be obliged to pay for her share of the Continental money, shilling for shilling. He asked gentlemen who had been in high authority, whether there were not some state speculations on the matter. He

had been informed that some states had acquired vast quantities of that money, which they would be able to recover in its nominal value of the other states.[82]

The arguments made by Cincinnatus, delegate Locke, and Patrick Henry reflected the feeling held by many Americans that the Constitution favored the rich over the poor, the wealthy merchant over the farmer, and the northern states over the southern states. In a more contemporary setting, this sort of analysis formed the basis for historian Charles Beard's thesis that economic gain was the primary motive behind the Constitution. Many Anti-Federalists and state legislators, as Beard pointed out, desired to renegotiate or break their contractual obligations with creditors and moneylenders.[83] If the Constitution was ratified in its final form, these transactions previously made on the grounds of a devalued currency would be paid their face value in specie, which, as Patrick Henry claimed, benefited speculators. The matter of who would gain by the payment of the war's debts soon contributed to the split between Alexander Hamilton and Thomas Jefferson, as described in the next chapter, which would have a profound effect on American politics. Even at the Virginia state ratifying convention, James Madison essentially agreed with Henry's assessment of the situation, and he admitted that "there might be some speculations on the subject. . . . The old Continental money was settled in a very disproportionate manner."[84]

Following the Constitutional Convention and during the debate over ratification, the Federalists repeatedly identified the Anti-Federalists as supporters of paper money and easy public credit.[85] The Anti-Federalists did defend the states' right to emit bills of credit, largely on the basis that governments must act when the public is threatened by economic crisis or war, and emitting bills of credit, and therefore engaging in deficit spending, was a legitimate act by sovereign governments. The Federalists, ironically, agreed with this logic. In the *Federalist Papers*, Hamilton argued that the federal government should be granted the revenue generating and spending authority required to meet national emergencies. The real issue between the Federalists and the Anti-Federalists, however, was determining what government or governments were sovereign, with the right to spend and tax as it or they thought proper. The debate was a political one about power and authority, and not about economics, devalued currency, or inflation. The Anti-Federalists saw in the Constitution some of the same oppressive features that plagued the colonial governments under parliamentary rule. Before the Revolution, the central government in England restricted the colonies from emitting bills of credit under the pretext of controlling inflation and speculation. The Anti-Federalists believed that now another central authority was attempting to pursue this same course of action, and the outcome would be just as pernicious. The Anti-Federalists distrusted a powerful executive branch, an aristocratic Senate, and a central government geographically removed from the public.

Maintaining the states' authority to print bills of credit was just one device the Anti-Federalists endorsed to protect state power. At the New York ratification convention the Anti-Federalist Gilbert Livingston proposed that an amendment be added to the Constitution: "That no money be borrowed on the credit of the United States without the assent of two thirds of the senators and representatives present in each house."[86] Both New York and Rhode Island included such amendments in their statements of ratification delivered to the Congress. The Federalists who controlled the Congress evidently never discussed these proposed amendments, and they were probably lost in the shuffle during the transition to the new system of government. The imposition of such an amendment and the intended maintenance of state-emitted bills of credit would have had very real economic consequences, but their obvious purpose was to preserve states' rights against the federal government and the Constitution.

The Federalist solution to the weaknesses found in the Articles of Confederation was, of course, adopted by the states and the Constitution became the supreme law of the land. Hamilton and Madison received what they requested in the *Federalist Papers*: Article 1, Section 8, of the Constitution empowered the national government to collect taxes, provide for the common defense, and borrow money on the credit of the United States. Article 1, Section 10, prohibited the states from issuing bills of credit, and it required debts to be paid in specie. The responsibility for directing the nation's war effort was centralized, and with it, so Hamilton thought, the need for states to emit bills disappeared. The Federalists had their Constitution, but their next challenge required them to use the document to govern the nation and provide for its finances.

The Anti-Federalists played an important role in American politics by expressing the fears that many people had about the presence of a strong central government. These concerns retained their significance, as the Jeffersonian and Jacksonian "persuasions" demonstrated. At the time, the Anti-Federalist distrust of a strong central government appeared quite reasonable considering the nation's negative experience with Parliament. Moreover, many Americans continued to see themselves primarily as citizens of their respective states; this raised questions of political allegiance which could only later be answered by the Civil War. Meanwhile, just as the Anti-Federalists understood the issue, the ability of a government to obtain revenues, whether through taxation or deficit spending, and to spend those revenues as it deemed necessary defined that government's power and authority. The debate that soon took place between Alexander Hamilton and Thomas Jefferson over the federal government's proper role in society revolved around this same point. Jefferson's political and philosophical victory over Hamilton turned out to be the decisive factor in shaping American attitudes about balanced and unbalanced federal budgets in the nineteenth century, but Jefferson's triumph only recognized what the Anti-Federalists knew, that restricting a government's ability to unbalance its budget limited its sovereignty.

4

Creating a Symbol: Balanced Budgets and the Concept of Corruption

The second branch of the system is high duties . . . first, to protect the manufacturer, by enabling him to sell his wares at higher prices, and next to produce an excess of revenue. The third branch of the system is internal improvements, which is the sponge which is to suck up the excess of revenue.

JAMES K. POLK, on the Whig's "American System" and the relationship between tariffs, federal spending, and public debt, 1830

The democracy of this country never can be overthrown. The true democratic spirit is endued with immortal life and strength. Our star glitters far above; clouds may now and then pass under it, but there it shines undimmed and untouched, and there it will shine when the factions who decry it, with all that belongs to them, shall be remembered as the creatures of a day and the offspring of corruption. Nor can the Democratic Party become essentially corrupt, either. For true democracy has within itself a perpetual spring of health and purity.

WALT WHITMAN, 1847

The young republic fought its revolution and soon adopted a constitution prohibiting what passed at the time for state deficit spending. The complex, controversial, and pressing issue of administering the great debt incurred during the war remained to be settled. This task quickly shattered the unity of the governing Federalist party and provided Alexander Hamilton's opponents with a powerful reason for avoiding future federal deficit spending. Balancing the national budget rapidly assumed a sym-

bolic meaning, certainly to selected elite figures, far surpassing any pro-
saic bookkeeping notion of balance, or what might be considered by
modern standards the "macroeconomic" effects produced by federal deficits and debt. Instead, budget balancing took on a widely understood,
comprehensive symbolic purpose that is now largely forgotten but remains astonishing for its consistency of thought, influence on public
policy, and force underlying the development of American political and
economic institutions. Indeed, this crucial post-Revolutionary period is
principally responsible for this country's rejection of national deficit
spending in the early nineteenth century as a matter of principle, while
foreign governments freely engaged in the practice.

The issues of debt management, deficit spending, the nature of federal
expenditures, and the organization of the country's financial system polarized Americans from the earliest days of the young nation's existence.
Federalists opposed Jeffersonian Republicans, and Whigs opposed Jacksonian Democrats. Behind many an American's fear of federal deficits
and debt was the concept of "corruption." This concept symbolically
joined the Jeffersonians and the Jacksonians and their rural ethic of small
government and small business against their Federalist and Whig adver-
saries, causing Jefferson to call eventually for an amendment to the Constitution requiring balanced federal budgets to prevent the "corruption"
of the people and their government. Derived from ancient, neoclassical,
and English political philosophy, "corruption" identified the ways a
public debt could undermine a democratic republican government. The
concept dominated American thought and public policy during this period, and the symbolic meaning of balanced budgets became rooted in the
nation's politics until the Republican party's ascendancy during the Civil
War.

Alexander Hamilton and the Public Debt

The new federal government and its first secretary of the treasury, Alexander Hamilton, faced a bleak financial situation in 1789. The nation's
public sector was in debt some $77 million, with over $50 million of this
sum consisting of the federal government's own foreign and domes-
tically held debt. At the same time the nation lacked anything resembling a comprehensive banking or financial system, as the entire country
possessed only three banks, which made financing the debt through
private institutions an impossible proposition.[1] The federal government's revenue came by way of customs duties, consisting of approximately $2 million a year between 1789 and 1791.[2] This amount was
insufficient to meet the government's interest payments on outstanding
debt in addition to its normal administrative functions. Consequently, as
one of its first actions, the government in 1789 was forced to borrow

$170,000 from the semipublic Bank of North America, placing the country further into debt. Hamilton's monumental task of reorganizing the federal government's financial position was made all the more difficult by the multiple forms of bonds, securities, bills of credit, and promissory notes circulating throughout the country, each providing a different rate of interest. Despite Robert Morris's valiant struggle to centralize and standardize the debt, Hamilton's initial significant undertaking as secretary was simply to identify how much money the government owed and to whom, and report this information to Congress. Hamilton's reports to the Congress are significant because they articulated his views on the importance of budget balancing, and because Hamilton's plan for financing the debt provoked substantial opposition from within the Federalist party. Those who opposed Hamilton, for example, Madison and Jefferson, eventually left the Federalists to form their own party, emphasizing the need to balance budgets, retire the nation's debt, and limit federal expenditures in order to prevent Hamilton's vision of a strong central government from becoming reality.

In January 1790, Hamilton submitted to Congress his famous "Report Relative to a Provision for the Support of Public Credit." The report outlined Hamilton's strategy for financing the public debt, and it explained why Hamilton's immediate concern was focused less on achieving balanced budgets or retiring the debt than it was on establishing the nation's credit. Hamilton had little or no hope of quickly retiring the debt, which actually grew by several million dollars while the Federalists controlled the presidency. Only in 1796 and 1797, Washington's final two years in office, did federal revenues rise higher than $8 million, with surpluses over $2 million each year. Hamilton could hardly have expected surpluses of this limited size to reduce the debt in any significant manner. Instead, Hamilton was preparing the nation for any future emergencies that might force the government into deficit spending. Hamilton believed deficit spending to be the normal course of action "in times of public danger." Thus, Hamilton wrote:

> That exigencies are to be expected to occur, in the affairs of nations, in which there will be a necessity for borrowing.
>
> That loans in times of public danger, especially from foreign war, are found an indispensible resource, even to the wealthiest of them.
>
> And that in a country, which, like this, is possessed of little active wealth, or in other words, little monied capital, the necessity for that resource, must, in such emergencies, be proportionably urgent.[3]

Interestingly enough, Hamilton foresaw deficit spending occurring in war and peacetime, as long as such government expenditures were necessary. The report goes on to describe the beneficial effects of a well-maintained public credit. Hamilton pointed out that governments possessing good credit records would find new loans readily accessible and offered at reasonable rates of interest, but "when the credit of a country is in any degree questionable, it never fails to give an extravagant premium." Meanwhile, lenders would willingly make loans to responsible governments, for "the advantage to the public creditors from the increased value of that part of their property which constitutes the public debt, needs no explanation." Hamilton recognized that perhaps the most difficult task he faced in obtaining congressional permission to enact his program was to mollify the fears of the traditional debtor class of farmers and small merchants, who believed from prior experience that the public debt would primarily benefit wealthy creditors. Hamilton reminded his audience that debt instruments, like bills of credit, often functioned as circulating currency, thus relieving debtors of the need to deal only in specie. "It is a well-known fact," he wrote, "that in countries in which the national debt is properly funded, and an object of established confidence, it answers most of the purposes of money. Transfers of stock or public debt are there equivalent to payments in specie; or in other words, stock, in the principal transactions of business, passes current as specie." With this paper currency added to the circulating specie, "trade is extended by it; because there is a larger capital to carry it on. . . . Agriculture and manufactures are also promoted by it" and "the interest of money will be lowered by it."[4]

Hamilton directed his statements to farmers and landholders, for the United States was predominantly an agrarian society. He acknowledged that rural America was hard-pressed by the withdrawal of state bills of credit, but with the federal government exercising responsible restraint in its financial affairs, new editions of federal securities acting as circulating currency could stimulate the nation's agricultural sector. As Hamilton saw it, the nation would truly be bound together and economically enhanced through its debt: "This decrease, in the value of lands, ought, in a great measure, to be attributed to the scarcity of money. Consequently whatever produces an augmentation of the monied capital of the country, must have a proportional effect in raising that value. The beneficial tendency of a funded debt, in this respect, has been manifested by the most decisive experience in Great-Britain."[5] Remarkably, Hamilton offered to those who trusted him the least a financial solution similar to the one states and colonies employed during the previous century, but this time Congress would play the role of Parliament.

The heart of Hamilton's proposal called for the federal government to renegotiate the terms of its foreign and domestic debt.[6] Holders of outstanding national and state securities would be offered new federal "stock" paying attractive interest rates, usually between 4 and 6 percent. Payment of the principal and sometimes the interest was deferred for as much as ten years. In addition, the government would allocate $600,000 from its customs revenues for administrative purposes, with the balance of revenues used to finance the debt. In this way, balanced budgets and surpluses were encouraged, as excess revenues could be applied to financing and eventually retiring the debt. Nevertheless, Hamilton's most pressing motivation to balance the budget and avoid deficits came from his need to obtain surplus federal funds to make interest payments on the outstanding debt, rather than from an orthodox view that deficits were harmful. These arrangements were favorably received by foreign lenders, particularly France and Holland. Impressed by Hamilton's actions, Holland later willingly made new loans to the federal government for $9.4 million during the 1790s. Hamilton's plan for financing the foreign debt was approved by Congress, but his method for accommodating the domestic debt proved to be ideologically divisive and difficult to get adopted.

The "Report" contained two very controversial proposals regarding domestic debt, with a third discordant recommendation made in his "Second Report" on public credit. First, Hamilton urged the federal government to assume financial responsibility for the states' Revolutionary War debts. Centralizing the nation's debts was a idea dating back to Robert Morris's administration at the Treasury Board. By assuming these debts the states would be unable to claim the Constitution oppressed them by forcing states with large debts to press debilitating taxes on specie-poor citizens. Furthermore, Hamilton believed assumption would centralize the gathering of tax revenues, thereby preventing the "collusion and confusion" over governments competing for revenues. Assumption of these debts allowed Hamilton to request the imposition of domestic excise taxes to support the added state debts, continuing the centralization of the public sector's revenues, expenditures, and debt. Hamilton also reasoned that assumption would increase public support for a strong central government, particularly support from those who might lend funds to the new national government: "If all the public creditors receive their dues from one source, distributed with an equal hand, their interest will be the same. And having the same interests, they will unite in the support of the fiscal arrangements of the government."[7]

Objections were raised to the planned assumption because it benefited "creditor" states at the expense of "debtor" states (Virginia, North Carolina, Delaware, Maryland, Pennsylvania, and New York). During the Revolution some states were forced to borrow heavily to finance the war effort, thereby incurring substantial debts, but after the war they were prevented from retiring their debts because postwar economic hardships curtailed the collection of adequate tax revenues. These were the debtor states, that had borrowed funds from the Continental Congress to maintain their wartime commitments. The more fortunate states were able to pay their debts soon after the war with cheap, devaluated paper currency. These were the creditor states, and Hamilton planned to reimburse them with specie and notes at their nominal value. The creditor states would be handed a windfall gain, the difference between the deflated currency's value and the worth of the new federal stock. On the other hand, the debtor states owed money to the federal government and they were now obligated to pay the government in specie or notes at their current value.[8]

In the second controversial aspect of his report, Hamilton proposed to pay to the bearer the full nominal value on outstanding debt instruments. Redeeming government securities at nominal value plus interest, Hamilton argued, was a fundamental practice needed to establish the federal government's reputation as a good credit risk. Hamilton's opposition, however, pointed out that during the war and afterward, many of the original purchasers of government securities, who were often Continental soldiers, were forced by their financial plight to sell their bonds at less than full value to speculators and wealthy creditors. Speculation was rampant, and neither Hamilton nor his supporters denied that the practice reached into every state, or that speculation allowed some individuals to realize tremendous financial gains. In response to Hamilton's report, his opponents, including James Madison, proposed several alternative repayment plans benefiting the original bond holders and giving the creditor or speculator the interest only on the devaluated security. Hamilton vigorously rejected such designs, claiming any "discrimination" between the original and current debt holders was unreasonable, for "it is inconsistent with justice, because in the first place, it is a breach of contract; in violation of the rights of a fair purchaser." Moreover, Hamilton feared that such discrimination reduced the government's future ability to obtain loans at less than exorbitant cost, as lenders would charge the government high interest rates to protect their investment.[9]

On December 14, 1790, Hamilton sent to Congress "The Second Report on the Further Provision Necessary for Establishing Public Credit (Report on a National Bank)." The second report outlined the need for a bank of the United States, the third leg of Hamilton's plan for the nation's finances. Occasionally the federal government relied upon Robert Morris's Bank of North America for small loans, but Hamilton believed that the country's financial needs required a bank with larger assets and additional economic authority. The Bank of North America's capital stock was limited to $2 million, while the proposed bank's stock was set at $10 million. Hamilton asserted that with these additional assets the Bank of the United States would invaluably assist the nation's economic development: "The tendency of a national bank is to increase public and private credit. The former gives power to the state for the protection of commerce among individuals. Industry is increased, commodities are multiplied, agriculture and manufacturers flourish, and herein consists the true wealth and prosperity of a state."[10]

James Madison, William Branch Giles from Virginia, James Jackson from Georgia, and others, opposed the bank, but they did not argue against its economic value to the republic. Rather, Hamilton's bank was opposed on constitutional grounds, for the Constitution failed to provide the direct authority they argued was required to create such an institution. Thomas Jefferson also wrote against the bank, claiming any congressional authorization violated the Constitution's intent, and "to take a single step beyond the boundaries thus specially drawn around the powers of Congress is to take possession of a boundless field of power, no longer susceptible of any definition."[11] By preventing the Congress from chartering the bank, Madison and his friends sought to constrain Hamilton and limit an interpretation of the Consitution that might leave the central government with undefined and excessive powers.

Hamilton won on all three issues. Assumption and redemption were approved by Congress in the 1790 Funding Act, while the First Bank of the United States received its charter in 1791, proving to be a valuable financial resource for the federal government as all sides believed it would. Assumption of state debts became law only after Hamilton offered the permanent placement of the nation's capital as a bargaining chip, convincing some southern delegates that locating the capital at Georgetown on the Potomac was worth assumption. "So two of the Potomac members," Jefferson later observed, "(White and Lee, but White with a revulsion of stomach almost convulsive) agreed to change their votes, and Hamilton undertook to carry the other point."[12] Hamilton obtained the bank's charter on a highly sectional, North-South vote in Congress. Attorney General Edmund Randolph and Secretary of State Jefferson, both Virginians, appealed directly to President Washington to veto the measure. Washington rejected their appeal after reading Hamilton's defense, "Opinion on the Constitutionality of the Bank." Jacob Cooke, a modern editor of Hamilton's works, evaluated the essay and later wrote: "Hamilton's opinion is the most brilliant argument for a broad interpretation of the Constitution in American political literature. His bold assertion of federal sovereignty provided a firm foundation for the exercise of governmental powers which our later history proved to be essential."[13] Indeed, when Jefferson and Madison became presidents they left virtually intact Hamilton's financial system.

Jefferson and the Concept of Political Corruption

Hamilton's victories were paid for at the highest political price. The Federalist party, though not yet formally divided, was hopelessly and permanently polarized. Madison and Jefferson, once closely allied with Hamilton, now were his most vocal and intense political enemies. Jefferson wrote in *The Anas*, almost twenty years after Congress approved state debt assumption in the Funding Act, "This measure produced the most

bitter and angry contest ever known in Congress, before or since the
Union of the States."[14] The division between Hamilton's Federalists and
what was to become the Democratic-Republican party had a decisive
effect on the way the public regarded federal expenditures and balanced
budgets, certainly through Jacksonian Democracy and up to the Civil
War. Because the colonies first issued bills of credit in 1690, a residue of
sympathy remained in the American psyche for the occasional need for
deficit spending in times of war and economic crisis; as demonstrated by
the Anti-Federalist position taken during the ratification process, these
feelings were not yet extinguished. After the Constitution was ratified
with its provisions against state-emitted bills of credit, many states continued to deficit spend and borrow heavily until economic disaster struck
in 1837. By comparison, federal deficit spending and borrowing were
viewed with suspicion even by those who condoned such behavior by
state governments. One explanation for this divergence in opinion lies in
the distrust for the federal government Hamilton sowed in the minds of
Jefferson, Madison, and their allies. Jefferson and Madison feared and
opposed Hamilton's efforts to create a strong central government—and
the reasoning behind their fears is best explained by examining the
concept of "corruption," as Jefferson and later Andrew Jackson knew it.

Jefferson's fullest recollection of this period is contained in his work
The Anas, composed over a number of years with the relevant sections
written on February 4, 1818. From his historical vantage point Jefferson
outlined his compelling distaste for Hamilton's philosophy of government. Jefferson described his adversary in this fashion: "Hamilton was,
indeed, a singular character. Of acute understanding, disinterested, honest, and honorable in all private transaction, amiable in society, and duly
valuing virtue in private life, yet so bewitched and perverted by the
British example, as to be under thorough conviction that corruption was
essential to the government of a nation."[15]

Hamilton was to be opposed because he wished to impose a system of
government resembling the English Parliament and monarchy on the
American people. The influence of English thought and institutions on
Hamilton's thinking was well known; the Bank of the United States
imitated the Bank of England's financial and economic purpose as well as
administrative structure in nearly every respect. At the Constitutional
Convention, Hamilton presented a plan of government Jefferson considered "a compromise between the two parties of royalism and republicanism," where the executive and one house of Congress served life terms
and appointed all state governors. The financial plan Hamilton proposed
to Congress only furthered his monarchical and royalist vision: "Hamilton's financial system had then passed. It had two objects; 1st, as a puzzle,
to exclude popular understanding and inquiry; 2d, as a machine for the
corruption of the legislature. . . . And with grief and shame it must be
acknowledged that his machine was not without effect."[16]

How could Hamilton succeed if his monarchist tendencies were so obvious and odious to a nation which only recently fought against such principles? In the first place, Jefferson believed Hamilton "got unchecked hold of General Washington." Jefferson pictured Washington as so old and senile that he was willing "to let others act, and even think for him." Next, the assumption policy allowed speculators to reap huge profits "filched from the poor and ignorant," while enabling "the stock-jobbing herd" to gather the number of followers needed to overwhelm those of loyal republican virtue. Finally, Hamilton outwitted his opponents in Congress by dividing his enemies and gaining their votes. Jefferson wrote,

> I know well, and so must be understood, that nothing like a majority in Congress had yielded to this corruption. Far from it. But a division, not very unequal, had already taken place in the honest part of that body, between the parties styled republican and federal. The latter being monarchists in principle, adhered to Hamilton of course . . . so that the whole action of legislature was now under the direction of the Treasury. Still the machine was not complete. The effect of the funding system, and of the Assumption, would be temporary; it would be lost with the loss of the individual members whom it has enriched, and some engine of influence more permanent must be contrived, while these myrmidons were yet in place to carry it through all opposition. This engine was the Bank of the United States.[17]

Jefferson's *Anas* contained some of the most powerful political imagery of the period. His frequent references to Hamilton's financial system as a "machine" and to the Bank of the United States as an "engine" signaled to the American people these were things alien and unwanted in a republic. Most Americans lived in the rural sections of the country and engaged in an agrarian economy. This circumstance was particularly true for Americans living in the lower half of the United States, people who were Jefferson's natural constituency. "Machines" and "engines" represented to these individuals a foreign way of life, something common to urban manufacturing centers, Hamilton's New York City for example, not pastoral America. More frightening than the machine, however, was the power of political "corruption."[18]

In the language of the times, corruption identified the political decay eating away at the foundations of republican and parliamentary governments, with England serving as the prime example of a corrupt state.[19] True republican governments provided for representation of contentious social forces and groups in a stable parliamentary setting. Any single group's ability to seize political power over the others would be prevented by parliament's institutional arrangements that "mixed" or "balanced" opposing factions. In England, the House of Lords, the House of Commons, and the monarchy acted to represent and balance the aristocracy's and the general public's interests and authority. The notion of "checks and balances" guiding the American Constitutional Convention arose from this line of political philosophy that had its roots in classical and neoclassical thought. This balance, Jefferson believed, could be upset by corrupting influences seeking to pervert a constitutional or parliamentary government in order to dominate the polity. Contemporary connotations referring to corruption in terms of graft and patronage may also apply in this case, but, in Jefferson's sense, graft and patronage were merely methods by which the balance of government was subverted to achieve a "corrupt" state.[20]

For Jefferson and other Americans, England provided the textbook example of corruption's insidious nature. After the English Restoration in 1660, Parliament appeared to fall increasingly under the spell of its ministers; not only did they act as an avenue of communications between the monarch and Commons, but over time the ministers' authority over affairs of state grew progressively independent and autocratic. The potential and real powers of the Chancellor of the Exchequer in particular were extraordinary, given the obvious role money plays in political life. Historian Lance Banning described this power in his exceptional work *The Jeffersonian Persuasion*:

> Ministers could . . . call upon additional inducements in the form of governmental offices or pensions for their parliamentary supporters. Patronage and governmental influence in elections, which made it possible for ministries to exercise a certain measure of executive control of Parliament, were one of the foundations for the great stability of eighteenth-century England. Yet the use of these techniques, the rise of cabinet direction of the state, was also an essential starting point for eighteenth-century oppositions. . . . Yet parliamentary influence was but one of many symptoms of a growing evil. Court money was employed in parliamentary elections, purchasing the representatives and debasing the electors: "the little beggarly boroughs" were "pools of corruption."[21]

Corruption, therefore, referred both to the means and the end whereby republican government was subverted. This state of degradation existed because powerful administrative agencies under the direction of their respective ministers acted to undermine and thwart the government's structural balance and its electoral process. Corruption was most easily achieved when unscrupulous ministers took advantage of speculative opportunities offered by a large public debt and the government's need for revenues. The presence of a substantial public debt, or an abundance of excess revenues, justified a minister's claim that his agency required additional employees to administer the government's finances, thus enlarging his ability to offer graft and patronage.

The concept of corruption surfaced and resurfaced in English politics, to be used by those out of power as a charge against the regime in power, who were portrayed as perverting the nation's republican virtues. Such was the case in the contest between Viscount Bolingbroke and Sir Robert Walpole. Bolingbroke claimed Walpole's ministry to be a corrupting influence whose power derived from the ability to bribe and offer patronage. Banning paraphrased Bolingbroke to explain how corruption and government revenues were intertwined:

> Growing revenues and higher rates make it possible for ministers to create a horde of officers, who fill the Parliament and exercise a rising influence in elections. The civil list provides vast funds for the corruption of Parliament, and the practice of anticipating revenues creates additional supplies. In fact, the means available to ministers have grown to such a great extent in recent years that the crown has now, through influence, powers just as great as it once had by prerogative. The fate of English liberty depends on a union of good men against the progress of corruption.[22]

This understanding of corruption was part of America's political baggage brought over from England, and was available to Jefferson in his fight against Hamilton.

Jefferson's application of the concept was damning, as he charged "Hamilton was not only a monarchist, but for a monarchy bottomed on corruption."[23] Certainly Hamilton's financial program fit perfectly into the corruption model: the public debt and public sector revenues were centralized; the Bank of the United States was created in a mirror image of the Bank of England; Hamilton expressed interest in the *Federalist Papers* for combining the state civil service lists under a single, national corps of civil service, thus adding to the federal government's patronage powers; and his explication on the positive benefits accruing to the economy from a well-financed debt provided economic justification for the system.[24] Just as English ministers increased their following through patronage, Jefferson argued that Hamilton offered millions of dollars to speculators and favored states through assumption and redemption, and thereby "the phalanx of the Treasury was reinforced by additional recruits."[25]

Jefferson's great fear was that a central government burdened by deficits and debts would undermine its republican and constitutional foundations while it promoted widespread social and economic inequality. While speculators, bankers, and the moneyed aristocracy would benefit from the unearned financial leverage and profits derived by financing the national debt, the government would spend its added revenues by promoting an industrialized economy through Hamiltonian policies that resembled those of mercantilist and corrupted England. Once again England served as the model to be avoided, for just as its government was corrupted in no small way due to its enormous debt, English society and its moral values were also corrupted by a system of manufacturing and industry that created vast social and economic divisions.

Jefferson's widely shared distrust of industry was such that he wrote in *Notes on the State of Virginia*, "Corruption of morals in the mass of cultivators is a phenomenon of which no age nor nation has furnished an example . . . the proportion of which the aggregate of the other classes of citizens bears in any state to that of its husbandmen, is the proportion of its unsound to its healthy parts, and is a good-enough barometer whereby to measure its degree of corruption."[26] At the heart of the matter for Jefferson was his opposition to political and economic systems that prevented individuals from achieving their natural station in life. He believed in a specific form of social equality, one that allowed for the development of a "natural aristocracy," which opposed the "artificial aristocracy" created through hereditary titles or by the brutal exploitation present in industrial economies. The social conditions that best enhanced personal freedom and human development, Jefferson claimed, were evident in an agrarian community where independent yeomen participated in a republican government, versus the misery and inequity found in corrupt England's industrialized urban slums. Thus, corruption defined in terms of political economy the relationship between the citizen and the state which inhibited public and personal virtue. The concept of corruption extended to the administrative malfeasance that undermined the republic's constitutional balance of powers and to the decay of the ideal polity, America's agrarian democratic republic.

How was Hamilton's corrupting influence on the young republic to be curbed? By eliminating the Treasury's capability to pervert the Constitution's republican balance, by retiring the public debt, by balancing the federal budget to keep the debt from expanding, by limiting government expenditures so budget surpluses could provide necessary revenues for a "sinking fund" from which earmarked funds would be used to retire the debt, and by opposing the Hamiltonian scheme for employing the government's finances to promote manufacturing. From 1801 until 1808, every year but one of Jefferson's administration, the federal government ran moderate budget surpluses. Jefferson did add $15 million to the national debt to pay for the Louisiana Purchase, but payments on this added debt were financed in a manner that did not restrict the government's ability to achieve surpluses. The Louisiana Purchase itself was regarded as a device to prevent corruption, for Jefferson argued that the new territory would provide the needed land to preserve America's agrarian nature and to prevent the crowding and deprivation associated with the slums of industrialized cities. Declared Jefferson in a letter to James Madison: "This reliance [on the people] cannot deceive us, as long as we remain virtuous; and I think we shall be so, as long as agriculture is our principal object, which will be the case, while there remains vacant lands in any part of America. When we get piled upon one another in large cities, as in Europe, we shall become corrupt as in Europe, and go to eating one another as they do there.''[27] Only in this context did Jefferson willingly add to the national debt.[28]

Jefferson's political and economic policies were greatly aided by a resurgent economy that provided substantial federal revenues and by a friendly Congress that endorsed Jefferson's desire to limit expenditures. Once Jefferson defeated John Adams, his Republican party controlled the presidency for nearly three decades, while presidents James Madison and James Monroe followed Jefferson's formula for preventing the federal government's corruption. Jefferson's philosophical and political triumph over Hamilton was decisive. His concerns about corruption, preserving states' rights, avoiding the development of a strong centralized government by limiting federal expenditures, retiring the debt, and obtaining balanced if not surplus budgets, passed on to Andrew Jackson and the Democratic party. After Hamilton met his death at Aaron Burr's hands, many years would pass before anyone argued with such intelligence and conviction about the benefits a public debt and deficit spending might bring to the nation.

The War of 1812

The War of 1812 exemplified the political divisions separating the Federalists and Republicans. It also identified the republic's difficulty in managing a wartime economy, which ultimately drove the government deeper into debt. The war itself was the greatest military and financial debacle in American history. In each year of the war the federal government ran deficits, while the national debt grew from $45 million in 1811 to $127 million by the end of 1815. Running deficits in wartime proved to be common enough practice, but the nation's weak military showing partially stemmed from the financial frugality exercised by Jefferson and Madison over the government's military expenditures, and the war's financial crisis was exacerbated by Madison's failure to recharter the Bank of the United States once its twenty-year charter expired in 1811. In addition, Madison's failed wartime administration validated to some extent Hamilton's belief that a centralized financial system and a viable national government were necessary for a stable public credit and a responsible national defense.

Jefferson's fears of Hamiltonian corruption greatly influenced his military thinking. Under the Federalists, the government had been intent upon strengthening coastal fortifications and increasing the navy's size through the acquisition of such large fighting ships as the *United States*, the *Constitution*, and the *Constellation*. Moreover, the Federalists sought to expand the professional army due to their distrust of the general populace and the state militias. Aided by Americans' traditional fear of standing armies and navies, Jefferson and Madison reduced military spending from the Federalist levels and rejected the Federalist strategy of building additional frigates in favor of small 50-foot gunboats manned by militia sailors, sporting one gun as opposed to the *Constitution's* forty-four cannon. Jefferson viewed the Federalist desire to enlarge and professionalize the military as just one more step taken to separate the people from their government. Consequently, excluding Jackson's postwar conquest at New Orleans, American military victories were far and few between and won almost exclusively at sea by privateers and Federalist-funded regular navy frigates.[29]

The war's financial crisis came about almost by design. Albert Gallatin, Madison's treasury secretary, proposed before the conflict began that government borrowing be the primary source of revenue if war with England did occur. He informed Congress in the December 16, 1808, Treasury Department's *Annual Report* that "loans should be principally relied on in case of war."[30] Gallatin planned to maintain taxes at peace-time levels, while deficit spending covered the war's added costs. At the time such a plan seemed reasonable, for until the war began the American economy enjoyed an extended period of prosperity. But the military disasters inflicted upon the country produced uncontrollable and unforeseen expenses, draining the Treasury and the state banks. Four months after the war began Gallatin gloomily informed the president that the government required at least an added $21 million to fund the military in 1813. But additional bank loans were "unattainable," as the banks "already lent nearly to the full extent of their facilities."[31] The government found itself issuing millions of dollars worth of public stock and Treasury notes that acted as paper currency. The situation was made decidedly worse by the refusal of Congress to accept Gallatin's latest advice to raise internal taxes, thereby forcing the Treasury to offer unusually high interest rates on government securities to make them acceptable as currency and to prevent their rapid devaluation. Not until late in the war would Congress authorize a series of "war taxes" by increasing duties and excise taxes on a variety of commodities and possessions. Nevertheless, by the end of the war, "the credit of the government was gone."[32] Only the continual emissions of paper money and public stock allowed the government to muddle through until the war's conclusion in 1815.

After the War of 1812 the need for a new national bank to repair the nation's finances was obvious to everyone concerned. All sorts of scrip, state bank stock, and federal notes circulated throughout the country at widely fluctuating interest rates, most of it devalued, resulting in inflation which drove rare specie currency out of circulation. On May 10, 1816, Madison signed into law a bill chartering the Second Bank of the United States. Granted a twenty-year charter and $35 million in capital stock, as opposed to the First Bank's $10 million, the new bank's primary responsibilities were to control inflation and place reasonable restraints on the states' ability to expand credit.

The most interesting aspect of the war's financing was Gallatin's proposal to pay for it through deficit spending. Gallatin's reasoning was threefold. First, Secretary Gallatin and most of Congress believed that even in wartime the economy would remain healthy, and thus adequate bank loans would be available to the government. Second, the war's expenses were grossly underestimated by all involved. The House Ways and Means Committee, the committee in Congress most responsible for federal finances, planned for financing a war at far less than its actual cost.[33] Third, and most important, Gallatin and Congress feared the wrath of angry taxpayers and state governments more than they feared deficit spending. Gallatin's failure to propose adequate internal taxes and the reluctance of Congress to increase taxation can largely be explained by their desire to avoid infringing upon a source of revenue long claimed by the states.

The war's effect on the economy did little to enhance the public's affection for deficit spending. Private debtors may have been aided temporarily by the expanded money supply, but the economic dislocation was severe enough to persuade the Republicans to accept the ghostly presence of Hamilton's national bank, with all its potential for corrupting the republic. The bank, and the matter of its recharter in the 1830s, later proved to be the dominant political issue in Andrew Jackson's presidency. If the War of 1812 provided economic evidence to reinforce Jefferson's position on the evils of deficit spending, the national bank issue tested of the nation's willingness to allow such a powerful centralizing force to exist.

Jackson, the Bank War, and Liquidation of the Debt

The rapid development of the nation's banking system in the early nineteenth century had major consequences for both federal and state deficit spending. In the absence of private-sector banking, colonial and later state governments often emitted bills of credit to supplement specie currency not only to finance their normal operating expenses, but also to expand their money supplies in times of economic hardship. Operating under mercantile arrangements where the line separating the public and private sectors often remained undefined, governments took this responsibility upon themselves rather than permit the establishment of private banks that might stray from government control. Thus, after a fashion, colonial governments acted as central banks, allowing credit to grow in times of crisis. As described earlier, bills of credit constituted deficit spending, for these interest-bearing securities imposed future obligations on tax revenues.

When the number of banks in the United States increased from three in 1789 to nearly one hundred state-chartered banks by 1811, the necessity for a state government to behave as a regional bank greatly diminished, and deficit spending could be limited to accommodate just the government's operating expenses.[34] Oddly enough, while the federal government limited its expenditures to prevent corruption and to retire the national debt, state governments found they were freely able to engage in deficit spending by borrowing from banks within their own state boundaries, principally to finance the construction of canals, roads, and other "internal improvements." The Bank of the United States played a crucial role in this regard. The bank both held the federal government's bank deposits and it regulated the amount of the credit the state banks could provide their customers, including the state governments. When Andrew Jackson successfully destroyed the corrupt "monster" Bank of the United States, its control over state banks also disappeared, permitting state governments to borrow at record levels for activities far more expensive than operating costs.

Alexander Hamilton recognized the role colonial governments played in their embryonic attempts to stabilize local economies, and he anticipated the powerful position a true central bank would have in an American economy to control and expand private as well as public credit. The benefits that a well-serviced public debt and a national bank might bring to the economy served as the keystone of Hamilton's thinking. His belief in the value of a public debt was largely derived from David Hume's essay "Of Public Credit." In the essay, Hume wrote: "In short, our national debts furnish merchants with a species of money, that is continually multiplying in their hands, and produces sure gain, besides the profits of their commerce. . . . More men, therefore, with large stocks and incomes, may naturally be supposed to continue in trade, where there are public debts; and this it must be owned, is of some advantage to commerce, by diminishing its profits, promoting circulation, and encouraging industry."[35] In fact, the bulk of Hume's essay denounced public debt, but it was this section that strongly influenced Hamilton in his first report on public credit. Hamilton was still left with the problems of speculation and inflation resulting from excessive emissions of bills of credit and government debt, in addition to providing for the nation's commercial credit in the most efficacious manner. To this end he looked to Adam Smith's *Wealth of Nations* for guidance on central banking, where Smith stated:

> The stability of the Bank of England is equal to that of the British government. All that it has advanced to the public must be lost before its creditors can sustain any loss. . . . It acts, not only as an ordinary bank, but as a great engine of state. . . . It is not by augmenting the capital of the country, but by rendering a greater part of that capital active and productive than would otherwise be so that the most judicious operations of banking can increase the industry of the country.[36]

As Hamilton later wrote in his second report on public credit, where he proposed that a national bank be established, such a bank could best control the nation's distribution of paper currency and stimulate the country's commerce.[37] Under the powers granted by congressional charter, the Banks of the United States operated in much the manner foreseen by Hamilton and Smith, but efforts by the bank to control credit expansion and inflation were not always appreciated by a public that was specie-poor. Moreover, bank policies were intimately tied to deficit spending at both the federal and state levels, for when the bank contracted credit to limit inflation, much as the Federal Reserve does in twentieth-century America, the economy could suffer from recession, thereby reducing government revenues and creating the conditions responsible for deficit spending.

The Second Bank of the United States had the power to control state banking operations by presenting these banks with their own paper certificates for redemption in specie, which the bank had previously purchased in the nation's money markets. Hence, both credit and specie supplies could be controlled by the central bank. In 1819 Langdon Cheves, the bank's president and former Speaker of the House of Representatives, undertook a major effort to contract state bank credit. State regulatory controls over their own banks were extremely lax, and the inflationary situation had deteriorated to such an extent that even the famous supporter of states' rights, John C. Calhoun, endorsed the central bank's program. During congressional debate over the bank's charter in 1816, for example, Calhoun pointed out that the state banks issued over $170 million in bank notes on the basis of less than $15 million specie.[38] The bank's actions soon forced the state banks to reduce their issues of notes to $45 million.[39] The bank's credit contraction, as necessary as it might have been to control inflation, contributed to a severe depression in the United States lasting for some five to six years.

The federal government consequently ran deficits in 1820, 1821, and 1824 but avoided other potential deficits through an extensive "retrenchment" of federal operations and expenditures, particularly military spending. During James Monroe's administration federal expenditures fell from $21.5 million in 1819 to as little as $14.7 million in 1823. What remains significant about the depression is that for the first time since the Constitution's ratification and since the federal government took power, the nation experienced a long-term economic crisis and the policy of the day clearly identified federal retrenchment rather than expansion as the desired course to follow. One reason the government acted in this manner was its fear of adding to the national debt, which swallowed up some 40 percent of all federal revenues between 1817 and 1819.[40] Therefore, the cry went out to trim the budget. In the Sixteenth Congress in 1820, for instance, Representative Howell Cobb from Georgia introduced eight measures into Congress requiring reduced spending, stating in his defense, "To me, there has always been something highly objectionable, if not immoral, in the idea of burdening our posterity, for the support of our extravagances."[41] Cobb's concern, echoed throughout American history, was that deficit spending and the debt it creates constituted a burden on future generations of taxpayers and citizens.

The election of Andrew Jackson in 1828 signaled the continuation of Jeffersonian policies in government, on the debt's retirement, and on the evils of deficit spending. Jackson, like most of his predecessors, believed in the strong maintenance of states' rights, though not at the cost of national unity, and frugality in the federal government's expenditures. Budget surpluses were needed to retire the debt, a goal finally realized under his administration in 1834, and when the debt was retired Jackson felt that what surpluses remained should be turned over to the states. Jackson's policies and a healthy economy provided the government with surpluses in every year of his administration. Jackson outlined his thoughts on these matters in his first inaugural address:

> Some of the Topics which shall engage my earliest attention as intimately connected with the prosperity of our beloved country, are, the liquidation of the national debt, the introduction and observance of the strictest economy in the disbursements of the Government. . . . a Just respect for State rights and the maintenance of State sovereignty as the best check of the tendencies to consolidation; and the distribution of the surplus revenue amongst the States according to the apportionment of representation, for the purposes of education and internal improvement, except where the subjects are entirely national.[42]

For Andrew Jackson, as for many other Americans, retiring the debt was a point of national honor and public morality. The debt materially represented the sacrifices made by the founding fathers to give the nation life, and the debt's liquidation validated their republican experiment. In the spirit of the "City on the Hill," the United States would demonstrate to the European powers that a republic could indeed be financially responsible and avoid the Old World's corrupt excesses.

Jackson had this to say in 1831 about the debt's anticipated retirement: "We shall then exhibit the rare example of a great nation, abounding in all the means of happiness and security, altogether free from debt." In 1836 he again declared, "The experience of other nations admonished us to hasten the extinguishment of the public debt." Jackson's treasury secretaries concurred with their president's sentiments. Louis McLane believed a retired debt would have a "moral influence . . . throughout the world," gaining "new confidence in our free institutions." Levi Woodbury reported to Congress in 1835 that by retiring the debt an "unprecedented spectacle is thus presented to the world." Later, President John Tyler wrote in 1842 that Americans were a "people rendered illustrious among nations by having paid off its whole debt." In 1844 President James Polk wrote about the debts of Europe, saying, "Melancholy is the condition of that people whose government can be sustained only by a system which periodically transfers large amounts from the labors of the many to the coffers of the few," and that the United States "owes to mankind the permanent example of a nation free from the blighting influence of a public debt."[43] The budget was to be balanced and the federal debt retired to prove the worth of the Revolutionary War to the entire world, if not to the Americans themselves.

However much Jackson was motivated by morality, patriotism, or practical finance, his hostility toward the federal debt and deficit spending characterized a broader set of attitudes familiar in Jacksonian Democracy. Jackson and his most devoted followers opposed debt and credit in all its forms, public and private. This antagonism stemmed from both Jackson's personal experiences with credit and the general state of the economy. Nearly ruined financially as a young man in a transaction involving the sale of land on credit, Jackson's animosity toward debt and credit in favor of hard money commerce was deeply rooted. At a time when bankruptcy laws were extraordinarily harsh, people who failed to pay their debts could receive long prison terms; the man to whom Jackson sold his property died in debtor's prison.[44] This situation was particularly acute on the frontier and in the South, for specie remained concentrated in the large Eastern banking and financial centers, leaving much of the country to rely on credit and the local banks that issued it. This extensive dependence on unbacked bank credit left farmers, small merchants, and debtors extremely vulnerable in times of United States Bank-induced credit contractions, speculative ventures gone astray, failed banking schemes, or recessions. In other words, the people most severely affected were Jackson's natural constituency. Banks, credit, speculators, and the wealthy who owned the banks and made their fortunes on the basis of credit, were vehemently denounced by the Jacksonians, who believed their president represented the common public's interests.

The Jacksonians considered bank credit the primary device employed by the moneyed aristocracy to gain an unfair and permanent economic advantage over the honest working man and woman. Jacksonian William Gouge wrote in 1833 that banks produced inequality, luxury, and corruption. Banks, noted Gouge:

> lay the foundations of an *artificial* inequity of wealth; and, whenever this is done, the wealth of the few goes on increasing in the ratio of compound interest, while the reflex operations of the very causes to which they owe their wealth, keep the rest of the community in poverty. . . . But banking has a more extensive effect on the moral character of the community, through that distribution of wealth which is the result of its various direct and remote operations. Moralists in all ages have inveighed against luxury. To it they attribute the corruption of morals and the downfall of nations.[45]

Credit and debt either allowed the rich to fortify their economic position or provided the speculators with the capital to finance their schemes that all too often brought grief to the nation. Moreover, when recession or economic disaster struck, the moneyed aristocracy who owned the bank stock continued to collect their profits while the banks foreclosed on tradespeople and farmers.

In the same way the rich were seen to profit from their ownership of bank stock and their manipulations of private credit and debt, the Jacksonians believed public debt only benefited the "tyranny of wealth and power." Jackson wrote in 1824 that the federal debt was "a national curse, [and] my vow [if I become president] shall be to pay the national debt, to prevent a monied aristocracy from growing up around our administration that must bend it to its views, and ultimately destroy the liberty of our country."[46] Samuel Ingham, another of Jackson's treasury secretaries, noted, "Interest [on the debt] is now paid to capitalists out of the profits of labor; not only will this labor be released from the burden, but the capital, thus thrown out of an unproductive, will seek a productive employment."[47] If the working classes were to be liberated from the aristocracy, as Jackson saw it, the national debt required liquidation and the credit-making Second Bank of the United States had to be denied its request for an extended charter.

Jackson's fight to the death with the "monster" bank was inevitable. Though Jackson opposed the bank's recharter for pragmatic political reasons, as branches of the bank fought Jackson's election and donated money to anti-Democratic candidates, his determination to bring the bank to its knees paralleled Jefferson's argument that the bank provided a destabilizing source of power in the republic. The bank often did cooperate with the Treasury and the president in office, yet the bank remained essentially autonomous, answerable only to its Board of Directors and run by the bank's president who exercised tremendous authority. The Bank of the United States was truly vulnerable only when it required rechartering. Its independence from public control, the unwillingness on the part of the bank's president, Nicholas Biddle, to compromise with Jackson, and the great efforts the bank made to engage in partisan political warfare, enraged Jackson.

Not surprisingly, during his struggle with the bank Jackson invoked the language of Jefferson and the concept of corruption to express his position. So, Jackson wrote, "The result of the ill-advised legislation which established this great monopoly was to concentrate the whole moneyed power of the Union, with its boundless means of corruption and its numerous dependents, under the direction and command of one acknowledged head."[48] Again, Jackson used precisely the same words as Jefferson to describe the bank and its effects on the republic, calling it an "engine" that produced corruption with its paper currency:

> But if your currency continues as exclusively paper as it now is, it will foster this eager desire to amass wealth without labor; it will multiply the number of dependents on bank accommodations and bank favors; the temp-

tation to obtain money at any sacrifice will . . . inevitably lead to corruption which will find its way into your public councils and destroy, at no distant day, the purity of your Government. . . . Recent events have proved that the paper money system of this country may be used as an engine to undermine your free institutions; and that those who desire to engross all power in the hands of the few and to govern by corruption or force are aware of its power and prepared to employ it.[49]

Jackson's attorney general, Roger B. Taney, argued against the bank's recharter, citing "its corrupting influence . . . its patronage greater than that of the Government—its power to embarrass the operations of the Government—& to influence elections." When the Congress in 1834 failed to override the president's decision to remove all federal deposits from the bank and place them in selected state "pet" banks, Jackson declared, "I have obtained a glorious triumph. . . . The overthrow of the opposition in the House of Representatives . . . was a triumphant one, and put to death, that mamouth of corruption and power, the Bank of the United States."[50] With Jackson's successful veto of the bank's charter and his removal and redistribution of federal deposits to the state banks, the victory over the Bank of the United States and its "corrupt aristocrats" was complete. Reduced to state-chartered bank status in Pennsylvania, the bank ignominiously collapsed in 1841.

With the bank's demise and the federal government's debt retired, both events taking place in 1834, Jackson secured the conquest over corruption long sought and prescribed by Jefferson. But two significant and unanticipated consequences resulted from Jackson's victory. The first was that the power of the presidency was extended far beyond anything "King Andrew's" predecessors realized. Jackson used the veto more than all previous presidents and he legitimized the veto power in nonconstitutional issues by vetoing the bank's recharter. Furthermore, his control over cabinet officers, the nation's financial structure, and his direct appeals to the public for support against his opposition in Congress on the bank question, set new precedents in American politics. The other consequence of the Bank War resulted from Jackson's failure to provide the nation with a serious proposal for a financial and institutional arrangement to replace the bank. Not until the crisis posed by the Civil War did there exist anything resembling a centralizing force or system for regulating the country's finances. In the absence of the Bank of the United States, state banks were free to create credit largely as they saw fit, and state governments wasted little time in taking advantage of the situation.[51]

Internal Improvement, State Debts, and Federal Surpluses

An American living in the first half of the nineteenth century had to look neither hard nor far to find objections to the federal government's deficits or debt. First, continued deficit spending made the debt's retirement a more difficult proposition. Second, the debt's existence enabled foreign investors and America's moneyed aristocracy to buy securities and thereby profit at the expense of the taxpaying public who bore the debt's "burden." Third, the debt's presence was an affront to the nation's honor, and it placed the United States in the same category as oppressive and corrupted England, the greatest debtor of all time. Fourth, the preeminent American and European economists of the day found a public debt to be an economic weight on the community, as an elementary notion of the public "crowding out" of private investment and productivity circulated among scholars.[52] Fifth, large debts justified an expanding bureaucracy or a national bank to administer federal finances, thus creating patronage and corruption within the structure of republican government. The debt was considered morally outrageous, politically unjust, and economically debilitating. Although this and more could be said on the evils of deficits and debt no matter whether they be incurred by federal, state, or local governments, these objections were mostly directed toward the national debt and federal deficits. For all the animosity that might be mustered against federal deficits and debt, the nation lacked a unified, orthodox "balanced budget" mentality applying to all levels of government. Instead, there existed a very decided tolerance of state deficits and debts, even as retrenchment and rigid economies were exercised in the federal government to liquidate the national debt.

This double standard is demonstrated in a fascinating letter Thomas Jefferson wrote to his friend John Taylor on November 26, 1798, in which Jefferson called for a balanced budget amendment to be added to the United States Constitution. The letter deserves to be quoted at length:

> I wish it were possible to obtain a single amendment to our constitution. I would be willing to depend on that alone for the reduction of the administration of our government to the genuine principles of it's [sic] constitution; I mean an additional article, taking from the federal government the power of borrowing. I now deny their power of making paper money or anything else a legal tender. I know that to pay all proper expences within the year, would, in case of war, be hard on us. But not so hard as ten wars instead of one. For wars would be reduced in that proportion; besides that the State governments would be free to lend *their credit* in borrowing quotas. . . . It is a singular phenomenon, that while our State governments are the very *best in the world*, without exception or comparison, our general government has, in the rapid course of 9. or 10. years, become more arbitrary, and has swallowed more of the public liberty than even that of England.[53]

Jefferson, of course, was engaged in his bitter rivalry with Hamilton. He wrote to Washington as early as 1792 on the matter, claiming that "this exactly marks the difference between Colonel Hamilton's views and mine, that I would wish the debt paid tomorrow; he wishes it never to be paid, but always to be a thing wherewith to corrupt and manage the Legislature."[54] By attaching this amendment to the Constitution, Jefferson determined such an action would prevent the federal government's corruption. Such proposals were not unique in American history. As noted earlier, at the state conventions held to ratify the Constitution, Anti-Federalists and others expressed concern over the national government's revenue-gathering powers, and had proposed limitations on congressional borrowing authority.

Jefferson followed in the path trod by the Anti-Federalists, for he too favored the states' credit rights over the federal government's, even if war should become a reality. Jefferson's motivations clearly had to do with preserving state power and using this power as a countervailing force to control Hamilton's corrupting influence, rather than balancing the budget for what might be considered fiscal purposes. During the War of 1812 Jefferson later violated his own proposal by suggesting in 1814 to President Madison that the federal government issue $200 million in paper money to finance the war.[55] The lack of industry available to support the war effort also led Jefferson to be somewhat more tolerant of manufacturing. In addition, though he strongly supported free trade, Jefferson as president employed a trade embargo against the British as an instrument of foreign policy. Apparently after Hamilton's death and with the presidency and Congress in friendly hands, Jefferson felt the nation was safe from corruption for the time being. Moreover, after he became president, Jefferson failed to act on his own suggestion and propose a budget balancing amendment to Congress; instead he found it in the nation's best interest to borrow $15 million to finance the Louisiana Purchase only four years after he wrote to Taylor.

Before reviewing the history of state deficits and debt, some attention should be paid to the revolution occurring in public finance. Prior to the development and growth of private banking in the United States, which took place after 1800, colonial and state governments financed their deficits by emitting bills of credit and other interest-bearing securities which acted as paper money. These deficits were incurred to cover everyday operating expenses, as well as government attempts to provide a source of credit for commercial and private purposes. In the wake of an expanded banking system, these state governments were relieved of this function, for the citizenry was then able to obtain credit directly from the banks. Consequently, the state governments were freed from a major expense that created deficit spending. Furthermore, the states were then able to finance their deficits and debt without emitting bills of credit, by selling noncirculating securities to these state-chartered banks and to other private investors. This new method of financing public debt allowed the states to comply with the Constitution's provisions prohibiting state-issued bills of credit, but at the same time the states could borrow as they saw fit. The sale of noncirculating bonds and securities by states to banks and the various money markets formed the basis for public financing that is still the method employed by state governments in the twentieth century. These state-chartered private banks, therefore, limited the need for deficit spending by state governments because the banks assumed the economic responsibilities once exercised by the colonial and state governments, but these banks also provided the institutional capability for supplying the credit the state governments might use to borrow at new and record levels.

Still, the credit available to state governments or anyone else was regulated by the First Bank of the United States from 1791 until 1811, and by the Second Bank of the United States during the years 1816 through 1836. When the banks endeavored to control the nation's inflation by curbing excessive credit expansion, they acted as a "natural" constraint limiting state borrowing and deficit spending. This forced reduction in the amount of available credit made borrowing an increasingly expensive and unattractive proposition, and it supplemented the moral and political pressures that worked against state deficit spending. Accordingly, before 1840 no state felt it necessary to incorporate a mandatory budget balancing amendment into its constitution. The central bank that Jefferson and Jackson so freely and regularly inveighed against ironically supplied much of the constraint such an amendment would provide. Nevertheless, state deficit spending was not unknown before Jackson destroyed the Second Bank of the United States and these deficits should not be unexpected considering the long and bitter defense the Anti-Federalists and other states' rights supporters made in behalf of paper money and state-issued bills of credit.

Between 1800 and 1820 the several states rarely ran deficits, principally because the state governments provided only minimal levels of service to their citizens. Consequently, in this period the states functioned on administrative budgets limited even by standards of the day. Average annual state expenditures ran between $100,000 to $200,000, with Pennsylvania recording one of the largest budgets for a state when its expenditures reached $440,802 in 1820. The primary cause of deficit spending before 1820 came during the War of 1812, when national defenses were in such ruin that many states provided their own protection, forcing them to borrow a collective $5 million, of which $3,710,000 was repaid by the federal government. Other than these wartime deficits, New York passed as the great state debtor, running deficits to finance administrative operating expenses and the large-scale capital expenditures associated with the state's internal improvement projects.

From 1797 until 1820, New York ran deficits every year except 1801 and 1817 to provide revenue for this purpose.[56] The state's other major expense requiring deficit spending was the construction of the Erie Canal, the first great state-funded public works project. Construction on the canal began in 1817 and was not completed until 1825, but it proved to be economically rewarding for the state and politically rewarding for its public mentors. "The success of the Erie Canal was immediate and sensational," Reginald McGrane, author of *Foreign Bondholders and American State Debts*, wrote in 1935:

> Before the work was finished the tolls exceeded the interest charges and within ten years the bonds issued for its construction were selling at a premium. The cost of freight from Buffalo to New York dropped from $100 to $15 per ton, and the time from twenty days to eight. Villages and cities sprang up along the route; the price of farm products in western New York doubled in value, and that of the states north of the Ohio River was increased with a corresponding rise in land values. New York City became the emporium of western trade.[57]

The canal's success served as the beacon lighting the way for the other state governments to assist their own economies, and the relatively quick and well-managed retirement of the large federal debt encouraged state legislatures to believe they too could retire their debts once internal improvements spurred local commerce.

After 1820 state deficits increased in size and frequency, particularly during the years 1830 through 1838. Table 12 indicates the level of funds borrowed from banks and private, especially foreign, investors between 1820 and 1838, and the debt levels reached by the states in the years 1841, 1853, and 1860. The magnitude of this borrowing is suggested by comparing it to total federal expenditures made during the same period. In the six-year span 1830–35 the states borrowed $41.5 million, while total federal expenditures reached $83.8 million, slightly more than twice state borrowing. When the Second Bank of the United States collapsed in 1836 the states rapidly accelerated their rate of borrowing. In four years, 1835 through 1838, state borrowing jumped to $107.8 million, nearly equal to federal expenditures of $119.5 million spent during this period. Even more astounding, the states borrowed more in these four years than all the combined federal deficits totaling $99.7 million incurred from 1789 through 1838! Between 1820 and 1838 the states borrowed a collective $174.3 million, with most of this debt being assumed at the very same time the federal government made such great efforts to liquidate the national debt. How did the states put these borrowed funds to use? Table 13 outlines the distribution of the outstanding state debt level reached by 1838 and its breakdown by functional use. The states' outstanding debt at the time was $172.3 million, with $60.2 million employed in canal con-

Table 12. State borrowing and debt, 1820–1860 (thousands of dollars)

State	Borrowing levels					Debt levels		
	1820–25	1825–30	1830–35	1835–38	Total: 1820–38	Debt, 1841	Debt, 1853	Debt, 1860
Ala.	100		2,200	8,500	10,000	15,400	4,479	3,445
Ark.				3,000	3,000	2,676	4,103	3,092
Calif.							3,267	3,824
Conn.								
Del.								
Fla.			1,500			4,000		383
Ga.						1,310	2,802	2,670
Ill.			600	11,000	11,600	13,527	17,000	10,277
Ind.			1,890	10,000	11,890	12,751	7,712	10,179
Iowa							55	351
Ky.				7,369	7,369	3,085	5,571	5,479
La.	1,800		7,335	14,000	23,135	23,985	9,589	4,561
Me.	58		555		555	1,735	471	699
Md.		577	4,210	6,648	11,493	15,215	15,356	14,876
Mass.				4,290	4,290	5,424	6,445	7,132
Mich.				5,340	5,340	5,611	2,359	2,316
Minn.								318
Miss.			2,000	5,000	7,000	7,000	7,271	5,753
Mo.				2,500	2,500	842	802	25,952
Neb.								52
N.H.							74	50
N.J.								
N.Y.	6,873	1,624	2,205	12,229	22,931	21,797	24,323	33,570
N.C.		4,400	1,701		6,101		2,224	9,129
Ohio	1,680	6,300	16,130	3,167	27,277	10,924	15,218	16,927
Pa.						36,336	40,272	37,969
R.I.								
S.C.	1,250	310	500	4,000	5,560	3,691	1,925	4,046
Tenn.				6,648	7,148	3,398	3,653	20,898
Texas							5,341	
Vt.								199
Va.	1,030	469	686	4,133	6,318	4,037	12,089	33,248
Wis.						200	100	
Total	12,791	13,680	41,513	107,824	174,307	192,945	192,527	257,406

Source: B. U. Ratchford, *American State Debts* (Durham, N.C.: Duke University Press, 1941), pp. 78–107.

Table 13. State debts outstanding in 1838 and their purposes (in thousands of dollars)

State	Banking	Canals	Railroads	Turnpikes	Miscellaneous	Total
Alabama	7,800		3,000			10,800
Arkansas	3,000					3,000
Florida	1,500					1,500
Illinois	3,000	900	7,400		300	11,600
Indiana	1,390	6,750	2,600	1,150		11,890
Kentucky	2,000	2,169	350	2,400		7,369
Louisiana	22,950	50	500		235	23,735
Maine					555	555
Maryland		5,700	5,500		293	11,493
Massachusetts			4,290			4,290
Michigan		2,500	2,620		220	5,340
Mississippi	7,000					7,000
Missouri	2,500					2,500
New York		13,317	3,788		1,158	18,262
Ohio		6,101				6,101
Pennsylvania		16,580	4,964	2,596	3,167	27,307
South Carolina		1,550	2,000		2,204	5,754
Tennessee	3,000	300	3,730	118		7,148
Virginia		3,835	2,129	355	343	6,662
Total	54,140	60,202	42,871	6,619	8,475	172,306

Source: B. U. Ratchford, *American State Debts* (Durham, N.C.: Duke University Press, 1941), p. 88.

struction, $54.1 million supplying the capital used to charter state banks, $42.8 million was spent on building railroads, with the remainder distributed among turnpike construction and miscellaneous uses.

The states were willing to engage in this extensive borrowing because they believed internal improvements offered substantial economic and political opportunities, and because they felt forced to follow this course of action since the federal government under Andrew Jackson's leadership declared these were functions best left to the states. One of America's great nineteenth-century economists, Henry C. Adams, observed in his 1887 book *Public Debts* that the most significant aspect of Jackson's domestic policy was the way "the Federal government rolled certain duties from off its own shoulders on to those of the States, and this may be the best perceived by tracing the development of the idea of internal improvements."[58] When, in 1941, B. U. Ratchford wrote *American State Debts*, he followed Adams's analysis and concluded that Jackson's "political creed called for a curtailment of federal activities at a time when the demand and the need for governmental services were increasing. Consequently, the states had to supply the services." Because "funds were limited, it was natural that the states should consider borrowing, especially as a large part of the planned expenditures were for projects which were expected to be self-supporting."[59] The decision to decentralize internal improvements in favor of state rather than federal construction was at the heart of the philosophical disagreement between Jacksonian Democrats and the Whig opposition.

In contrast to Jackson, his Whig opponents favored not only a widespread program of federally funded internal improvements, but also a strong protective tariff and national banking system to assist the growth of the nation's manufacturing industry, as well as a stronger central government than the Jacksonians envisioned. The Whig attitude on internal improvements and the federal government's role in the matter was neatly addressed by Daniel Webster, who spoke on the virtue of these improvements by pointing to the Delaware breakwater project, a federally funded artificial harbor then under construction: "It will cost several millions of money. Would Pennsylvania ever have constructed it? Certainly, never, . . . because it is not for her sole benefit. Would Pennsylvania, New Jersey and Delaware have united to accomplish it at their joint expense? Certainly not, for the same reason. It could not be done, therefore, but by the general government."[60] Nevertheless, even the Whigs felt constrained to fund their proposed internal improvements either from funds present in the budget or through budget surpluses. The most systematic Whig plan for these improvements was designed by Henry Clay; it was designated the "American System."

In 1818 Clay addressed the Congress in defense of federally funded internal improvements, stating: "In regard to internal improvements, it does not follow, that they will always be constructed whenever they will afford a competent dividend upon the capital invested. . . . But, in a new country, the condition of society may be ripe for public works long before there is, in the hands of individuals, the necessary accumulation of capital to effect them. . . . The aggregate benefit resulting to the whole society, from a public improvement, may be such as to amply justify the investment of capital in its execution."[61] But Clay carefully went on to say, "Of all the modes in which a government can employ its surplus revenue, none is more permanently beneficial than that of internal improvement."[62] Webster, Clay, and the other Whigs realized they could only fund their program of internal improvements from budget surpluses because of public opposition to any plan that added to the national debt. Consequently, the Whigs supported the use of high tariff rates to generate the huge surpluses needed to fund the proposed public works projects. Moreover, the tariffs also protected the country's industrialists, who generally were located in the Northern states and who were politically allied with the Whigs, against foreign economic competition.

How these potential federal surpluses would be used was another source of discord between the Jacksonians, who wanted these funds to be distributed to the states, and the Whigs, who wished to complete their system of internal improvements. Historian Daniel Walker Howe noted in *The Political Culture of the American Whigs* that "the reactions of the two parties to the extinction of the national debt during Jackson's administration typify these observations. The Democrats welcomed the chance to liberate people from the burdens of taxation. The Whigs favored redeeming the people by retaining the taxes and spending the money on worthwhile improvements."[63] Jackson successfully defeated most of the Whigs' internal improvement projects, and the states assumed responsibility for their own systems of public works.[64] Furthermore, with the national debt retired the Democrats were making provisions to distribute budget surpluses when they occurred to the various state governments.

Then disaster struck in 1837. Held afloat on a sea of state bank credit, the nation's economy sank into a depression surpassed only by the Panic of 1893 and the Great Depression. The 1837 panic resulted from a number of factors, including the recent demise of the Second Bank of the United States. In the bank's absence the state banks were relatively free to expand credit, as the state governments were reluctant to impose adequate specie reserve requirements that would tie the amount of available bank credit to a bank's specie supply. The states had little motivation to restrain their banks, for the state treasuries often received a substantial portion of bank stock and profits as the price for awarding a bank a state charter. In addition, during Jackson's war with the bank, the president dispersed the federal government's bank deposits into the state "pet" banks, presenting the pets with specie required to expand credit. From 1835 to 1837 the number of banks grew from 704 to 788, and bank loans increased from $365.2 million to $525.1 million.[65]

This explosion in state bank credit provided speculators with all the venture capital they needed to exploit the economy. "Madness ruled the hour," wrote John C. Calhoun, "the whole community was intoxicated with imaginary prospects of realizing immense fortunes."[66] Speculators particularly took advantage of the situation to purchase federal land in the Western territories, as the federal government allowed purchases to be made in bank notes, in other words, in bank-issued credit. In an attempt to control this rampant speculation and to control credit expansion without a central bank to guide policy, the Treasury Department issued its famous "Specie Circular" on July 11, 1836, which required all future federal land transactions be made in specie. The consequences were catastrophic. The nation's complex and interwoven system of credit tumbled like a house of cards. Specie fled the Eastern states to accommodate land transactions in the West, leaving Eastern businesses and Southern agriculture to wither on the financial vine, which in turn caused the hoarding of specie.[67] Foreign bank failures, reduced demand for American goods abroad, and domestic crop failures further aggravated the economy, forcing the nation to wallow in depression until the economy recovered some seven years later.

One way to measure the depression's influence on the economy is to examine its effect on the federal budget. Federal revenues steadily fell from a record high of $50.8 million in 1836 to only $8.3 million in 1843, the smallest amount received since 1809. Deficits ran consecutively from 1837 until 1843, interrupted by the 1839 surplus. Faced with these new deficits, President Martin Van Buren and the Congress no longer had to concern themselves with how to dispose of the government's surplus. The recently liquidated federal debt increased anew, never again to be retired in the nation's history. Parenthetically, the federal government later ran deficits to finance the Mexican-American War and in the years 1858 through 1860, as a consequence of the 1858 panic, brought on by yet another state bank-induced credit expansion and collapse.

State governments were also affected by the Panic of 1837. Deprived of credit like the rest of the country and holding little in the way of specie reserves, the states were placed in a tight financial bind and were unable to meet their budgetary obligations. As a result, the states borrowed when and wherever they could to keep their governments operating. The states' "canal and railroad systems were not completed, and brought in little, if any, revenue. The states had to complete those projects or lose everything." In addition, "there were many who refused to accept the panic at its true value; they regarded it as merely a financial phenomenon." As the depression grew in severity so did the states' financial plight. In 1841 several of the states defaulted on their loan payments. First Florida, Mississippi, Arkansas, and Indiana defaulted in 1841, and then Illinois, Maryland, Michigan, Pennsylvania, and Louisiana joined their ranks in 1842.[68] Alabama, New York, and Ohio were in a condition of near default. To overcome this string of financial embarrassments the proposal was made in Congress in 1842 that the federal government once again assume responsibility for the states' debt, as it had after the Revolutionary War at Alexander Hamilton's urging.[69] The proposal was defeated, and these debtor states were forced to raise their taxes and renegotiate their loans, often at much higher interest rates.

This second planned assumption failed for a number of reasons, including state pride. John C. Calhoun spoke on the matter in the Senate on February 5, 1840. He argued against assumption, declaring, "There is not a State, even the most indebted, with the smallest resources, that has not ample resources to meet its engagements." Calhoun went on to say that even his native South Carolina "has spent her thousands in wasteful extravagance," and would pay its debts without the federal government's aid or "I would disown her."[70] Calhoun quickly rejected assumption to preserve his state's financial honor and to prevent the type of national bonding Hamilton once claimed a federal assumption of state debts would produce, as the planned assumption clearly clashed with Calhoun's fervent defense of states' rights and his efforts to maintain the states' financial autonomy.

His concern for states' rights also laid the foundation for Calhoun's stand against federal budget surpluses. In his Senate speech Calhoun recalled how the nation's economic crisis developed. At the heart of the problem, he believed, was the "vast revenue which had been poured into the treasury by the tariff of 1828, and which had accelerated the payment of the public debt. . . . And a surplus began to accumulate in the treasury." Between the time of the debt's retirement in 1834 and the panic's beginning in 1837, the budget surplus grew to some $30 to $40 million. Placed under the second bank's administrative care, the ongoing surplus became the irresistible target of "the cupidity of many of the leading State banks and some of the great brokers of New York." With the surplus in their grasp, said Calhoun, the banks would be free to expand their credit, "hence their war against that institution," the Second Bank of the United States. The bank collapsed, and the government's surplus was distributed to "the vaults of certain State banks," thus provoking the nation's uncontrolled credit expansion.[71]

The real culprit in Calhoun's conspiracy theory was the tariff of 1828 that provided the surplus, "the source in which has originated that very derangement of the currency." Calhoun's speech revealed his causal reasoning: "Now I ask, in the first place, is it not certain, if it had not been for the surplus revenue, the deposits would not have been removed? And, in the second, if there would not have been a surplus had it not been for the tariff of 1828?"[72] The tariff Calhoun described was designed and supported by Northern manufacturing interests for profit, and by the Whigs who believed as a matter of public policy in insulating the nation's infant industrial concerns from foreign competition. The Whigs furthermore hoped to employ this tariff produced surplus in federally funded internal improvement projects. Andrew Jackson opposed the then growing surplus because the revenue would be used to finance the Whig programs, as Calhoun opposed the tariff to protect Southern agriculture and political concerns. "Many powerful interest are continually at work," Jackson stated in his 1837 Farewell Address, "to procure heavy duties on commerce and to swell the revenue beyond the real necessities of the public service . . . in order to fasten upon the people this unjust and unequal system of taxation, extravagant schemes of internal improvement were got up to squander the money and purchase support. . . . The Federal Government cannot collect a surplus for such purposes without violating the principles of the Constitution and assuming powers which have not been granted."[73] Moreover, Jackson argued, budget surpluses as well as budget deficits could prove harmful to the republic, for they would allow the Whigs to realize their system of centralized government, "a system of injustice, and, if persisted in, [it] will inevitably lead to corruption and must end in ruin."[74]

Calhoun, like Jackson, opposed the federal surplus for reasons of political economy. The surplus was the end product of protectionist policies imposed by the central government Calhoun saw threatening the South's political liberty in addition to harming its economic well-being. The nation previously had endured the nullification crisis pressed by Calhoun's South Carolina against the tariff passed by Congress in 1828. The South Carolina government held that a state had the right to declare federal law null and void, thereby asserting state sovereignty.[75] Aside from actual secession, nullification served as the pinnacle of states' rights doctrine. Significantly, Calhoun referred to the 1828 "Tariff of Abominations," and not to later tariffs such as the 1833 "Compromise" tariff which substantially lowered the nation's tariff rates. These latter tariffs produced the budget surpluses that troubled him, not the 1828 tariff, for the federal government did not acquire large surpluses until the national debt was retired in 1834. Nevertheless, Calhoun recognized the powerful symbolic effect the "Tariff of Abominations" and the national government's budget surpluses would have on the South. Though by 1840 Calhoun and Jackson were bitter political enemies, Jackson too attacked surpluses because they represented the outcome of policies created by the Whig opposition and their centralizing political ethic.[76]

Although men like Jefferson and Jackson clearly believed in national union, they also employed the concept of corruption with its disposition favoring decentralized government to guide and clarify their policies. Jackson willingly mobilized the army to threaten South Carolina during the nullification crisis to preserve the union, but the opportunity existed for individuals who felt less positively about the union to incorporate the corruption theme into some form of extreme states' rights doctrine. This particular use of the idea of corruption may indeed be found in Calhoun's famous monograph "A Disquisition on Government." Stated very briefly, Calhoun argued that individual freedom is best served by requiring actions of the federal government to be approved through the consent of affected sectional or major interest group majorities to produce a "concurrent majority." A government operating under the principle of concurrent majority is superior to simple majority rule, or a "numerical majority," because among other reasons the system of majority rule produces factionalism, partisan conflict, the oppression of minorities, and the corruption of government and public virtue. Revenues would be raised to an unwarranted degree, just to enrich the majority. Thus, said Calhoun:

> It is, accordingly, found that in the violent strifes between parties for the high and glittering prize of governmental honors and emoluments . . . slander, and breach of faith are freely resorted to as legitimate weapons, followed by all their corrupting and debasing influences. . . . These vibrations would continue until confusion, corruption, disorder, and anarchy would lead to an appeal to force—to be followed by a revolution in the form of the government.[77]

Calhoun happily declared that a concurrent majority could "purify and regenerate" even a "corrupt and degenerate community," whereas a government operating with a numerical majority "would just as certainly corrupt and debase the most patriotic and virtuous people."[78] So Calhoun suggested that unless the system of numerical majority underwent reform—a system he believed allowed the North to dominate the South—a "revolution" would occur. In this way the concept of corruption that Jefferson and Jackson invoked to preserve and protect the republic was employed by Calhoun to undermine that very same system of government.

Later, in the wake of the states' financial disgrace created by the 1837 panic, a movement began in the various states to impose state constitutional requirements on the legislatures to eliminate or severely constrain the states' borrowing privileges. Table 14 lists the dates these "balanced budget" amendments were adopted by the respective states. In 1842 Rhode Island became the first state to adopt such an amendment requiring "the express consent of the people, to incur state debts to an amount exceeding fifty thousand dollars, except in time of war."[79] These amendments, adopted for the most part between 1842 and the Civil War, usually

Table 14. States' debt limitations and year of adoption

State	Year	State	Year
Alabama	1867	Nebraska	1866
Alaska	1958	Nevada	1864
Arizona	1867	New Jersey	1844
Arkansas	1934	New Mexico	1911
California	1849	New York	1846
Colorado	1876	North Carolina	1936
Florida	1885	North Dakota	1889
Georgia	1877	Ohio	1851
Hawaii	1959	Oklahoma	1907
Idaho	1889	Oregon	1857
Illinois	1848	Pennsylvania	1857
Indiana	1851	Rhode Island	1842
Iowa	1846	South Carolina	1868
Kansas	1855	South Dakota	1889
Kentucky	1850	Texas	1845
Louisiana	1845	Utah	1895
Maine	1848	Virginia	1870
Maryland	1851	Washington	1889
Michigan	1843	West Virginia	1872
Minnesota	1857	Wisconsin	1848
Missouri	1875	Wyoming	1889
Montana	1889		

Source: A. J. Heins, *Constitutional Restrictions against State Debt*, p. 10. © The University of Wisconsin Press, used with permission.

contained three elements: "(1) a nominal debt was allowed to cover casual deficits; (2) beyond this, the consent of the people was required; and (3) the state might not endorse obligations of others."[80] These constitutional provisions generally succeeded in controlling the growth of the states' debt level. Nineteen states adopted these amendments between 1842 and 1860, and during the same time thirteen states witnessed a drop in their debt load.

Despite the examples of these provisions and the lessons learned from the recent panic, several states either did not pass such amendments or were not deterred from borrowing and increasing their debt. After 1845 another wave of state borrowing began, with Virginia the largest debtor. As shown in Table 12, Virginia's debt grew from $4 million in 1841 to over $33 million in 1860, with most of these funds used to support canal, railroad, and turnpike construction. Missouri increased its debt load from less than a million dollars in 1841 to about $26 million by 1860 in order to enlarge the state's railroad system. To link its railroads to those of adjoining states, Tennessee incurred a debt that grew to $20.9 million in 1860 from $3.4 million in 1841. On the eve of the Civil War, the collective state indebtedness stood at $257.4 million, $67.5 million greater than in 1841, and four times the size of the $64.8 million national debt.

Balanced Budgets and Symbolic Politics

The nation's early historical landscape is pockmarked with deficits incurred by governments at every prominent level of authority. They found it necessary or desirable to engage in deficit spending, and not always when the nation was at war or experiencing economic calamity. Some of these deficits were incurred through methods often unknown to modern analysis, such as the widespread distribution of bills of credit. In the coming years the state and federal governments would master the art of off-budget spending, thereby allowing the states to comply with their balanced budget constitutional restrictions. To be sure, governments that did engage in deficit spending often met with fierce public resistance. Significantly, however, in the face of this opposition deficits and debt continued to be incurred in the public sector. Furthermore, the case can be made that had the federal government rather than the states assumed authority for the construction of internal improvements projects, many of those state debts would have instead belonged to the national government. Yet, despite the reality of deficit spending's widespread presence in the nation's heritage, the period before the Great Depression, and especially before the Civil War, is commonly thought to be free from deficits and debt except in times of crisis. Why is this so?

After Thomas Jefferson's election to the presidency the republic's political agenda up to the Civil War was set by people who held a fairly consistent political philosophy, in spite of the cultural and social differences separating the Jeffersonians and Jacksonians. Though the Federalists and the Whigs offered spirited opposition, they never seriously controlled the federal government after John Adams's defeat, as the Whig presidents William Henry Harrison and Zachary Taylor died during their first few months in office and Millard Fillmore enraged his Whig colleagues by ignoring most of their suggestions and political philosophy. For these reasons, the concerns Jefferson, Jackson, and their allies expressed about the federal government's centralizing tendencies dominated American political thought.

That Americans should reject the Federalist and Whig plans for a strong central government is hardly surprising considering the nation's highly independent and sectional colonial past. Moreover, the aristocratic tendencies displayed by many Federalists and Whigs did little to endear them to the average citizen. Into this broad philosophical contest over the merits of centralized versus decentralized government was thrust the unifying issue of the debt's corrupting influence on the republic. If the debt could be employed to promote one faction's rise to political and economic dominance, many Americans responded by calling for its retirement and the prevention of any further growth in the debt by way of deficit spending. This rejection of deficit spending, except when the nation confronted the most desperate circumstances, also applied to budget surpluses. Once the moneyed aristocracy represented by the Federalists and Whigs obtained control over either federal securities that financed the debt or over surplus federal funds, they could manipulate the government and the economy for their own political and financial profit. In Andrew Jackson's mind, therefore, there was a single remedy for the nation's political difficulties. "There is but one safe rule," he warned, "and that is to confine the General Government rigidly within the sphere of its appropriate duties. It has no power to raise a revenue or impose taxes except for the purposes enumerated in the Constitution; and if its income is found to exceed these wants, it should be forthwith reduced, and the burdens of the people so far lightened." Jackson's faith ultimately rested with the people to preserve the republic: "And while the people remain, as I trust they ever will, uncorrupted and incorruptible and continue watchful and jealous of their rights, the Government is safe, and the cause of freedom will continue to triumph over all its enemies."[81] To secure the republic, both federal deficits and surpluses were to be avoided, for only a truly balanced budget could prevent corruption.

On the other hand, although the federal government might not be trusted with deficits or surplus revenue, state governments were considered more politically reliable and less likely to offer the same type of corrupting threat to the nation. Paradoxically, a number of intended and unintended federal actions made large-scale state borrowing possible, including the deposit of federal funds in state banks and the destruction of the central bank, which was regarded at the time to be another corrupting influence in American life. These actions allowed the states to borrow more rapidly and in greater quantities than the federal government in order to carry out the tasks Jefferson and Jackson felt properly belonged to the states. Only the most disastrous of depressions forced the states to curtail temporarily their borrowing and adopt constitutional restrictions on deficit spending to eliminate abuses in their local financial systems.

In other words, what most Americans found objectionable was not the principle of running deficits or incurring debts, but rather incurring *federal* deficits and debts. Thus, the more parochial and less visible state governments continued to borrow heavily even while the federal government avoided its corrupting deficits and aimed for balanced budgets. By the outbreak of the Civil War, balanced budgets symbolized the nation's ability to control the federal government's political powers, particularly in its relationship with the states, and to guarantee the maintenance of the checks and balances established in the Constitution. Unbalanced budgets, therefore, in terms of political economy, symbolized a powerful threat to the nation and its republican government.

5

Distorting a Symbol: Republican Party Government, 1861–1932

We are spending great sums in useless "public
improvements," and are paying pensions under a law which
seems framed but to put a premium upon fraud and get away
with public money. And yet the great question before
Congress is what to do with the surplus.

HENRY GEORGE, 1883

On this, as on so many other points, Hamilton's political
philosophy was much more clearly thought out than that of
Jefferson. He has been accused by his opponents of being the
enemy of liberty. . . . But he also realized that genuine
liberty was not merely a matter of a constitutional
declaration of rights. It could be protected only by an
energetic and clear-sighted central government, and it could
be fertilized only by the efficient national organization of
American activities.

HERBERT CROLY, on the Jefferson–Hamilton dispute, 1909

Thomas Jefferson, Andrew Jackson, and their followers provided America with what might be called a republican critique of government and society. Central to this critique was the concept of corruption that saw unbalanced federal budgets undermining constitutional government and republican virtue. Budget deficits and unnecessary surpluses enabled the moneyed aristocracy, who owned the banks and corporate "monopolies," to gain access to the Treasury and exert unwarranted influence over the government and the economy. While speculators and moneylenders manipulated public finances, the Jeffersonians and Jacksonians believed budget surpluses and deficits would provide the federal government with the revenue needed for expanding its authority at the political cost of sacrificing states' rights. Public leaders who, like Jefferson and Jackson, employed this corruption theme in their political thought feared that excessive federal revenues would be used to bribe public officials, influence elections, enlarge the federal "civil list," justify the presence of a national bank, and supply the revenues required for a system of federal internal improvement projects. All of these activities, in their view, compromised the nation's freedom.

After the Civil War the term "corruption" lost its elegant constitutional meaning, and it was instead applied to the common graft, fraud, and abuse of public office occurring at all levels of government. Perhaps the term's more elaborate definition disappeared because the Civil War itself was fought to save the republic by defending the federal government against the excesses of dissident state authorities, and against the ideas of individuals like John C. Calhoun who invoked the concept of corruption in the Southern cause. The Union victory, moreover, was financed by massive deficit spending, thus preserving rather than threatening the Constitution. In addition, the Democratic party, which historically opposed the Whig and Republican centralizing tendencies and was most likely to employ the corruption theme in its political language, was crippled by the Civil War. Most important, however, the modern Republican party was hardly motivated to invoke the very same symbolism that damned its Federalist and Whig predecessors. In other words, the circumstances surrounding the traditional and functional meaning of "corruption" in this new political context radically changed after the Civil War.

With the Democrats severely weakened and offering only limited opposition, the Republicans enacted their Hamiltonian-like policies by increasing the federal government's tariff rates, leaving the government with huge budget surpluses. Like Hamilton, the Republicans sought to promote and protect industries, chiefly located in the North and Midwest, through a system of high tariffs. These tariffs were not always popular, as they were considered by many small merchants and farmers—regardless of political affiliation—to be a direct subsidy for the wealthy manufacturing interests which provided them with an unfair advantage in the marketplace. To reduce these enormous surpluses, and thereby legitimize the need for high tariffs, the Republicans dramatically increased federal expenditures in the late nineteenth century. By spending at such a rate that the government might be forced into running deficits, tariffs were made to appear as a national necessity for providing revenues to balance the budget and to retire the national debt. These surpluses, tariffs, and greenback paper money, all legacies from the Civil War's deficit spending, dominated American politics.

Louis Hartz characterized this period in the country's history as the rise to power of the "New Whiggery" who "marched into the Promised Land after the Civil War and did not really leave it until the crash of 1929."[1] The New Whigs, in contrast to the Whiggery of Clay and Webster, employed the language of Jefferson and economic competitive individualism, but these Republicans were supportive of federal policies that included high tariffs to promote industrial capitalism. "The principle at work here," said Hartz, "was obvious enough: big capitalism was able now with the major exception of the tariff, to dispense with the Hamiltonian promotionalism on which it had relied in the days of its weakness."[2] Although Hartz mentioned the tariff, he underestimated its importance and how the tariff system altered the pattern of federal expenditures established by the Jeffersonians and Jacksonians. Also at issue was how the Republicans' method of financing the debt mobilized their Democratic and agrarian political opponents. As Andrew Jackson observed in the 1830s, the creation of unbalanced federal budgets through the manipulation of the tariff could dramatically alter the nature of American life. The years 1861 through 1932 indeed witnessed a decisive transformation in the nation, one in which the dominant Republican party rejected the policies of the Jeffersonians and Jacksonians and forever changed the country's political and economic institutions. At the same time, the Republicans perpetuated but distorted the meaning of balanced federal budgets in American political thought.

Financing the Civil War

Abraham Lincoln's presidential victory in 1860 appropriately marked the nation's transformation from a preindustrial to an industrial America. Lincoln ran for office as a Republican, but his younger days were spent in the Whig party, and he adhered to the Whig's basic political values regarding the economy and the federal government's place in society. Lincoln supported federally funded internal improvements, defended the Bank of the United States against Andrew Jackson, and endorsed the federal government's tariff wall to promote and protect domestic industry. "As president, Lincoln signed every bill for raising import levies that crossed his desk—and there were ten of them."[3] Lincoln was the first president since John Quincy Adams to complete at least one term in office and hold true to the centralizing political ethic associated with the Whig and Federalist parties. Still, Lincoln was a transition figure who probably identified with the small farmer ethic of the Free Soilers rather than the industrial capitalism of the Gilded Age Republicans.[4] Although the Civil War justified the rapid expansion of federally promoted industry, railroads, and internal improvements, it is likely that some of this infrastructural development would have occurred in any case considering Lincoln's Whig disposition. The war did dominate the Lincoln presidency and produced massive deficit spending, however, while the wartime crisis and Republican economic policy changed the nation's financial structure.

As the Civil War became a reality, the federal government found itself unprepared to finance a war on such an enormous scale. Owing to the Panic of 1857 the government had already run deficits in the three years preceding the war and the Democrats' low tariff rates restricted the government from collecting the revenues needed to meet even peacetime spending. Furthermore, the government had only limited control over the nation's banks and money supply. In 1846 the Democrats passed the Independent Treasury Act requiring the Treasury to use only specie when conducting transactions, and it placed all federal deposits in decentralized "subtreasuries" reminiscent of Jackson's "pet" banks. At the same time, the state governments continued to control their own state banks' distribution of notes and certificates that often acted as circulating paper currency. This decentralized financial system, the prohibition of federally issued paper money, and state control over most banks in the country "marked the complete triumph of Democratic hard money philosophy and the absolute separation of the Treasury and the banks."[5] What worked well enough in peacetime did not meet wartime exigencies, however, and during the course of the war the Republicans restructured the country's finances.

Treasury Secretary Salmon Chase soon realized that even the new and higher tariffs enacted by the Republicans in the 1861 Morrill Tariff Act failed to increase revenues adequately; the federal government would be forced to deficit spend at a fantastic rate. Federal deficits incurred during the war dwarfed any previously recorded. In 1865 the federal deficit reached nearly one billion dollars. Still, as in the War of 1812, Congress avoided imposing significant levels of internal taxation until late into the war. In his 1863 annual report to the Congress, Chase acknowledged the administration erred by not proposing adequate taxation. Chase believed taxes were best avoided rather than "increase the burdens of the people at a time when the sudden outbreak of flagitious rebellion had deranged their business, and temporarily diminished their incomes."[6] The government therefore suspended specie payments, turned to direct borrowing from banks and the public, and distributed paper money, better known as "greenbacks," to finance the war.

Congress agreed to issue greenback paper currency reluctantly, for some of its members argued that the Constitution prohibited the distribution of "bills of credit." Only the overwhelming need to supplement specie currency to carry out commercial transactions and government activities convinced the Congress to approve the greenbacks. This greenback currency was in fact a noninterest-bearing federal debt instrument that paid specie only on its face value. But because greenbacks carried no redemption date for when they might be redeemed for specie, the Treasury could keep them in circulation as long as Congress allowed. Despite these qualities, greenbacks technically constituted a portion of the federal government's deficit and debt. Greenbacks, consequently, were "in effect a forced loan upon the people. . . . The notes were, in fact, printing press money."[7] By refusing to make greenbacks directly redeemable and by suspending specie payments for public and private debts, the government sought to control speculation and currency devaluation. To protect its currency and limit specie hoarding, moreover, the government left the gold standard in 1861 and returned to it only in 1879. Nevertheless, as the supply of greenbacks and other federal notes increased so did the rate of inflation, as the general price index rose from 98 in 1861 to 179 in 1865. Under conditions set by the three Legal Tender acts authorizing greenback distribution, the Treasury emitted some $431.5 million worth during the Civil War, leaving $428 million in circulation in 1865.[8]

In addition, to strengthen its control over the country's finances the government took steps to recentralize the banking system, in a fashion, President Lincoln declared, "which promises so certain results and is at the same time so unobjectionable."[9] The National Banking Act was the most important piece of banking legislation passed during the war. It created a system of federally chartered national banks located throughout the country which were permitted to issue national bank notes. For the first time since Jackson defeated the Second Bank of the United States, the federal government's banking system was in direct competition with the state banks. Later, in 1865, the Congress passed a law that taxed state bank notes, thereby supplying an incentive for state banks to use federal notes and join the federal system as national banks. Over time, this newly enacted banking legislation evolved into the Federal Reserve System.

This elaborate financial structure designed to underwrite the Civil War and its deficits and debt reflected on the one hand the economic burden thrust upon the federal government, and on the other hand the particular political philosophy representative in the Republican party. The National Banking Act and the Legal Tender acts served to further the Republicans' drive to centralize the country's finances in order to repair what they perceived as the anarchy inherent in the state banking system. Furthermore, by reducing the influence and prestige of the state banks the Republicans hoped to increase public support for the national government. Senator John Sherman, who introduced the Banking Act and later became treasury secretary, considered the legislation, said one historian, a "contribution toward a growing American nationalism."[10] Although the national banks were elevated in status above the state banks, the federal government acted through its 1865 tax on state bank notes to make the federal notes more financially attractive while reducing the public's loyalty for their state banks. Certainly the financial emergency posed by the war motivated many Republicans to support these policies. Yet voting records from this period indicate Congress was largely divided along partisan lines, with the Democrats remaining generally opposed to the Legal Tender and Banking acts.

These economic measures passed by Congress to finance the deficit had lasting political significance. First, the high tariffs used to generate revenue to finance the debt created huge budget surpluses after the war. These surpluses enabled the federal government to expand its support for internal improvements and other expenditures far beyond the level permitted by the Jacksonian Democrats in antebellum America. Second, the federal government's efforts to contract the greenback money supply and return to the gold standard sparked the Populist movement in rural America and the Democratic silver movement in the West. Third, the national banking system developed into the Federal Reserve System, ensuring that the country's banks would be subject to a centralizing authority. High tariffs and protectionist policies, paper money, federal internal improvements, and centralized banking were symptomatic of the corruption that Jefferson and Jackson feared. Nevertheless, however potent the corruption theme had been before the war to limit the growth of large public and private centralizing institutions, the reality of total war, the economic evolution into industrialization, and Republican party policies turned the United States from its preindustrial heritage.

Selected Observations on the Management of the War Debt

After the war two powerful themes emerged in the public's rhetoric: a growing sense of nationalism, particularly in the North, and a widespread desire to retire the federal debt. Nationalism provided the Republican party with its philosophical mandate to rule, whereas the desire to retire the debt and keep the budget from running deficits enabled the Republicans to gain the public support they required to enact their protectionist policies. Euphoric nationalism, the legacy of a powerful wartime government, and Republican policies led many people to consider the social and economic benefits that might accrue from an activist federal government. "Not since the time of Alexander Hamilton had men of education and intellectual influence reveled so openly in the potentialities of an active, powerful state. . . . publicists, intellectuals, and politicians indulged in a rhetoric of triumphant nationalism."[11] These nationalistic sentiments were well suited to the Republicans who embraced their Federalist and Whig predecessors' activist political philosophies. Subsequently, the Republican party's own policies, as reflected in the federal government's rapidly growing revenues and expenditures, served to consolidate the central government's political authority gained during the war and guarantee it a major role in the nation's economic development.[12]

Before reviewing the Republicans' spending, tariff, and debt reduction policies, some attention should be paid to the sometimes complex and contradictory public discourse that surrounded the issue of the debt's retirement. Although the American people generally wished to see the debt retired, the public also appreciated the economic benefits that resulted from having the greenback money supply and other government debt instruments in circulation. These greenbacks served to expand the country's money supply far above its prewar levels, and thus it both promoted and accommodated an increase in economic activity. The conflicting desire to see the debt retired and the rate of economic growth sustained, was widely evident in the nation's postwar discourse and politics.

Retiring the debt was a national obsession, as perhaps best suggested by foreign observers. In 1886 the London-based *Economist* reported, "There is scarcely a provincial town [in the United States] in which some financial person—some banker or stockbroker—has not made and published calculations as to the quickest and best mode of paying off the great debt."[13] The Treasury Department at the time estimated the debt would be retired in some thirty years. In 1869 Francis Walker, secretary to the British legation in the United States, wrote, in an article called "The National Debt," that "the majority of Americans would appear disposed to endure any amount of sacrifice rather than bequeath a portion of their debt to future generations." There was a "strong and controlling sense that debt was always and everywhere an evil; that it was a good thing to 'work off' the mortgage, even if it involved working very hard."[14]

A correspondent for *Lippincott's Monthly Magazine* claimed in 1868 that the debt served as an economic foundation for the same type of political oppression the English people labored under with their corrupting public debt, which benefited "moneyed institutions and heavy capitalists, who have immense sums to invest, and would like to have the nation guarantee the annual interest upon the same to themselves and their successors." He called a national debt "in fact a great calamity, an incubus upon industry, and an increasing source of official corruption."[15]

The tax burden required to pay the interest on the moneylenders' bonds would fall upon the working people, *Merchant's Magazine* declared in 1867: "The present pressure of a National debt upon the resources of the people does not depend so much upon the nominal aggregate of that debt, as upon the amount of the annual interest it calls for, the methods of taxation used to collect the amount, and the sacrifices which these taxes entail by the interruption of the industry of the toiling masses of the population.''[16] These interest payments not only were made to domestic moneylenders, but also to foreign lenders who held some $600 million in federal securities in 1866. If these brief observations are to be believed, the debt was generally considered to be a true economic hardship on taxpayers, on future generations of Americans, and a source of unwarranted economic gain for the bankers, speculators, and moneylenders who financed the debt.[17]

Confronted with the public's fear of the debt even during the war, President Lincoln tried to assure the people the debt could be managed in a socially equitable manner. In his 1864 Annual Message to Congress, Lincoln remarked:

> The public debt on the first day of July last, as appears by the books of the treasury, amounted to $1,740,690,489.49. Probably, should the war continue for another year, that amount may be increased by not far from five hundred millions. Held as it is, for the most part, by our own people, it has become a substantial branch of national, though private, property. For obvious reasons, the more nearly this property can be distributed among all the people the better. . . . The great advantage of citizens being creditors as well as debtors, with relation to the public debt, is obvious. Men can readily perceive that they cannot be much oppressed by a debt which they owe to themselves.[18]

Lincoln made three important points in his address to Congress on the debt. First, as more Americans held federal securities Lincoln argued the debt would be increasingly democratized, and therefore made tolerable to Americans who feared the debt benefited the wealthy. Second, because the debt was held "by our own people," Lincoln indicated the public could feel secure the interest payments on the debt would go to American citizens and not to foreign nationals. Therefore, Lincoln was saying the debt compiled with the economic notion that "internally" held debt simply created a domestic or internal transfer of funds among citizens. Third, Lincoln referred to the debt becoming a "substantial branch of national, though private property." Thus, he claimed, federal debt instruments such as bank notes and securities, and even greenbacks, constituted wealth, an investment for the future, and a form of circulating currency. Through such efforts as this, Lincoln attempted to temper the public's concern about buying and using paper money.

Lincoln's last point was crucial; it pointed to the political and financial difficulties the nation would endure in the coming years. Americans wanted to retire the debt but they had grown accustomed to the extra paper money supply then in circulation. Contracts and other legal and economic agreements had been made on the basis of this inflated money stock, and to reduce the money supply or deflate the currency could produce economic disaster. So, the major public issue for some time to come was determining how the debt might best be managed. There were signs this was not going to be an easy task. By 1869, it was clear that the "early enthusiasm for reducing the debt" had lessened. The "seductive philosophy of 'fructification'—namely, that money left with the people increased more rapidly than if transferred into the public treasury—was gaining ground."[19] Government bonds and federal bank notes supplemented greenbacks as paper currency, and thus when held by the public they could "fructify," as this added currency encouraged commercial transactions and economic prosperity. Without a well-regarded and reliable paper currency, as opposed to specie, the nation continued to depend on federal debt instruments for its economic health.

While the nation was off the gold standard this reliance on federal debt as capital and currency in place of specie provided some members of the financial community with a powerful reason for tolerating the debt. In 1865 an article in the journal *Commercial and Financial Chronicle* found the Civil War's expenses to be no different than the cost of making capital improvements, as both stimulated the nation's economy: "A national debt . . . may be so managed as to stimulate productive power and augment the force of inventive genius, to economize capital and open a beneficent reservior for gathering together and rendering more productive ten thousand little fertilizing streams of national wealth."[20] The most cogent expression of this view is to be found in a pamphlet titled "How Our National Debt May Be a National Blessing: The Debt Is Public Wealth, Political Union, Protection of Industry, Secure Basis for National Currency, the Orphans' and Widows' Savings Fund." The booklet was written by Samuel Wilkeson in 1865 and distributed by Jay Cooke, who was among America's most wealthy and powerful bankers, to reflect Cooke's attitude toward the debt. Cooke's banking house acted as the subscription agent that sold nearly all the federal government's bonds and securities for the Union during the war. Thus Cooke had a unique perspective and understanding of the debt's financing, as well as a financial interest in its fate.

Wilkeson wrote that rather than considering "a permanent debt" to be an economic or social burden it should be regarded as "so much capital added to our wealth," for "the interest of the debt only becomes the measure of its burden."[21] As long as interest payments were made on the debt it could serve to invigorate the nation. Wilkeson looked to England's debt as the great example of a nation's financial liability enriching the public: "For half a century this seemly and nominally huge and burdensome debt has served to vitalize the manufacturing and trading genius of the English people, and as money, has enabled the British to do for that long time the marine carrying for the world."[22] Retiring America's debt, Wilkeson argued, "WOULD BE TO EXTINGUISH THIS CAPITAL AND LOSE THIS WEALTH. TO EXTINGUISH THIS CAPITAL AND LOSE THIS WEALTH WOULD BE

AN INCONCEIVABLY GREAT NATIONAL MISFORTUNE."[23] The public needed currency to pay their debts and engage in commercial transactions, and the government's war bonds and national bank notes acted as currency to aid these economic activities. These bonds "are cash capital, literally, absolutely and without figure of speech."[24]

Alexander Hamilton had exclaimed in 1781, "A national debt if it is not excessive will be to us a national blessing; it will be a powerful cement of our union."[25] Eighty-four years later Wilkeson and Cooke echoed Hamilton's analysis, as Wilkeson noted, "This, our National War Debt, should be held forever in place as the political tie of the States and the bond forever of a fraternal nationality."[26] Amazingly, Wilkeson believed that if the nation had owned a large and permanent debt before the war the bloody conflict would have been avoided: "Had we possessed a huge Union debt in 1860, and had as much of it been diffused among the mountaineers and planters of South Carolina as is now held in Rhode Island, as much in Alabama as now in Indiana . . . the war for slavery had never been waged. While holding the Union bonds the South would never have made war upon the Union."[27] The war's debt also justified a "permanent revenue tariff" and would provide the nation with "a uniform bank-note currency that shall be money all over the Republic."[28] Furthermore, the debt's very presence would bring honesty to government, for as the public scrutinized the debt's financing, "integrity would be more and more demanded of public men, and of candidates for office."[29]

Cooke's position on the debt's social and economic benefits is truly fascinating, and not simply because his attitudes toward the debt, paper money, tariffs, national union, and the British financial system matched Alexander Hamilton's. Cooke's pamphlet, first of all, suggests just how deeply ingrained paper money's use had become in the United States. Cooke in his own fashion anticipated the economic and social disruption that would occur once repayment of the debt was under way and these debt instruments were withdrawn from the nation's economy. Cooke's pamphlet was also a polemical tract, aimed at convincing not only the American people, but also the banking and financial community of the debt's economic usefulness. Cooke's banking colleagues largely disagreed with him, for they sought a paper money contraction through debt reduction, and a speedy return to the gold standard. These bankers stood to gain huge profits from a reduction in the paper money supply and the resulting deflation. Many contracts and financial agreements during the Civil War were based upon an inflated currency, and with a deflated currency these loans would be repaid to the lenders in money worth substantially more than it had been during the war. Finally, Cooke's suggestion about how the presence of a large debt could justify high tariff rates indicates that the idea was considered seriously by prominent Republicans and members of the financial community. As events later demonstrated, the Republicans did attempt to justify these large tariffs on the grounds that rising federal expenditures and debt reduction required greater revenues. Currency contraction, budget surpluses, and tariffs were the three dominant political issues in post–Civil War America, and on each issue the Republican party played the decisive role in determining public policy.

Federal Expenditures in Post–Civil War America

The Republican party's influence on national policy can best be understood by examining the changing nature of federal expenditures after the Civil War, and the primary cause of this change, the Republicans' protection of the tariff system. The late nineteenth century's great federal budget surpluses created by the tariff permanently altered expenditure patterns in two ways. First, expenditures greatly increased in size. Before the war the largest single-year expenditure reached $65 million in 1859, but after the war expenditures never fell below $240 million. Between 1865 and 1900, federal spending annually averaged $325 million. Even after accounting for inflation and excluding interest payments on the national debt, the Republicans elected to reject the spending patterns of Jacksonian Democracy.[30]

In the second place, expenditures changed in substance as well as in scale. Federal spending for internal improvements rapidly increased after the war, far beyond the level permitted by Jacksonian Democrats. Expenditures for river improvement and harbor construction grew from a total of $3.7 million spent between 1850 and 1860, to $53.8 million from 1869 to 1879. Between 1880 and 1890 the government spent $102 million on rivers and harbors, whereas all federal support for this activity from 1831 through 1860 was only $12.4 million.[31] Some attempts were made to limit the cost and extent of these waterway projects. In 1882 President Chester Arthur took an unusual step for a Republican president by vetoing that year's $18 million River and Harbor Bill "on the grounds of its unconstitutionality and unwarranted diversion of public funds," wrote economist Alexander Noyes in 1909.[32] Yet, "within twenty-four hours the bill was passed over this Presidential veto, and the majority of votes to override the veto came from Administration Congressmen."[33] Where Jackson's vetoes prevailed Arthur's failed, though both presidents employed similar constitutional arguments when vetoing these expenditures. Later, in 1898 the government spent $20.8 million on river and harbor construction, the most ever for that purpose.[34]

In addition to increasing expenditures for constructing and improving harbors, public buildings, rivers, bridges, roads, and lighthouses, the federal government became a major partner in building America's railroads. Federal aid for national railroads is a famous chapter in the country's history, but before the Civil War federal expenditures on railroads were almost nonexistent. State and local governments supplied the greatest portion of public funds for railroad development and other internal improvements. Before the war state governments spent some $300 million for internal improvements, and local governments provided an additional $125 million.[35] After the war, however, federal support rapidly increased, with the single largest grant of $65 million spent to aid the Union Pacific and the Central Pacific build the transcontinental railroad. In addition, some 100 million acres of public land were granted by the federal government to the railroads, who often sold this land for substantial profit. Significantly, where state and local governments led the way in providing subsidies for railroads before the war, after the conflict the federal government became the prime supplier of public funds for railroad construction.[36]

Pensions for the Grand Army of the Republic proved to be a third reason for increasing federal expenditures. These pensions rose in cost from $27.1 million in 1878 to $159 million in 1893. By 1880, pensions accounted for 21 percent of the total federal budget, 34 percent in 1890, and 27 percent in 1900.[37] Pensions served not only to honor and care for the war's veterans, but they also provided valuable patronage for the Republican party's most loyal followers. "The Bureau of Pensions was the most uncompromisingly political branch of the late nineteenth century bureaucracy. . . . The Pension Act of 1880 made almost every northern Civil War veteran and his dependents eligible."[38] Quite clearly the Republicans responded to the powerful political influence exerted by the Grand Army, but the pensions were also increased because the "Republicans sought to spend off this surplus in order to maintain the protective tariff system."[39] "God save the surplus!" James Tanner, the director of the Pension Bureau, proclaimed in 1880.[40] Whereas the Democratic president Grover Cleveland vetoed pension legislation, such as his February 1887 veto halting an effort to give full pension rights to anyone who served three months in the war, the Republicans worked to expand the rolls to unjustifiable limits. Only when the government began running deficits in the 1890s did "the importance of pension expenditures as a prop to the tariff decline."[41]

Patronage politics also contributed to the increase in postal expenditures. The Post Office appropriations bill accounted for 10 percent of federal spending in 1875, 18 percent in 1895, and 26 percent in 1915.[42] More revealing, post office workers comprised nearly 60 percent of all federal employees during these years. Although the nation's postal needs grew during the late nineteenth century, so too did the demands of patronage politics. Historian Morton Keller has pointed out that Republican politician James Tyner considered the Post Office to be "second only to the Treasury in political importance" as "the keeper of Administration politics," with its thousands of appointees "scattered everywhere, the walking representatives of the dominant party constantly within the gaze of the people."[43] Both postal worker positions and post offices, which grew in number by almost 80 percent between 1880 and 1900, were often allocated for patronage purposes. Moreover, Grover Cleveland's replacement of 40,000 postmasters during his presidency suggests that neither party refrained from using the postal system in this manner.

Another form of public expenditure reflecting Republican policy was the deficit spending incurred by Republican elected and appointed governors in the old Confederacy. After the war the rebellious states found their governments directed by federally appointed civilian and military governors, and these governors financed economic reconstruction in the South through state borrowing. These Republicans soon authorized the physical reconstruction of the South's ruined infrastructure, but these repairs did not take place without scandal and fraud in the assignment of government contracts. How much illegal activity occurred is still subject to historical debate, but such actions were regularly publicized by the occupied Southerners as justification for disowning their states' Reconstruction debt altogether. The South had largely repudiated its Confederate Civil War debt, with one consequence being the total collapse of its banking and credit system.[44] Later, "when the Democrats had succeeded, slowly and painfully, in wrestling control from the carpetbaggers, they proceeded to make good their warnings that the Reconstruction debts would not be paid."[45] Eight former Confederate states acted to repudiate or scale down all or a portion of these debts, for a combined $115 million in debt reduction.

For the South, these Reconstruction debts represented the power of a repressive federal government controlled by the Radical Republicans in Congress. Moreover, state deficits had been employed to assist and educate newly freed slaves, and this also antagonized the South and the predominant racist element in the Democratic party. "So far from the expenditures of the reconstruction era being totally lost in waste and fraud," noted historian Kenneth Stampp, "much of this physical reconstruction was accomplished while the radicals were in office. They expanded the state railroad systems, increased public services, and provided public school systems—in some states for the first time. Since schools and other public services were now provided for Negroes as well as for whites, a considerable increase in the cost of state government could hardly have been avoided."[46] Many of these public services were immediately eliminated or greatly reduced in scale once the Republicans left the South, and not unexpectedly the former slaves fared the worst under restored Democratic rule.

To accommodate the increased spending taking place at the federal level the Congress restructured its committee system. "The major consequence of these revenue measures and the rapid rate of economic expansion after the War was that the most pressing problem faced by almost any budget arrangement would be how to dispose of the chronic surpluses that kept appearing in the Treasury."[47] In the 1870s and 1880s the House Appropriations Committee was slowly stripped of its responsibilities, and its spending powers were divided among numerous authorization committees. The Appropriations Committee previously exercised control over the budget process, but many Republicans and Democrats considered this centralized authority, placed as it was in the hands of congressmen reluctant to spend these surplus funds, to be an objectionable barrier to a more liberal spending pattern.

The Democrats in the Congress had a very strong incentive to decentralize the spending process. It was during their control over the House in the years 1877 to 1885 that the initial decentralization occurred.[48] The fragmentation of the Appropriations Committee's powers appeared to be an attractive prospect particularly to Southern Democrats, because although the Republicans dominated the presidency, the new budgetary system would allow them to influence and control more legislation and gain the federal support needed to help rebuild the South. Congressman John H. Reagan of Texas, chairman of the Commerce Committee which assumed many of these new spending powers, engineered the effort to deprive the Appropriations Committee of its control over rivers and harbors spending. As Reagan later noted, "I took an active interest in securing the necessary appropriations for the improvement of the rivers and harbors, as a means of promoting the interests of commerce."[49] Not surprisingly, the South, as well as the Midwest, benefited greatly from this new distribution of federal funds.[50] Once the Republicans regained control over the House, they supported the fragmentation initiated by the Democrats, as Republican Speaker Thomas Reed declared: "When economy is carried to extreme and becomes parsimony, it is only a hindrance and a stumbling-block instead of a virtue. In 1885 economy had become parsimony, and the real needs of the country had been repeatedly sacrificed to a mere show of figures."[51] This decentralization of spending power from a single appropriations committee to numerous authorization committees later took place in the Senate, which was controlled by the Republicans for all but twelve years between 1861 and 1932, thus furthering the Republicans' spending efforts and their desire to protect the tariff.

So, the Republican party sought to justify their high tariffs on the grounds that the pressing cost of government required the added revenues they produced. The Republicans claimed the Treasury needed the extra funds to make ends meet, but "the major fiscal problem facing the federal government . . . was not raising but spending its revenue. Rising national wealth and the protective tariff produced a surplus every year from 1866 to 1893. The annual average during the 1800s was $100 million. The need to protect the tariff by spending off the surplus and the use of federal funds to finance a costly system of party politics . . . were the prime determinants of late nineteenth century federal expenditure."[52]

The Republicans offered no substantive plan for spending the surplus, such as Henry Clay's "American System," and so the traditional devices of party politics, logrolling, patronage, and pork-barrel spending for internal improvements determined the fate of the federal government's vast budget surpluses. In addition to protecting the tariff and improving the Republican party's political fortunes, the government's spending was considered in itself representative of the nation's purpose and power. "Regarded from the economical side," economic historian Albert Bolles wrote in 1886, "the government in most cases could hire much more cheaply than build; these structures, therefore, cannot be defended on the ground of economy. But our country having grown rich and populous, public sentiment very generally has favored the erecting of buildings for use and adornment and symbols of national greatness."[53]

While tariff rates and federal expenditures grew dramatically, the Republicans continued to express fear of deficits and debt throughout Reconstruction, the Gilded Age, and after, and no doubt some Republicans genuinely believed deficits and debt were harmful or at least undesirable. Nevertheless, a modern examination of only the Republicans' political statements intended for public consumption, without a review of public policy, is misleading. In 1981, the Senate Judiciary Committee's "Report" on a possible constitutional balanced budget amendment had this to say about the Republicans: "President William McKinley took the position that, even during unsatisfactory economic conditions, 'the government should not be permitted to run behind its debt.' President Benjamin Harrison described unnecessary public debt as 'criminal.' "[54] The "Report" failed to point out that during Harrison's term in office federal spending increased from $299 million in 1889 to $383 million in 1893. Although Harrison's predecessor left the budget with a $111 million surplus, Harrison's last budget contained a meager $2.3 million surplus, and in the following year, 1894, the government began running deficits. Similarly, the Judiciary Committee's selection of McKinley was another doubtful choice, for McKinley presided over deficits in 1897, 1898, and 1899, and only one surplus in 1900. Not surprisingly, as a member of Congress McKinley supported and helped author legislation significantly increasing the tariff rate, and as president he nearly doubled the federal bureaucracy's size.

In summary, the Republican party dramatically increased spending at the federal level, and noticeably at the state level during Reconstruction. Many of these expenditures were usefully employed, including support for the railroads and for social spending in the South. Other expenditures, including internal improvement projects and veterans' pensions, were often made in order to protect the tariff or for patronage purposes. Though some modern observers underestimate the importance of tariff politics in nineteenth-century America, to farmers and small businesses the tariff was often considered an unwarranted subsidy to the large Eastern industrial concerns that raised the price of many goods beyond their normal cost.[55]

The huge surpluses produced by these tariffs only reinforced the opinion that tariffs were unfair and unnecessary. Consequently, to limit the political repercussion stemming from the tariff issue, the Republicans altered the budgetary process and engaged in unprecedented spending to reduce the surplus and legitimize the need for more tariff revenues. All the while, the Republicans continued to trumpet the Jeffersonian call for balanced federal budgets as they introduced Hamiltonian policies. Still, to appreciate fully how the tariff system guided federal expenditures and the government's debt reduction efforts, further examination of the protectionist system is in order.

Republican Tariffs and Republican Deficits

The Republicans were obsessed with protecting the tariff wall, and the best way to justify the tariff, they reasoned, was to spend the government's accumulated surplus revenues. Besides increasing federal expenditures, however, the Republicans legitimized their tariffs by their efforts to reduce the national debt. Debt reduction won public support, but these reductions were not carried out without significant financial cost. In 1871 R. Dudley Baxter wrote *National Debts*, a comparative study of debt management throughout the industrialized world. Baxter made these instructive comments about the federal government's debt reduction activities:

> These figures are astonishing; that a young nation like the United States should have paid off in little more than five years nearly £90,000,000 of capital, or twenty-eight millions more than the net reduction by Great Britain in the fifty-five years since 1815. . . . But this reduction has been effected by a severity of taxation, and a mistaken system of imposts, that have crippled many branches of industry, and have probably cost the public of the United States—by the artificial prices of protected articles, and the check to trade and the increase in wealth—more than £250,000,000 of actual payments. . . . For a State to pay off its debt by high protective duties, is as unwise a policy as it would be for a merchant to pay off his by levying a toll at his shop door upon all his customers. A more judicious system of taxation might have accomplished a considerable reduction without such disastrous consequences. No State in the world has less need than the United States to make sacrifices for a rapid reduction of the Debt, since in no

other State will the Debt so surely and rapidly reduce itself by the natural growth of the nation.[56]

Baxter perhaps underestimated the Republican party's desire to limit imports and promote domestic industry by imposing high tariffs, all in the name of debt reduction. He did, however, point out that if the Treasury mismanaged the debt's retirement by reducing it with unwarranted haste, this policy could impose serious economic costs as well as benefits.

In the 1880s, for example, the Republicans did indeed mismanage the debt's reduction to justify their high tariffs. At first the Treasury bought as many high-interest-yielding outstanding federal securities as it could, said Treasury Secretary John Sherman, "simply to invest the surplus money."[57] These purchases actually reduced federal interest payments on the debt, but soon the government was buying its own unmatured securities at premium rates, thus causing the Treasury to lose money on its transactions. Moreover, by removing the securities from public use the Treasury in effect contracted the money supply: "To the world at large, this spectacle of public debt redemption, to the extent of nearly half a billion dollars . . . was sufficiently astonishing. But admiration was at least tempered by the contempt for the wild extravagance of the policy. . . . But these very redemptions were extinguishing the bank-note currency, thus actually contracting circulation."[58] The nation still lacked any serious alternative to specie currency other than national bank notes and federal securities, which were tied to the national debt level. Retiring the debt meant pulling these paper currencies into the Treasury's vaults and out of circulation, thereby limiting the public's ability to engage in economic activities. The economy's health became imperiled, and the Republicans were forced to halt their drive to retire the debt.

Unfortunately, these efforts at debt retirement were not curtailed quickly enough to prevent a major disruption of the nation's financial markets. To reduce the debt the Treasury had purchased an enormous number of national bank notes and other securities with gold, thereby greatly reducing the government's gold supply. While the Treasury redeemed securities for gold, the country's imports exceeded exports, causing the nation's private gold stocks to be sent abroad in payment for foreign goods. This debt reduction and foreign trade imbalance precipitated a severe depression in 1893. For as the government's gold flowed from the Treasury, and eventually was sent overseas by consumers to buy foreign goods, the public lost faith in the specie redeemability of its national bank notes and federal securities. "Severe economy alone could have averted the approaching retribution," one economist noted in 1909, "and instead of practicing economy the people, like the Government, were indulging in renewed extravagance."[59] The panic's worst effects lasted several years, and as a consequence the government ran deficits from 1894 until 1897, while the national debt grew by nearly half a billion dollars. A great portion of this newly acquired debt was incurred when the Treasury *bought back* the gold it originally spent to retire the debt, in order to reestablish public confidence in the government's gold supply.

As the Panic of 1893 took shape, the federal government engaged in its largest peacetime spending effort in American history. In 1890 the Republicans passed the McKinley Tariff Act, which was expected to produce a budget surplus that year of $105 million. To spend this huge surplus and those projected for future years, the Harrison administration proposed an expenditure program of enormous scale. "The surplus, indeed, was obviously doomed to speedy destruction."[60] The combination of accelerated spending and an unexpected decline in tariff revenues, in spite of the new rates, produced a deficit in the Treasury's accounts in the last quarter of the 1891 fiscal year and in two quarters of the 1892 fiscal year. The overall annual budget continued to show surpluses, but the quarterly deficits portended things to come. The actual 1890 surplus registered at $85 million, but the 1892 surplus was $9.9 million, and just $2.3 million in 1893, as the government spent money hand over fist:

> Through tortuous compromises and weird half-measures on other issues the Republican majority in the Billion Dollar Congress of 1889–91 moved steadfastly enough toward its object of doing away with the large government surplus which the thrifty Grover Cleveland had left. . . . President Harrison, too, had promised that he would not be found ungenerously "weighing the claims of old soldiers with an apothecary's scales." This served to spur on to extravagance a Congress which needed no encouragement. . . . To the cry of "The old flag and an appropriation!" The Fifty-first Congress enacted also a long series of public-works bills, acts for the improvement of rivers, harbors, coast defense, ships of war—and all that passes under the name of "pork-barrel" legislation, until the total sum of approximately $1,000,000,000 by various measures had been signed away, and the great Treasury surplus turned into a deficit.[61]

The Fifty-First "Billion Dollar" Congress infuriated the public not only with its record-breaking spending, but also with the high tariff rates set in the 1890 McKinley Tariff Act. House Speaker Thomas Reed defended the Congress, declaring, "This is a billion-dollar country!"[62] Nevertheless, the electorate turned control of the House of Representatives over to the Democrats in the midterm election. Reed lost his speakership and McKinley lost his seat in Congress, though, remarkably, he later became president.

The Harrison administration was replaced in 1892 with Grover Cleveland's second term as president. In each of his terms in office Cleveland attempted to reduce the high tariffs and lower the government's expenditures. Faced with huge deficits, the 1894 deficit was $64 million, Cleveland and his Democratic Congress searched for an alternative revenue source, rather than raise the tariff, as his protectionist Republican opponents desired. The Democratic party's political base rested with its rural constituency located in the South and West, whose people saw the tariff only serving the wealthy manufacturing industries in the East at their expense. The tariff functioned as a tax, making the purchase of foreign goods prohibitively expensive, forcing farmers, miners, and the like to purchase overpriced domestic goods. The revenue solution designed by the Democrats consequently combined lower tariff rates with the establishment of a personal income tax. Clearly, the anticipated federal deficits encouraged the Democrats to enact the income tax, as one observer wrote in 1911: "The advent of President Cleveland to power was, therefore, understood to mean a modification of the tariff, and the urgency of fiscal reform was emphasized by the fact that the country was facing a series of deficits."[63]

The fiscal reform provided by the Democrats was a new and lower tariff rate incorporated in the 1894 Wilson-Gorman Tariff Act, which included provisions for an income tax. Somewhat progressive, the tax required individuals and corporations to pay a 2 percent tax on all income above $4,000. Pressure for the tax and its progressive nature came from the Democrats' rural membership who voted for Cleveland. "The adoption of a limit of exemption at $4,000 was largely due to the strenuous efforts of the Populist Party. Almost the entire support of the measure came from the South and West; from New England, Pennsylvania, and New York there were but few votes in the House of Representatives in its favor."[64] As it turned out, the Congress split over the new tariff, with the Senate favoring higher rates than the House. The Senate version of the tariff, the Gorman bill, restored some tariff reductions made in the House's Wilson bill. Cleveland was so furious he refused to sign the legislation as it finally emerged from Congress, letting the act become law without his stamp of approval. The income tax portion of the bill remained intact, however, even when the tariff appeared to provide the revenue needed to offset the deficit. The Populists and their congressional allies believed the bankers and industrialists exercised an excessive degree of power, and they kept the income tax provisions in the act to control and tax the wealthy: "The Gorman bill put sugar back on the dutiable list, and made many other changes which so weakened the radical nature of the House bill that all danger of a deficit seemed to be at an end. The income tax was no longer a fiscal necessity. Yet all attempts to expunge it from the bill were utterly unavailing. The farmers' influence was too strong."[65] Still, neither the income tax nor the tariff delivered sufficient revenues to balance the budget during the next five years. The income tax, moreover, was soon rendered useless, as the Supreme Court ruled in 1895 in *Pollack* v. *Farmers' Loan and Trust Company* that the tax was unconstitutional.[66]

When the Republicans regained power in the famous realigning 1896 election, not unexpectedly they set about raising the tariff. In 1898 the Congress passed the Dingley Tariff Act which increased rates even beyond those imposed to finance the Civil War. These changes in the tariff are shown in Figure 3, indicating the shift in rates from the 1861 Morrill Tariff until 1975. The Republicans' protectionist intent was clear: "In so far as the Dingley Tariff was designed to correct the deficit in the Government's finances—a matter of importance—it was not an effective measure."[67] Free trade advocates argued that the high tariff rates placed on imports actually lowered rather than raised federal revenues by discouraging Americans from importing foreign products. As the volume of imports declined, so did the government's revenues. "The deficit con-

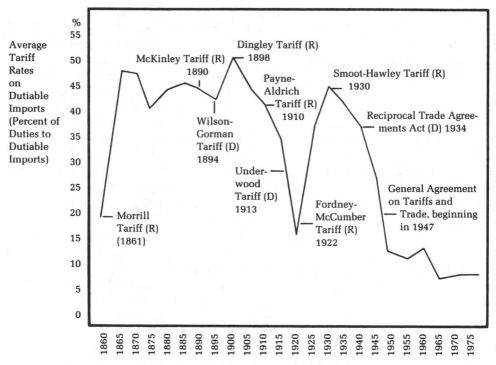

(R): Supported primarily by the Republican party.
(D): Supported primarily by the Democratic party.

Sources: *Historical Statistics of the United States*, p. 888; R. A. Pastor, *Congress and the Politics of U.S. Foreign Economic Policy* (Berkeley: University of California Press, 1980), p. 78.

Figure 3. Average tariff rates on dutiable imports

tinued; customs revenue itself, during the twelve months after the law's enactment, was smaller than in either year under the Wilson Tariff."[68] The tariff rates had finally reached such a level under the McKinley and Dingley tariffs that they reduced rather than increased the government's revenues, although they served the Republicans' protectionist intentions.

There were still more federal deficits before the economy was reduced to shambles in the Great Depression. The government ran deficits in 1898 and 1899 due to the expenses associated with the Spanish American War and the tail-end effects of the 1893 panic. These war-related deficits totaled $127 million. In 1904 and 1905 federal financing for building the Panama Canal forced the government into deficit spending for a sum of $65.5 million. "To meet the cost of constructing the canal, treasury surpluses were used and money was borrowed by the sale of bonds. The total expenditures for this great public undertaking, between 1904 and 1916, amounted to $400,000,000, for which approximately a third came from borrowing."[69] The nation experienced another major bank panic in 1907, which created a terrible depression that lasted for some three years. American demand for foreign goods fell sharply, thus producing fewer tariff revenues for the Treasury. Revenues fell from $665.8 million in 1907 to $604.3 million in 1909. Despite the decline in revenues, the Congress, with its decentralized appropriations process, continued to spend at a brisk pace, thus producing deficits of $57 million in 1908, $89 million in 1909, and $18 million in 1910.

The 1909 deficit shocked the Congress and the American people, for it was the largest peacetime deficit yet recorded in the country's history. Reaction to the deficit subsequently produced reforms in the budgetary process, as will be shown, and reforms in the banking system. In 1913 the Democrats passed the Federal Reserve Act, designed specifically to maintain some form of coordinating authority while preserving the banks' still largely decentralized structure. The present-day Federal Reserve System was authorized by Congress in place of the large bankers' preferred Aldrich Plan that called for one dominant central bank. "To progressive Democrats, the adoption of the Aldrich plan could mean only the perpetuation of existing Wall Street control—nothing less, in fact, than a resurrection of the second Bank of the United States, which Jackson had destroyed."[70]

In addition, after Woodrow Wilson was elected president in 1913 the Democrats immediately introduced legislation to reduce tariff rates by way of the 1913 Underwood Tariff. The federal government had difficulty adjusting to its newly reduced revenues, forcing the Treasury to run small deficits of some $400,000 in both 1913 and 1914. Wilson's aversion to the Republican tariff was expected, for he promised throughout the presidential election to reduce the high rates. He quickly received political support on the tariff issue from Progressives, what remained of the Populists, and other rural groups that formed the Democratic party's political base:

> The first item on Wilson's legislative agenda was the smashing of the system of privileged tariff protection that the Republican party had carefully erected since 1861. . . . So largely has the tariff been eliminated from the politics of the present day that it would be easy to minimize the difficulties that Wilson and his supporters faced. . . . Ever since the Civil War the high protective tariff had been to progressives one of the symbols of privilege. Cleveland had tried hard to lower the rates and had almost wrecked his party in the effort. Taft had promised tariff revision, and his failure had hastened the disruption of his party.[71]

Other than the deficits stemming from World War I, the federal government's budget was in surplus until 1931 and the Great Depression.

What had firmly taken hold during these years of Republican party rule was what Jefferson and Jackson would have called Hamiltonian government. "The renewal of the Hamilton-Webster system," wrote historians Charles and Mary Beard in 1927, occurred "in the field of domestic affairs after 1861—protective tariffs, sound currency, centralized banking, and federal benevolence for business enterprise."[72] So many of the things Jefferson and Jackson feared most came to pass during the Republican hegemony, in addition to those mentioned by the Beards, including a growing federal bureaucracy, federal funding for internal improvements, and federal budgets in deficit or excessive surplus. Indeed, the budget surplus was instrumental in maintaining the Republicans' protectionist tariff wall and had supplied the funds for internal improvements. The Republican deficits, moreover, played a direct role in the development of the nation's banking institutions and the structure of Congress. This fundamental change in government and public policy was not simply an evolutionary one, but was rather the consequence of a significant shift in the ideology guiding the republic.

In a broad sense, Hamiltonian government emerged when the central political authority began to employ the centralized state apparatus to promote business, in an almost mercantile fashion, through direct and indirect government intervention, often by assuming the political and economic authority that once rested with lesser, decentralized governments. As an economic development strategy, Hamiltonian government during this period encouraged industrial and manufacturing expansion through tariffs and regulations often at the expense of America's agrarian economy. These forms of protectionism were widely perceived to be the most obvious federal activities altering the structure of the marketplace while contributing to social and economic inequality.[73] Furthermore, in a manner consistent with Hamiltonian government, the Progressives provided Americans with a new and highly coherent purpose for eliminating federal deficit spending through the idea of "administrative efficiency," as the nation's professional middle class reacted to the excesses of Gilded Age Republicanism.

Progressive "Efficiency" and Balanced Budgets

The Progressives' major contribution to American politics was their legitimation of the federal government's activist presence in the economy. The Progressives considered the national government to be a countervailing force, the only institution powerful enough in society to lessen the undesirable behavior and qualities of corporate trusts and industrial capitalism. The Radical Republicans, what remained of the old Whigs, and the Gilded Age Republicans employed federal power to assist industrial capitalism's rapid development. The Progressive Republicans emerged as a political force because of their response to "machine" politics and through their attempt to lessen the social and economic problems created by industrialization. Thus, Hamiltonianism ironically employed the federal government to encourage industrial capitalism's expansion while it attempted to provide a federal solution to mitigate capitalism's worst side effects. To achieve social and economic harmony the Progressives viewed federal regulations administered by a professional and politically neutral bureaucracy as one device for mediating conflict. Furthermore, the Progressives, who drew much of their strength from middle-class professionals, academics, and merchants, looked to administrative reform to cure the evils of party politics and the big city machines employed by both Republicans and Democrats.

This Progressive sentiment for a professionalized federal administration operating on the basis of scientific management and "sound" business principles focused on budgetary reform at the federal and local levels of government. While the state governments' debt load grew relatively slowly after the Civil War (see Appendix 1), America's largest cities experienced a tremendous increase in debt. "In 1861 the nation's townships, villages, cities, and counties had obligations of about one hundred million dollars; in 1870 over five hundred million; in 1880—despite the pressure for reduction in the seventies—over eight hundred million"[74] These municipal debts were often symptomatic of bossism and machine politics, and by introducing businesslike strict accounting methods into the budget process, Progressives and reform groups, such as the New York Bureau of Municipal Research, the National Municipal League, and the Chicago Merchant's Club, hoped to fight the big city machines. In addition to applying these business and scientific management practices to the budgetary process, the Progressives sought to centralize this process through the executive budget. Thus, strong mayor governments became the bulwark of municipal reform, as the Progressives asserted that by giving the mayors the task of designing the budget the chief executives' powers would be strengthened at the expense of the bosses.[75]

The Progressives proposed similar reforms for the federal budget, but these reforms came at a time when the Republicans were under increasing pressure to control federal spending. Before the Panic of 1907 the Republican party could both publicly scorn deficits and debt and raise tariff rates and increase expenditures. But the panic modified the party's thinking about its traditional support for heavy spending. The deficits of 1908, 1909, and 1910 greatly embarrassed the Republicans, forcing them to consider how the decentralized congressional budget process limited their ability to control spending when such controls were desired. In 1909 Congress requested that President William Howard Taft investigate and report on how the government could more effectively ensure the budget would be balanced in the future. Taft soon organized a presidential "Commission on Economy and Efficiency" to look into the matter. Appointed to the commission were some very prominent Progressive academics and public officials. Included in the group were political scientist Frederick Cleveland, a famous budget expert and technical director of the New York Bureau of Municipal Research, and Frank Goodnow, first president of the American Political Science Association and author of *Politics and Administration*, which was published in 1900.

The commission recommended to the president, who presented these suggestions to the Congress, that the budget originate in the executive branch of government rather than in the Congress. The executive office would contain a new agency, the Bureau of Central Administrative Control, with a Budget Division located in the bureau, and a revitalized Civil Service Commission. "With the centralization and consolidation of these tasks the commission believed that 'each process would become a part of a well-considered *plan* for providing complete, accurate and prompt information on each subject.' "[76] Goodnow's influence is visibly evident in the Taft Commission's report, for in *Politics and Administration* he points to the need for a centralized bureaucracy, made free from politics in the day-to-day performance of its administrative tasks:

> This centralization of administration toward which we have gradually, and it would seem irresistibly, tended, appears therefore to involve the recognition of a sphere of government in which politics are to have much less influence than has been accorded to them in the past. . . . It is also made necessary if we are to hope for any great administrative efficiency, and if the party is to be kept in its proper position, i.e., as a means and not an end, an aid and not a hindrance to the expression of the popular will.[77]

The Budget Division proposed by the commission would assist the president in designing the budget and, the commission report stated, deliver "the annual *program of business* for the Federal Government."[78] So, "here was the commission's answer to Congress's request for advice on balancing revenues with expenditures."[79]

Congress never acted on the commission's report or on the sample executive budget Taft submitted in 1913. Motivated to control expenditures following the massive spending associated with World War I, however, Congress did pass in 1921 the Budget and Accounting Act, legislation originally drafted by W. W. Willoughby who served on the Taft Commission staff. The act authorized an executive budget, but Congress elected not to follow Willoughby's recommendation for a completely separate executive office budgeting agency. The Bureau of the Budget was placed in the Treasury Department to make the bureau's director answerable directly to the president while guaranteeing Congress access to the bureau. Furthermore, the Congress recentralized its appropriations process, long since decentralized in the 1870s and 1880s to accommodate larger federal spending. In 1920 the House, and then the Senate in 1922, returned to the Appropriations Committee central authority for setting spending levels.

In addition to rethinking the budgetary process and exercising organizational efficiency, the Progressives also believed larger federal revenues would help balance the budget. The drive for a federal income tax had come to a standstill after the Supreme Court ruled the 1894 tax unconstitutional; the defeat of William Jennings Bryan and the Populists in 1896 and 1900 also reduced the impetus for such a levy. The Progessives, however, continued to support the graduated income tax, as the government's deficits encouraged Congress to search for new revenues. Furthermore, as a political trade-off the Republicans found themselves offering to support the income tax in return for Democratic and agrarian tolerance of the proposed Payne-Aldrich Tariff. In any case, the Progressives considered the tax to be one more federal device to manage social conflict and limit the political appeal of radical elements in society. The income tax, said President Theodore Roosevelt, was to be levied on "those fortunes swollen beyond all healthy limits."[80]

The presence of federal deficits and the political power of the Progressives and agrarian Democrats forced Congress in 1910 to pass those sections of the Payne-Aldrich Tariff Act that placed a 1 percent tax on corporate incomes above $5,000. The Supreme Court approved this tax and the Treasury collected $20.9 million in 1910, $33.5 million in 1911, $28.6 million in 1912, and $35 million in 1913.[81] Congress merged this tax with the general income tax established by the Sixteenth Amendment. The Progressives supported the 1913 income tax and 1910 corporate income tax not only to reduce the government's deficits, but also to employ federal power as a regulating mechanism to preserve social harmony.[82]

Balancing the budget at all levels of government became an important measure of bureaucratic professionalism and efficiency, as well as a method for controlling party government and machine politics. Through such devices as administrative reform, federal regulations, and the income tax, the Progressives sought to exert public control over the excesses of industrial capitalism. Nevertheless, balancing the budget did not mean the federal bureaucracy would shrink in size or that the powers of the president would decrease rather than increase, nor did it mean the surrender of federal authority to the states. Theodore Roosevelt, for example, proudly proclaimed in his autobiography, "During the seven and a half years of my Administration we greatly and usefully extended the sphere of Governmental action, and yet we reduced the burden of the taxpayers; for we reduced the interest-bearing debt by more than $90,000,000."[83] Roosevelt's progressive instincts about railroad and antitrust regulations and the implementation of the income tax did not encourage him to lower traditional Republican tariff rates or limit spending for internal improvements. As late as 1908 Roosevelt endorsed the tariff and "the improvement of our inland waterways."[84]

The Progressive Republicans' understanding of the balanced budget as a symbol of administrative efficiency differed greatly from the notion that balanced budgets symbolized the containment of "corruption." For Jefferson and Jackson, balanced budgets suggested that the national government's power to create social and economic inequality through Hamiltonian policies would be constrained. The Progressives presumed the opposite, for they believed the federal government could lessen the inequality created by an industrialized world, where laissez-faire no longer functioned in a socially desirable fashion. Henry C. Adams, cofounder of the American Economic Association and an advocate of railroad regulation, typified the Progressive attitude by calling for stronger federal intervention in the economy because, he wrote in 1886, "the collapse of faith in the sufficiency of the philosophy of laissez faire, has left the present generation without principles adequate for the guidance of public affairs."[85] The federal government, despite its expanding authority, the Progressive argued, could be kept under public control by ensuring the bureaucracy was honest, efficient, professional, and separated from politics. Balanced budgets were considered an easily understood, publicly accessible, businesslike measure of that efficiency.

This Progressive, middle-class conception of the balanced budget held sway over much of the public, and in all likelihood it replaced any lingering notions resembling the corruption theme. The consequences of the Progressive vision of government and the budget were indeed significant. The ideological constraints against federal expansion were further weakened, and if federal spending was "efficiently" administered the burden of controlling expenditures then rested with limiting revenues. Yet through their adept handling of the tariff issue the Republicans had already demonstrated that revenues could be adjusted to suit a particular conception of government. Other political groups, the Populists, Bryan Democrats, and Progressive Democrats, in addition to writers such as Edward Bellamy and Henry George, endorsed the general idea that a strong central authority was required to bring industrial capitalism under public control. Nonetheless, the Progressive Republicans played a crucial role in the federal government's development in this direction, for they were the first "establishment" group in power to articulate this theme so clearly.

Return to "Normalcy"

After World War I and President Warren G. Harding's election in 1920, the country, in Harding's words, "returned to normalcy." Normalcy, in one sense, meant returning to the basic policies characterizing the Republican's Hamiltonian approach to government and the economy. The Republicans, for example, soon passed the Fordney-McCumber Act in 1922, thereby increasing tariff rates to protect American business and to help finance the war debt. Still, these postwar Republicans have received the reputation for being decidedly unique in their concern for reducing government expenses.[86] Federal expenditures did diminish during the Harding administration by $3 billion, from $6.4 billion in 1920 to $3.4 billion in 1922, as the wartime administrative apparatus and military were demobilized. Furthermore, whereas Gilded Age presidents Harrison and McKinley approved increases in veterans' benefits, Harding and Hoover opposed the distribution of veterans' "bonuses." Whereas the Progressive Republicans supported the income tax imposed on the wealthy, Andrew Mellon led the fight to reduce corporate taxes. "During his first eight years as Secretary of the Treasury, Mellon's refunds" to corporations totaled "$3.5 billion, including several million dollars returned to the various Mellon interests."[87] Although these Republicans expressed the desire to limit federal spending, the government's expenditure pattern was in fact higher than what had existed before World War I. In 1915 expenditures reached $760 million; between 1921 and 1931 annual expenditures, excluding debt payments, were over $2 billion, a growth in spending far greater than the rate of inflation.[88] High Republican tariffs allowed for increased expenditures and provided surplus budgets from 1921 to 1930.

Though balanced budgets always suggested economy in government, after the graduated income tax became law the Republicans had an added incentive to keep the budgets from running deficits, if only to reduce the tax burden levied on its traditional business constituency. Indeed, the corporate income tax was the decisive element in the nation's finances that forced the spendthrift Republicans to restrain federal spending.

Harding, Calvin Coolidge, and Herbert Hoover in this regard resembled their Gilded Age predecessors more than the progressives, for they opposed the income tax and attempted to make the Treasury rely instead upon the tariff for revenue. Republican rhetoric and policy endorsed limited government in the 1920s because it was clear to those who sought "normalcy" that after Roosevelt, Taft, and Wilson, an activist federal government, Progressive regulations such as the Sherman Antitrust Act, and the corporate income tax could work against the party's business constituency.[89] Consequently, not only did these presidents weaken the income tax, they limited the federal government's intervention in the economy by appointing corporate leaders to direct the nation's regulatory agencies to an extent that suggested a return to the Gilded Age.[90] The response to these appointments by those who agreed with Senator George Norris was decidedly unfavorable. These appointments "set the country back more than twenty-five years," Norris declared in 1925: "It is the nullification of federal law by a process of boring from within. If trusts, combinations, and big business are to run the government, why not permit them to do it directly rather than through this expensive machinery which was originally honestly established for the protection of the people . . . against monopoly and control?"[91]

The Democrats, on the other hand, had little to offer as an alternative to Republican "normalcy." Like the Progressive Republicans, the Progressive Democrats embraced the notion that balanced budgets equated administrative efficiency and good government, without prohibiting an increase in federal authority. "The New Nationalism and the New Freedom," noted Arthur Schlesinger, Jr., "alike affirmed the necessity of active intervention in economic life by the state."[92] Wilson's New Freedom was short-lived, for although William Jennings Bryan referred to the Congress of 1922 as "the most progressive . . . we have had in years," by the end of the decade the Democratic party appeared even more concerned about cutting taxes and aiding big business than the Republicans.[93]

Following their terrible losses in the 1924 election, congressional Democrats abandoned Progressivism and instead endorsed policies they hoped would gain the support of big business in future elections. When Andrew Mellon proposed a $330 million tax cut in 1925, the Democrats countered with a plan for $500 million in tax reductions. The Democratic proposal included $94 million in corporate tax cuts more than Mellon's tax cut, as well as an added $54 million in reductions for individuals with incomes ranging between $20,000 and $1 million. The Democratic intent was clear, as Senator Furnifold Simmons of the Finance Committee declared the tax reduction's purpose was "to make businessmen realize that the Democratic Party is not bent on taxing them or their enterprises exorbitantly."[94] The magnitude of these Democratic and Republican tax reductions threatened the budget's expected surplus, for "the great difficulty with this Congress was to restrain its members, who had seen a great light on the last election day, from voting a deficit in the treasury."[95] By 1926, the Democrats, to gain favor with corporate leaders, labeled the Republicans "big spenders" and accurately pointed out that the Coolidge administration spent "four times as much money as had President Wilson ten years earlier."[96] By the mid-1920s both parties proclaimed the virtues of unfettered industrial capitalism and openly courted the nation's corporate powers.

The nation had by now reached the watershed point in its economic and political development where paradoxically the diminution of progressive federal government, as well as its presence, encouraged Hamiltonianism. "Who was the real disciple of Jefferson," asked Louis Hartz, "the man who wanted the Anti-Trust Act or the man who opposed it?"[97] The paradox applies to such men as Harding and Coolidge who attempted to restore the national government to normalcy by limiting its regulatory and taxing powers, while at the same time they endorsed high protective tariffs. In fact, the two ambitions were compatible, for the Republicans maintained their tariffs and spent off the large budget surpluses they produced, but Harding and Coolidge also rejected spending beyond the point that might require any meaningful corporate taxation. Theirs was an unabashed Hamiltonianism cloaked in Jeffersonian garb.

The Jeffersonians and Jacksonians feared not only a dominant central government, but also the powers exercised by the "moneyed aristocracy" and their "monopolies." Large omnipotent private institutions, like the Banks of the United States, were regarded as much a threat to republican government, republican virtue, and individual freedom as a national government conducting Hamiltonian policies. The competitive balance of commercial power that Jefferson and Jackson once hoped to see in the marketplace had been distorted by Republican economic policies and the presence of monopolistic trusts. By hampering the effectiveness of federal regulations while preserving the tariff, Harding, Coolidge, and Hoover did little to rectify those marketplace distortions. On the other hand, the Progressives identified these distortions, but rather than looking toward the state governments to restore the lost balance, they enhanced federal authority and provided the national government with a "neutral," "efficient," and more powerful federal bureaucracy. Nevertheless, the Progressive notion of the federal government as countervailing power also acknowledged the legitimacy, as Roosevelt said, of "good" trusts. If after these many years of Republican party government the United States could only be governed by some form of Hamiltonianism, there remained the question of whether Hamiltonian government in the future would serve the interests of social equality or social hierarchy.

The Republicans closed their long history of tariff legislation by raising tariffs with the infamous 1930 Smoot-Hawley Tariff Act. The legislation passed through the Republican-controlled Congress with ease, though Senator Lawrence Harrison, the Democratic minority leader, declared the tariff was "obnoxious and indefensible."[98] President Hoover signed the Smoot-Hawley Act, in keeping with his earlier position on the tariff as a presidential candidate: "I am sure the American people would rather entrust the perfection of the tariff to the consistent friend of the tariff than to our opponents, who voted against our present protection to the worker and the farmer, and whose whole economic theory over generations has been the destruction of the protective principle."[99]

The tariff caused imports to fall from $4.4 billion to $1.5 billion in four years, but exports fell as well because other countries retaliated by raising their tariffs. World trade dropped from $34 billion in 1929 to $12 billion in 1933. Many economists of the day identified the Republicans' Smoot-Hawley Tariff as a major cause of the Great Depression.[100] The Republicans, in any case, once again justified their protectionist policies by employing the tariff revenue to increase public works and to make payments on war debts. President Hoover estimated the "normal rate" of expenditures for public works to be $250 million in 1928, and he pledged to increase that figure to $500 million in 1931.[101] Though total federal spending in 1929 constituted only some 3.0 percent of the GNP, the federal government's size and purpose had indeed dramatically changed under Republican rule.

The Populist Critique of Republican Party Government

The American people in this post–Civil War era could find many moral and economic reasons for objecting to federal deficits and debts, but perhaps the most powerful reason was the widespread belief that deficit and debt financing benefited the wealthy at the expense of common taxpayers. Consequently, while deficit and debt financing played a central role in the Republicans' economic policies, this financing also helped to mobilize their political opposition. To combat these Republican policies, two economic programs were proposed during the late nineteenth century to limit the benefits gained by the moneyed interests, but which paradoxically employed the large-scale expansion of the national debt. During the 1860s the Democrats proposed the Pendleton Plan, and later in the 1880s the Populists endorsed what they called the Subtreasury Plan. The Populist plan in particular deserves special attention, for many sympathetic historians believe the Jeffersonian and Jacksonian republican critique of government is most readily identifiable in agrarian groups like the Populists. Ironically, what became of the agrarian "revolt" only strengthened Hamiltonian government.

Many of the political differences that agitated Americans in the last half of the nineteenth century stemmed from the deficits and debt incurred in the Civil War. During the war, as noted earlier, the federal government left the gold standard and employed paper greenbacks and federal bank notes to replace specie currency. Paper money's introduction into the economy was inflationary, but it also stimulated the economy by increasing the amount of currency available for business transactions. Yet business contracts executed during and immediately after the war were set in terms reflecting the paper currency's lessened value. The greenback's inflationary effect therefore encouraged many small businesses, working people, and farmers to extend their debt load, for the borrowing public could expect to repay their loans at a future date with cheaper money.

After the Civil War, the Republicans, especially Treasury Secretary Hugh McCulloch, anxiously sought to return the nation to the gold standard. This goal was eventually accomplished by bringing specie legally back into circulation and by contracting the paper money supply, which consisted of the government's debt instruments. As the money supply shrank, the deflationary trend forced debtors to pay their debts with increasingly valuable currency. The Treasury slowly contracted the currency by withdrawing paper from circulation and by allowing the greenback supply to grow smaller relative to an expanding population and economy. Between 1865 and 1868 the greenback supply fell from $428 million to $356 million, while the total volume of currency, including bank notes, decreased by $45 million.[102] This paper money was more than simply printing press currency, for greenbacks and bank notes represented the federal government's outstanding debt incurred during the Civil War.

There were now two issues at hand. First, how much of this paper money, particularly greenbacks, should be allowed to circulate in place of specie, and second, how should the interest-bearing federal bank notes be redeemed by the government once their owners presented them for payment? If the notes were redeemed by the Treasury for gold, the wealthy holders of these notes would reap huge profits, for the notes were purchased with relatively inexpensive greenbacks during the war. To obtain the gold to pay the note-holders the federal government would be forced to raise revenues, and the specie-poor workers feared that the burden of these revenues raising efforts would fall on them. Specie redemption terrified many working people, as "gold and silver virtually disappeared from circulation after the suspension of specie payments in December, 1861. The only thing laboring men knew of gold during the war years was what they read in the newspapers about the activities of the gold gamblers in New York, activities which had a considerable effect on the price level."[103] These Republican policies of specie redemption and currency contraction alienated many workers and drove them into the Democratic party.

The Democrats hoped to attract these workers and rebuild their political base in the Middle West and North by focusing on these financial issues. Though divided themselves on the redemption matter, the 1868 Democratic party platform incorporated the Pendleton Plan, authored by Ohio congressman George H. Pendleton, who argued that the national debt could be retired quickly, fairly, and painlessly by substituting greenbacks for federal bank notes. By paying note-holders with greenbacks instead of gold the government would no longer need to increase taxes to gather specie. Greenbacks, unlike the bank notes, paid no interest and could be redeemed for their face value in specie only when the Treasury chose to do so. Pendleton declared in 1867:

> The non-interest paying debt, consisting of greenbacks and unliquidated debt, amounts to about eight hundred millions of dollars. . . . The proposition of the Republicans is to convert this debt into bonds which pay interest in gold. The interest on these bonds will be forty-eight millions in gold annually. The result will be to increase by that amount the expenses, to convert active capital into inactive capital, and thus to increase the number of those who do not pay taxes, and to increase the burden of those who do pay taxes. . . . these bonds should be redeemed in greenbacks. . . . The greenbacks would take place of the bank notes, which would be called in, and that eighteen million dollars of interest would be saved.[104]

The Republicans viciously attacked the plan, fearing it would "repudiate" the debt. General Joseph Hawley, governor of Connecticut, for instance, announced at the 1868 Republican national convention that "every bond, in letter and in spirit, must be as sacred as a soldier's grave."[105] The Republicans did respond to the widespread criticism of the Treasury's currency contraction by temporarily suspending greenback contraction in 1867. Radical Republicans Benjamin Butler, John Logan, and Thaddeus Stevens, among others, eagerly assailed the contraction; they argued that both high tariffs and an expanding currency were needed to spur industrial development.

Northern labor was deeply divided between supporting the Democrats and the Republicans. The Republican party remained attractive because its tariff policy favored industrial workers, and most Northerners continued to consider the Democrats the party of "Southern supremacy." On the other hand, the Democrats opposed currency contraction, specie redemption, and the big banking interests. This split among workers, Ulysses S. Grant's appeal as a war hero candidate, and the rural Democrats' apathetic behavior brought the Republicans victory in 1868. Surprisingly, the Democratic cotton farmers in the South and wheat farmers in the West showed little interest in the election, despite the political and economic appeal of the Pendleton Plan. In spite of the currency contraction, prices for farm goods remained high and the farmers prospered. "It seems safe to say that in the years 1865 to 1870 . . . farmers were the least concerned of all economic groups in the general question as to whether the volume of currency should be expanded or contracted."[106]

The Republicans immediately took advantage of their victory by passing the 1869 Public Credit Act, requiring specie redeemability of all bank notes. Labor groups, such as the National Labor Union, one of the country's most powerful, reacted in anger. The union declared in its publication: "The keynote of the present administration is the legalization of gold contracts, or virtually legislating out of the people one hundred dollars, with six per cent gold interest for every forty dollars furnished by the capitalists. This kind of legislation has a gold basis and a specie-returning in it with a vengeance and is only equalled in enormity by furnishing to capitalists the cash means to build the Pacific Railway at enormous profit."[107] The Republicans, however, regarded President Grant's 1868 and 1872 victories as national mandates to continue specie redeemability for federal bank notes, and there was little the Democrats could do about it.

These events were hardly likely to encourage Northern workers to condone any future peacetime deficit spending. Deficits and debts were still feared for the same reasons advanced by the Jeffersonians and Jacksonians. To finance the debt the federal government necessarily sold securities to those who could afford to purchase them, namely the large Eastern banks, corporate powers, and speculators. Pendleton's plan attempted to minimize the worst social and economic consequences of this financing; had it been adopted there is a possibility that some of the stigma attached to deficit financing would have diminished, and deficit spending might have become a more acceptable instrument of federal policy. Moreover, despite their support for Republican tariffs, Northern workers who demanded greenback money had something in common with the hard currency Jeffersonians and Jacksonians:

> The thread of consistency which connects the monetary ideas of the pre–Civil War and post–Civil War labor movements is a general hatred and distrust of banks, bankers, and bank-notes. The importance of this thread as a means of understanding the two movements cannot be overemphasized. Experience with the worthless shin-plasters issued by the state banks during the Jacksonian period as well as with the political overtones of central banking as practiced by Nicholas Biddle had convinced the leaders of the labor movement that the workingmen could put their confidence only in gold or silver. The Civil War introduced a new set of conditions to which adjustments had to be made.[108]

These adjustments included accepting federal greenbacks as currency rather than paying wealthy investors gold for their bank notes, thereby employing the national debt to limit the economic and social power exercised by the banking interests. With the Democrats' electoral defeat and the Pendleton Plan's abandonment, however, labor remained torn between endorsing Republican tariffs and Democratic money policy.

Later, the nation's financial situation drastically changed for the worse due to the Bank Panic of 1873. The panic resulted in a severe depression lasting from 1873 until 1879, the longest economic contraction yet recorded in the country's history. The economic difficulties presented by bank failures, closed businesses, and rising unemployment were magnified by a money stock that grew only 17 percent from 1867 to 1879. This astonishingly low monetary growth was matched only by the years of the Great Depression.[109]

The panic encouraged the greenback forces to press again for an increase in the paper money supply. In 1874 congressional Republicans finally reacted by passing the "Inflation Bill," authorizing an increase in greenbacks, but President Grant quickly vetoed the measure. Later that year Congress reversed itself again, and with Grant's approval it ordered the greenback supply fixed at the 1874 level. The decision was costly, as an enraged electorate turned the House of Representatives over to the Democrats for the first time since the Civil War in the 1874 midterm elections. The negative consequences of the Republicans' economic policy spilled over into the 1876 presidential election, where the Democratic candidate Samuel Tilden received more popular votes than the Republican Rutherford B. Hayes, but Hayes gained one extra electoral vote and became president. Some Democratic voters were diverted from Tilden; they instead supported the short-lived, tiny Greenback party consisting of splinter agrarian and labor groups that called for an end to specie redemption.[110]

The panic's effects were initially felt by urban labor, but labor's concerns would soon be mirrored by rural America. Despite the economy's recovery in the 1880s, the farmers continued to suffer from falling prices and an inadequate money supply. From 1879 until 1897 prices fell nationwide by more than 1 percent a year and farmers were particularly hard hit.[111]

The farmers' problems were cultural, however, as well as economic. America was changing, becoming more industrialized, more urban, and the rural population felt socially threatened as its numbers declined.[112] These people simply did not know how to cope with the industrialization altering their traditional way of life, or with the large corporations, like the railroads, that invaded their homeland. They were at once dependent on and fearful of the changes taking place and yet accepting of what benefits these changes might bring to their lives. In the 1890s the Southern Populists were especially beleaguered: "They and those around them were sliding quickly into a poverty and dependence from which it became more and more difficult to escape. . . . In response to the unfavorable elements of this new American industrial society, the Southern Populists tried to elaborate a social order which would preserve what they wanted to keep and get rid of what they did not. . . . They drew on the material available to them—their rural Southern experience, their evangelical Protestant heritage, and their Jeffersonian-Jacksonian tradition."[113]

The Populists searched for a political solution to the challenges of industrialization, big business trusts, and banks by turning to the power of the federal government. "Their solution was a two-tier economic structure which combined essentially a simple market society for the large number of independent producers with democratic government ownership and operation of those elements of industrial society which for one reason or another could not be controlled by individuals."[114] To preserve 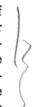 their understanding of the marketplace, based on the individualistic notions of self-determination, the right to work, and success or failure determined by one's own efforts, the Populists sought the expanded use of federal and state power to nationalize the railroads and utilities. This attempt to gain the benefits of a "two-tiered economic structure" never met with success, nor did the Populists fully reconcile the philosophical contradictions and practical political problems associated with designing and implementing such a society. Furthermore, the exact role the Populists played in American political history is still subject to intense debate. What is significant about the Populists in a narrower sense is that their solution to remedy the economic difficulties at hand included expanding the national debt.

To alleviate their financial plight, where the specie-poor Western banks lacked the gold necessary to extend credit, many Populists united behind the 1889 Subtreasury Plan. The plan essentially called for the federal government to operate a "subtreasury" office in every county in the nation where at least $500,000 in agricultural commodities were produced. The federal government would store these products and pay the producer greenbacks worth 80 percent of the goods' local value. The currency would be loaned to the producer at 1 percent interest, and if the goods were not reclaimed by the farmer within one year, the federal government would be authorized to pay the farmer's debt.[115]

This shift to greenbacks from specie signaled a dramatic reversal in agrarian America's long-standing distrust of paper money dating back to Jefferson and Jackson. This reversal, however, complemented the Jeffersonian and Jacksonian hostility toward the powerful financial institutions based primarily in New York, Boston, and Philadelphia. By employing the federal government as banker, the Subtreasury Plan "promised to destroy credit, interest, and the lien system by providing an effective mechanism for putting the country on a cash basis and by allowing the federal government rather than merchants and bankers to furnish needed capital cheaply to the producers."[116] The Subtreasury Plan called for an expanding greenback money supply, which in effect required an expanding federal debt and perhaps deficit spending. Greenbacks, once again, were federal debt instruments that paid no interest and could be redeemed for their face value in specie only when the federal government considered redemption worthwhile.

This Populist solution ran counter to the Democratic plan for strengthening the economy, as the Democratic solution simply called for an increase in the amount of specie making up the money supply.[117] The Democrats' salvation was silver specie, and on this point the Populists and Democrats sharply and profoundly disagreed. Aside from their flirtation with greenbackism in the 1860s and 1870s, as in the Pendleton Plan, the Democrats opposed policies intended to increase the national debt. To emphasize their opposition to deficit spending by all agents of the federal government, the Democrats and Republicans in the Congress took action during the Cleveland administration by way of the 1886 Harrison Act to limit territorial governments from indebting themselves beyond newly established limits.[118] Furthermore, Cleveland, a Democratic president, greatly angered the Populists by proposing unsuccessfully to Congress that the government employ the budget surplus to redeem a portion of the outstanding greenbacks and federal bank notes for specie. The effect of such an action would have been a contraction of the paper currency while retiring some of the national debt.[119]

Many Populists, particularly those located in the deep South far from the Western silver mines, found Bryan's silver program too limited to end the control they believed the bankers and industrialists exercised over the economy. Adding silver to the currency simply increased the money stock. On the other hand, the Subtreasury Plan attacked those social institutions responsible for manipulating the country's economy and the financing of the national debt. "Free silver meant nothing more than an expansion of the currency supply; legal tender fiat currency was the leading edge of an antimonopoly greenbackism that questioned the legitimacy of the central institutions of American capitalism, including the role of the government in the social and economic life of the country."[120] The Populist candidate for president in 1892 received 1 million of the 12 million votes cast in that election, but the Populists realized they would have to support or "fuse" with the Democrats and Bryan in 1896 if their reforms were to be realized. This alliance was ideologically costly, for the Populists were forced to subsume their Subtreasury Plan in favor of the Democrats' silver program.[121]

The 1896 and 1900 elections left the Populists and the Democrats devastated. The Republicans won because they successfully united Northern labor behind the tariff threatened by Bryan and they gained assistance from the bankers and other Eastern financial and industrial interests that sought to maintain the gold standard. In addition, the nation's money supply was expanding, as new gold fields opened in Alaska and Colorado, without relying on silver or greenbacks. This expanding specie currency relieved the debtors' and farmers' worst financial problems, particularly as prices for farm products and other goods climbed. The money supply grew by about 7.5 percent a year and prices rose more than 2 percent annually between 1879 and 1914.[122] Improving economic conditions and a solidified Republican party defeated the Democratic and Populist alliance, along with their silver and Subtreasury programs.

The effects of political defeat and economic vitality greatly reduced rural America's political rage and economic demands. "Prices did rise after 1896, and agrarian politics did subside. A golden age for agriculture preceded the First World War. It was a period of both favoring prices and political calm upon the land."[123] Bryan's defeat broke the back of Populism politically and spiritually. The Populists envisioned their movement to represent not only the farmers, but industrial labor as well. As in the days of Jefferson and Jackson, the Populists believed the primary political and social division in the land separated the "working people" from the "moneyed aristocracy." When labor supported McKinley rather than Bryan, this conception of American political life crumbled. The farmers no longer considered themselves united with labor in a common struggle; as a result agrarian America's economic and political goals, and the method for achieving them, changed dramatically. Farmers soon organized themselves in agricultural interest groups, seeking specific remedies for particular grievances, instead of a mass social movement demanding widespread institutional conversion.[124]

Populism was dead, and with Populism went what numerous historians regard as the last vestige of true Jeffersonian-Jacksonian agrarian democracy.[125] The Populists sought equality not in the socialistic collective sense, but in the equality of opportunity and economic competition where the individual remained responsible and free to determine his or her fate. This emphasis on the individual producer alienated the socialists. Daniel De Leon, the "ideologue-leader" of the Socialist party, dismissed the Populists, declaring, "It was a middle class movement, a movement aiming at the impossible achievement of preserving the system of small production."[126] The Populists looked to Jefferson and Jackson rather than socialism for their republican critique of society. Considering the Populist heritage of hard money and fear of centralized authority, however, they ironically turned to paper currency and to the federal government in order to nationalize railroads and establish federal "subtreasuries."

After the demise of Populism, agricultural political interests became remarkably adept at gaining federal legislation favoring their concerns.

The list of such legislation is indeed impressive, and includes the 1902 Reclamation Act guaranteeing federal water to small farmers, the 1906 Pure Food and Drug Act, the 1916 Federal Farm Loan Act, and others.[127] Almost all of this legislation was supported by Progressive Republicans and Democrats, but, significantly, the Farm Bureau and the bipartisan "farm bloc" in Congress also achieved substantial interest group victories in the 1920s. In 1923 Congress passed the Agricultural Credits Act, signed by President Harding. The act provided a system of "intermediate credit banks" operating under the supervision of the Federal Loan System created in 1916. After this victory the farm bloc sought direct farm price subsidies through the McNary-Haugen subsidy plan. In effect, the farmers endorsed the legitimacy of the Hamiltonian tariff system, for the subsidy plan looked specifically to tariff revenues and federal budget surpluses to supply the funds needed to pay the subsidies.[128] Though the Republicans rejected the McNary-Haugen plan, the Hoover Administration did support the 1929 Agricultural Marketing Act, providing $500 million in federal loans for cooperative farming associations. Rural America was now less the standard-bearer of Jeffersonianism and Jacksonianism defending the free market or combating monopolies and instead was just another interest group ratifying federal authority while receiving federal benefits; certainly the Republicans and Democrats responded to the farmers in this fashion.

Balanced Budgets and Symbolic Politics   *reprise from ch. 4*

By the time of the New Deal the notion of balanced federal budgets had passed through two distinct phases in American politics and public policy. In the first phase, during the age of Jefferson and Jackson balanced federal budgets symbolized the public's ability and willingness to prevent the "corruption" threatening republican government and republican virtue. Deficit spending and excessive surpluses were thought to encourage this corruption's development by placing unnecessary revenues at the federal government's disposal, ultimately compromising the nation's constitutional balance of powers while enriching the moneyed aristocracy who financed the deficits and debt. Thus, unbalanced federal budgets contributed to the growth of the large public and private institutions that Jefferson and Jackson believed threatened individual liberty, agrarian democracy, and the authority of the state governments.

In the second phase, the Republican party, the philosophical and political heir to the Federalist and Whig parties, was the dominant political party in the United States from 1861 until 1932. The Republicans enacted policies long rejected by those who invoked the concept of corruption, but because the Treasury gathered its revenue largely through tariffs, the fear of deficits actually worked in favor of Republican policies. The

Republicans paradoxically benefited from the symbolism employed by the Jeffersonians and Jacksonians. The Republicans could expand federal power in the manner they desired even while opposing deficit spending. The more they opposed deficits but created the conditions where deficits might exist, the more tariff revenues flowed into the Treasury. In this sense, the concept of corruption was seriously flawed, for it failed to take into account how the fear of deficits vindicated larger tariff rates and the need for more revenues to balance the budget. In any case, the Republican party had little incentive to perpetuate the political symbols and ideology aimed at defeating the very policies it held so dear.

The Republican party essentially replaced the corruption theme's reasoning for opposing unbalanced budgets with the Progressives' notion of administrative efficiency. The Progressives viewed the federal government as a stabilizing force in society, acting in a neutral fashion to mediate social and political conflict between capital, labor, and rural America. Balanced budgets represented to the Progressives the government's administrative efficiency, professionalism, and freedom from the graft and abuse of public funds common to machine and party politics. The Progressive understanding of efficiency and budgets in balance or surplus suggested a bureaucracy independent of party control and the traditional spoils system, but also one administering a federal government with expanding activities and responsibilities. Finally, the Progressives pushed for administrative reform by way of the executive budget because they reasoned that centralizing the budgetary process through the executive branch would increase the likelihood of achieving a balanced budget. Contrary to Progressive expectations, however, history would demonstrate that in future years it would be the presidency that led the federal government into incurring deficits as a matter of acceptable public policy.

Nevertheless, the Republican party's justification for rejecting deficit spending during most of the period described here stemmed from the pragmatic need to protect the tariff system. Even the Progressive notion of administrative efficiency failed to address the issue of excessive surpluses, but as the federal government's revenue base depended less on tariffs and more on income taxes the Republicans had an added incentive to oppose deficits in earnest. Although tariffs were in effect taxes levied on foreign goods, thus protecting domestic industries, the graduated income tax placed the direct cost of running the government on the Republicans' business constituency. Before the federal income tax was enacted, the Republicans could accept, even encourage a rapidly growing budget, for large federal expenditures required, and thereby justified, high tariffs.

In late-twentieth-century America, when deficit spending is indeed "chronic," observers may glance nostalgically back at the surpluses gathered during this period of Republican government. Yet many Americans living at that time objected strenuously to those surpluses, often for the same reasons they opposed deficit spending. Balanced budgets were desired, not budgets in excessive surplus, and this desire allowed the Republicans to spend the surplus as quickly as possible while maintaining high tariffs. Deficits, of course, justified the need for more tariff revenue and they were opposed for the same reason as budget surpluses.

The Republican party responsible for those tariffs acted in just the manner fearfully predicted by the Jeffersonians and Jacksonians: unbalanced budgets provided the federal government with the revenues required for bureaucratic expansion, federal internal improvement projects grew in number and cost, the banking system was centralized, high tariffs benefited the wealthy and corporate monopolies, and states' rights were eroded through federal regulations. Balanced federal budgets continued to symbolize the public's financial and political control over the federal government, even as the language of political corruption was lost to history. The great irony of Republican party government, however, was that the public's fear of unbalanced budgets led to the greatest enhancement of federal power yet known in the country's history.

6

Transforming a Symbol: Democratic Party Government, 1933–1980

Nearly 150 years ago Thomas Jefferson wrote, "The new circumstances under which we are placed call for new words, new phrases, and for the transfer of old words to new objects." New words, new phrases, the transfer of old words to new objects—that is truer today than it was in the time of Jefferson, because the role of this country is so vastly more significant.

John F. Kennedy, on deficit spending and the "myths" associated with the national debt, 1962

Discredit an economic theory and you discredit its attendant politics.

Kevin Phillips, 1983

The Great Depression ushered in a period in American history that witnessed the dynamic growth of federal authority and the purposeful use of deficit spending to stabilize and strengthen the economy. This "fiscal revolution," as Herbert Stein called it, developed first in the Hoover administration, but it flowered during the New Deal and again in the New Frontier and Great Society of the 1960s. Although still very much a part of public policy in the 1980s, particularly in the form of deficit spending, during the 1970s the revolution exhausted much of the public legitimacy it once enjoyed when presidents and public officials declared deficit spending was a necessary and positive federal activity.

This loss of legitimacy was not due to the economic consequences of deficit spending. No matter what adverse economic effects the Reagan deficits may have on the economy in the late 1980s and beyond, most serious economists believe that the deficits incurred in the 1970s and

161

early 1980s did little harm to the economy. Nor was the loss of public legitimacy due to the criticism of the federal government's deficit spending voiced by the Republican party. Though Republicans since the Hoover years regularly denounced peacetime deficit spending, Richard Nixon proclaimed, "We are all Keynesians," and the Gerald Ford administration presided over the largest peacetime deficits in American history prior to Ronald Reagan. Instead, the loss of legitimacy was largely caused by Democratic leaders who failed to defend the policy of deficit spending when it most needed defending, during the mid and late 1970s. Rather than explain to the American public that deficits incurred in the midst of a recession were often beneficial, prominent Democratic leaders, for example Governor Jimmy Carter of Georgia and Governor Jerry Brown of California, attacked the Ford deficits on the basis that they created havoc in the economy. Since the days of the New Deal the Democratic party worked long and hard to educate the public about the useful application of deficit spending, but for the sake of defeating President Ford in the 1976 election the Democrats abandoned and discredited the cornerstone of their economic policies. In the process, they also discredited their attendant politics, and the confusion that ensued among Democrats over deficit spending and fiscal policy only served to favor Ronald Reagan in 1980.

Certainly any policy that employed prolonged deficit spending, like full-employment economics, required a competent and continuous public defense. The Democrats during the New Deal and post-Roosevelt years were engaged in the difficult process of reversing the symbolism that by the 1930s had traditionally become associated with balanced and unbalanced federal budgets. From the republic's earliest days, unbalanced federal budgets represented an unwarranted expansion of national authority carried out at the expense of state governments, in order to benefit the interests of the moneyed aristocracy, bankers, and industrialists. The Jeffersonians and Jacksonians first articulated this fear of an excessive federal presence, symbolized by unbalanced budgets, through their understanding of political corruption. After the Civil War, the Republicans found they could manipulate federal revenues by adjusting tariff rates and achieve the same policy results once sought by the Hamiltonian Federalists and Whigs without requiring the Republicans to object to a policy of balanced budgets.

In each case, those who favored either decentralized or centralized government supported balanced budgets to realize their own particular visions of politics and society; balanced budgets assumed symbolic qualities far more complex than any accountant's understanding of balance. Though the reasoning underlying the positions staked out by these conflicting political groups became increasingly vague and lost to history, what had emerged through time was a uniquely American tradition favoring balanced federal budgets. To achieve their own political vision that ostensibly sought Jeffersonian ends through a Hamiltonian centralization of federal power, the Democrats were forced to contend with this traditional concern for unbalanced budgets, and substitute in the public's mind an alternative understanding of unbalanced budgets and beneficient federal power.

Jefferson, Hamilton, and FDR

Although the fiscal revolution had its intellectual foundation in the Populist and Progressive movements, the Democratic party, more than the Republicans, lacked the historical and philosophical background to support an activist stance by the federal government. Given his party's past, Franklin Delano Roosevelt's attempt to come to grips with the Democrats' Jeffersonian legacy is significant. Writing to his mother in the autumn of 1927, Roosevelt declared that Jefferson "had a better insight into the Republican form of government than did G. Washington or A. Hamilton."[1] Urged by his mother to read Jefferson, Roosevelt was so taken with the great statesman that during the closing weeks of the 1932 election he centered several major campaign speeches on the clash between Jefferson and Hamilton. By examining Roosevelt's interpretation of Jefferson's thought, some additional light may be shed on the fiscal revolution that was taking place in American public policy.

Roosevelt's difficult task was to reconcile Jeffersonian individualism and decentralized government with his own belief that the economic exigencies of the day required enhanced federal power. Roosevelt began by describing the bitter feud that divided Hamilton and Jefferson, which Roosevelt said focused on the issue of who should govern the nation. Whereas Hamilton favored a "dominant centralized power" governed only by "certain sections of the Nation and certain individuals within these sections," Jefferson's vision of America called for a broad national solidarity in which "the interests of all groups in every part must be considered."[2] But Jefferson's firm belief in individual liberty tempered this solidarity so that "individualism was made the great watchword of American life." This individualism expressed itself through "two sets of rights," the right of private ownership and the right of "personal competency." Some federal authority was necessary to protect property rights, but to preserve personal competency, which included freedom of speech and "freedom of personal living," the "Government must so order its function as not to interfere with the individual."[3] Thus, according to Roosevelt, Jefferson successfully assimilated personal liberty and the need for national unity in preindustrial America by limiting government to protecting property rights.

The notion of personal competency was a crucial element in Roose-

velt's thinking, for it encouraged him to believe he had conciliated Jeffersonian individualism with an active and powerful central government. In
Jefferson's time, "the happiest of economic conditions made that day
long and splendid. . . . No one, who did not shirk the task of earning a
living, was entirely without opportunity to do so." The social and political formula of individualism and limited government succeeded because
at the very least the open frontier enabled farmers and workers to rebuild
their lives in the American wilderness. Even in the early days of the
industrial revolution, said Roosevelt, an individual's hard work, ambi-
tion, and personal competency resulted in substantial achievement, for
"there was equal opportunity for all." But by 1900 the conditions that
nurtured this equal opportunity were greatly diminished, for "at the
request of businessmen themselves," the federal government's new function was "to assist in the development of industry."[4] Roosevelt cited the
protective tariff, railroad subsidies, and grants to the maritime industry as
examples of federal support to these industrialists. To rectify the economic and social disadvantages created by these federal activities, in
addition to combating the misery of depression, Roosevelt argued that the
federal government was obligated to extend its benefits to the entire
nation, rather than only to privileged bankers and industrialists.

How would the federal government under a Democratic administration
accomplish its new responsibilities? By adjusting its structure and purpose to meet the reality of an industrialized and depressed America.
Whereas Herbert Hoover engaged in "unscientific, belated—almost frantic—economy in Government," Roosevelt's presidency would promote
"enlightened administration." "Our task now," declared Roosevelt, "is
not discovery or exploitation of natural resources, or necessarily producing more goods. It is the soberer, less dramatic business of administering
resources and plants already in hand . . . of distributing wealth and products more equitably, of adapting existing economic organizations to the
service of the people."[5] Organized along lines resembling the ad hoc
structure of Woodrow Wilson's World War I administration, Roosevelt
promised to reshape the federal government in the image of the War
Industries Board, the War Trade Board, and the Food and Fuel Administration. Jefferson would have approved these changes, said Roosevelt,
for Jefferson "did not deceive himself with outward forms. Government
to him was a means to an end, not an end in itself; it might be either a
refuge and a help or a threat and a danger, depending on the circumstances." Furthermore, "if Jefferson would return to the councils of the
party, he would find that while economic changes of a century have
changed the necessary methods of government action, the principles of
that action are still wholly his own."[6] By serving the nation as a whole,
Roosevelt argued that he could recreate the national union that existed
under Jefferson.

In fact, when Roosevelt considered reorganizing the federal government's purpose and structure he looked to the Progressives rather than to Jefferson for guidance. What alarmed Roosevelt more than centralized government was a "highly centralized economic system, the despot of the twentieth century," for "where Jefferson had feared the encroachment of political power in the lives of individuals, Wilson knew that the new power was financial."[7] Therefore, an efficacious central government was needed to counterbalance the power of industralized capital, and to aid the "forgotten man" who suffered at the hands of nefarious bankers and "moneychangers." All this would be achieved through principles of "enlightened administration" and planning.

Roosevelt endeavored to separate himself from the legacy of Hamiltonian government, where a strong federal authority was historically equated with social and economic inequality. His grasp of American history made Roosevelt more than a little uneasy about how this equation might be applied to his own presidency, as this remarkable effort to dissect the Jeffersonian-Hamiltonian feud in the midst of an election suggests. Still, the content of federal policies mattered more to Roosevelt than did the government's centralized form, and as long as these policies favored all interests rather than only the moneyed aristocracy Roosevelt reasoned the federal government would be freed from the specter of Hamiltonianism. But Roosevelt presented a rather embellished portrait of Jefferson, for Jefferson cared greatly about form, as he declared that decentralization enabled the public to participate fully in the nation's political life. "Divide the counties into wards of such size," Jefferson said, "as that every person can attend, when called on, and act in person. . . . These wards, called townships in New England . . . have proved themselves the wisest invention ever devised by the wit of man for the perfect exercise of self-government . . . the whole is cemented by giving to every citizen, personally, a part in the administration of the public affairs."[8] Roosevelt gambled that federal policies would produce more freedom, opportunity, and participatory democracy than the federal government's centralizing tendencies might prevent.

The Democratic party accepted Roosevelt's understanding of history and his principles of government, and in the years following the 1932 election the Democrats became the major source of social change in America. The Jeffersonian goals of equal opportunity and personal competency, as Roosevelt saw them, would be pursued by a progressive central government, one that over time came to acknowledge deficit spending as a necessary and pragmatic, if not legitimate, tool of social and economic policy. This tolerance for deficits came slowly, was never completely agreed to even among Democrats, and stemmed primarily from Roosevelt's desperate search for policy instruments that could defeat the Depression. Later, Keynesian economics and the notion of the full-employment budget embedded deficit spending in macroeconomic theory, thereby adding to the legitimacy of unbalanced federal budgets.

In one sense, the toleration shown toward the federal government's deficits by key political leaders and by many academic economists was almost inevitable. The concept of corruption employed by Jefferson had its origins in the study of "political economy." Social, political, and economic theories were examined as a joint concern, thereby encouraging scholars and legislators to consider systematically the moral and political outcomes produced by any given set of economic activities. The twentieth century witnessed the division of political economy into its distinct subfields, mostly through the influence of Alfred Marshall's work in economics published in the late nineteenth century. One consequence of this division, suggested Daniel Bell, is that formal "economics moved from the moral (or political) and normative to the instrumental and scientific."[9] At the same time, efforts to reform government through scientific management and public administration accompanied this revolution in the academic study of economics. If politics was unseemly and could not be counted on to care for the public's business, then perhaps science could. If economists determined through their scientific analysis that deficits were sound, then the nation's political leaders were under some obligation to accept this advice. By the time of the New Frontier and Great Society such counsel was commonplace.

Building Pyramids and the New Deal Deficits

The deficits associated with the Great Depression and the New Deal initiated the third phase in the nation's symbolic understanding of balanced and unbalanced budgets. In the first phase, unbalanced federal budgets produced before the Civil War symbolized the federal government's potential corruption that threatened agrarian democracy and the Constitution's balance of powers. Next, the massive budget surpluses created by Republican tariffs, in violation of the corruption theme, supported federal expansion and activities that were widely perceived to be a major source of the inequities feared by Jefferson and Andrew Jackson. The deficits incurred in the 1930s, regardless of their economic effects, symbolized the federal government's growing presence in the economy and society for both those people who supported and opposed this intervention.

The federal government's responsibility to incur deficits was best spelled out by John Maynard Keynes. In order to stimulate aggregate demand and save the country from economic ruin, Keynes argued, the national government should increase public spending, even if this meant running deficits. Keynes had this to say about deficits and government spending in his classic work, *The General Theory of Employment, Interest, and Money*, published in 1936:

> Public works even of doubtful utility may pay for themselves over and over again at a time of severe unemployment, if only from the diminished cost of relief expenditure, provided that we can assume that a smaller proportion of income is saved when unemployment is greater; but they may become a more doubtful proposition as a state of full employment is approached. . . . If this is accepted, the above reasoning shows how "wasteful" loan expenditure may nevertheless enrich the community on balance. Pyramid-building, earthquakes, even wars may serve to increase wealth, if the education of our statesmen on the principles of the classical economics stands in the way of anything better.

Keynes used the term "loan expenditure" as a "convenient expression for the net borrowings of public authorities on all accounts, whether on capital account or to meet a budgetary deficit."[10]

The notion that public works projects might aid a troubled economy was not a Keynesian or Democratic invention. Economists Simeon Leland at the University of Chicago and Summer Slichter of Harvard University, among others, wrote early in the Depression that greater levels of federal spending were necessary to reduce the dimensions of the crisis. Moreover, President Hoover was not automatically inclined to reject such advice, for Hoover sought to increase the number of federally funded projects to end the Depression. Thus, Hoover's willingness to employ federal funds in this fashion made its own contribution to the development of the fiscal revolution. In his memoirs Hoover defended his use of public works and attacked Roosevelt for suggesting in the 1932 campaign that only under a Democratic administration would there be public works to aid the unemployed:

> [Roosevelt] either ignores or is ignorant of the fact that as far back as 1922, in our unemployment conference of that year under my chairmanship, we developed the idea of making use of public works to assist in the stabilization of employment in times of depression and laid the foundation for its operation. . . . This total of nearly $2,000,000,000 Federal public works [for 1929 through 1932] was greater than the whole expenditure during the previous thirty years, including the Panama Canal. It accounted for a considerable part of the deficit.[11]

In addition, while Hoover left it to the states to provide individuals with unemployment relief, he agreed to make federal loans available through the Reconstruction Finance Corporation to banks, railroads, and insurance companies. Roosevelt later argued that the corporation was an excellent example of Hamiltonian government, for Hoover willingly used federal resources to protect the interests of the wealthy, but forced workers to seek aid from the impoverished states.

Hoover was well known for his opposition to deficit spending. After his defeat at Roosevelt's hands, Hoover proclaimed in 1935 that deficits were prolonging the Depression. "It is not overstatement to say," he declared, "that had the Republican principles of balancing the budget been accepted in 1931 and 1932, the final stone in the foundation of permanent recovery would have been laid three years ago instead of deferred for years hence."[12] Though Hoover certainly favored balanced budgets he was not dogmatically tied to budget balancing. Hoover and his advisers concluded that cutting taxes would stimulate the economy and bring the government increased revenues in the long run, despite the possibility of creating deficits. Herbert Stein analyzed Hoover's economic policies and found "the administration knew that 'balancing the budget' is an elastic concept. . . . They knew in the first place that balancing the budget did not mean balancing it every year. Surpluses in some years could make room for deficits in other years." Indeed, in 1930 Hoover told the nation: "When we recollect that our Budget has yielded large surpluses for the last 11 years, which have enabled us to retire the public debt, in addition to retirements required by law, to the extent of nearly $3,500,000,000, we can confidently look forward to the restoration of such surpluses with the general recovery of the economic situation, and thus the absorption of any temporary borrowing that may be necessary."[13] The economic situation did not allow for Hoover to implement his tax cuts, however, for he decided that an increase in federal borrowing that took place while the money supply was contracted could not help but limit private borrowing and thus choke off recovery. Reacting to these conditions, Hoover pressed the Congress to raise taxes and therefore reduce the size of the projected deficits.

Thus, a restrictive monetary policy that influenced interest rates, bond prices, and the flow of gold played a crucial role in Hoover's decision to avoid deficit spending, principally by raising taxes. Had Hoover found the size of the nation's money supply more encouraging he might not have called for a tax increase, and instead allowed some of the projected deficits to occur as scheduled.[14] But even without these tax increases the amount of deficit spending projected for FY 1931–33, a total of some $3.2 billion, was not overwhelmingly large. In the preceding ten years the Treasury had reduced the national debt by over $9 billion, suggesting that the slack economy could have absorbed the deficits had the Federal Reserve produced a more accommodating monetary policy.

Regardless of the size of the money supply, the government's ability to run deficits was considerably constrained by its limited capability to digest and make use of the extra expenditures. The federal government throughout much of the 1930s was simply not organized to spend the tremendous amounts of money that Keynes, for one, felt was necessary to end the Depression. Nevertheless, Hoover's public works projects "helped to lay the groundwork for the New Deal efforts."[15] Hoover's interest in public works was not so surprising, considering that he engineered American assistance to Europe after World War I, and he understood the government's potential ability to assist a depressed economy. In any case, under the Hoover administration the 1931 deficit reached $461 million, and was rivaled only by the $89 million peacetime deficit of 1909. The 1932 deficit registered at $2.7 billion. Significantly, federal expenditures grew during the Hoover years from $3.3 billion in 1929 to $4.7 billion in 1932, a 42 percent increase.

Accepting deficits did not come easily to Franklin Roosevelt, who as a presidential candidate dedicated himself to restoring balanced federal budgets. Consequently, though Roosevelt eventually came to accept deficit spending, his deficits during those crucial New Deal years of 1933–40 never climbed above $4.4 billion, nor did federal expenditures in any year exceed $10 billion. When measured as a proportion of the GNP, Roosevelt's deficits were in the same range as those incurred, for example, by the Ford and Reagan administrations. As shown in Table 15, Roosevelt's largest deficit, that of 1936, reached 5.3 percent of GNP, as compared to 4.0 percent in 1976 and 5.7 percent in 1983.

Roosevelt never felt comfortable with deficit spending or Keynesian economics. The president actually tried to reduce projected federal spending in 1933 by cutting veterans' benefits by $400 million and federal salaries by $100 million. Roosevelt warned Congress that "too often in recent history liberal governments have been wrecked on the rocks of loose fiscal policy." Historian William Leuchtenburg wrote about the

Table 15. Federal deficits and GNP, 1931–1940 (in billions of dollars)

Fiscal year	Deficit	GNP	% GNP
1931	−0.5	76.3	0.6
1932	−2.7	58.5	4.6
1933	−2.6	56.0	4.6
1934	−3.6	65.0	5.5
1935	−2.8	72.5	3.8
1936	−4.4	82.7	5.3
1937	−2.8	90.8	3.1
1938	−1.2	85.2	1.4
1939	−3.9	91.1	4.3
1940	−3.9	100.6	3.9

Source for GNP: Bureau of the Census, *Historical Statistics of the United States* (Washington, D.C., 1961), p. 139.

1933 budget, Roosevelt's first, observing that "under the leadership of Franklin Roosevelt, the budget balancers had won a victory for orthodox finance that had not been possible under Hoover." Roosevelt was under great pressure from members of the Democratic party, including party leaders Robert Wagner and Bernard Baruch, to balance the budget. "With the monotony and persistence of old Cato," declared Baruch, "we should make one single and invariable dictum the theme of every discourse: 'Balance budgets. . . . Cut governmental spending—cut it as rations are cut in a siege. Tax—tax everybody for everything.' " In April 1933 Roosevelt wrote to Colonel Edward House about his firm conviction that the deficits should be limited, saying, "I realize well that thus far we have actually given more of deflation than of inflation. . . . It is simply inevitable that we must inflate and though my banker friends may be horrified, I still am seeking an inflation which will not wholly be based on additional government debt." Nevertheless, the deficit continued to grow, and on August 30, 1934, Lewis Douglas, Roosevelt's budget director, resigned to protest the deficit. "I hope, and hope most fervently," he informed the president, "that you will evidence a real determination to bring the budget into actual balance, for upon this, I think, hangs not only your place in history but conceivably the immediate fate of western civilization."[16]

By 1937 the economy recovered somewhat from the darkest days of 1932 and 1933, and soon Roosevelt became concerned less about unemployment and more about anticipated inflationary growth occurring during the predicted recovery. In response, the administration made plans to reduce federal spending for FY 1938:

> Roosevelt, inordinately worried about the danger of inflation, slashed spending sharply. He cut WPA [Works Progress Administration] rolls drastically and turned off PWA [Public Works Administration] pump-priming. At the very same time, Washington collected two billions in new social-security taxes. The government had not only stopped priming the pump but was even "taking some water out of the spout." If business had been ready to take over, none of this would have mattered, but business still lacked the confidence to undertake new investment. . . . The "prosperity" of early 1937, which rested on an insecure base of mass unemployment and a sluggish construction industry, had been achieved largely by the government's deficit spending.[17]

Roosevelt's budget cuts were made in an attempt to reduce the deficit and eventually balance the budget. "I have said fifty times," noted Roosevelt, "that the budget will be balanced for the fiscal year 1938. If you want me to say it again, I will say it either once or fifty times more. That is my intention."[18] Treasury secretary Henry Morgenthau supported these budget reductions because he considered these deficits to be inflationary, and because he feared the government's credit would be impaired if the Treasury flooded the bond market with federal securities. Federal Reserve Board chairman Marriner Eccles acted as the administration's foremost proponent of deficit spending, but in 1937 even he warned Morgenthau that *"in his opinion it was imperative that assurance be given that the budget would be balanced in 1938* [Eccles's emphasis]."[19] Liberal Democrats Harry Hopkins, Harold Ickes, William Douglas, Jerome Frank, and others opposed Roosevelt's call for balanced budgets and reduced spending. They argued unsuccessfully that the $1.6 billion reduction in the FY 1937 deficit from FY 1936 was weakening the economy, and that more spending, not less, was needed to preserve the recovery. The FY 1936 deficit was $4.4 billion, Roosevelt's largest, but the GNP also made its greatest gain in any year during the Depression. Roosevelt's budget reductions produced a relatively small $1.2 billion deficit in 1938, but the president's inflationary fears vanished as the economy plunged deeper into the depression.

The president acted on this new economic crisis by increasing government spending and deficits; subsequently the deficit grew to $3.9 billion in both 1939 and 1940. Roosevelt had disbanded the Public Works Administration, but he soon proposed that a reinvigorated PWA be granted a budget of over $1 billion, while Harry Hopkins's Works Progress Administration would receive a budget of over $1.4 billion. For the first time in his presidency, Roosevelt accepted deficit spending as a positive and necessary federal activity if the economy were to recover. He accepted these deficits so that Americans would have immediate access to employment though public works jobs, but historians contend that Roosevelt refused to acknowledge or failed to understand the need for the large-scale federal spending required in Lord Keynes's macroeconomics theory. R. F. Harrod, Keynes's official biographer, said about Roosevelt, "It is not clear that he acted on the principle that it was the deficit, rather than the public works themselves, that was the potent agency in reducing unemployment."[20] Similarly, James MacGregor Burns observed in his biography of Roosevelt:

> The idea of boosting spending and holding down taxes and of doing this year after year as a deliberate policy, the idea of gaining prosperity by the deliberate creation of huge deficits—this idea in its full dimensions seemed but another fanciful academic theory, and Roosevelt by 1938 had had a bellyful of such theories. Pump priming as a temporary emergency measure he could understand—but not deficit spending as the central, long-term approach to full-scale economic recovery. . . . The trouble with deficit spending was that halfway application did not work. It had utility only through full and determined use; otherwise it served only to antagonize and worry business by increasing the public debt without sufficiently raising spending and investment. A Keynesian solution, in short, involved an

almost absolute commitment, and Roosevelt was not one to commit himself
absolutely to any political or economic method.[21]

Roosevelt did little publicly to embrace a Keynesian interpretation of
deficit spending. To Roosevelt, deficits were extraordinary expenditures
that differed from normal government expenses, and only their extraordinary nature made them tolerable. As late as 1938 Roosevelt was still
accounting for his failure to meet his 1932 campaign pledge and the
Democratic platform to balance the budget: "Immediately upon assuming
office, I recommended and effected drastic economies in the regular
expenditures of government. . . . The great increase in the expenditures of
Government came from the new extraordinary agencies of Government
created to meet the emergency and from the necessities of meeting the
widespread needs of the unemployed. Neither the platform nor the
speech intended, in letter or spirit, to permit the emergency and the
distress of the unemployed to go on without assistance from the Government's treasury."[22] Roosevelt's view that deficits constituted at best an
unpleasant necessity no doubt contributed to the public's distaste for
deficit spending. A public opinion survey conducted in 1939, for example,
asked the question, "If you were a member of the incoming Congress,
would you vote yes or no on a bill to reduce federal spending to the point
where the national budget is balanced?" More than 61 percent of the
respondents replied yes, including 54.8 percent of those classified as poor,
and 57.5 percent of those who were unemployed.[23] As Roosevelt's administration came to an end, neither the public nor the president accepted the
Keynesian strategy of producing "pyramid-building" deficits.

Roosevelt's political enemies vilified the New Deal, its programs, ex-
penses, and deficits. To them, and even to some of Roosevelt's allies, the
New Deal signaled the ascent of fascism and socialism in America. In the
Senate, Henry Hatfield, the chairman of the Republican party's Senatorial
Campaign Committee, declared, "The New Deal, while it sings the
praises of Jefferson and Jackson, is more in keeping with the preachings of
Norman Thomas, Stalin, Mussolini and Hitler."[24] Hatfield was not alone
in his charge against the New Deal programs or the president. B. C.
Forbes, the owner of *Forbes Magazine*, editorialized against "the rampant
Fascism raging at the moment" in the federal government. The *Wash-
ington Star* argued that "there can be little quibbling over the advised use
of the word 'dictator' in reference to the new authority given to the
President." The *Wall Street Review* declared in an editorial, "In short,
Mr. Roosevelt has constitutionally asked for the power to become our
Dictator."[25] In an article in *Current History*, another writer found America to be on the road to fascism: "The essential element of fascism is its
economic program, which seeks to insure for the middle class their old
security through an adaption of the fundamentals of capitalism, but

under government control, to a new social and economic system that will benefit the nation as a whole rather than a few individuals. That is the program of the Roosevelt administration."[26] Indeed, where Roosevelt saw Jeffersonian unity and nationalism, his foes saw fascism. Herbert Hoover wrote, for example, "The effort to crossbreed some features of Fascism and Socialism with our American free system speedily developed in the Roosevelt administration. The result was that America failed to keep pace with world recovery."[27]

These deficits represented more than wasted expenditures and obstacles to recovery, for the enemies of the New Deal also saw deficits as a threat to democracy and a stimulus to totalitarian government. In a 1939 issue of *Harper's Magazine*, Roy Helton asked, "Must America Go Fascist?" and said the answer was inevitably tied to the nation's deficits and debt. The pattern of totalitarian rule and debt was clearly set in recent European history:

> What is it that gave Italy back to an absolute ruler? The answer is in her history: twenty-seven billion dollars of war borrowings on top of an already heavy debt structure was more than her government could handle as a democracy. Was it only the burning self-assertion of Adolph Hitler that has made him a ruler of Germany more absolute than Frederick the Great?. . . . What but national despair under the immense load of debt that had been saddled upon Germany by the Allies and by our own super-salesmanship, creating a burden which a Republic could not carry? A master had to appear, and the basic reason, as in Italy and in Russia was debt.[28]

Democracies burdened with debt and deficits faced the choice of raising taxes to eliminate the debt or passing the burden on to future generations. As the European experience suggested, democracies lacked the will or the political incentive to retire their debts, thus forcing their economies beyond the brink of disaster. Such a scenario was possible in the United States, the author wrote, for "under the American system no political party, whether local or national, can impose a serious increase in general taxes and hope to remain in office after the ensuing election."[29] At this point, Helton said, democratic countries become vulnerable to demagoguery and the potential transformation into totalitarian systems of government.

Roosevelt's opponents obviously held an intense hatred for the New Deal, and the government's deficits provided them with a convenient issue in attacking the Democratic programs and the president. The choice of this issue was all the more obvious because deficits not only troubled the public, but Roosevelt as well. Deficit spending, in any case, clearly symbolized more than the economic harm it might create or inefficiency and waste in government. Instead, unbalanced budgets and New Deal creations, such as the Tennessee Valley Authority and the rest of the

"alphabet agencies," represented the presence of those European ideologies that threatened to end American democracy and capitalism. The
National Association of Manufacturers restated this theme in 1947, declaring:

> A policy of continued deficits on the part of the government must mean
> ultimately the elimination of competition and the loss of that freedom of
> choice which is characteristic of a system of democracy and individual
> enterprise. . . . Believers in democracy. . . . are unwilling to turn over the
> welfare of our 140 million people to the whims of a small clique of "plan-
> ners" and politically appointed bureaucrats . . . it is not possible to have
> individual freedom and bureaucratic dictation simultaneously.[30]

English debt and the "corruption" it created once persuaded Americans
to avoid unbalanced budgets. Less than a century later, some Americans
again regarded European debt to be a source of tyranny and a model of
finance to be rejected.

Balanced and unbalanced federal budgets continued to assume a symbolic quality that was political in nature and extended beyond simple
accounting notions of deficit or surplus budgets. Deficit spending symbolized the federal government's presence in the economy and society, a
presence that was perceived to be either a bureaucratic intrusion threatening the nation's liberty or the necessary product of a responsible government's policies that provided for the country's well-being. In retrospect, the fear that deficit spending and "managed money" constituted
"the first step toward fascism, communism, socialism, stateism, planned
economy, or whatever name collectivism happens to be using at the
moment," as Herbert Hoover declared, appears exaggerated and certainly
less sophisticated than Jefferson and Jackson's opposition to federal deficit spending.[31] Nevertheless, these sentiments underscored the symbolic
power that unbalanced federal budgets exercised in American politics.

Despite the uneasiness and open hostility directed at federal deficits,
however, important elements in both the Democratic and Republican
parties agreed that federal action, including deficit spending, was necessary to compensate for the weakened forces of an unstable economy. No
political party could expect to govern if it allowed another depression to
occur without making every effort to end such a catastrophe. The Employment Act of 1946 constituted the government's formal declaration
that it had the responsibility and authority to use its fiscal and monetary
powers to prevent high unemployment. The government would seek
balanced budgets when the economy was strong, and run deficits to
stimulate aggregate demand when the economy was in recession. This
basic Keynesian formula was accepted not only by a generation of fasci-
nated young economists, but also by the nation's political leadership.
President Dwight Eisenhower made reference to the formula in 1953:

Balancing the budget will always remain a goal of any administration. . . .
That does not mean to say that you can pick any specific date and say,
"Here, all things must give way before a balanced budget." It is a question of
where the importance of a balanced budget comes in; but it must be the aim
of any sound money program. . . . When it becomes clear that the Government has to step in, as far as I am concerned, the full power of Government,
of Government credit, and of everything the Government has will move in
to see that there is no widespread unemployment and we never again have a
repetition of conditions that so many of you here remember when we had
unemployment.[32]

Eisenhower matched his words with deeds when he approved an increase in federal spending to counter the 1957–58 recession, thereby
helping to create deficits in FY 1958 and FY 1959. The great fiscal revolution, in which the government would pursue balanced budgets but run
deficits when required, was consolidated.

The Full-Employment Budget

Incurring deficits in a deep recession or during a national emergency
became acceptable public policy, even for many reluctant Republicans
like Dwight Eisenhower. The federal government had indeed developed
into what Marriner Eccles once described as the economy's "compensatory agency."[33] The next significant step in the formation of fiscal policy,
however, encompassed much more than simple countercyclical policy.
Even before the end of World War II, prominent economists Beardsley
Ruml and Richard Gilbert and others explored the idea that a "gap" often
formed between the economy's potential GNP produced at full employment and its actual performance. To bridge this gap, the federal government might be forced to stimulate the economy by running deficits even
when the economy was in less than dire straits.

Just as the economy was measured in terms of potential and actual
performance, the budget also would have two measures. The first measure essentially was an accountant's understanding of expenditures and
revenues; the second measure, the full-employment budget, reflected the
economists' estimate of what the surplus or deficit would be if the economy was operating at full capacity. Thus, what normally might be considered a deficit could be regarded as a deficit of smaller proportions or even
a surplus at the full-employment level, as the strength of an economy at
full capacity would be calculated to provide the government with increased revenues. A full-employment deficit indicated the budget was
unusually stimulative, whereas a full-employment surplus acted as a
source of economic restraint. Optimally, the full-employment budget
would be balanced when the economy achieved its full-capacity, full-
employment potential. Thus, for example, Eisenhower's FY 1960 budget

surplus of $270 million was also estimated to be a fiscally restrictive $13 billion full-employment surplus.

The full-employment budget represented not only an approximation of the budget given certain economic conditions, but it also served as a symbol of the government's new responsibilities. For the full-employment notion called upon the government to stimulate the economy when it failed to reach its potential as well as in crisis. "The power of Keynesian ideas," Walter Heller wrote, "could not be harnessed to the nation's lagging economy without putting them in forms and terms that could be understood in the sense of fitting the vocabulary and the values of the public. At the same time, men's minds had to be conditioned to accept new thinking, new symbols, and new and broader concepts of the public interest."[34] The key to this particular symbol's desired effect was in its prefix, the term "full-employment."

John F. Kennedy, whom Heller served as chief economic adviser, was elected in the midst of an economic recession. Though unemployment approached 7 percent in 1960, President Eisenhower, like President Harry Truman, feared inflation more than recession during this postwar period. Consequently, Eisenhower pursued deflationary policies during his last two years in office, and vowed to balance if not achieve a large surplus for the FY 1960 budget. Despite advice from Vice-President Richard Nixon and economist Arthur Burns to stimulate the economy by cutting taxes to reduce the size of the surplus, perhaps creating deficits in the process, Eisenhower maintained his surplus-gathering strategy. Economists generally agree that Eisenhower's deflationary plan was "the main fiscal policy mistake of the twenty years" between World War II and Vietnam.[35] Moreover, the economy did not fully recover from the recession until 1965. Nixon later blamed Eisenhower's failure to stimulate the economy as a major cause of his loss to Kennedy, and the lesson Nixon learned from this "crisis" later influenced his own ideas about the federal government's economic role.[36] It was this ill-fated combination of recession and unemployment mixed with a policy of deflationary balanced budgets that Heller hoped would be replaced with the symbolically appealing "full-employment" budget calculation and its implication for federal action.

Kennedy did not immediately accept Heller's thoughts about deficit spending and the full-employment budget. Nevertheless, Heller greatly influenced Kennedy and succeeded in encouraging the president to downplay his commitment to budget balancing. For example, Heller successfully "watered down" Kennedy's first State of the Union Message with "seven escape hatches" for the president to climb through if the budget eventually proved to be in deficit. Heller and fellow economist Paul Samuelson later convinced Kennedy to abandon a plan for tax increases to fund the Berlin crisis military buildup of 1961.[37] Kennedy became increasingly convinced that Heller and his other economic advisers were correct about the full-employment budget, and in 1962 Kennedy made his historic speech at Yale University on the role of deficit spending and fiscal policy. Kennedy recognized that as president the primary responsibility for promoting the language of the new economics was his, and he undertook this task at Yale, where he observed:

> The myth persists that Federal deficits create inflation and budget surpluses prevent it. . . . Obviously deficits are sometimes dangerous—and so are surpluses. But honest assessment plainly requires a more sophisticated view than the old and automatic cliché that deficits automatically bring inflation. . . . What we need is not labels and clichés but more basic discussion of the sophisticated and technical questions involved in keeping a great economic machine moving ahead.[38]

Balancing the budget remained important to Kennedy, but the new standard was balancing the budget at the full-employment level.

Although the economy improved in early 1961, the expansion was sluggish throughout the latter part of the year and into 1962, while the gap between potential and actual GNP stood at $50 billion. To close the gap, Kennedy initially turned to stimulative fiscal policy in the form of increased federal spending. Consequently, FY 1961 expenditures grew by more than $5 billion above the previous year, thereby creating a $3.4 billion deficit. But measured in full-employment terms the budget contained a $10 billion surplus that still acted as a drag upon the economy. As the recovery faltered in 1962 the administration attempted to generate economic growth by other means that would reduce the surplus. The administration next sought to increase private investment activities through targeted investment tax credits and depreciation allowances, which remained in effect throughout most of the decade. These credits later proved to be a powerful economic incentive, but they did not produce the immediate effect the administration desired, and so Kennedy searched for additional stimulus. Although a rapid expansion of federal spending was the preferred solution, Kennedy realized he lacked the political power to push a dramatic expenditure increase through a generally conservative Congress. Instead, if the administration was to reduce the full-employment surplus it would have to do so on the revenue side of the budget. Thus, in August 1962 Kennedy called for a major across-the-board tax cut for 1963 that was designed to eliminate approximately $11 billion of the surplus and create the first balanced budget measured in terms of full employment. Soon after Kennedy's death, under Lyndon Johnson's sponsorship the tax cut became law in 1964.

The tax cut quickly became the classic textbook example of the new neo-Keynesian economics in action. "The big tax cut," Arthur Okun reflected, "was the first major stimulative measure adopted in the postwar era at a time when the economy was neither in, nor threatened imminently by, recession. And unlike U.S. tax reductions in the 1920s, late 1940s, and 1954, the 1964 action was taken in a budgetary situation marked by the twin facts that the federal budget was in deficit and federal expenditures were rising."[39] The government's stimulative fiscal policy, an expanding money supply, increases in consumer demand, and a healthy rate of private investment finally produced a full-employment economy in 1965. Although the federal budget contained a $1.5 billion deficit in 1965, the full-employment budget was balanced. Additionally, the healthy economy produced new tax revenues that offset the tax reduction, thereby providing the golden example for future supply-side economists. Successful fiscal policy of this sort would yield the funds required for a larger federal government, even under unfavorable political conditions. "The upsurge of tax revenues flowing from economic expansion," wrote Walter Heller, "would finance higher levels of local, state, and Federal spending than we would have had without the tax cut's stimulus—a stimulus that the country was unwilling to provide by deliberately enlarging the Federal budget."[40] Though economists continue to debate the true cause of the economy's vibrant condition, there was no question that between 1961 and 1969 the economy experienced its longest recorded cyclical expansion. Remarkably, this unique period began with five years of nearly noninflationary growth, during which the CPI grew at an average annual rate of only 1.3 percent.

Kennedy's decision to seek a tax cut reflected the tremendous influence Walter Heller and his fellow economists had on the president. Heller clearly understood his task was the "economic education of, by, and for presidents," and the use of the new budget and economic terminology was precisely that of training presidents, Congress, and ultimately the public in a fundamentally different understanding of economics.[41] The images of deficit spending Heller had to overcome to convince others to use his new symbolism were truly formidable. James Sundquist has remarked:

> One cannot read the continuing public debates over fiscal policy in the decade prior to 1963—or even the academic debates, for that matter—without being impressed with the extent to which the principle of the balanced budget had been not just an economic but a moral percept. The enemies of deficit spending not only attacked deficits as "inflationary," employing economic arguments, but associated them with patterns of personal conduct that bore a moral stigma—"waste," "profligacy," "recklessness," "spendthrift," "living beyond one's means," "insolvency," and even "immorality." And they described the balanced budget in words that embodied a positive set of personal moral values—"responsibility," "prudence," "thrift," "soundness," "solvency." . . . They were seeking to identify themselves with the voters' image of what constitutes virtue in public men.[42]

Despite the pressure on them to maintain an orthodox understanding of the balanced budget, Heller praised Kennedy and Lyndon Johnson for being good students who possessed a willingness to learn, for "they had insatiable appetites for memoranda written by their economic advisers."[43] Legislators, too, could be educated in the new economics. Democratic congressman Richard Bolling, for instance, commented on the administration's 1962 economic report by complimenting Heller for bringing "out very clearly that there are a variety of budgets and that the budget is a great deal more than the symbol it has become in, let's say, political terms. I have been extremely disturbed by the general public's acceptance of the notion that there is something almost sanctified in a balanced budget, and . . . by the general view that our public debt is in a dangerous situation."[44]

By 1965 the new economics was also accepted by segments of the nation's media. In January of that year a writer for the *New York Times Magazine* confidently reported that after President Johnson issued his budget for the coming year, "the headlines Tuesday morning will once again read 'Deficit' and some Americans will again murmur 'inflation' and 'burden on our grandchildren' and 'unsound fiscal policy.' But probably more Americans than ever before will say, 'Good for the President. It's the right policy.' "[45]

President Eisenhower's administration, in contrast, had evoked dismay among many economists when the president pushed for surpluses in 1959 and 1960. Eisenhower opposed deficits because among other reasons he believed they weakened the country's balance of trade position. Eisenhower "never explained the connection between balancing the federal budget and 'America's ability to pay her debts' to the rest of the world," wrote Herbert Stein, "but his references to the matter always implied that the connection was direct and close. In fact, the connection is at most indirect and loose."[46] The government's economic victory in the early 1960s appeared to ensure the stature of presidential economic thinkers for some time to come, since "at that point, for a brief moment, even congressmen were using the appellation 'professor' as a term of respect and approval" for economists, but "the high-water mark of the economist's prestige in Washington was probably reached late in 1965."[47] The Vietnam War undermined both the economists and their prosperity without inflation.

Inflation, Vietnam, and Deficit Spending

The creeping inflation that accompanied the Vietnam War had its origins in sources other than federal deficit spending. Instead, the inflationary trend was created by a rapid monetary expansion, an increase in consumer demand, and the growth in federal expenditures due to the war.

The Kennedy administration greatly benefited from the deflationary policies pursued by the Eisenhower administration, which not only brought inflation under control but also provided the Democrats with the wide margin of a large full-employment budget surplus to work with and stimulate the economy. In the process, the nation suffered through three recessions during the Eisenhower presidency, but the low levels of inflation recorded in the early 1960s were due in part to Eisenhower's policies. As the economy rebounded and private sector credit demands increased, so did the money supply. From June 1965 until May 1966 the money supply grew at an annual rate of 6 percent. "This was not a case of monetary policy being forced by circumstances to underwrite heavy Treasury borrowing. As Vietnam expenditures rose, federal receipts initially rose just as fast."[48] In the last two quarters of 1965 military expenditures climbed by an average annual 6.5 percent, and then 25 percent in 1966. Still, the FY 1966 deficit was just $3.8 billion, lower than the deficits of FY 1962–64. Deficit spending did not really get "out of hand" until FY 1967 when the deficit was $8.7 billion, and later in FY 1968 when the deficit reached $25 billion. The FY 1969 budget contained a $3.2 billion surplus. Because only two deficits of appreciable size were incurred during the late 1960s, placing the blame for the inflation registered in this period on these deficits becomes a difficult task.

The task that did face the Johnson administration was controlling inflation in wartime without employing the various forms of wage and price controls that the government imposed during America's previous three wars. This time the administration relied upon normal fiscal and monetary policy to beat inflation. The government, however, responded slowly to the inflationary threat. Despite the recommendation of his economic advisers that a general tax increase was needed to reduce the rate of economic growth in 1966, President Johnson argued that Congress would refuse to implement an across-the-board tax. He instead proposed a "bits-and-pieces" revenue program that Congress did approve. "The economists in the administration," Arthur Okun later reported, "watched with pain and frustration as fiscal policy veered off course. . . . The January 1966 budget marked the first defeat of the new economics by the old politics since Kennedy's decision in August 1962 to delay a tax-cut recommendation."[49] Although the economists failed to get their tax increase adopted, they did influence President Johnson and the Congress to reduce the rate of growth in nondefense expenditures. Johnson's advisers nicknamed the 1966 spending proposal the "little budget" in recognition of the president's reductions in domestic spending. This decline in the growth of nondefense expenditures was apparent throughout the rest of Johnson's tenure in office. From mid-1965 through mid-1969 domestic spending, aside from interest payments on the debt and social security, grew by $19 billion. If the economy had continued along the path it was taking before Vietnam, these expenditures would have increased by more than $30 billion.[50]

Yet budget reductions and smaller deficits by themselves were unable to slow the economy or beat inflation. The nation's monetary authorities finally acted in 1966 to contract the expanding money supply and produced seven months when monetary growth was essentially zero. The economy responded, and from late 1966 through mid-1967 the country experienced a mild recession. At the same time reductions in the rate of domestic expenditures created a budgetary surplus in the first half of 1966, although "the surplus was too small and occurred too far beforehand to account for the slowdown in the economy in the fourth quarter." Later, in 1968, the Congress passed a 10 percent tax surcharge on corporate and individual incomes, after rejecting Johnson's proposed 6 percent surcharge in 1967. The new revenue, combined with a $6 billion reduction in nondefense spending, quickly turned a full-employment deficit of $11 billion recorded in the first half of 1968 into a $10 billion full-employment surplus in 1969. Nevertheless, "economic activity did not slow down during the third quarter, and inflationary forces even gained strength." The budget surplus failed to counteract the stimulative effects of an expanding money supply which once again had been accelerated in 1967, and which grew at an annual rate of 8.5 percent from April to December 1968. Deficit spending had neither caused inflation to develop in the late 1960s, nor could surpluses single-handedly conquer inflation. Ironically, once the budget went into surplus the Treasury became a net supplier of funds to the nation's credit markets rather than a borrower, thereby providing funds to the private sector, and thus contributed to economic growth and inflation rather than inhibiting inflation.[51]

The Vietnam War weakened the American economy, which has yet to recover the exuberant rate of growth it experienced in the early 1960s. The economic comparisons with the prewar years were obvious. Interest rates climbed as the Consumer Price Index rose from a 1.9 percent annual growth rate in 1965 to 6.1 percent in 1969. Although the 1964 tax cut appeared so carefully crafted and timed for its economic effect, the government's economists, particularly its monetary authorities, misjudged the inflationary trend developing in 1965.[52] The Treasury, meanwhile, incurred its largest deficits since 1946, while federal expenditures doubled between 1960 and 1969. The Johnson administration experienced the greatest difficulty in managing simultaneously a wartime economy and an expanding nondefense budget. Given these circumstances, only a short time would have been expected to elapse before President Richard Nixon dismantled the principal economic "symbol" of the New Frontier and the Great Society. Remarkably, both the Nixon and Ford administrations perpetuated the full-employment concept with its obvious implications for federal intervention in the economy and justification for increased future federal spending.

Rather than attack the fiscal revolution and revert to a more orthodox understanding of budget balancing, President Nixon adopted the full-employment terminology and accompanying policies. Nixon learned his lesson that the federal government had more than passing interest in promoting economic well-being when he suffered defeat at John Kennedy's hands in 1960, after Eisenhower failed to stimulate the economy and pushed for budget surpluses in 1959 and 1960. The days when a president could, as Teddy Roosevelt had, call in J. P. Morgan and the banks to save the economy from collapse while the government remained idly by, had long since passed. Nixon also watched, perhaps bitterly, while Kennedy received accolades from economists and business leaders alike for proposing deficit-inducing tax cuts. The 1969 budget contained a surplus, and Nixon's immediate concerns focused on Vietnam and inflation, but the president's position on deficits would soon be tested. The decade of stagflation began quickly as a restrictive monetary policy once again contributed to the recession taking shape in 1970. The unemployment rate climbed, growing to 4.9 percent in 1970 and then 5.9 percent in 1971, never to return to the 1969 full-employment rate of 3.5 percent for the rest of the decade.

The administration's initial statements on fiscal policy warned the Congress and the nation against excessive spending and deficits. "The goal of policy should therefore be moderately more rapid economic expansion in the latter part of 1970," Nixon informed the Congress, and "keeping the Federal budget in balance, as I have recommended . . . will help achieve this result."[53] Nevertheless, the forces in the administration that favored an increase in spending won important budgetary decisions from the president over advisers such as Arthur Burns and Budget Director Robert Mayo, who desired a greater degree of fiscal restraint:

> The budget balancers in the administration were defeated. Arthur Burns, in particular, felt that Nixon had lost the golden opportunity to check federal spending. He realized that the highly publicized budget cuts were largely cosmetic, without seriously drawing back long-range spending programs. As Budget Director, Mayo tried manfully to bring the budget into line but failed. . . . Many of his most important initiatives to cut expenditures were not backed up by the President. The reduction of $1.1 billion for the Pentagon would have been still larger had Nixon sided with Mayo instead of [Defense Secretary Melvin] Laird. Nor was the space-exploration program cut to Mayo's specifications. Nixon overruled Mayo's attempt to eliminate the costly supersonic transport (SST) subsidy program. And he lost his argument with the President that the proposed new program of income maintenance for the poor, whatever its long-range savings, was fiscally irresponsible in the short range.[54]

As the recession deepened, the administration became more overt in its attempt to stimulate the economy through full-employment tactics.

Nixon again reported to Congress that there were "powerful upward pressures" at work, "but existing and foreseeable expansionary forces in the economy are not strong enough to assure that output will rise by as much as is desired and feasible. These forces must, therefore, be supplemented by expansive fiscal and monetary policies."[55] Nixon's economic program for 1971 called for a 7.5 percent increase in spending and a $2.7 billion tax reduction. The proposed deficit stood at $18.5 billion, which the president estimated would fall to $11.5 billion if the economy recovered as planned. The deficits, however, grew to $23 billion for both 1971 and 1972, and then fell to $14.8 billion in 1973. Nevertheless, Nixon was later able to inform Congress that "from 1971 through 1973, the full-employment budget principle permitted and called for substantial actual budget deficits."[56] Despite Nixon's famous battle with Congress over impoundment of federal funds, which often involved the transfer of money from Democratic- to Republican-sponsored programs rather than true budget cuts, the president was not unwilling to incur deficits.[57]

When should the budget be balanced? Logically enough, Nixon called for balanced budgets at the full-employment level:

> Some people have forgotten the crucial point that the full-employment principle requires that deficits be reduced as the economy approaches full-employment—and that it establishes the essential discipline of an upper limit on spending at all times. The full-employment budget principle permits fiscal stimulation when stimulation is appropriate and calls for restraint when restraint is appropriate. But it is not self-enforcing. It signals us what course to steer, but requires us to take the actions necessary to keep on course.[58]

Nixon's FY 1975 budget proposal, his last, predicted full-employment surpluses for the 1974, 1975, and 1976 budgets. In fact, the 1974 budget did register a full-employment deficit of only $2.2 billion, the closest the budget had come to being balanced at the full-employment level since 1970.

In 1975 the full-employment deficit grew again to $22.6 billion as the economy went into a deep recession in 1974 and 1975. In response to the recession, the Ford administration proposed a stimulative package of tax cuts and increased spending that necessarily increased the deficit. Ford's budget called for a $16 billion tax cut and, while cautioning Congress "to keep a tight rein on spending," an 11 percent increase in budget outlays. "I regret," said Ford, "that my budget and tax proposals will mean bigger deficits, temporarily, for I have always opposed deficits. We must recognize, however, that if economic recovery does not begin soon, the Treasury will . . . incur even larger deficits in the future." Ford publicly stated that his deficits were not inflationary and were economically beneficial for the nation, yet he did advise against future "deficits that would be inflationary when the economy returns to high employment."[59]

This brief excursion through fiscal policy reveals four ways in which elite attitudes toward deficit spending and the relationship between deficits and the economy had changed since the beginning of the fiscal revolution. First, by the time Jimmy Carter became president, every chief executive from Hoover to Ford had engaged in deficit spending, most doing so in a manner that consciously induced deficits through increased spending or tax cuts. Despite party affiliation or ideological orientation, these men concluded that deficits would accelerate the economy and were valuable policy instruments. Congress, meanwhile, concurred with presidential intent by voting for these fiscal measures. Certainly the idea that deficits constituted "extraordinary expenditures" to be used only during great hardship had been transcended by 1971, when Richard Nixon supported deficit spending during a relatively minor recession when unemployment was 6 percent. Despite their rhetoric against deficit spending, every modern Republican president, including those who, like Herbert Hoover, had impeccable conservative credentials, proposed economic and federal budgetary programs that included deficit spending. The difference between Republicans and Democrats on this matter was one of degree rather than of kind. Republicans actively employed deficit spending as a part of fiscal policy, but Democrats generally supported deficits of greater magnitude. Gerald Ford's 1977 budget, for example, contained a deficit ranging over $50 billion. The Democratically controlled Joint Economic Committee in the Congress found the president's FY 1977 budget "so restrictive that it does not serve as a useful starting point for budget policy deliberations."[60] The most serious budgetary issues separating the two parties focused on the total amount of expenditures and how they were to be used, rather than on employing the deficit itself.

Second, when examined strictly from an economic perspective, the various administrations had good reason to employ policies that tolerated deficit spending. The idea that public sector deficits could stimulate economic recovery and growth had been accepted by many economists before Franklin D. Roosevelt became president. The economic problems deficit spending posed included its effect on long- and short-term interest rates, inflation, and the crowding out of private investment. Certainly by Carter's 1976 election, however, economists lacked the data needed to prove recent deficits had adversely influenced the economy. In fact, because the Ford administration's huge deficits failed to create high interest rates, as well as inflation, academic investigation of the crowding out effect temporarily declined after 1976.[61] Thus, the failure of deficit spending to produce discernible harm and the government's apparent ability to control deficit spending—two budgets produced by the Nixon administration were nearly balanced at the full-employment level—no doubt reinforced the use of deficit spending. Finally, the full-employment notion with its implications for deficit spending was widely accepted among academic economists and government officials, and by 1976 no economic doctrine was more powerful an influence on policymakers.

Third, this book's emphasis on the presidency reflects that office's increasingly central role in the making of the federal budget and fiscal policy since the creation of the executive budget in 1921 and the beginning of the fiscal revolution during the 1930s. Congressional attempts at "reforming" the budgetary process in 1946 and 1974 by establishing spending ceilings were in part a response to concerns about deficit spending. (The inability of Congress to agree on budget targets led to the abandonment of the 1946 Legislative Reorganization Act; the 1974 Congressional Budget Act's effect on altering the budgetary process is described at the beginning of Appendix 2.) Congressional budgetary reform, particularly in 1974, however, also represented efforts to compete with the president in directing fiscal policy.[62] As Congress soon discovered:

> The [1974] Budget Act . . . did not insulate Congress from presidential influence. When a President announces a deficit or attacks Congress for deficit spending, he is shaping political expectations about the size of the deficit. Congress must accommodate to the President because the way a deficit is perceived politically depends on how the President defines it. Congress could have safely produced a $60 billion deficit for fiscal 1976 because Ford had given it his stamp of approval. . . . Congress added a little stimulus to the economy—and several billions more to the estimated deficit—but its options had been narrowed by the President.[63]

In the forty years following World War II, despite numerous instances of budgetary conflict between the president and the Congress, presidential spending requests were met by congressional appropriations that on an average annual basis varied marginally and were only $800 million smaller than the president's budget.[64] Presidential leadership, therefore, was the decisive factor in the setting of fiscal policy and, as in the case of John Kennedy's speech at Yale, the "shaping of political expectations" about the budget.

Fourth, the emphasis on "fiscal policy" signaled the decline of such traditional economic issues as tariffs, gold, and paper money, which once were so intimately tied to deficit spending. The Democrats under Franklin Roosevelt finally accomplished their long-held dream of greatly reducing tariff rates after Roosevelt was elected.[65] Federal revenues were increasingly dependent on income taxes rather than tariff duties, and soon the connection between tariffs and deficits was lost to modern politics. Furthermore, the Democrats also set the value of gold at a fixed rate of $35 an ounce and prohibited the private ownership of gold. Later, President Nixon closed the "gold window," thereby preventing the redemption of gold for dollars. Simply put, the government's decision to engage in deficit spending no longer was influenced by the country's supply of specie. In addition, banking regulations and the establishment of the Securities and Exchange Commission helped to reduce fears that "speculators" and "moneychangers" would benefit from gambling on the worth of federal credit.[66] Although these economic issues and old symbolic meanings receded from contemporary discussions about deficit spending, other sets of concerns and symbols took their place.

The Issue of Spending Control and the Decline of the Full-Employment Budget

As the first Democratic president in eight years, Jimmy Carter's success was vitally important to the Democrats' political fortunes and the perpetuation of their philosophy of government, which remained essentially unchanged from Franklin Roosevelt's broad description of neo-Jeffersonian government in the 1932 presidential campaign. That vision called for a powerful federal government to pursue national goals through a centralized administrative apparatus, with the intent of increasing "personal competency" in an age of industrial capitalism. The Democrats quickly discovered during the New Deal that federal programs and transfer payments to aid the unemployed, socially outcast, and downtrodden were of greatest value during depression or recession, and supplying these programs often produced budget deficits. In addition, the development of full-employment economics, which went hand in hand with the idea of an activist federal government and was adopted by the Democrats, also called for deficit spending. As a result, the Democrats had a great deal at stake in continuing the public's economic "education" begun by John Kennedy, for despite the fact that Republicans also engaged in deficit spending, the Democrats inevitably were identified by the public as the party of big government and big spending. If this was to be their image, the Democrats had to make that image and the symbols that represented their party positive ones. Thus, after an eight-year hiatus from the presidency, the Democrats urgently needed their new leader to be someone who could either supply the Democrats with a new vision of government or articulate the virtues of current Democratic programs and, more specifically, who could educate the public about the proper economic use and effect of deficit spending. The Democrats, in other words, had to defend Walter Heller's symbol, the full-employment deficit, against competing symbolic interpretations of the deficit. Unfortunately for the Democrats,

Jimmy Carter proved to be uninterested or unwilling to accomplish this task.

Even if Carter had attempted such an effort, the job would have been quite difficult. By the mid-1970s, deficit spending and "big" government were under attack from both the ideological right and left. During these years numerous examples of spending that was "out of control" were offered as proof of the evils of big government and deficit spending. New York City's fiscal crisis was often cited as an example of liberal mis-management, where excessive spending and "give-away" programs brought the nation's most populous city to its financial knees. The city's deficits, confused bookkeeping, defaulted loans, laid-off workers, and inefficient public services served as evidence for the entire nation of the fiscal catastrophe that could occur again at any moment. Conservative political leaders and thinkers, such as former Treasury Secretary William Simon, warned that New York was "a terrifying dress rehersal of the fate that lies ahead of this country if it continues to be guided by the same philosophy of government."[67]

In California, the voters' approval of Proposition 13 in 1978 became the opening shot in the "tax revolt" that quickly spread to other states and cities.[68] Although aimed at obtaining property tax relief, Proposition 13 came to represent the public's broader displeasure with rapidly expand-ing state and local governments that accumulated huge budget surpluses without providing tax relief. Governor Jerry Brown, who was principally responsible for the growth of the state surplus and the failure of Califor-nia's legislature to grant tax relief, opposed Proposition 13. Then, as a candidate in the 1976 Democratic presidential primaries, Brown attacked the Ford deficits and supported a U.S. consitutional prohibition against deficit spending. Brown later pointed to Proposition 13 as a successful instance of such a provision: "I believe that the time has come for this nation to balance what it produces with what it spends." He noted that the "magnitude of the reductions forced by Proposition 13 is greater than the reductions that would be required under a balanced-budget constitu-tional amendment," but declared, "We are enduring . . . and our programs are functioning effectively."[69] Had Brown balanced his own budgets instead of creating multibillion dollar surpluses, perhaps Proposition 13 would have been less likely to occur, but he apparently remained unaware that American history demonstrated repeatedly the nation cared little for huge surpluses or for huge deficits. Brown, in any case, effectively chal-lenged Carter for the Democratic nomination in the closing months of 1976, forcing Carter to consider the California governor's position on balanced budgets.

Meanwhile, political scientists and economists continued to debate the causes of governmental growth and its effect on the economy. One explanation offered by Morris Fiorina, a political scientist, for big, ineffectual government appeared particularly interesting. The notion that constituency demands, entrenched bureaucratic self-preservation, and political self-interest invariably caused government programs and budgets to grow had long been a part of American political lore. What lawmaker was not concerned about bringing more dollars to his or her district, and becoming a local hero? But Fiorina proposed a new and depressing interpretation of this traditional formula for growth. Fiorina claimed that not only did legislators take credit for establishing federal programs, but, in addition, powerful incentives existed to create a bureaucracy so large and unwieldy that constituents could not be but incensed and inconvenienced with big government. At that point members of Congress could respond to constituent complaints and receive their thanks for taming the bureaucratic monster in Washington. "The system is connected when congressmen decry bureaucratic excesses and red tape while riding a grateful electorate to ever more impressive electoral showings. . . . Was the increase in the debt limit good policy? Who knows? Who cares?"[70] If Fiorina was correct, this indeed resulted in a dismal interpretation of government, for at least the traditional understanding of public sector growth included the idea that the true intent of big government was to aid the public rather than do it a conscious disservice. The budgetary decisions made by Congress seemed even more inept, irrational, and self-serving while the deficit rocketed to its highest point in American history during 1975 and 1976.

Viewed strictly from a theoretical standpoint, Keynesian and neo-Keynesian economics could easily accommodate the planned chaos and budgetary extravagance Fiorina described. Notions of efficiency familiar to students of public administration, scientific management, and progressive political thought were essentially unimportant to Keynes and his "pyramid-building" deficits. Keynes would have had little interest in the benefit/cost ratio of some highway project in Illinois or waterways program in California. What mattered to him was the existence of the deficit itself, and its timing and effect on the macroeconomy. Although at some level Keynes and his followers no doubt favored putting public expenditures to their maximum and most effective use, the purpose of deficit spending was to stimulate the general economy, and theoretically even spending on inefficient programs eventually filtered down and benefited the economy. The problem facing Keynesians, neo-Keynesians, and believers in the efficacious use of deficit spending, was the charge that their macroeconomic policies were not working as promised.

A fundamental building block of the new economics was the Phillips Curve, which identified the trade-off occurring between inflation and unemployment. By following the curve a government could control inflation by increasing unemployment, or stimulate the economy through inflationary policies. The nation's economic experience during the mid-1970s, however, appeared to negate the Phillips Curve, or so critics of the new economics claimed, as inflation, unemployment, and federal deficits all grew seemingly in tandem. In other words, the country suffered from stagflation, in which fiscal policy and deficits, claimed economists James Buchanan and Richard Wagner, made conditions worse, not better:

> The Phillips curve, it came to be realized, described only a short-run not a long-run trade-off. Expansions in aggregate demand, accompanied by some inflation, could reduce unemployment in the short run, but only because the inflationary effects were not fully anticipated. Once the predictable effects of inflation on real wages came to be understood, permanent structural features of the economy would reassert themselves. . . . To attempt to maintain "full employment" is an act of delusion. The readjustments can be postponed, though with ever-increasing difficulty, but they cannot be prevented, at least within the context of a free society. The inflation-unemployment spiral that results from short-sighted efforts at demand stimulation will simply increase the dissonance between people's aspirations and their realizations. As a result, democratic institutions become more fragile.[71]

Buchanan and Wagner's economic assumptions about the connection between deficits and the state of the economy were criticized by economists as varied as James Tobin and William Niskanen, but their research and Buchanan's long-term crusade against deficit spending kept the issue alive after many of their colleagues adopted full-employment economics.[72] Parenthetically, while conservative economists like Buchanan argued against deficits, Marxist and neo-Marxist economists also found reason to fault deficit spending. James O'Connor, Manuel Castells, and Ernest Mandel, among others, argued that inflation and debt-run economics were the logical outcome of "late capitalism," where the liberal state protected corporate profits and pacified worker demands while masking the contradictions of capitalism with "a continuous expansion of demand."[73]

In an atmosphere charged by Proposition 13 and New York City's uncertain financial status, perhaps Jimmy Carter had no choice except to attack the Ford deficits. Carter's candidacy and administration, however, expressed itself in an ambivalent fashion on the issue of deficit spending. Carter sometimes acknowledged the full-employment understanding of deficits but elsewhere declared them the cause of economic ruin. In April 1976 candidate Carter issued "An Economic Position Paper for Now and Tomorrow," which stated: "For the current fiscal year, an expansionary fiscal and monetary policy is necessary. Social needs and the need for economic stabilization may require from time to time unbalancing of the budget. But, we should strive toward budget balance, *within an environ-*

ment of full employment, over the long term. The surplus years should balance the deficits. *I therefore call for balanced budgets over the business cycle.* This can be achieved by 1979. At the present time, there is clear need for stimulus in order to return the economy to full employment [Carter's emphasis]."[74]

Carter apparently understood and accepted full-employment economics and the need for large, stimulative deficits. The Ford deficits of 1975–76, approved by a Democratic Congress, certainly seemed reasonable considering the economy's poor showing, and Carter's paper condoned these deficits. By September, however, Carter ripped into the Republicans' deficit spending: "The Republicans say they are the party of fiscal responsibility. But their record shows the worst fiscal mismanagement in our history. . . . The deficit for the year just ended is $65 billion. That is the largest deficit in our history. It is larger than the deficits of all eight Kennedy-Johnson years combined." Again Carter attacked the Ford administration: "Mr. Ford's budgets will account for the largest single deficit and more than one-third of the public debt incurred during our 200 year history. The increase in the public debt during the Nixon-Ford years will be greater than the total public debt incurred under all other Presidents in our history."[75] Although Ford's deficits in 1975 and 1976 rose to $45 billion and $66 billion, when measured in full-employment terms they were $22.6 billion and $18.7 billion, reflecting the economy's weakened condition.

Despite President Carter's displeasure while on the campaign trail with Ford's deficit spending, his "Economic Recovery Program" sent to Congress in January 1977 called for a two-year $31.2 billion stimulative package of tax cuts and increased spending. Consequently, the full-employment deficit grew to $19.4 billion in 1977, and again to $20.3 billion in 1978. With a gap of $132 billion between actual and full-employment GNP, Carter's stimulative policies appeared to be an appropriate partial remedy. At the same time, Carter pledged his administration would achieve a balanced budget by 1981; to achieve this goal the Recovery Program consisted of "temporary" tax rebates and spending proposals. Carter was adamant about balancing the budget, as he said in March 1977: "I intend to cut down the expenditure of Government programs well enough to bring about a balanced budget by 1981. I am deeply comitted to this goal." Nevertheless, in May, Carter described in different terms the need to cut expenditures in order to end deficit spending: "It's not legitimate spending on human needs that causes Federal deficits. It's principally the inadequate revenues that come in from a sluggish economy that creates those deficits. . . . The other important point I want to make is that I'm unalterably opposed to fighting inflation by keeping unemployment high and factories idle."[76]

By December, Carter was less certain about how the administration would maintain its stimulative fiscal policies and still achieve a balanced budget: "If there was an absolutely rigid fixation on a balanced budget, then there would be no chance for tax cuts. . . . I just can't give a firm commitment on how we will balance tax cuts versus a balanced budget by 1981."[77]

Although Carter was uncertain about how exactly the deficits would be reduced, the administration's Recovery Program and an increasingly healthy economy lowered the unemployment rate to 5.8 percent by 1979, the lowest rate since 1974. The deficit accordingly fell to only $27.7 billion, the smallest deficit recorded since 1974. Carter, obviously proud of these accomplishments, declared:

> I was very concerned in 1976 about the high Federal Government deficit. When I ran for President, the Federal deficit was over $66 billion. I've not been in office yet 2 years, but the Congress and I together have already reduced the deficit by $25 billion. I'm now preparing the 1980 fiscal year budget. I'm going to cut the Federal deficit to less than half what it was when I was elected.[78]

These comments, and numerous others made by Carter about the government's deficits, quickly revealed that the administration had stopped talking publicly about the full-employment budget. During the 1976 campaign Carter referred to balancing budgets "within an environment of full-employment," but during most of his presidency he clearly meant balancing the unified budget. Ironically, Carter did come close to fulfilling his original campaign pledge, for the FY 1979 full-employment deficit stood at only $2.4 billion, as shown in Table 16. Moreover,

Table 16. Three measures of the federal deficit, FY 1970–1981 (in billions of dollars)

Fiscal year	On- and off-budget deficit	Unified budget deficit	Full-employment deficit
1970	−2.8	−2.8	−1.5
1971	−23.0	−23.0	−10.6
1972	−23.4	−23.4	−8.8
1973	−14.9	−14.8	−13.6
1974	−6.1	−4.7	−2.2
1975	−53.2	−45.2	−22.6
1976	−73.7	−66.4	−18.7
1977*	−53.6	−44.9	−19.4
1978	−59.2	−48.8	−20.3
1979	−40.2	−27.7	−2.4
1980	−73.8	−59.6	−18.0
1981	−78.9	−57.9	−0.8

Source: U.S. General Accounting Office, "An Analysis of Fiscal and Monetary Policy," August 31, 1982, p. 35.
*Does not include transition quarter deficit.

throughout 1980 the Commerce Department regularly reported that the
FY 1981 budget contained a large "high-employment" surplus. In February, for example, the surplus was projected to be $55.4 billion. Although
the surplus dwindled due to changing economic conditions, during the
election year the high-employment budget estimates predicted there
would be a surplus. Only in 1982 did the Commerce Department revise
its calculations to indicate that the FY 1981 budget had slipped into a
high-employment deficit of $800 million.[79] Thus, the long-sought-after
goal had nearly been achieved as early as 1979, but who knew? Jimmy
Carter certainly made little effort to "educate" the public in the new
economics. "Carter wasn't about to try to sell the public the concept of
the full employment budget," observed Charles Schultze, Carter's chairman of the Council of Economic Advisors. "But I doubt if another president would have done so. Such things aren't really their cup of tea."[80]

Although conservative economists objected to the validity of the Phillips Curve, the decline in unemployment occurred as the inflation rate
grew in 1978, and then hit 13.3 percent in 1979. For President Carter, the
source of this inflationary trend was self-evident. "I'd had unexpected
success in implementing the first programs to create jobs and stimulate a
lagging economy," Carter wrote in his memoirs, "but after a few months
the threat of rising inflation and budget deficits preyed on my mind."[81]
The basis for Carter's thinking is something of a mystery, for Carter's top
economic advisers, at least in retrospect, questioned their president's
contention that deficits created inflation. Did deficit spending produce
inflation in the context of the late 1970s? "Only moderately. Only a little.
I think it was principally, not solely, oil prices in 79–80, and food prices
in 78," recalled Chairman Schultze.[82] "I think he gave it greater weight
than I would personally have," remembered Stuart Eizenstat, Carter's
chief domestic policy adviser. "My feeling is that [deficits do] have some
impact on inflation and interest rates," said Eizenstat, but deficits are
"only one of many factors that influence inflation . . . the biggest cause of
inflation in 1979 was the run up in oil prices, not the increase in the
deficit, and indeed increases in the deficit often occur more because they
tend to follow economic trends than for any other reason."[83]

If Carter's aides had serious doubts that the FY 1979 budget, for example, with its $2.4 billion full-employment deficit was creating double-
digit inflation in a $2.4 trillion economy, they apparently made little
effort to convince Carter to adopt their way of thinking. For in response to
the perceived relationship between deficits and inflation, the administration submitted a restrictive FY 1980 budget to Congress. Alice Rivlin,
director of the Congressional Budget Office, noted that "although the
President's proposed budget cuts are disproportionately in the domestic
areas of the budget, the intent of the Administration is that these reductions will not reduce benefits or services to the poor." Nevertheless, the

budget proposal included a $3.1 billion cut in Comprehensive Employ-ment and Training Act (CETA) training programs, a $2.6 billion reduction in health care funds, and a $600 million proposed drop in social se-curity.[84]

The Carter administration's position on the supposed effects its deficits were having on inflation is all the more curious because it lacked the empirical economic evidence needed to make such conclusive state-ments. Noting this lack of empirical evidence, Schultze later observed: "The standard econometric equations, and the standard way of looking at" the deficits' effect on inflation "would probably suggest that a small part of the increase in inflation during [Carter's] administration was due to having some excessive stimulus in late 77, 78, probably, but it wasn't very big."[85]

The Council of Economic Advisors was unable to find a strong casual relationship between inflation and deficits, and apparently the Office of Management and Budget (OMB) also lacked such evidence. As Carter's OMB director, James McIntyre, Jr., recounted: "In the course of putting together our proposals for discussion . . . with the President," OMB con-sidered "what the sources of the budget deficit would be, [and] we did take into account the size of the deficit, what it meant in terms of percent-age of the GNP. We looked at its effect on . . . credit markets, particularly with respect to crowding out. But, we never really . . . [produced] a specific study on the impact of deficits . . . specifically on things like inflation, or the size of the deficit as it might effect the credit markets themselves. We looked at those things, but we didn't have a definitive study that I can recall on the particular impacts."

According to McIntyre, when OMB did examine the deficit's effect on crowding out, it looked at "how much of the credit market would actually go to finance the federal deficit," as shown, for example, in Table 7, which is based on OMB data.[86] By following such a simple procedure, however, there was little opportunity for OMB to have measured the possible "crowding in" of private investment activities created by deficit spend-ing.

Although the economic relationship between deficits and inflation was at best questionable, by 1979 and 1980 the political pressure, some-what self-induced, on Carter and the Democrats to balance the budget mounted. By mid-1979, twenty-nine states, of the thirty-four required, had approved some form of resolution calling for a constitutional con-vention to study the addition of a balanced budget amendment. A July 1978 Gallup Poll found 81 percent of respondents favoring such an amendment.[87] Meanwhile, elements within the Democratic party pushed for a balanced budget as the 1980 election grew closer. In August 1980, only three months before the election, the newsletter *Democratic Congressional Views*, issued by the Democratic Campaign Committee, carried as its cover story an interview with Congressman Timothy Wirth. Wirth repeatedly declared that in order to beat inflation, "it is imperative that the United States Government balance its budget."[88] Finally, in January 1980 the president released his proposed FY 1981 budget which included a projected $15.8 billion deficit. Within days, private estimates of the deficit indicated it would climb to the then dizzying heights of $50 or even $60 billion, and the nation's financial markets began to panic. In response to these fears, the Democrats huddled together, cut $13 billion from the budget, and proposed new revenues that turned the projected deficit into a projected $16.5 billion surplus. The Democrats' need to counter Wall Street's budget balancing obsession produced the paradoxical situation in which despite their ostensible concern about inflation, Carter was asked, as part of the new budget package, to impose an oil-import fee to raise revenues to reduce the deficit. "I welcomed the suggestion," Carter later wrote, "although the impact of the import fee would be felt in gasoline price increases of about ten cents a gallon."[89] Such a regressive tax, while providing revenues to divert attention from the federal budget, would promote inflationary tendencies of its own within the economy.[90]

By the end of Jimmy Carter's presidency the Democratic party appeared thoroughly confused about the role deficit spending should play in fiscal policy, as it seemingly discarded the full-employment budget idea. The unemployment rate climbed back to over 7 percent, which under normal circumstances would have had the Democrats proposing a stimulative fiscal policy that included deficit spending. The inflation rate in 1980 stood at 12.4 percent, however, and, because flawed economic reasoning identified deficit spending as the principal cause of this inflation, the Democrats sought to balance the budget. The 1980 Democratic National Platform reflected this confusion. On the one hand, the platform stated, "Fiscal policy must remain a flexible economic tool. We oppose a Consitutional amendment requiring a balanced budget."[91] This statement echoed the tradition of John F. Kennedy. On the other hand, this was also Jimmy Carter's Democratic party, and the platform went on to say, "We support the discipline of attempting to live within the limits of our anticipated revenues. . . . Between FY 1978 and 1981, real federal spending will have *declined* at an average annual rate of 0.6%."[92] Finally, the platform added this bewildering comment: "The federal budget has not been and must not be permitted to be an inflationary nor a recessionary force in our economy, but it also must not be permitted to ignore pressing human needs."[93] If the budget was neither "an inflationary nor a recessionary force," then why all the fuss about deficit spending?

The Democrats failed to legitimate the full-employment budget with the public, and kept it at best an elite concept. In the name of short-term political gain the Democrats discredited the very foundation of their macroeconomic policy, leaving nothing substantial in its place. By abandoning deficit spending on the basis of highly questionably economic pretense the Democrats also discredited their attendant politics. For any new Democratic budget proposal that added a single dollar to the deficit instantly lost legitimacy on the grounds, supplied by the Democrats themselves, that it helped to cripple the economy. Without educating the public on the difference between "good" and "bad" deficits, all deficit spending became identified as a primary source of inflation or high interest rates. After repudiating deficit spending, and thus the new economics, the Democrats in 1980 lacked any serious alternative framework that defined the party's role in shaping economic policy.

Balanced Budgets and Symbolic Politics

Beginning with the New Deal, the Democratic party briefly transformed the largely negative symbolism associated with unbalanced budgets and deficit spending into something more positive, where deficits were considered helpful policy instruments that benefited the economy. The Democrats had not altogether rejected the idea of balanced budgets, of course, for during the New Frontier they adopted the full-employment balanced budget as the new symbol of fiscal prudence. By the end of the Carter administration, however, deficit spending was once again transformed into the symbol of inefficient and wasteful public expenditure produced by a bureaucratic and insensitive "big government." As Democratic congressman Leon Panetta noted, deficit spending elicited several highly negative interpretations:

> [Deficit spending is] symbolic of the feeling that you can just spend whatever you want at the federal level, and even if it involves deficit spending somehow it doesn't make much difference. It's symbolic of programs that have been enacted that were supposed to help people that were not very effective in helping people. It's symbolic of an economy that has been tough to analyze to begin with as to its basic problems, but it's symbolic of the fact that we've had a high inflation high unemployment, and there seems to be lack of discipline generally throughout the economy. So obviously running high deficits is symbolic of that lack of discipline.[94]

Aside from these political connotations, the Democrats encouraged the public to fear the economic effects of deficits, regardless of their size or the condition of the economy. President Carter's firmly held belief that deficit spending was a principal source of the nation's economic difficulties had much to do with this regression in Democratic thinking. Whatever Carter's shortcomings as a leader, his relatively conservative presidency nevertheless reflected a growing national hostility toward "big government," which deficit spending ultimately symbolized.[95] Furthermore, the Democrats' difficulties, as suggested by the federal government's intergovernmental relations, predated Carter.

Writing about federalism in 1966, Walter Heller had declared, "My basic premise, then, is that to the simple question, 'Do you want stronger state government?' the country's answer is unequivocally, 'We do.' If we do not accept that basic premise, if we are unrelenting Hamiltonians . . . then all of the succeeding syllogisms . . . will not convince us that Federal revenues should be shared more generously with the states."[96] Yet while federal grants to the states rapidly increased in size and number, the autonomy and decision-making power of state governments declined. Under Lyndon Johnson's "creative federalism," traditional federal-state relations were altered in favor of government programs that emphasized federal-local cooperation, where local governments served as the national government's primary agent for social change and economic development. Liberal Democrats believed they had good reason to bypass conservative state legislatures that were dominated by rural interests, but all too often even local governments in the big cities were deprived of initiative and power. Although local participation and decision making were often explicit goals of the "war on poverty" programs, in numerous instances local programmatic initiatives were constrained by federal directives. By 1968, for example, two-thirds of all federal funds for local projects created by Community Action Agencies operating out of the Office of Economic Opportunity (OEO) were already earmarked by Congress for such federally designated programs as Head Start, despite the specific intent of OEO to encourage locally initiated programs.[97] In 1980, the federal government's Advisory Commission on Intergovernmental Relations (ACIR) reported that even general revenue sharing funds, those "designated specifically to have the fewest possible federal requirements," carried major restrictions on state and local decision making.[98]

The Democrats practiced Hamiltonian government through a powerful and centralized administrative apparatus and, though its purpose was to promote social equality rather than social hierarchy, one consequence of this structure was to promote a widespread sense of public disillusionment with the federal government during the 1970s. Considering Franklin Roosevelt's great efforts to disassociate his 1932 campaign from the specter of Hamiltonianism, the direction taken by the Democrats was often self-defeating. The form and structure of government *did* matter, as Jefferson argued, and by the mid-1970s a number of Democrats expressed their dissatisfaction by voting for such candidates as Jimmy Carter and Jerry Brown and by toting the pop-political science and economics bestseller *Small Is Beautiful.*[99]

The condition of American federal-state relations was paradoxically captured by Samuel H. Beer, a political scientist, in a 1982 edition of the *New Republic* magazine. Beer described the historical evolution of the "national idea" from Hamilton and the Federalists through the Whigs, Teddy Roosevelt, FDR, and LBJ; he pronounced himself a believer in the Hamiltonian "idea of the nation." Minimizing Hamilton's affection for the moneyed aristocracy, his obsession with the English monarchy and government, and his desire to merge state "civil lists" into the federal government's, Beer opposed Ronald Reagan's "new federalism and his proposals to cut back on the activities of the federal government." Instead, Beer wrote, "I plead with the new federalists: come out from behind that Jeffersonian verbiage, and take up the good old Hamiltonian cause."[100] Ironically, the *New Republic*, whose founder Herbert Croly had trumpeted Hamilton's virtues at the turn of the century, had cast Ronald Reagan in the role of Thomas Jefferson.

7

Coming to Grips with a Symbol: Ronald Reagan and Unbalanced Budgets

> The Republican Party no longer worships at the altar of a balanced budget.
>
> CONGRESSMAN JACK KEMP, Testimony before the House Budget Committee, 1981

> It commits to what Ronald Reagan promised in 1981—to balance the budget.
>
> SENATOR PHIL GRAMM, on the Gramm-Rudman-Hollings balanced budget legislation, 1985

Ronald Reagan's presidency will forever be remembered for the massive federal deficits incurred during his administration. Yet the long-term political significance of these deficits extends beyond their immediate economic consequences, the instrumental outcome of a given year's budget battle, or an evaluation of the budgetary process. Instead, what matters most in this regard is the persistence of the balanced budget idea in the making of American public policy. Opinions differed, of course, during Reagan's first term over the meaning of balanced budgets and how they could be achieved. Whereas Ronald Reagan campaigned in 1980 on the platform that federal deficits produced inflation and high interest rates, by 1984 this conservative Republican president regarded deficits to be economically tolerable, if not innocuous. Reagan persisted with his call for a constitutional limitation against the government's deficits, however, because though they might be economically benign, Reagan considered them to be the product of exorbitant domestic spending. More to the point, Ronald Reagan distinguished between deficits created by tax reductions made in the service of restraining federal expenditures, and deficits caused by what he regarded to be a spendthrift national government.

Meanwhile, Reagan's moderate and liberal Democratic opponents, reeling from their 1980 defeat, were determined to press the deficit issue against the president. Continuing their retreat from neo-Keynesian economics begun under the Carter administration, the Democratic party decried the deficits, claiming Reagan's unbalanced budgets produced economic chaos, while the Democrats sought major tax increases during the country's worst economic decline since the Great Depression. The Democrats' argument was principally an economic one; additional taxes were necessary to lower Reagan's deficits which by themselves, the Democrats said, would derail the expected economic recovery. They also contended that new taxes were required to fund needed social and domestic programs. The historically reversed positions of Ronald Reagan and the Democrats on the matter of deficit spending reflected their contrasting interpretations of the federal government's proper place in American life. Furthermore, their differences over budget balancing set the stage for future opportunities and constraints for the Democratic and Republican parties.

Ronald Reagan's "Constitutional Government"

Two hundred years of American history demonstrated the remarkable political volatility attached to the issue of balancing the federal budget, though the avowed purpose for balanced budgets changed repeatedly. Prior to the Civil War, in the days of Jefferson and Jackson, balanced federal budgets represented the prevention of "corruption" in the federal government; excessive revenues were thought to enable the moneyed aristocracy to exercise an unwarranted degree of financial and political influence over the national government. The Jeffersonians and Jacksonians believed agrarian democracy, social equality, and the Constitution's balance of powers would be grievously threatened by the forces of social hierarchy that sought to expand federal authority, at the states' expense, to promote the interests of bankers, manufacturers, and the moneyed elite of the Federalist and Whig parties. Following the Civil War, the Republicans found the public would tolerate higher tariffs if the revenues they produced were applied toward reducing the national debt and balancing the federal budget. These tariffs, not coincidently, protected the industrialists against foreign competition, and the revenues they provided enabled the Republicans to increase federal expenditures substantially. Thus, the Republicans employed the Jeffersonian and Jacksonian call for balanced budgets while enacting the Federalist and Whig policies that enhanced federal authority. The Jeffersonians and Jacksonians balanced the federal budget to control the national government, whereas the Republican party balanced budgets to expand federal powers.

Over time, the desire to balance budgets derived strength from history itself, as balancing the federal budget became a tradition others sought to emulate, as well as from the idea that balanced budgets symbolized government efficiency. The Progressives contributed to the view that governments could safely expand their powers if they were properly managed and balanced their budgets. Economic and administrative efficiency, in the Progressive sense, largely supplanted the older political ideologies as the standard for judging the worth of balanced budgets. This transformation in standards paved the way for the growing influence of Keynesian economics and the fiscal revolution taking place in the 1930s. Macroeconomic theory legitimized deficit spending in specified circumstances despite the political symbolism and tradition associated with balanced budgets. Furthermore, the Democrats argued that an expansionary federal authority was required to restore Jeffersonian and Jacksonian political equality and economic opportunity damaged during the years of Republican rule. Large public institutions—principally the federal government—would counterbalance the influence of large private institutions, while public resources distributed through the federal budget would accommodate a broader range of interests than those benefiting from the Republican's brand of Hamiltonian government.

If an economic understanding of unbalanced budgets were to supersede a political and symbolic interpretation, this economic theory needed to be thoroughly comprehended by political elites and explained to the general public. In other words, the notion that federal deficits were acceptable public policy instruments for economic reasons had to overcome the symbolism that associated unbalanced budgets with an unwarranted expansion of federal powers. Though Keynesian and neo-Keynesian thinking as exemplified by the full-employment budget idea influenced the policies of every president since Franklin Roosevelt, the resulting presidential attempts to educate the public in the new economics were cautious and limited in scope. Thus, the charge that an administration's deficits were fiscally irresponsible, a sign of bureaucratic inefficiency, as well as a symbol of government operating beyond the scope of public control, remained politically potent particularly as federal social interventionism became less popular during the 1970s.

The 1976 Carter candidacy demonstrated just how useful the balanced budget issue could be even against a moderately conservative Republican president like Gerald Ford, who incurred deficits in the midst of a deep recession. President Carter promised he would balance the budget by his last year in office because, he said, deficits created inflation and were economically harmful. The best economic evidence suggested Carter's view of the deficits' economic effects was misplaced, however. Alice

Rivlin, director of the Congressional Budget Office, reported in 1980, for instance, that a balanced budget would reduce inflation by only "tenths of a percent."[1] Carter, the self-proclaimed Washington outsider, confused the balanced budget's political symbolism with its economic consequences. Given Carter's professed belief in a restrained federal authority, he might better have argued that balanced budgets were necessary to restrict the federal government's revenues, and thus its bureaucracy and programs, without claiming balanced budgets would cure the nation's inflationary ills. In any case, by attacking deficit spending on economic grounds, especially at times when the budget was nearly balanced by full-employment measures, Carter helped to undermine the politics and policies initiated by the Democrats during the preceding fifty years.

The Democratic party pursued Jeffersonian equality while producing Hamiltonian centralization, but could the Republicans achieve Jeffersonian decentralization without creating Hamiltonian inequality? Taken at face value, this appeared to be the challenge facing the Republicans in 1981, for Ronald Reagan, the disaffected New Deal Democrat, declared that his budget policies and New Federalism were necessary to reclaim Jeffersonian and Jacksonian government. Reducing the federal government's expenditures and revenues, balancing its budget, trimming its regulatory activities, and enhancing states' rights, Reagan announced, would reinvigorate the public's political liberties and the nation's economy. Like Franklin Roosevelt before him, Ronald Reagan invoked Jefferson's name to frame and justify his administration's economic and budgetary policies.

In a theme heard repeatedly during the 1980 campaign and into his presidency, Reagan portrayed his administration as one seeking a "renewal" of basic principles defended during the Revolutionary War and outlined by the "founding fathers" in the Constitution. At the core of these principles was the importance of decentralized political authority exercised by the state and local governments. These constitutional "duties and rights" once reserved for the states had been "usurped" by the "expanding Federal monolith," Reagan said, which "undermined the system of checks and balances and the division of power that long protected the freedom of our people."[2] Moreover, these usurpers, these present-day liberals, Reagan identified as modern Tories who worked against the Constitution's balance of powers, and who would have rallied around "the central power of the King" during the War of Independence. On the other hand, observed Reagan in an interview, "the people whom we call conservatives today would have been the liberals [then], the ones fighting the Revolution."[3] (In a similar manner, Reagan later called for a "second American Revolution" in his 1985 State of the Union Address following his 1984 reelection).

How would Jeffersonian government, as Reagan interpreted it, be reclaimed? First, by trimming federal spending. Invoking Jefferson's views on federal spending, Reagan remarked, "For all governments [Jefferson's] admonition was straightforward: 'A wise and frugal government . . . shall restrain men from injuring one another . . . shall leave them otherwise free to regulate their own pursuits . . . and shall not take from the mouth of labor the bread it has earned.' "[4] Therefore, argued Reagan, "our program of budget cuts will discipline the Federal Government to live within its means," for "it has proven incapable of managing" the programs and responsibilities once delegated to the states.[5] Next, Reagan not only sought to shrink the national government, but also enlarge the role state governments played in the American political system. Observed the new president, "It was Jefferson who reminded us that against the invasion of the people's liberty, the only 'true barriers . . . are the state governments.' "[6] So, Reagan announced: "Our intention . . . is to renew the meaning of the Constitution. . . . Together then, let us restore constitutional government. Let us renew and enrich the power and purpose of States and local communities and let us return to the people those rights and duties that are justly theirs."[7]

This shift in favor of the states was needed, Reagan said, to correct a historical imbalance of power, similar to that faced by Andrew Jackson in his contest with the Whigs. Commented Reagan: "As history passes, we find our system of government pulled and twisted, first in this direction and then in that. Jackson's contemporaries sought to destroy it by tipping the balance too far toward the States. In our time, it is threatened by those who would place all the weight in a centralized National Government. Like Jackson, we must cleave to that well-charted course first laid out for us by our Founding Fathers."[8] Thus, the renewal of "constitutional government" would be achieved by reducing federal spending and, said Reagan, by "turning back to states and local communities, programs which the federal government has usurped."[9]

Because he considered the federal government to be administratively inefficient and inept, Reagan argued that the transition to constitutional government through his Program for Economic Recovery would be economically and socially painless, a pledge Herbert Stein later called the "economics of joy."[10] At the very least, Reagan promised to preserve the nation's "social safety net," those federal programs that assisted people during times of extreme hardship, while disciplining the government through budgetary and programmatic reductions. As Reagan claimed in his single presidential debate with Jimmy Carter, the federal government was bloated with fraud, waste, and abuse. When asked how he would balance the budget while cutting taxes and increasing defense spending, Reagan replied:

Well, most people when they think about cutting government spending they think in terms of eliminating necessary programs or wiping out some service government is supposed to perform. I believe there is enough extravagance and fat in government—as a matter of fact, one of the secretaries of H.E.W. [Health, Education, and Welfare] under Mr. Carter testified that he thought there was $7 billion worth of fraud and waste in welfare, and in the medical programs associated with it. We've had the General Accounting Office estimate that there is probably tens of billions of dollars that is lost in fraud alone, and they have added that waste adds even more to that. We have a program for a gradual reduction of federal spending based on these theories.[11]

Although even Reagan's Republican primary opponents, George Bush and John Anderson, claimed his economic program consisted of "voodoo economics" and that the budget would only be "balanced with mirrors," Reagan declared in the debate with Carter that if his Program for Economic Recovery was enacted there could be "a balanced budget by 1983, if not earlier."[12]

When Reagan talked about the federal government and his quest for balanced budgets in this manner, he clearly drew upon a host of symbolic associations that had evolved and gathered strength since the earliest days of the republic, which had become firmly embedded in the nation's political culture. Rather than limit the federal government to activities designated in the Constitution, such as providing the country with an adequate defense, Reagan charged that the Democrats violated the founding fathers' intent with their liberal vision of an expanding national government. Federal budgets were unbalanced, Reagan said, because a profligate centralized bureaucracy usurped the states' rights and duties by imposing costly programs of its own design. Reagan promised to place these programs under the states' authority, in addition to "the tax sources to pay for them."[13] Cutting federal revenues and expenditures, therefore, was intimately tied to Reagan's view of a new federalism. Fewer tax dollars diverted to the federal government implied that more funds would be made available for the states, in a manner indeed reminiscent of Jefferson and Jackson's attempts to restrain federal authority.

Furthermore, Reagan's complaint that the government's deficits were a product of an undisciplined bureaucracy's fraud, waste, and abuse, was more than faintly Progressive in tone. The Progressives' solution had rested on scientific management and improved administrative efficiency, but Reagan looked to budget and tax cuts, and ultimately to a consitutional amendment requiring balanced federal budgets. By adding such an amendment to the Constitution, Reagan believed he was proposing the necessary institutional reforms required to limit federal growth while promoting personal freedom. Most conservatives shared Reagan's symbolic goal, including "New Right" leader Richard Viguerie, who wrote in 1980: "Congress has shown again and again that it cannot discipline itself. We must, as Thomas Jefferson said, 'bind them down with the chains of the Constitution'. . . . We can do it by amending our Constitution and plugging up the loopholes by which the federal government is gradually destroying our economic freedom and thereby all our freedoms."[14] Thus, the presence of unbalanced federal budgets assumed far greater meaning than simply an accountant's understanding of deficit spending. According to these conservatives, deficits symbolized a significant threat to consitutional government and American freedom.

In addition to employing the deficit as a symbol of the federal government running outside the bounds of constitutional and popular control, Reagan claimed the government's deficits were the principal cause of inflation and high interest rates. "Yes, you can lick inflation," Reagan said during his debate with Carter, "by increasing productivity, and by decreasing the cost of government to the place that we have balanced budgets and are no longer grinding out printing press money, flooding the market with it, because the government is spending more than it takes in."[15] Reagan argued that the Democrats' deficits were monetized by the Federal Reserve, thereby creating the double-digit inflation of the late 1970s. In fact, these deficits were almost exclusively financed through borrowing rather than monetization, and they were not the cause of inflation or high interest rates, as President Reagan himself later admitted. Reagan used the "deficits are economically harmful" issue against Jimmy Carter, as Carter used the issue against Gerald Ford, and Reagan soon ran into difficulties similar to those Carter encountered when the budget failed to balance. Like Carter, Reagan combined and confused the symbolic with the economic aspects of deficit spending. A balanced budget might somehow represent a "disciplined" and "constitutional government," in Reagan's language, but it would not result in the nation's economic salvation when unemployment was above 7 percent and rising.

There was nothing particularly new in Reagan's claims that deficits were the necessary consequence of an overspending, bloated, liberalized federal government, or that these deficits caused inflation and high interest rates. Most Republicans and even some Democrats had been saying the same for decades. Reagan's innovation rested with how he chose to go about balancing the budget. For Ronald Reagan, the way to balance the budget and constrain future federal expansion was to cut the budget and reduce—not raise—taxes. Both Democrats and traditional budget-balancing Republicans had raised taxes, and all this accomplished, said Reagan, was to provide the revenues and justification required to increase federal spending rather than cut the deficit. In this manner, Reagan would be breaking with the Republicans of his day, and also with those Republicans of the late nineteenth and early twentieth centuries, who used the fear of deficits to raise revenues through higher tariff rates for the purpose of enhancing federal authority and protecting domestic industry. In contemporary America, Jimmy Carter's 1980 plan to balance the budget was just more of the same, Reagan claimed: "I believe that this plan presented is deceitful and is based very simply on balancing the budget which the President has promised to do simply by increasing taxes. And they are going to increase in the neighborhood of $100 billion next year. That budget will be $45 billion bigger than the present budget. The present budget is also expanding because Congress voted recently to enlarge it, because they are meeting more spending needs than they had estimated."[16]

Reagan stated that his tax cut would stimulate the economy, encourage productivity, reduce inflation and interest rates, and bring the government more revenues to balance the budget without encouraging an expanding budget: "I believe that this 'supply-side economics,'" he said in May 1980, "would result in a re-flow by the stimulation of the economy and would create jobs, and broaden the base of our prosperity. We've done this four times in this century, the last time under John F. Kennedy. And, every time it was against the advice of economists who believed that government spending was more stimulating to the economy than private spending. However, each time the government wound up with more revenues at the lower rates."[17] Balancing the budget by increasing taxes made possible more spending, which was counterproductive, Reagan argued, because the purpose of budget balancing was to contain and control the federal government, not legitimate its expansion.

Despite Reagan's strong support for the tax cuts, some question exists about the extent of his commitment to the supply-siders' economic doctrine.[18] Reagan and the supply-siders, for example, disagreed on the importance of balancing the federal budget. The leading supply-siders, among them Congressman Jack Kemp, agreed with Reagan that excessive government spending created deficits, but, they added, so did a weak economy. Therefore the supply-siders' principal solution for trimming deficits included tolerating these deficits, at least for an interim period following the reduction of marginal tax rates. The supply-siders reasoned that cutting taxes promoted economic productivity even if short-term deficits were produced, but in the long run the tax cuts provided the Treasury with the larger revenues required to fund needed federal programs. Consequently, supply-siders like Kemp did not automatically oppose deficit spending, as Kemp noted in 1978: "These historical examples [of tax reductions] increase our confidence that even if a slightly larger federal budget deficit were to emerge temporarily, the resources of increased state and local revenues and private saving could easily finance the federal deficit without creating a need to print more money."[19]

If tax rates were to be manipulated to simulate the economy in the fashion of John Kennedy's neo-Keynesian tax cut, however, there could be no place for a constitutional amendment intended to ban deficits. "I have opposed a constitutional amendment which would mandate a balanced budget," Kemp wrote, "because such a decree does not address the economic causes of budget deficits. Attempting to balance the budget by raising tax rates, for example, would further slow down growth and increase demand for still more spending. Slashing the safety net, if it succeeded, might do away with the numerical problem, but not the human one."[20]

Kemp contended, therefore, that greater economic prosperity was possible when the government ran tax cut-induced deficits than when the budget was balanced through tax increases. Incidentally, as his comments suggest, Kemp and a few other supply-siders, for example, economist Arthur Laffer, were less inclined than Ronald Reagan to cut the social safety net's means-tested entitlement programs, because they believed the tax cut's new revenues could support these federal activities.[21]

Although Reagan and the supply-siders were highly confident about the tax cut's effect on the economy, other members of the administration were less sanguine. Before a single vote was cast in the coming FY 1982 budget deliberations, several of Reagan's top advisers worried that the administration would run deficits of major proportions, much larger than Jimmy Carter's. In his celebrated interview with William Greider, Office of Management and Budget Director David Stockman revealed that even when employing the most optimistic economic assumptions, OMB's computers predicted "a series of federal deficits without precedent in peacetime—ranging from $82 billion in 1982 to $116 billion in 1984."[22] Stockman found these January 1981 estimates "absolutely shocking." These forecasts assumed the best possible economic conditions, but the administration's first budget proposal, the "white paper" February 1981 budget, predicted growing unemployment for 1981. As Murray Weidenbaum, chairman of the Council of Economic Advisors, told the Joint Economic Committee of the Congress in 1982, the administration's early economic forecasts indicated a recession was on the way.[23] Indeed, amid the white paper budget's extremely optimistic language about the economy's future, the budget indicated unemployment would increase to 7.8 percent in 1981 from 7.1 percent in 1980.[24] Thus, as the budget's automatic stabilizers took effect the deficit would grow anyway, with or without the implementation of supply-side tax cuts and increased defense spending.

David Stockman's budget projections and his views on the deficit were strongly in conflict with those held by the supply-siders. Though Stockman accepted some aspects of supply-side economics, he was more in agreement with the expectations school of economic thought, which significantly differed with the supply-siders on the matter of balanced budgets. Though the two schools both argued that "economic actors" responded to incentives, they disagreed about what those incentives were. In the case of curing inflation, the expectations model suggested that deficits created inflationary expectations and incentives in the economy, and thus balancing the budget played a crucial role in regaining economic stability. The supply-siders argued that tax cuts provided the strongest incentives, and consequently balanced budgets were less important in altering inflationary behavior. Stockman's interest in expectations theory appeared throughout the white paper budget, as discussed in Chapter 2, as did his emphasis on eliminating deficits. The supply-siders quickly became alienated from Stockman and accused him of attempting to undermine the president's faith in the tax cuts. According to supply-sider Paul Craig Roberts, the former assistant treasury secretary, Stockman "elevated" the importance of balanced budgets in the Reagan agenda during 1981 and in later years to enhance the status of OMB's budget cutting responsibilities.[25] Whatever the validity of Roberts's claim, Ronald Reagan seemed to need little encouragement from Stockman that a balanced budget was a worthy objective, or that cutting social programs in the FY 1982 budget—including means-tested entitlements—was an acceptable device to produce that goal. In any case, Stockman's budget projections indicated that trimming more than fraud, waste, and abuse was necessary if the budget was to be balanced in FY 1984.

Despite OMB's internal estimates of larger deficits to come and the supply-siders' view that deficits were economically tolerable, Reagan continued to argue throughout the 1980 presidential campaign and during his first year in office that he would balance the FY 1984 budget and that deficits were economically harmful. The quest for the balanced budget, the holy grail of Republican politics, galvanized Reagan's allies. "The glue that held us together," Republican senator Robert Packwood later told reporters, "was the drive toward a balanced budget."[26] Indeed, American politics focused on little else during Reagan's first term but the budget battles that consumed congressional attention throughout these four years.

The most dramatic of those budget battles occurred during the first eight months of the Reagan presidency. Ronald Reagan's budgetary revolution in 1981 marked the most impressive beginning for a new president since Franklin Roosevelt's fabled first one hundred days and the early months of Lyndon Johnson's Great Society. Many descriptions of Reagan's early success exist, including the detailed summary provided in Appendix 2, so at this point it is only necessary to recount that between January and August 1981, Reagan won a series of stunning budget victories against a dispirited Democratic opposition.[27] The budget and tax legislation Reagan signed on August 13 provided for a three-year budget cut of $130.5 billion, and a tax cut over the same period of $787 billion. Reagan's success was astonishing, in part, because of the unanimity required among the conservative ranks to reverse previous spending trends and to make the deepest budget cuts in modern American history. Party loyalty and ideological zeal obviously played a crucial role, but

Reagan's followers were also inspired by the president's pledge to balance the budget. Driven by this goal, Republicans and Democrats alike
overcame regional, partisan, and ideological differences, as well as constituency needs, to support the administration's economic program.

Contributing to Reagan's success was his often-repeated message that
federal deficit spending harmed the nation's economic well-being, and
that his economic program, once approved, would produce a balanced
FY 1984 budget. Reagan communicated this message to the public most
effectively, as for example during his first television address delivered on
February 5, 1981. At that time, the deeply worried president informed the
nation, "I regret to say that we are in the worst economic mess since the
Great Depression."[28] The reason for this mess, which consisted of high
inflation and unemployment rates, the president claimed, was primarily
due to the federal government and its "out of control" budget. The big-
spending federal government produced huge deficits, Reagan said, and
"we know now that inflation results from all that deficit spending."[29] One
possible solution to the country's inflationary problem rested with the
Democratic formula of raising taxes, but such a course was self-defeating.
First, from an economic perspective, "excessive taxation of individuals
has robbed us of incentive" and the resulting lack of productivity contributed to the economy's inflationary pressures. In the second case, rather
than serve to eliminate the deficit, extra revenues only encouraged more
federal spending. The answer, said Reagan, in perhaps the most important section of the speech, was to reduce the deficit by reducing the
incentive to spend, and that meant cutting taxes: "Over the past decade
we've talked of curtailing Government spending so that we can then
lower the tax burden. Sometimes we've even taken a run at doing that.
But there were always those who told us taxes couldn't be cut until
spending was reduced. Well, we can lecture our children about extravagance until we run out of voice and breath. Or we can cure their extravagance simply by reducing their allowance."[30] Trimming the government's allowance "means above all," the president continued, "bringing
Government spending back within Government revenues, which is the
only way, together with increased productivity, that we can reduce and,
yes, eliminate inflation."[31] Reagan's presumed link between tax cuts and
reduced inflation was exceedingly dubious. Nevertheless, cutting the
government's revenues in the presence of large federal deficits would
create even larger unbalanced budgets if the Reagan economic program
failed, thus paradoxically placing additional pressure on the Congress to
slash government expenditures.

Reagan's rhetoric that combined symbolic and economic attacks on
deficit spending acted as a powerful force in mobilizing his allies, but it
also produced some ironic consequences. After 1981, economic and political events forced Reagan to acknowledge that deficit spending was not

so economically harmful after all. As a result, Reagan placed himself in the awkward situation of calling for a constitutional amendment to restrict deficit spending for symbolic reasons, while recanting his earlier statements about its economic effects. In order to preserve his tax cuts and defense spending, President Reagan tried to weed out symbol from economic fact, but by mid-1982 this behavior appeared publicly confusing and opportunistic. Meanwhile, desperately searching for issues to attack the president, the Democrats attempted to turn Reagan's own earlier statements on deficits against him. Incredibly, the party of Roosevelt, Kennedy, and Johnson then proposed major tax increases in the midst of the worst recession since the 1930s to reduce the deficit. Still, the Democrats opposed Reagan's constitutional amendment and rejected his symbolic argument against deficit spending, that unbalanced budgets were the residue of an oppressive federal government. The Democrats would have left themselves ideologically bankrupt had they accepted such a conclusion. These remarkably reversed Democratic and Republican policy positions over the deficit could only have evolved during the course of an unprecedented four years of budgetary warfare.

Reagan's Deficit Metamorphosis

President Reagan's position on the economics of deficit spending altered as the federal government's deficits grew steadily larger and dwarfed OMB's early optimistic budget projections. As the deficits increased, so too did the domestic and international criticism directed at the administration's tax and defense spending policies, forcing Reagan to defend the deficits against charges that they produced inflation and high interest rates. If the deficits were not the source of economic harm, as the president began to argue, then raising taxes and cutting defense spending to produce an immediate balancing of the budget as an economic imperative were unnecessary. Moreover, with the deficits considered economically tolerable by the president, Reagan could maintain his tax and defense policies while continuing to push the Congress toward trimming more domestic spending. Reagan's stand on the deficit, however, greatly limited the effectiveness of his leadership role in future budget battles. The president's tolerance of the deficit also contributed to the demise of his Jeffersonian-styled program of New Federalism outlined in the 1982 State of the Union Address. At the same time, Ronald Reagan's self-proclaimed Jeffersonian emphasis on reducing the federal government's size and scope through his social spending and tax cuts produced a Hamiltonian-like outcome, in which the burden of the budget cuts fell on lower- and middle-income Americans and the principal benefits of the tax cuts were distributed to upper-income groups.

Reagan's reversal on the economics of deficit spending, in one sense,

should not be surprising. The president's administration had not been guided by the coherence of a single economic doctrine. Instead, Reagan's 1981 Program for Economic Recovery consisted of an amalgam of supply-side, monetarist, expectations school, and traditional budget-balancing thinking. Of the four strains, the supply-side and monetarist schools deemphasized the importance of deficits, the supply-siders to magnify the role of tax cuts, and the monetarists to support the claim that monetary policy served as a more effective economic tool than fiscal policy. Thus, when elements of the Republican party and the administration downplayed the deficit, these claims came from individuals sympathetic to these economic ideas.

The first break with the "deficits are economically harmful" argument came from Congressman Jack Kemp, who declared in a statement before the House Budget Committee in 1981 that the Republicans had shifted from their fixation with balancing the budget. The Democrats on the committee remembered Kemp's statement vividly. "And all of a sudden," recalled Norman Mineta, "Jack Kemp at the Budget Committee one day says, 'We Republicans no longer worship at the altar of a balanced budget.' We [were] all sitting there looking at each other. 'Excuse me, Mr. Kemp. Would you repeat that again, we didn't catch that.' And, you know, Jack came right back, 'We Republicans no longer worship at the altar of a balanced budget.' And so that's when . . . all of a sudden there [was] a flip-flop."[32] Added fellow Democrat Leon Panetta: the Republican shift "probably culminated in a phrase that Jack Kemp used in the Budget Committee, which is that Republicans shouldn't worship at the altar of the balanced budget anymore. Well if that isn't a total reversal of everything the Republicans have been saying for a number of years, I don't know what is."[33] In fact, Kemp's remarks were not so unusual, considering that since at least 1978 he had been writing that deficits should be tolerated to allow for supply-side tax cuts. Nevertheless, though well known, Kemp was not part of the administration and in the course of the ongoing budget battle his comments were soon forgotten by the news media.

A more important break in the Republican's ideological ranks came in December 1981, when Murray Weidenbaum and William Niskanen, respectively the chairman and a member of the president's Council of Economic Advisors, stated publicly that people needed, in Niskanen's words, "to change their perception of the deficit," for deficits were not connected to inflation and interest rates.[34] Niskanen later commented, "Once you get closer to Washington deficits almost become a religious issue, and it's harder to reflect on the issue or even talk intelligently about it."[35] "Deficits," continued Niskanen "have . . . no direct effect on inflation. Which is [to say], they do not by themselves perceivably affect aggregate demand. Which is consistent with the general monetarist position, not the Keynesian position. . . . The way I read the evidence is that deficits don't have any consistent effect on money growth. So they don't have an indirect effect on inflation either. The somewhat more surprising conclusion from the studies that I've seen, and some that have been done in government, is that deficits don't appear to have any effect on real or nominal interest rates."[36] Niskanen added that despite these findings, he disapproved of deficits because they distorted the time distribution of taxes, thus encouraging current spending that would have to be paid for by future generations.[37] Niskanen's remarks in particular caused a brief uproar, especially among conservative congressmen who had been battling the Democrats to balance the budget to save the economy. Like Kemp, however, Niskanen had been making these statements about the deficit in print since the late 1970s.[38]

At the press conference held less than two weeks after Weidenbaum and Niskanen made their comments, the president defended his aides: "What they were trying to explain was—not that a deficit is all right and not that we shouldn't continue a program to eventually get us back, as I've said, within our means. . . . And I think what they're pointing out is—you can balance the budget by robbing the people by imposing a punitive tax system on the people. . . . The only proper way to balance the budget is through control of Government spending."[39]

Reagan's statement avoided any direct refutation of his aides' assessment of the relation between deficits and the economy, and instead shifted the issue to one of taxation versus budget reductions to reduce the deficit. Reagan also made the famous claim at the press conference that his campaign pledge to balance the budget "was our goal, not a promise."[40] Reagan's admission, according to one weekly newsmagazine, was "an acute political embarrassment for the conservative Republican who has made a point of blaming large federal deficits as a basic cause of inflation."[41] The president's denial was necessary because by December 1981 the targets set in the president's FY 1982 budget had become meaningless. After Reagan's great budget victories in early 1981, David Stockman convinced the president in September of that year to request an additional $13 billion in budget cuts to keep the administration's deficit forecast on track. The Congress, increasingly disillusioned by the inability to produce a balanced budget despite deep cuts in politically sensitive programs, agreed to just $3.7 billion of Reagan's request.

Though the deficit grew larger, Ronald Reagan remained true to his symbolic conception of the federal budget and its relation to domestic spending and taxation. Higher taxes, the president argued, produced greater amounts of social spending and were to be avoided even if the deficit continued to expand. At the same time, to fend off the pressure to raise taxes and reduce defense spending because the government's deficits supposedly weakened the economy, the president moved further away from the idea that deficits were economically destabilizing. Jack Kemp had made his remarks about Republicans and deficits before the House Budget Committee, but Kemp was a congressman speaking for himself. William Niskanen argued that deficits were unrelated to inflation and interest rates, but Niskanen's claim was mildly sidestepped by the president. By early 1983, however, other, more visible members of the administration began to attack the commonly assumed links between deficits and the economy.

Most notable among these administration figures was Treasury Secretary Donald Regan. Sympathetic to the supply-siders' view of tax cuts and deficits, Regan spoke out as early as Febraury 1983 against the idea that deficits were the sole cause of high interest rates. With inflation increasingly under control, the latest charge against deficits was that they produced economically deadening high interest rates. Regan was asked to comment on the matter. In testimony before the Senate Appropriations Committee, Secretary Regan stated that the major reasons interest rates remained high were bankers' fear of a stimulative monetary expansion creating inflation, treasury borrowing, and "I think the third one, being very candid, is bank earnings. I think that banks, faced with a lot of problem loans, both domestic and international, are doing their utmost to keep their eanings by keeping their interest rates up."[42] The banking industry immediately castigated Regan for his statement, but in May of that year the Treasury Department formally dismissed the supposed relationship between deficits and interest rates.

May 1983 marked the eighth year of the Western powers' economic summit meetings. The conference that year was held in Williamsburg, Virginia, and the major subject that troubled America's allies was the threat of the federal government's deficits to the worldwide economic recovery. Prime Minister Pierre Trudeau of Canada publicly called the deficits "destructive" and Chancellor of the Exchequer Geoffry Howe of Britain seconded his comments.[43] To counter such remarks, the Treasury Department released in May a study that contradicted the claim that deficits created high interest rates. The twenty-two page report concluded that "economic theory yields only an ambiguous answer to the question whether large Federal deficits cause high interest rates, which then lead to a stronger dollar. Attempts to resolve the ambiguity by appealing to historical data have revealed no conclusive evidence to support the assertion that large deficits cause high interest rates."[44] Though the report received little public notice, it represented Regan's solidified thinking on the matter, for the treasury secretary became increasingly vocal in his criticism of those individuals who argued that deficits produced high interest rates.

Regan's most famous conflict over this matter occurred during his feud with the new chairman of the Council of Economic Advisors, Martin

Feldstein. Feldstein encouraged the president and the Congress to raise taxes and cut defense as well as domestic spending in order to reduce the deficit, which Feldstein declared to be economically harmful. Responding bluntly, Regan declared, "Economists who continue to claim that deficits make for high interest rates should climb down from their celestial observatories and acquaint themselves with terrestrial facts."[45] After Feldstein wrote in the council's 1984 annual economic report that, once again, deficits produced high interest rates, Regan told the Senate Budget Committee that with the exception of the president's statement contained in the report, "as far as I'm concerned, you can throw the rest away."[46]

How much the treasury secretary influenced the president on this subject is uncertain, but by 1984 Ronald Reagan repeatedly insisted that deficits did not cause high interest rates. In February 1984, Reagan told reporters that over "the last couple of years, even though our deficits vastly increased, our interest rates went down to half of what they were."[47] Two months later, at a convention of home builders and bankers, Reagan informed the gathering that while the deficit doubled during his administration, interest rates dropped from 21.5 to 11 percent: "So obviously, with the interest rates coming down at the same time that the deficit is going up indicates that there isn't that tie. . . . I'm not pessimistic about the deficit or any of the challenges we face. . . . I have to say that I'm convinced that [there] is nothing but . . . pessimism out there."[48]

Finally, the president restated his position during his presidential debate with Walter Mondale: "Yes, the connection that's been made again between the deficit and the interest rates—there is no connection between them. . . . Now if there was a connection, I think that there would be a different parallel between [the] deficit getting larger and interest rates going down."[49] Inflation was at its lowest level since the early 1970s, and if interest rates were unusually high, then according to the president pessimism was at fault, not the deficit. As the "pessimists" continued to argue that large-scale deficit spending would derail the economic recovery, Donald Regan countered, "I wish those economists would sit back and relax. This will be one of the greatest recoveries in history."[50]

During the course of Ronald Reagan's first term, the president became increasingly forceful in his argument that deficits were economically tolerable. This proposition, however, did not mean that Reagan approved of deficit spending. Reagan still opposed deficits because they symbolized to him unwarranted and wasteful federal domestic spending. Furthermore, Reagan contended the budget should be balanced, not to revitalize the economy as he once argued, but in order to constrain the operations of the federal government. Ironically, most respected economists pronounced that during Reagan's first term the government's deficits helped to fight the recession and aid the recovery. Reagan's stand on the deficit, nevertheless, was politically very costly. The president's resolve to preserve the tax cut while boosting defense expenditures resulted in the loss of Reagan's direct leadership in the budget battles following his FY 1982 victories.

In fact, the president's release of his FY 1983 budget request on February 6, 1982, became the turning point of the Reagan Revolution. The budget contained an estimated $91 billion deficit for FY 1983, together with an 18 percent increase in defense spending, $25.9 billion in social program cuts, and no new revenues. The projected deficit stunned Republicans and Democrats alike, and the reaction to the budget's proposed programmatic mix and lack of a tax hike was overwhelmingly negative. Reagan overruled his advisers on the matter of revenues, rejecting the suggestions of such aides as David Stockman and White House Chief of Staff James Baker to raise $45 billion in new "sin" taxes. As the president reiterated in his 1982 State of the Union Address, raising taxes would not lower the deficit, but only stimulate more spending. In response to Reagan's budget, the Budget Committee in the Republican-controlled Senate voted 16 to 1 to reject the economic assumptions used in the proposal, signaling the committee's intent to draft its own budget and discard the administration's. In the House, the Republicans refused to introduce Reagan's budget, which enabled the Democrats to submit the budget in order to have it defeated and thereby embarrass Reagan and the Republicans. Later, under tremendous pressure from Senate Republicans to reduce the projected deficit, Reagan promoted new tax legislation that increased revenues by $98.3 billion. Reagan received less than $7 billion in domestic spending cuts for FY 1983.

What made Reagan's FY 1983 budget proposal so crucial for the administration was the president's need to regain both the confidence of his congressional allies and his own momentum in the budgetary process. Given the growing deficit and the worsening economy, all factions of the Republican party once again needed to believe that supporting the president would produce a balanced budget in the near future if they were to maintain their cohesion in the coming FY 1983 budget battle. The White House failed to provide that needed unity. Instead, it indicated clearly that preserving the tax cut and the defense buildup was a higher priority to the president than balancing the budget. As Reagan stated in a speech he made in early 1982 to defend his proposal and argue against a tax increase, deficits were a lesser evil than raising taxes that promoted greater domestic spending and the expansion of the federal government: "Now, no one sympathizes more with the idea of a balanced budget than I do—you may remember that I've mentioned that a few times over the years. But the deficits we propose are much larger than I would like, but they're a necessary evil in the real world today. And bear in mind, they would not be significantly reduced, if at all, by raising taxes, which is the common element in most of the curb-the-deficit proposals that are being bandied about."[51] Though deficit spending had become for Reagan a "necessary evil in the real world today," most Republicans still considered deficits of the size proposed by the president to be the source of economic and political disaster. Consequently, even many conservative Republicans willingly reduced the proposed defense increase and supported the tax bill.

Reagan's difficulties with the FY 1983 budget foreshadowed the remaining budget battles of his first term. The 1982 congressional elections, held when the unemployment rate registered at more than 10 percent, sent enough liberal Democrats to the House of Representatives to break the president's working majority of Republicans and conservative "Boll Weevil" Democrats. Subsequently, after Reagan submitted his FY 1984 budget to Congress, the Republican House leadership offered neither the president's budget nor one of their own for consideration. For the first time since Ronald Reagan became president, the liberal and moderate Democrats in the House passed their own budget resolution. Moreover, moderate "Gypsy Moth" Republicans were more willing to reject the president's call for deep social and domestic program reductions. The president's submission of the FY 1983 budget with its $91 billion deficit thus marked the end of that phase of the Reagan Revolution characterized by significant cuts in domestic spending. Instead, as Appendix 2 indicates, the budget battles entered another period, in which Reagan's requests for most domestic spending cuts were rejected, but the fear of presidential veto and of being labeled a "budget-buster" helped to contain the overall growth of the federal budget.

President Reagan tolerated the deficit to preserve the tax cuts, increase defense spending, and squeeze domestic expenditures. Consequently, Reagan lost his leadership role during the budget battles that followed the victories he had gained in 1981. In addition, Reagan's stand on the deficits contributed to the defeat of two other components of his drive to "restore constitutional government," the administration's New Federalism program and the initiative to add a budget balancing amendment to the Consitution.

Ronald Reagan's FY 1982 budget conquests produced some significant changes in the federal government's relationship with the states, particularly due to the consolidation of numerous categorical federal grants into fewer, large block grants. Important as these block grants proved to be in increasing state control over federal assistance funds, the president outlined his most ambitious program for strengthening the states' role in his 1982 State of the Union Address.[52] In this speech, Reagan described plans for a "single, bold stroke" for turning numerous federal programs over to the states. As part of the New Federalism, the states would accept administrative responsibility for such projects as Food Stamps and Aid to Families with Dependent Children, in addition to forty other major domestic programs, for a total programmatic cost of $46.7 billion to be absorbed by the states. The federal government, in turn, would take administrative control over Medicaid and related health programs. Furthermore, the federal government would help finance the states' new task through a $28 billion trust fund, while the states could expect to save $19.1 billion in the Medicaid takeover. Thus, federal funding for the states would be $47.1 billion compared to the states' new expenses of $46.7 billion.

Democrats at every level of government denounced New Federalism as nothing more than an attempt to shift the federal government's deficit burden onto the states. "It seems clear to me," announced House Speaker Thomas "Tip" O'Neill, "what the administration is up to. Faced with huge deficits, spawned by excessive, ill-conceived tax cuts and massive defense increases, they propose to escape by dumping ultimate responsibility for important programs on the levels of local governments."[53] Added California's Governor Jerry Brown, "We know that the President has a major problem; he has a $100 billion deficit that the Congressional Budget Office estimates will grow to over $200 billion in the next few years, and yet at the same time he doesn't want to raise taxes. And I see the potential in this New Federalism as a device to shift that onerous political responsibility onto the backs of taxpayers in cities and counties and states."[54]

Senator Milton Hamilton of Tennessee, another state Democratic official, remarked, "It looks to us like . . . a shifting of the deficits that the federal government has been running to the 50 states in order to balance that budget, which they have not shown they can do."[55] *New York Times* economics correspondent Leonard Silk was equally blunt in his review of Reagan's New Federalism proposal: "Confronted with huge deficits, high unemployment and high interest rates, President Reagan has decided to change the subject. He has elected to lift his eyes and the nation's from present woes to the 'new federalism,' . . . But when the euphoria generated by the President's State of the Union Message fades, the big deficits will remain."[56] Democrats throughout the country opposed the programmatic swap for numerous reasons, including David Stockman's admission that New Federalism would produce substantial revenue disparities among the states soon after the switch took place.[57] The argument that the administration was simply attempting to shift the deficit burden onto the states through New Federalism remained a centerpiece of Democratic rhetoric.

As Ronald Reagan discovered, deficit spending functioned as a two-edged weapon. If the federal government's deficits served to constrain domestic spending as the president desired, then they also acted to impede the success of Reagan's federal-state swap. In April 1982, the administration abandoned New Federalism's programmatic transfer, for the White House and the National Governors Association had failed to agree on the nature of the swap and the amount of federal financial support that would be provided to the states.

The federal government's growing deficits also undermined Reagan's attempt to add a provision to the Constitution which required balanced federal budgets. The Senate adopted the amendment in August 1982, but in October the measure failed to gain the necessary two-thirds majority needed in the House of Representatives. In both branches of Congress members voted against the amendment for various reasons, including the historically inaccurate argument that the Constitution's authors disapproved of adding strict economic rules to the governing document. Members of Congress also opposed the amendment because they regarded the resolution to be a ploy to divert attention from the president's toleration of the deficits.

Democrats and Republicans both contended the amendment amounted to simple subterfuge. "President Reagan has given us the biggest budget deficit in our history," wrote Alan Cranston, who led the Democratic opposition in the Senate: "By the time he leaves office he will have added half-a-trillion dollars to our national debt. Now he wants a constitutional amendment to stop him from doing what he's doing. Talk about irony!"[58] Jim Wright, the House majority leader, declared, "The amendment was a kind of hidden ball trick. But the public will keep its eye on the ball, on the central issues—unemployment, raging recession and a record number of business failures."[59] "We're dealing with the politics of symbolism and simple solutions," added Democratic congressman Les Aspin.[60] "It is a sign of the dire straits in which the Reagan administration and the Republican party find themselves today," said Senator Edward Kennedy, "that they have stooped to this political charade to shore up their failing economic policy."[61] Charles McC. Mathias, Jr., who led the Republican opposition in the Senate, argued that the amendment was an attempt by the administration and the Congress to divert attention from the deficit. "We are trying to paper that over with a new page in the Constitution," said Mathias, "this is a substitute for real action. . . . I do not think we should use the Constitution as a fig leaf to cover our embarrassment over the deficit."[62] The *New York Times* editorialized against the amendment, declaring, "As political camouflage, Mr. Reagan's enthusiastic endorsement of a constitutional amendment requiring a balanced budget made sense. The message seems to be, forget that it was he himself who has insisted on enormous permanent tax cuts before making proportionate spending cuts. Forget that in February it was he who said that the resulting deficits 'will not jeopardize the economic recovery.' "[63]

The *Washington Post* found Congress and the president's support for the amendment "grotesque," in light of the huge deficits fostered by the administration's policies:

> It is grotesque for senators and a president who cannot get their current deficit under $100 billion to support, piously, constitutional language to put it at zero. Conservatives in particular might note that there are only two ways to do it quickly—a tremendous reduction in Mr. Reagan's defense plans or a tremendous increase in taxes. Senators sponsoring this amendment might usefully be asked which alternative they support.[64]

The president's position on the deficit, taxation, and defense spending once again acted as a factor in the loss of one of the structural changes he argued was necessary to renew "constitutional government." Most of the legislators who voted against the amendment, and many of the newspapers that editorialized against the proposal, may have done so under almost any set of conditions, regardless of Reagan's policies. Yet Reagan's insistence on preserving his tax cuts and defense increases in the face of mounting budget deficits publicly undercut the seriousness of the budget-balancing amendment drive, and elicited charges that Reagan engaged in a cynical effort to manipulate the Constitution. The president was certain of his priorities, particularly regarding his persistent claim that tax increases only fueled domestic spending. Nevertheless, although Reagan's stand on taxes and controlling social spending may have produced comparatively short-term budgetary gains, the opportunity to make enduring changes in federal-state relations and fiscal policy through the Constitution was lost. The defeat of both New Federalism and the balanced budget amendment in 1982, within a year or so of the president's greatest budgetary triumphs, proved how costly and volatile the deficit issue could be.

On the other hand, President Reagan did achieve significant success with his strategy of cutting taxes to restrain domestic spending. One measure of Reagan's success is provided by an examination of the trend in federal appropriations enacted during the president's first term. Though not all federal spending is accounted for by the appropriations process, the appropriations bills do include funding for nearly all familiar federal agencies and for most controllable spending. Table 17 shows the appropriations levels for FY 1982 through FY 1985. (Appendix 2 includes tables that provide data on the complete budgets for this period.) The table indicates that total congressionally enacted appropriations approved by the president during the four years exceeded Reagan's request by less than 1 percent, or $3.3 billion. "The mix of money may have differed from that which the President requested," reflected Republican senator Mark Hatfield, chairman of the Senate Appropriations Committee, "but spending has been held under the overall level requested by the President."[65] The "mix of money," or the appropriations distributed by

Table 17. Federal appropriations, FY 1982–1985 (in billions of dollars)

Appropriations bills	FY 1982 Request	FY 1982 Enacted	FY 1983 Request	FY 1983 Enacted	FY 1984 Request	FY 1984 Enacted	FY 1985 Request	FY 1985 Enacted
Agriculture	30,486	30,857	37,820	38,448	32,408	32,486	31,618	31,689
Commerce, justice, state, judiciary	8,278	8,640	9,144	10,043	10,030	10,493	11,034	11,410
Defense	192,976	190,093	229,301	215,680	246,054	234,030	291,945	274,141
District of Columbia	570	557	580	524	570	601	503	533
Energy & water	11,889	12,611	12,660	14,813	14,866	14,541	15,875	15,372
Foreign assistance	11,681	11,968	12,112	11,972	21,107	21,921	18,230	18,150
HUD-independent agencies	33,211	37,044	27,460	33,634	30,301	36,625	35,267	37,525
Interior	6,794	7,484	7,005	8,563	6,711	8,649	7,975	8,126
Labor, HHS, education	25,448	28,168	20,869	29,738	26,171	33,804	28,882	33,041
Legislative	636	551	813	645	780	726	700	659
Military construction	7,513	7,112	8,208	7,221	8,747	7,178	10,318	8,405
Transportation	9,775	10,299	10,970	11,489	10,706	10,687	11,382	11,197
Treasury, postal service, gen. gov't.	5,245	5,495	5,718	6,193	6,245	6,635	6,641	7,058
Total	344,502	350,879	382,660	388,963	414,696	418,376	470,310	457,306
Distribution by function								
National defense	205,744	202,133	242,842	228,951	262,341	248,136	310,517	290,258
Foreign operations	11,681	11,968	12,112	11,972	21,107	21,921	18,230	18,150
Nondefense domestic	127,077	136,778	127,706	148,040	131,248	148,319	141,563	148,898
Percent domestic	36.9	39.0	33.4	38.1	31.6	35.4	30.1	32.6

Source: *Congressional Record*, February 5, 1985, p. S 1003.
Note: HUD—Housing & Urban Development; HHS—Health & Human Services. Table excludes synfuels recissions in FY 1984 and FY 1985.

budgetary function, reveals that nondefense domestic spending fell from 40 percent of the FY 1982 enacted total to 32.6 percent in FY 1985. What is more significant, the nondefense portion remained essentially steady-state before accounting for inflation at the $148 billion level between FY 1983 and FY 1985. This restraint in domestic spending was in part due to the Democratic party's fear of being labeled by President Reagan as the party of the budget-busting big spenders. Consequently, during the recession that extended through much of this period the Democrats refrained from proposing extensive public works and jobs programs that approached, for example, New Deal or Great Society efforts, largely because the Democrats were constrained by the deficit, just as Ronald Reagan had intended.

Finally, in 1980 President Reagan declared that his administration's goal was to restore constitutional government and Jeffersonian decentralization, without creating what has been called Hamiltonian inequality. On one level, Reagan's deep tax cuts and large deficits did indeed act as a huge fiscal stimulant that promoted aggregate economic demand. This stimulus lessened the effects of the recession and encouraged economic recovery, thereby assisting all Americans. In this fashion, the administration's fiscal policies conflicted with the Federal Reserve's monetary policies that acted to curb inflation by inducing the recession. On another level, the specific changes in the federal government's tax and spending programs enacted during Reagan's first term aided upper-income groups while lower-income Americans found their benefits reduced. According to the Congressional Budget Office, for example, the average combined tax and benefit changes per household followed the pattern outlined in Table 18. On average, families with incomes of less than $10,000 lost a combined $270 in cash and in-kind benefits in 1983, $390 in 1984, and $440 in 1985. Meanwhile, households with incomes of $80,000 or more received total benefit increases of $7,070, in 1983, $8,270 in 1984, and $8,930 in 1985, due to the tax cut.[66] Another study, conducted by the Congressional Research Service of the Library of Congress, examined the effects of the 1981 Omnibus Budget Reconciliation Act on the poverty rate. The act, which enforced the FY 1982 budget cuts, was found to increase the total poverty rate during that fiscal year by 2 percent, and by 2.9 percent among children.[67] The increase in childhood poverty was largely caused by the budget reductions that removed 493,000 cases from the Aid to Families with Dependent Children program.[68]

The administration's budget and tax changes that produced these effects raised the fairness issue that tarnished Ronald Reagan's Revolution. In fact, the poverty rate and the inequalities in income distribution were on the rise before Reagan became president.[69] Reagan's budget reductions, however, enacted during a deep recession, made life very difficult for many Americans. The administration could have avoided the fairness

Table 18. Net changes in taxes and benefits per household by income, calendar years 1983–1985

Calendar year	All households	Less than $10,000	$10,000– 20,000	$20,000– 40,000	$40,000– 80,000	$80,000 and over
1983						
Cash benefits	−80	−170	−100	−40	−20	−40
Taxes	810	10	230	880	2,260	7,140
Net	730	−160	130	840	2,240	7,100
In-kind benefits	−70	−110	−60	−40	−60	−30
Net, including in-kind benefits	660	−270	70	790	2,180	7,070
1984						
Cash benefits	−170	−250	−210	−130	−90	−90
Taxes	1,090	20	330	1,200	3,080	8,390
Net	920	−230	120	1,070	2,990	8,300
In-kind benefits	−100	−160	−90	−60	−80	−40
Net, including in-kind benefits	820	−390	30	1,010	2,900	8,270
1985						
Cash benefits	−190	−280	−240	−130	−90	−100
Taxes	1,320	40	440	1,480	3,720	9,070
Net	1,130	−240	200	1,350	3,630	8,970
In-kind benefits	−120	−200	−140	−70	−90	−40
Net, including in-kind benefits	1,010	−440	60	1,280	3,540	8,930

Source: Congressional Budget Office, "The Combined Effects of Major Changes in Federal Taxes and Spending Programs since 1981," April 1984, Table 5.

Note: Benefit reductions are treated as reductions in household income and tax reductions are displayed as increases. Details may not add to totals because of rounding.

problem by taking greater care to equalize the costs and benefits of the Reagan Revolution, rather than targeting the bulk of the budget cuts at those who David Stockman called the government's "weak clients."[70] Instead, the administration dissipated the sense of national self-sacrifice that existed in 1981, manifested by the public's general willingness to reduce the budget and shrink the deficit to fight inflation, and replaced it with the belief that the budget cuts were unfair.[71] Over time, the concern for equity encouraged many Democrats, moderate Gypsy Moth Republicans, and even some conservatives from both parties, to bring the big budget-cutting days of the president's first term to a halt.

During Ronald Reagan's first term his symbolic understanding of budget balancing remained remarkably consistent. Deficits represented the unsound domestic spending practices of a bureaucratically inefficient, socially and economically intrusive national government, whereas balancing budgets in an "appropriate" manner indicated this spending could be brought under control. According to the president, balanced budgets should only be achieved through domestic budget reductions, not by way of tax increases that justified higher levels of spending. This general rule governed Reagan's budgetary policies throughout this period. Even when he agreed to major tax increases in 1982, Reagan claimed he did so with the understanding that Congress would make substantial budget cuts, which in fact were never enacted. Reagan's concern with balancing budgets, therefore, had always been predominantly political rather than economic in nature. When Reagan attempted to isolate the political and symbolic qualities of the balanced budget idea by claiming the deficits were economically tolerable, however, the president's New Federalism program and the drive to add a budget balancing amendment to the Constitution suffered. The Reagan Revolution and the push to restore constitutional government thus were ironically constrained by Reagan's own misleading assertions made before he became president that deficits produced economic ruin.

The combined effects of Reagan's defense increase, the tax cuts, congressional unwillingness to approve most of the administration's requests for domestic budget cuts, and the recession, produced huge deficits. The president thereby failed to keep his 1980 campaign pledge to balance the budget, but the deficits—and their resulting interest payments—inhibited liberal and moderate Democrats from proposing significant new social programs. In this regard, Reagan fulfilled a more meaningful promise by profoundly disrupting the Democratic party's traditional political agenda. More than any president since Lyndon Johnson, Ronald Reagan forced the American people to reconsider the issue of just what role the federal government should play in the nation's economic and social life.

The Democrats and Unbalanced Budgets

How the Democratic party interpreted the balanced budget idea during the Reagan years was at least as important as the outcome of any given year's budget battle, for the Reagan presidency had more to do with political ideas and ideology than any particular set of spending reductions. President Reagan forcefully challenged the principles of neo-Keynesian economics, the legitimacy of most social expenditures, and the authority of a powerful centralized government. These components of Democratic public policy were intimately tied together by the federal budget, and ultimately by the Democrats' distinction between good and bad deficit spending as measured by the full-employment budget. The notion that deficits aided the economy when the unemployment rate and the level of economic growth were unsatisfactory served as the cornerstone of neo-Keynesian economics, which in turn justified additional social spending and an enhanced role for the federal government in guiding the national economy. The Democratic party's task, therefore, lay not only in limiting whatever short-term political losses might be incurred during the Reagan Revolution, but also in promoting a coherent balanced budget principle that could add consistency and legitimacy to the Democrats' policymaking once they returned to power. Failing in this matter, the Democrats' fate would be to accommodate Ronald Reagan's call for a balanced budget standard that constrained domestic spending regardless of the economy's condition. In other words, without a measure that distinguished good from bad deficits, the Democrats lacked a macroeconomic explanation for opposing either the president's efforts to add a budget-balancing amendment to the Constitution or to cut social spending when the budget was unbalanced.

The stunned Democrats who returned to Congress after losing the White House and control of the Senate in 1980, however, obtained little assistance from the failed Carter administration on the subject of balanced budget standards. It was Jimmy Carter who compared the federal budget to that of his peanut farm: "I have never known an unbalanced budget—in my business, on my farm, as Governor of Georgia. And I've set a goal for myself, which I intend to meet: that before my administration is over, the budget of the United States will be balanced."[72] President Carter refrained from publicly discussing the full-employment budget soon after his 1976 election, instead proclaiming his intent to balance the unified budget. Later, during the 1980 election year, the Commerce Department reported in February that the FY 1981 budget contained a large, anti-inflationary, fiscally constrictive $55.4 billion full-employment budget surplus. Although the surplus diminished in size, the full-employment budget remained in that condition throughout the election year, but Carter made no mention of the surplus in his contest with Ronald Reagan.[73] Though the 1980 Democratic platform rejected proposals for a constitutional balanced budget amendment, it provided no reference to the full-employment budget, or any other economic doctrine that justified deficit spending.

The Carter legacy, nevertheless, only reinforced the Democrats' interest in producing budgetary plans similar to Ronald Reagan's, such that every budget scheme offered by the Democrats in 1981 projected a balanced FY 1984 budget. These budgets were designed in this manner due to political necessity and the desire to match Reagan's balanced budget pledge. By 1981 the Democratic leadership reasoned that proposing anything less than a balanced budget plan was politically unacceptable. Congressman Leon Panetta, one of the "Gang of Four" that designed the Democrats' FY 1982 budget resolution, noted the constraints that limited the Democrats' budgetary options: "We can't afford to suddenly turn around and tell people that suddenly, you know, running deficit spending at the government level is okay folks. Let's do it. I don't think it could happen politically, because . . . the Democratic Party is labeled . . . the big spending party and suddenly doesn't care about the issue of running high deficits. . . . Politically we can't afford to do it."[74]

Furthermore, public opinion surveys not only suggested the nation strongly favored balanced budgets, as Panetta implied, but the Democrats' sporadic attempts at informing the public about the benign effects of deficit spending proved to be unrewarding. Congressman Norman Mineta, another member of the Gang of Four, sent a newsletter to his constituents, explaining that deficits were only one of many factors causing inflation, not the main one. "The kind of mail generated in return!" recalled Mineta. "People would see that and say, 'Hey Mineta, you're off your rocker!' "[75] For every Norman Mineta, however, there were other Democrats like James Jones, chair of the House Budget Committee, who proudly announced, "My whole political career in Congress for the last nine years has harped against the high deficits, and has said essentially what Candidate Reagan said before he came to Washington."[76] By ideological standards Jones was a moderate, and so if the Democratic leadership was to preserve party unity it needed to present a budgetary plan that appealed to Democrats significantly more conservative than the Budget Committee chairman. The Democratic budget proposals had to accommodate what the Democrats regarded as the external constraint of public opinion, and the force of the conservative factions within the party.

In addition, the Democrats attempted to prove they were as capable as Ronald Reagan when it came to budget balancing and that such a goal could be realized in a more equitable fashion. The first Democratic budget resolution proposed in the House of Representatives in 1981, the year of the Reagan Revolution, was introduced by the Black Caucus. These Democrats believed the promise of a balanced budget added political legitimacy to their efforts to oppose the president and indicated that more than one road led to a balanced budget. "We took them on their own terms," declared Congressman Ronald Dellums, a caucus member. "Balanced budgets can de done in a way without putting the burden on the backs of the people. By using [the Reagan administration's] assumptions, we could expose their hypocrisy."[77] Like the other Democratic proposals that followed, the Black Caucus budget protected domestic programs by reducing the growth in defense spending and, over the long run, increasing taxes. Moreover, particularly in light of the recent election, the Democrats reasoned that by balancing the budget they could alter their public image of being the wasteful, big-spending party. "I think if there's anything the Democrats have to learn," said Leon Panetta, "it's that we have to approach the economy in a disciplined sense, and we do not have that image. I think very frankly that we need to restore some trust and confidence in the American people. . . . So I think Democrats have got to make that issue ours."[78]

The demoralizing outcome of the 1980 election and the political reality of 1981 led the Democratic party's liberal and moderate factions to embrace a proposal aimed at balancing the FY 1984 budget. By doing so the Democrats intended to change their big-spender image by proving they were fiscally "responsible"; attempted to meet the demands of public opinion—as the Democrats interpreted the 1980 election; tried to appease their conservative colleagues; and matched the balanced budget pledge made by Ronald Reagan. Furthermore, many liberal and moderate Democrats genuinely believed that balancing the budget would reduce or eliminate inflation and that their own balanced budget plan could limit the reductions in domestic spending proposed by the president.

As the government's deficits grew larger rather than smaller despite the Republicans' budget victories, the Democrats sought to emphasize the Republicans' failure by intensifying their own declarations that deficits were economically harmful and needed to be greatly reduced. The Democrats' principal device for trimming the deficits, aside from cutting defense spending, rested with increasing taxes, a method ideologically and economically confusing, and one that ultimately helped to lead the Democrats to defeat in 1984. To demonstrate they were at least as concerned and willing to reduce the deficits as the Republicans, moderate and liberal Democrats pushed for tax increases even as the economy plunged into recession. By cutting the deficits in this fashion the Democrats attempted to counter the president's use of the deficits to squeeze domestic spending, but in the process the Democrats obscured the vital distinction between economically good and bad deficits. Commenting on Reagan's tax cut, for example, Leon Panetta observed that one deficit resembled most any other deficit: "I think it's very interesting that we've suddenly gone from the position that deficits created by spending programs are bad. But deficits created by loss of revenues through tax cuts, or what have you, are okay. I don't believe in that. I think, in fact, the economists who look at the figure don't believe that. Like a rose, a deficit is a deficit is a deficit."[79]

When deficits appeared alike there could be no excuse for anything less than balanced budgets, even during a recession. Consequently, raising taxes as the economy deteriorated became acceptable Democratic fiscal policy. In April 1982, Treasury Secretary Donald Regan soberly noted, "We're in a very steep recession at this point and the economy is dead in the water."[80] Yet during the very same month, Congressman Daniel Rostenkowski, Democratic chair of the House Ways and Means Committee, pressured the Republicans in an attempt to raise $35 billion in economically restrictive taxes for FY 1983 to trim the deficit.

Although more socially equitable than the Republicans' tax plans, the Democrats' tax proposals were economically puzzling considering their traditional fiscal policy. Even the Democrats experienced difficulty in explaining their purpose in raising taxes during a recession, as suggested by this exchange of questions and answers between *Washington Post* columnist David Broder and Congressman Jim Wright, the House Democratic majority leader, in November 1982:

> *Mr. Broder:* I want to understand the new Democratic theory of economics. Are you saying that the way out of this recession is to cancel the income tax cut and raise excise taxes? That's the way to get out of a recession?
>
> *Rep. Wright:* . . . I think the way to get out of a recession is to provide the stimuli that will encourage investment in those specific things that will modernize our aging industrial plant and machinery, create jobs [so] we can be more competitive on world markets. . . . Immediately, I think . . . we must . . . provide jobs for the jobless and homes for the homeless.
>
> *Mr. Broder:* Has the tax increase that the Congress passed last summer helped end the recession, or has it helped prolong the recession?
>
> *Rep. Wright:* I think all it has done has been to redress some of the enormous excesses of the tax decrease of the year before. I voted for it reluctantly . . . because I thought it was a necessary thing under the circumstances to reduce the raging deficit, which otherwise would have been much higher than it is.[81]

Wright's comments indicated the Democrats supported a major tax increase that had no purposeful macroeconomic effect. Its intent was solely to reduce a deficit that at that time crowded in, not crowded out, private investment. In the process, Wright and the Democrats failed to provide an alternative economic logic that could account for their willingness to raise taxes during a recession and abandon the fiscal policies that once guided them. If the majority leader endorsed huge tax increases in the midst of the worst economic calamity since the Great Depression simply to reduce deficits, then the Democrats could hardly expect the public to sanction peacetime deficits at any level. Furthermore, when the Democrats no longer attempted to legitimate deficit spending under these severe conditions or neglected to offer, say, a publicly comprehensible plan to phase in tax increases and equitable budget reductions during a period of economic recovery to achieve a balanced full-employment budget, their fiscal policy merely reflected Republican economic values, not their own. The Democrats, of course, had made their situation more difficult by having engaged in a bidding war with the Republicans in 1981 to cut taxes beyond even the administration's original request, thus unnecessarily increasing the deficit. Like the Democrats of the 1920s, the Democrats of 1981 attempted to appeal to their opponents' business constituency by cutting taxes. Like the Democrats of the 1920s, the Democrats of 1981 achieved minimal political success.

The Democrats also expressed their ambivalence toward deficit spending in their House Caucus publication *Rebuilding the Road to Opportunity: A Democratic Direction for the 1980s*, published in September

1982. This document constituted the Democratic party's sole comprehensive alternative economic program issued during Ronald Reagan's first two years in office. In *Rebuilding the Road*, the Democrats had this to say about deficit spending:

> We reject any economic program that projects annual federal budget deficits of $100 billion or more well into the forseeable future. Such deficits will keep interest rates high, choke off investment and, over time, prove inflationary. . . . Achieving a balanced budget is very important to our economic future. We do not believe that the federal government should continue to spend an ever-increasing percentage of the nation's wealth. We need to limit spending and to set tax rates in order to generate a balanced budget during periods of sustained economic growth.[82]

The Democrats filled their confusing statement with loopholes. Balanced budgets were necessary, they said, when the economy experienced "growth," but deficits apparently could be sky-high during recession as long as they did not "project" $100 billion "into the foreseeable future." Absent from the Democratic statement was any clear measure that identified when an unbalanced budget might be economically beneficial, or explained why a projected $99 billion deficit would be acceptable compared to another at $120 or even $200 billion. Instead, they apparently settled on the $100 billion figure because it was a rounded, easily recognized, convenient number. Through their evasiveness the Democrats failed to provide themselves, or the public, with a useful or justifiable measure to evaluate future balanced and unbalanced budgets.

Ironically, the new standard for judging deficits came from Ronald Reagan, and not the Democratic party. In a speech presented before the National League of Cities in November 1982, after the election, President Reagan first employed the term "structural deficit": "We have, as I've said, sizably reduced the annual increase in spending, but there is no way we can eliminate, by budgetary cuts alone, the structural deficit built into the budget, or can it be eliminated by raising taxes. . . . The answer lies in stimulating the economy and increasing productivity."[83] The term was Reagan's own, most likely adopted by the president after he listened to his advisers discuss the "structural unemployment" present in the economy. In any case, the media, politicians, and economists soon used the phrase to describe the difference between a deficit caused by recession and one created by insufficient revenue or excessive spending. Even economist Walter Heller, who once urged President Kennedy to proclaim the virtues of the full-employment budget symbol, converted to Reagan's term.[84] The structural deficit idea was strikingly similar to the Democrats' full-employment budget notion, but the two had significantly different symbolic and public policy implications. The full-employment budget represented the federal government's broad commitment to a fiscal policy stimulative enough to produce a "full-employment" economy. The structural deficit implied that while some portion of a deficit could be the consequence of a weak economy, an uninhibited federal government's extravagant domestic spending produced the remaining deficit. Thus, Reagan's use of the term fit neatly with his opposition to tax increases and his desire to cut social spending. By failing to defend their own symbolic interpretation of balanced and unbalanced budgets, and therefore of their understanding of the federal government's proper role in the economy and society, the Democrats instead allowed Ronald Reagan to replace their symbol with one of his own.

Not surprisingly, the Democrats' full-employment budget measure, with its largely forgotten ties to the Employment Act of 1946, suffered an unheralded death. In late 1983, after consultation with other units of the executive branch and the Congressional Budget Office, the Commerce Department stopped calculating the 4.9 percent full-employment budget, based on a 4.9 percent level of unemployment in the economy. Instead, a 6 percent "high-employment" budget continued to be calculated and published, based on a 6 percent level of unemployment, together with a new "middle-expansion, cyclical" budget that had no intended fiscal implications.[85] The difference between the full- and high-employment deficit estimate remains economically and politically significant. While, for example, the FY 1982 unified budget deficit stood at $110.6 billion, the full-employment deficit estimate reached only $32.6 billion, but the high-employment deficit registered at $57.2 billion, as shown in Table 19. Despite their obvious bearing on fiscal policy, the congressional Democrats raised no objections when the Commerce Department ceased to calculate and publish the full-employment figures. By the mid-1980s, the

Table 19. Three measures of the federal deficit, FY 1981–1984 (in billions of dollars)

Fiscal year	Unified deficit	4.9% Full-employment deficit	6% High-employment deficit
1981	−57.9	−3.2	−24.1
1982	−110.6	−32.6	−57.2
1983	−195.4	−53.7	−81.5
1984*			
1st Q.	−188.8	−55.2	−84.9
2d Q.	−190.2	−48.9	−79.6
3d Q.	−179.7	−52.1	−83.9

Source: Department of Commerce, *Survey of Current Business,* August 1983, Tables 2 and 6.
*FY 1984 annual projections at the full-employment budget level were calculated only for the first three quarters.

4.9 percent unemployment target may no longer have been economically realistic. The topic, however, was worth the Democrats' serious consideration.

With no alternative conception of the budget to defend, the Democrats attempted to convince the public in 1984 that they were more capable than Ronald Reagan and the Republicans at balancing the budget. During the Democratic presidential primaries, every major candidate denounced the government's deficit spending and pledged to reduce these deficits by increasing taxes and cutting defense expenditures. One reason to trim the deficits was to reduce the pressure they exerted on domestic spending. Senator Ernest Hollings, for example, claimed that Ronald Reagan tolerated the government's deficits for just that reason:

> [Reagan] knows what he's doing. He's not amnesiac. He's intentional. He not only cuts the programs, but he likes the fact that deficits will keep us Democrats from ever even discussing new programs. If we can ever get that White House again we'll have a hard time sort of restoring the programs and properly fund them. But with those high deficits for years we won't have any chance at all to talk about new programs.[86]

Still the Democrats' central argument raised against Reagan's deficits focused on their economic effects. At the Democratic National Convention, Walter Mondale declared in his acceptance speech: "Here's the truth about the future: We are living on borrowed time. These deficits hike interest rates, clobber exports, stunt investment, kill jobs, undermine growth, cheat our kids, and shrink our future. . . . I mean business. By the end of my first term, I will reduce the Reagan budget deficit by two-thirds."[87] Thus, Mondale pledged to cut the deficit to approximately $65 billion in FY 1988, but why reduce the deficit by two-thirds? Why not three-quarters or one-half, or eliminate it altogether?

Walter Mondale and the Democratic platform failed to explain why the deficits of the size he proposed were economically satisfactory. The Democrats simply no longer employed an agreed-upon measure to distinguish good from bad deficits, one that responded to changes in the economy and guided fiscal policy. Instead, they came to rely on fixed standards that lacked any intrinsic economic justification and were altered as the situation demanded. In 1982 the House Democratic Caucus economic program, *Rebuilding the Road to Opportunity*, stated that balanced budgets were an economic necessity during periods of growth, but that deficits running up to $100 billion were tolerable during recessions. In 1984 Mondale selected the fraction of one-third of the current deficit to demarcate acceptable deficits. Meanwhile, the Democratic platform added to the confusion. "The Democratic Party is pledged to reducing these intolerable deficits," the document stated; however, it continued, "We oppose the artificial and rigid constitutional restraint of a balanced budget amendment. Further we oppose efforts to call a Federal constitutional convention for this purpose."[88] If deficits "killed jobs," as Mondale argued, then why oppose a constitutional prohibition on deficit spending, or indeed tolerate deficits at any level? From an economic standpoint, the Democrats left this question unanswered in 1984.

The Democrats' assessment of deficit spending had truly been perplexing. For nearly eight years, since the early days of the Carter administration, the Democrats proclaimed that deficit spending first produced inflation, then high interest rates, and next killed jobs. They pushed for steep tax increases during a sharp recession to trim the deficit for no clearly explained macroeconomic purpose, then allowed the full-employment budget to die a silent death, and yet still rejected a balanced budget amendment. The Democrats' inconsistent position on deficit spending encouraged Ronald Reagan to make this assessment of the opposition in his own convention speech:

> We have heard a lot about deficits this year from those on the other side of the aisle. Well, they should be experts on budget deficits. They've spent most of their political careers creating deficits. . . . Now, however, they call for an end to deficits, calling them ours, yet at the same time the leadership of their party resists our every effort to bring Federal spending under control. For three straight years they have prevented us from adopting a balanced budget amendment to the Constitution. . . . Their candidate, it would appear, has only recently found deficits alarming. Nearly 10 years ago he insisted that a $52 billion deficit should be allowed to get much bigger in order to lower unemployment. . . . Was anyone surprised by his pledge to raise your taxes next year if given the chance? In the Senate, he voted time and again for new taxes.[89]

If the Democrats vacillated on the subject of deficit spending, as Reagan suggested, there was no question about where they stood on the matter of taxation.

Walter Mondale's efforts to focus attention on deficit spending and taxation as the principal domestic issues of the campaign proved to be an uphill struggle against public opinion. Peter Hart, Mondale's chief pollster, and Richard Wirthlin, the White House pollster, both concurred early in the campaign that many Americans had little concern about the deficit situation. Wirthlin's surveys indicated that only 3 percent of the public expressed great concern about the deficits, and Hart's surveys revealed that just 42 percent of respondents knew the deficit had grown during the Reagan presidency. According to Hart, only 10 percent of respondents voluntarily mentioned the deficit as a serious issue. Hart, nevertheless, still contended that the federal government's unbalanced budgets would develop into a major political problem for the Republicans. "The deficit is the Republican's claim to economic management,"

Hart stated, "and now that claim is gone. It changes the dynamic of this election."[90]

The administration, however, chose to stress its contribution to the growing economy, rather than to the presence of huge federal deficits. Senator Paul Laxalt, chair of the president's reelection campaign, called the deficit issue "a yawner." "We, as Republicans, have talked about deficits and balanced budgets since the days of Roosevelt, and the people simply haven't listened, because they can't relate to those huge numbers." The public would care about the deficits only "if those deficits should translate into higher interest rates or higher inflation."[91] The polls concurred with Laxalt's analysis. After three years of large-scale deficit spending, many Americans appeared to be desensitized to the federal government's unbalanced budgets, and in any case they did not hold the Reagan administration responsible for these deficits. The opinion polls indicated, for example, that respondents agreed that Reagan would be more effective in reducing the deficit than Mondale, and that Mondale's most potent issue was jobs, not the deficit and taxation.[92] A *New York Times/CBS News Poll* reported:

> Voters were asked which of four economic problems—the deficit, unemployment, inflation and interest rates—they thought was most important today. About a third of the respondents said unemployment was, and they divided almost evenly on whether they planned to vote for Mr. Reagan or Mr. Mondale. But among the two-thirds who cited the other three problems, Reagan supporters outnumbered Mondale supporters by margins of greater than 2 to 1.[93]

In other words, Mondale's strongest political support rested with those people who stated that reducing unemployment remained the most important domestic issue. Rather than address this group's concerns about unemployment as the central theme of his campaign, Mondale inevitably linked the subject to the deficit, and then told these same people he intended to tax them. On the other hand, those groups who cared most about the deficit found Mondale decidedly less politically attractive than Ronald Reagan.

On the subject of taxes, Mondale's situation proved to be even more desperate. Polls administered throughout the campaign indicated the public overwhelmingly rejected Mondale's plan to raise taxes. On election day, NBC News reported that 50 percent of exit-poll respondents opposed tax increases to reduce the deficit, with only 32 percent supporting higher taxes. The polls also indicated that early in Reagan's term the public opposed the tax cut in order to reduce the deficit, but as the tax cut took effect the public became unwilling to surrender their new income for deficit reduction.[94]

The Democrats' long-term difficulties with the balanced budget issue were more deeply rooted than the simple misreading of public opinion surveys during the 1984 election. Balancing the federal government's budgets remained predominantly a political matter. Ronald Reagan understood this and therefore pressed for a balanced budget amendment, avoided tax increases, and proposed major reductions in domestic spending to achieve his vision of government, even as he dismissed the deficits' presumably harmful effects on inflation and interest rates. The Democrats' task proved to be more arduous and complex. For in order to protect their own conception of government they had to identify, under hostile political conditions, the economic efficacy of deficit spending. Good deficits had to be distinguished from bad deficits in a consistent, publicly comprehensible manner. Instead, the Democrats seriously jeopardized their notion of the public good for short-term political gain by neglecting this responsibility. At the same time, some Democrats, including Senator Daniel Patrick Moynihan, accused the Reagan administration of harboring a strategy "to induce a deficit and use that as grounds for the dismantling" of social programs.[95] Yet, regardless of the accuracy of Moynihan's claim, no administration had been more vociferous than Reagan's in defense of deficit spending's benign economic effects. The Democrats, on the other hand, regularly denounced the government's deficits and thereby pressured domestic programs in a manner that paradoxically complemented the president's efforts to cut domestic spending. The Democrats never attempted to defuse the administration's drive on social programs by merely agreeing with Reagan that the government's deficits would not devastate the economy. The Democrats not only found Reagan's $200 billion deficits economically harmful, they also came to the same conclusion about Reagan's $110 billion deficit, and the $50 billion deficits of the Carter administration. By the end of Ronald Reagan's first term, the Democrats had helped to create a political climate that could produce the constitutional or statutory limitations on deficit spending they had long opposed.

Balanced Budgets, Symbolic Politics, and Gramm-Rudman-Hollings

From the earliest days of the republic, balanced and unbalanced federal budgets have been tied symbolically and instrumentally to competing visions of government and society. Two of these visions, Jeffersonian decentralization with its emphasis on balanced federal budgets, and neo-Keynesian centralization with its advocation of budgetary "flexibility," appear hopelessly incompatible. Yet the challenge of American politics remains to accommodate the two without promoting Hamiltonian inequality, to recognize the federal government's macroeconomic responsibilities while furthering the nation's experiment with federalism.

In a somewhat curious fashion, Ronald Reagan came close to blending elements of the two ideas together, though some of his policies did indeed lead to greater social inequality. "We who are in Government," President Reagan asserted in his 1983 State of the Union Address, "must take the lead in restoring the economy."[96] As a consequence of Reagan's fiscal policies, the federal government incurred deficits that no contemporary Democratic president could have dared produce and then survive politically. Many empirical economic assessments of these deficits indicate they lessened the recession's harsh effects and assisted the economic recovery of 1983–84. This very conservative Republican president ironically verified the macroeconomic efficacy of federal deficit spending even as he called for a constitutional amendment requiring balanced budgets.

At the same time, through his 1982 New Federalism program, Reagan pushed for the decentralization of federal programs into the administrative care of the state governments. This effort failed. Mainly because of his attempt to reduce federal domestic spending, the president's proposed financial support for the states' new responsibilities would have ended shortly after the programmatic swap had taken place. This probable outcome forced the states to oppose New Federalism. In effect, Reagan's commitment to reducing the size of the public sector, especially at the federal level, undermined and outweighed as a priority his plan for programmatic decentralization. The president did achieve some success with his block grant initiatives in 1981. On the other hand, the most significant change in federal-state relations may stem more from the size of the federal government's debt and the restraint imposed on federal spending due to the presence of large federal deficits than any program initiated by Ronald Reagan. Servicing the debt, for example, could require such a large portion of federal revenues that the national government will be forced to rely more upon the states to conduct domestic public policy.[97]

Jeffersonian decentralization and neo-Keynesian full-employment economics continue to be the ideological triumphs of the Democratic party, but the Democrats often experience difficulty reconciling the two ideas. Aside from criticizing the Reagan deficits, regardless of their size or the prevailing economic conditions, the Democrats' alternative conceptions of government offered in 1984 rested with such centralizing notions as "industrial policy" and the general discounting of state and regional solutions to public problems. In his analysis of the 1984 Democratic Convention, *Washington Post* columnist David Broder observed:

> The weakness of the Democrats' Electoral College situation reflects a flaw in the party's approach to politics: a preference for nationalizing its philosophy and procedures, and an inclination to ignore the federalism built into American politics and government. . . . The building blocks of the Demo-

cratic Party are no longer seen to be its state and local affiliates but its
national ethnic and interest group caucuses. . . . The irony is that the Democrats have forgotten the essential federalism of this political system at a time
when their greatest strength and greatest talent are in local and state government.[98]

Indeed, during the recession most state governments conducted public
policy in a manner largely consistent with liberal and moderate conceptions of how governments should act. The states, for example, accepted
responsibility for the block grant programs created by the Reagan administration and continued to fund them when federal assistance diminished.[99] Even as the federal government reduced its financial aid to the
states, state and local taxes were increased to maintain most social programs, with the notable exception of public aid for the working poor.
Furthermore, to provide for their states' future well-being, both Demo-
cratic- and Republican-controlled state governments engaged in economic development activities.[100]

An enhanced state role, however, should not obscure the continued
need for an active federal intervention in the macroeconomy, or for a
federal government that protects civil rights and liberties while financially assisting the states with their new administrative duties. Recent
efforts on the part of some states to lower their tax rates, for instance, are
made possible in large part by a generous federal government, rather than
the exclusive efforts of "fiscally responsible" state governments. In its
postelection evaluation of the Democratic party, the *New Republic* concurred with David Broder's assessment of the party's lack of interest in
the states and cited the governors' fiscal skills as an example of competent
leadership: "If any one group ought to be elevated in influence, it is the
[Democratic] party's governors [who] have been dealing creatively with
some of the nation's most difficult problems and balancing budgets at the
same time."[101] To a great extent those states that are able to balance their
budgets do so because the federal government has allowed its budget to
remain unbalanced, in part because of revenue transfers to the states. The
combined state surpluses equal a third of the federal deficit, and in FY
1985 the federal government provided the states and localities with one-
fifth of their revenues.[102] The states are therefore able to offer their social
programs and engage in economic development activities indirectly
through the federal treasury.

The Democrats' apparent difficulty in reconciling the competing visions of Jefferson and Keynes accounts for much of their current uncertainty and unrewarded search for "new ideas." The idea of a national
industrial policy is simply an extension of old Federalist and Whig
thinking but it is not as systematic or well considered. The Democrats
will continue to find that such notions are politically unsatisfactory. The

nation's population center, and its balance of political power, are moving inexorably West and South, to regions traditionally reluctant to accept strong, centralized political authority. Yet the emergence of strong state and local governments, active in their economies, is very much a part of the country's Jeffersonian and Jacksonian heritage, and is compatible with neo-Keynesian balanced full-employment budgets.

Regardless of the paths taken by either the Democratic or Republican parties, the balanced budget idea persists in American politics. Though this chapter focuses on 1981–84, President Reagan's first term, the enactment of the Gramm-Rudman-Hollings legislation in 1985 requiring a balanced on- and off-budget for FY 1991, later revised to FY 1993, deserves some mention. The significance of Gramm-Rudman-Hollings is that it reaffirms the political importance of balanced budgets, though mandated balanced budgets may harm the nation's economy rather than help it. Conservatives in the Congress initiated Gramm-Rudman-Hollings because even deficits incurred by Ronald Reagan symbolized big, wasteful, inefficient government living beyond its means. Moreover, the conservatives argued the law would break the apparent stalemate between the Congress and the president that prevented the elimination of the deficit. Liberal and moderate Democrats supported the legislation because the failure to do so after decrying the evils of the Reagan deficits would have been politically embarrassing. More to the point, the presence of those deficits served to constrain federal funding for programs cherished by congressional liberals and moderates. Furthermore, Gramm-Rudman-Hollings offered them a way to contain the president's increased defense spending. Whatever the motivation for voting for the legislation, Gramm-Rudman-Hollings further undermines the full-employment budget idea. The goal of achieving a balanced budget for its own sake, rather than for some specified macroeconomic purpose or measure, has now become law. Consequently, the pressure supplied by Gramm-Rudman-Hollings to reach a balanced budget, the existence of the deficits Gramm-Rudman-Hollings is intended to eliminate, and the presence of a revenue-neutral tax reform all contribute to limit an activist fiscal policy and the introduction of expensive social programs during the coming years.

For nearly two hundred years the federal government has operated under the principle that its budgets should be balanced. Yet the contemporary debate over the budget's instrumental and economic effects has failed to identify the origins of this principle or account for its persistence in American politics and political thought. Public discourse has to a great extent remained uninformed about this unique budget balancing tradition which has exercised such sway over public policy. History teaches that the tradition is regenerated through the day-to-day conflict of competing political visions and is articulated by the nation's political elite. This budget balancing principle is so deeply rooted in the nation's political culture that neither full-employment economics nor the presence of the huge deficits created during the Reagan presidency have shaken American politics free from its constraining influence. The sense that the federal government's unbalanced budgets are unacceptable remains most evident. Republicans and Democrats alike continue to proclaim the evils of deficit spending, and in this manner their words and deeds serve to preserve the balanced budget principle for future political confrontations.

Appendix 1

State Debts and the Development of Off-Budget Spending, 1860–1984

The Civil War and Reconstruction greatly increased the states' collective debt, as wartime expenses and the effort to rebuild state infrastructure overwhelmed the states' ability to generate revenues. In 1860 the states' combined debt was $257.4 million, but by 1870 the new debt level stood at $355 million, with many of these debts incurred by the South while under Republican rule. Post–Civil War state politics often revolved around questions related to debt finance and reduction, questions such as who would pay increased taxes to retire and finance the debt, and who would benefit financially from the debt's retirement. After Reconstruction the states made a massive effort to reduce their debts, and the collective debt loan did fall until about 1900, when it reached $249.4 million in 1902. After the turn of the century, state debts rose again; by 1931 the net debt load grew to some $2 billion, while the national debt had climbed to $16.8 billion. This increased debt was largely attributable to borrowing by New York, Illinois, California, Louisiana, West Virginia, North Carolina, and a few other states. "Internal improvements" by way of transportation costs contributed heavily to the states' indebtedness; by 1931 highway construction was the single greatest cause of the states' long-term debt. "The states borrowed mainly for highways, which accounted for nearly half of all loans. Unemployment relief and soldiers' bonuses and loan funds each accounted for about one eighth of the total."[1]

To accommodate their new borrowing needs, state governments found four devices to evade their constitutional limits by way of nonguaranteed borrowing: (1) state agency revenue bonds; (2) borrowing through public corporations, commissions, and authorities; (3) delegating state operations to local governments and agencies; and (4) lease-purchase agreements. In contrast to nonguaranteed borrowing, guaranteed borrowing describes the "full faith" constitutional guarantees made to lenders that their state bonds and securities will be repaid through the state's general fund revenues. Therefore, state borrowing obligated under the conditions set in state constitutions is considered legally different than off-budget nonguaranteed borrowing. In order to persuade the credit market to accept these off-budget securities, states often were, and still are, forced to pay higher interest on these bonds. Therefore, off-budget nonguaranteed debt is more costly to state governments, and consequently to the taxpayer, than is on-budget guaranteed debt. By 1963 over half of all state borrowing was made through off-budget nonguaranteed debt instruments.

State supreme courts began allowing state governments to issue revenue bonds in 1889, when Colorado's Supreme Court ruled bonds issued for canal building were legal, as the securities would be repaid from canal revenues. Because repayment did not depend on Colorado's general fund receipts, the court determined these securities did not constitute state debt in violation of Colorado's constitution. Montana's Supreme Court permitted that state to issue revenue bonds for building construction, and Minnesota's Supreme Court allowed the state to build prisons funded with special nongeneral fund generated taxes. Other states quickly followed these examples by selling their own revenue bonds to finance off-budget projects.

State governments also looked to local public authorities, corporations, and commissions to carry out state projects, and thus eliminate the need for direct general fund budgeting. The use of other public authorities for this purpose dates back at least to the Kennebec Water District operating in Maine in 1899, and later under the more expensive Port Authority of New York, established in 1921. State governments began authorizing these authorities in large numbers during the 1920s and the courts generally agreed the debts incurred were not constitutionally illegal.

State officials also found they could delegate state responsibilities to traditional local governments, that is, cities and counties. These local governments would carry out such mandated tasks, highway construction for example, and the states would agree to reimburse these other governments for their expenses. By delegating authority, many states were able to sidestep constitutional debt limitations through repayment schedules.

Finally, states found the lease-purchase agreement to be a useful device to avoid constitutional limitations. In 1860 the California State Supreme Court ruled state leasing agreements did not constitute state debt, as no payments were required until the contracted service was performed. A. James Heins wrote about these agreements in his 1963 book *Constitutional Restrictions against State Debt:* "The substance of this rather clear decision [in California] has been carried forward to make possible agreements by which a state may lease facilities built with funds borrowed by private corporations or other governmental units, at rentals sufficient to operate the facilities and amortize the debt. . . . The legal intricacies involved are significant, and it is never quite clear when a debt is a debt." Heins's assessment of these methods for avoiding constitutional restrictions led him to predict that "the practice of interagency lending of state funds will continue." Furthermore, because "nonguaranteed borrowing carries significantly higher interest cost than borrowing for which a state's credit is pledged," Heins added, "I propose that full borrowing power be restored to state legislatures, with no referendum requirements, nor any other restriction currently found in state constitutions."[2] Heins believed that suspending these restrictions was necessary because states simply evaded their constitutional limits, at further expenses to the taxpayer.

The presence of off-budget spending has enabled many states to incur huge debts while operating under the constraints of state constitutional prohibitions against deficit spending. For example, by 1984 the state of California had approximately $6.6 billion in outstanding general obligation bonds in circulation. Despite intense partisan conflict over the possible need to raise taxes to balance the state's budget during the recession years of 1982 and 1983, the state's voters approved some $600 million in bonds for the 1982–83 fiscal year, and over $800 million in 1983–84. At the same time, debt service on the bonds grew from $262 million in 1981, to $391 million in 1984, all of which was taken from the state's general revenue funds.[3]

Appendix 2

The Reagan Budget Battles, FY 1982–1985

The glue that held us together was the drive toward a
balanced budget.

SENATOR ROBERT PACKWOOD, 1982

This appendix outlines in a detailed fashion the budget battles of Ronald
Reagan's first term as president, supplementing the material presented in
the preceding chapters. Each fiscal year's budget fight took place under a
unique set of economic and political circumstances, and produced a
different budgetary outcome. One central theme surfaced time and again,
as the balanced budget idea acted as a form of political constraint on all
actors involved, despite the magnitude of the federal government's growing deficits. The FY 1982 budget battle serves as a worthy example of this
trend. Not only did it result in President Reagan's most dramatic and
significant victories, the FY 1982 budget deliberations also exemplified
how the political fortune that accompanied the Reagan Revolution ultimately was tied to the balanced budget issue. Regardless of the budgetary mix of programs proposed by any presidential or congressional alliance, each major budget package offered for FY 1982 sought public and
political legitimacy by promising a balanced FY 1984 budget. Whether
the solution for realizing this mysteriously unobtainable goal rested with
budget reductions, tax cuts, or tax increases, both the Republicans and
Democrats employed the balanced budget as a unifying principle and as
a political war cry.

Ronald Reagan rallied his forces during the presidential campaign and
in the early months of his administration by applying his combination of
symbolic and economic arguments against the government's unbalanced
budgets, claiming they produced inflation and were the product of a
national government that oppressed individual freedoms and states'

rights. Meanwhile, rather than call attention to the idea of full-employment budgets or other Keynesian notions, the Democratic leadership
rallied their own supporters by emphasizing the deficit's harmful economic consequences, while seeking to balance the budget by defeating
Reagan's tax programs and defense buildup. For Republicans and Democrats alike, in 1981 the balanced budget quickly became an end in itself,
regardless of what it might mean for an economy that rapidly headed into
a deep recession. In this regard, Reagan's election in 1980 structured the
nation's political discourse, in addition to the federal government's policy objectives.

The prospect of achieving a balanced budget soon disappeared, however, and after the president's success in 1981 the budget battles entered a
new phase. Despite the growing federal deficit, Ronald Reagan remained
committed to protecting his tax cuts and defense increase. Consequently,
the president's budget proposals for FY 1983–85 were formally rejected
even by his own Republicans in the Congress, fearful as they were of
creating larger deficits. The big budget-cutting days of FY 1982 and the
president's first term had come to an end. Nevertheless, despite the
Democrats' success in the 1982 congressional elections, there would be
no major increases in domestic spending. Neither the Democrats nor the
Republicans sought the label of "budget-buster," and so the latter budget
battles of FY 1984 and FY 1985 became frustrating efforts in deficit
reduction. Constrained by the president's resistance to raising taxes or
cutting deeply into defense spending, and by the Democrats' unwillingness to accept further serious reductions in domestic programs, the Congress still achieved some success in reducing the budgetary imbalance,
but not enough to bring the deficits much below $200 billion.

Before proceeding with this chronological review of the budget battles,
a brief summary of the formal budgetary process as it existed during this
period may bring some order to these events. According to the 1974
Budget Reform Act, the president is responsible for presenting his budget
proposal to Congress at the end of January. Once received by the Congress, the budget is distributed to all congressional committees for their
assessment of how the budget might influence programs falling within
their jurisdictions. By March 15, these committees must submit to the
appropriate House or Senate Budget Committee their "views and estimates" of the budget. The Budget Committees' task is to design a budget
resolution. This resolution sets nonbinding spending ceilings that guide
Congress in determining tax, authorization, and appropriations bills. The
Budget Committees take into account the competing priorities outlined in
the "views and estimates" reports, testimony presented at hearings by the
two budget committees, and economic estimates and programmatic analysis provided by the Congressional Budget Office and the Joint Economic
Committee of the Congress. The Budget Committees are expected to

present their proposed resolutions to their respective houses of Congress by April 15.

After the House and Senate have received these proposed resolutions, they are required to approve some form of budget resolution by May 15. The First Concurrent Budget Resolution then acts as a nonbinding guide for all congressional committees when they consider their various tax and spending bills. Furthermore, the resolution indicates congressional fiscal priorities and assumptions about the status of the nation's economy. Because the resolution is only an internal procedural device and not a law, it does not require presidential approval. With the First Concurrent Budget Resolution in hand, the committees of the Congress work to produce the relevant tax and authorization legislation and the thirteen appropriations bills that actually allocate funds to the government's agencies and programs. Before these bills may take effect, they must be signed by the president. The 1974 Budget Reform Act also provides for a second budget resolution. Unlike the first resolution the second is binding, but it still does not call for presidential approval. To enforce the Second Concurrent Budget Resolution, in the event, for example, that the appropriations bills exceed their ceiling, the Congress may include restrictive reconciliation language in the resolution. This language directs the relevant tax and spending committees to report legislation that would bring revenues and expenditures in line with the resolution. According to the Budget Reform Act, the budget process should be completed by the beginning of the new fiscal year, which starts on October 1. As the events described here indicate, however, budgetary timetables were largely bypassed, first resolutions were made binding, second resolutions rarely used, and continuing resolutions that extended funding from the preceding year were commonly employed to fund the federal government.

The Reagan Revolution: FY 1982

President Ronald Reagan fired the budget battle's first shot with his auspicious 1981 State of the Union Address, delivered to Congress on February 5. In his speech Reagan told the nation, "I regret to say that we are in the worst mess since the Great Depression" and that most of the country's difficulties could be traced directly to the federal government and its deficit spending. "We know now," Reagan said, "that inflation results from all that deficit spending. . . . And that means above all bringing Government spending back within Government revenues, which is the only way, together with increased productivity, that we can reduce, and yes, eliminate inflation."[1]

In the days that passed before the administration unveiled its proposals for the FY 1982 budget, rumors circulated about David Stockman's "black doomsday book" of OMB cuts. The Stockman hit list reportedly called for a $14 to $15 billion set of recissions in the FY 1981 budget, and $40 to $50 billion in reductions from Jimmy Carter's lame-duck FY 1982 budget proposal. Most responses to the suggested cuts were positive. The *New York Times* ran an editorial on February 15 titled "Why Federal Spending Must Be Cut." Echoing Reagan's theme that deficits created inflationary expectations, the editorial stated: "If people really believed that deficits mean inflation, then a nasty self-fulfilling prophecy unfolds. . . . Beyond psychology, there are clear economic reasons to stride towards a balanced budget. Mr. Reagan must do so to win room for the tax cut. . . . To avoid the risk, or at least the expectation, of even higher budget deficits, the Government must cut spending too."[2] A number of Democrats also initially endorsed the idea of reducing federal expenditures. Senator William Proxmire observed, "President Reagan's plan to cut $30 billion to $40 billion out of his 1982 budget still could leave the federal government with a more than $100 billion deficit. . . . Such a deficit could shove the inflation rate close to 20 percent. . . . but it's not enough. [The cuts] should be deeper and sharper."[3] Despite his questionable economic logic concerning deficits and inflation, Proxmire soon received his wish for major budget cuts.

Before the administration released its budget, however, two events occurred in early February that highlighted the divisions existing within the White House over the deficit issue, and the odd twist of fate that forced Senate Republicans to vote for higher debt levels and ultimately higher deficits. In the first incident, the cracks that deepened in the coming years were already evident in the administration. Reflecting on the one hand Treasury Secretary Donald Regan's supply-side learnings, and on the other hand David Stockman's emphasis on budget cutting and reducing the deficit, the two men publicly gave different interpretations of whether the proposed tax cuts would be tied to budgetary reductions. Regan declared the public was "entitled to be able to plan taxes and not have it 'if' and 'maybe.'" But Stockman countered that "they will be an integral part of the same package."[4] The two views were incompatible, for Stockman declared the tax cuts would be feasible only if budget cuts were approved, which elevated cutting the deficit as a policy goal over obtaining tax cuts. The administration's failure to distinguish symbolism from economics, to decide, in other words, whether balanced budgets were a guide to the president's political vision or an economic necessity, created disagreement among Reagan's top advisers even in early February.

In the second incident, the most difficult legislative task facing the administration before issuing the new budget was securing congressional approval for raising the national debt ceiling by $50 billion. Large numbers of Republicans, especially those in the Senate who had been the minority party for over two decades but gained control over the Senate in 1980, blanched at voting for such a measure. Now responsible for directing the nation's affairs, and following the request of a Republican president, the Senate Republicans fell into line. The Republicans' response to the debt ceiling issue left the Democrats to make the most of the situation, as they gleefully forced their opponents to vote for the measure by threatening to withhold their usual support for this kind of legislation. "The inmates have taken over the asylum," Senator William Armstrong told his Republican allies. "The Democrats, who have been telling us that it's all right to raise the national debt, are going to vote against it. And the Republicans, who have told us that it was morally wrong to raise the national debt, are voting for it."[5]

On February 18, President Reagan presented his momentous budget address to Congress and outlined the major provisions of his "Program for Economic Recovery." On the spending side, the program called for budgetary savings of $41.14 billion in FY 1982 from the Carter proposal, $79.7 billion in FY 1983, and $104.4 billion in FY 1984. Where Carter's FY 1982 budget included $739.3 billion in outlays, Reagan's budget stood at $695.5 billion. The Reagan budget predicted that the FY 1982 deficit would reach $45 billion, $22.9 billion in FY 1983, and the FY 1984 budget would contain a $500 million surplus. The big news, of course, was not just the cut in total spending, but where the cuts were to be made. The shift in spending priorities witnessed a reduction in the growth of domestic spending, and a dramatic increase in defense expenditures. By FY 1984, the Reagan program recommended that military spending increase to 32 percent of the total budget from 24 percent in FY 1981, while domestic spending aside from interest payments and "protected" safety net programs would shrink from 29 percent to 18 percent in FY 1984.

The new administration's defense budget stemmed neither from an assessment of military strategy nor from an evaluation of defense programmatic needs. Instead, the defense budget expanded as a result of a game of one-upmanship, with elements of the Reagan transition team viewing both Jimmy Carter and the Soviets as their opponents. The person principally responsible for the defense increase was William Van Cleave, a professor at the University of Southern California. It was Van Cleave who proposed that the defense budget grow 7 percent in real terms during the 1980 election, while other Reagan advisers Alan Greenspan and Martin Anderson favored 5 percent. The previous two Carter budgets allowed for a real increase of 3 percent, and during the campaign Carter endorsed a defense increase of 4 percent. After his defeat, however, Carter included a 5 percent real rate of growth in his FY 1982 lame-duck budget, thus seeking to match, and perhaps to embarrass Ronald Reagan. Van Cleave, then a member of the Reagan transition team, convinced Secretary of Defense Caspar Weinberger that the new president had to beat the Carter figure to send a clear message to Moscow of Reagan's intent to strengthen U.S. security, and that a 7 percent real increase was the appropriate signal. Weinberger agreed, and as the Reagan budget team designed the Program for Economic Recovery it added this increase to the 5 percent contained in the Carter lame-duck budget. Thus, the Reagan defense budget increase was actually twice as large as proposed by candidate Ronald Reagan during the 1980 election.[6]

The program's other principal components included a 30 percent tax cut for individuals, spread over three years, and significantly greater corporate tax credits for cost recovery allowances, as well as a commitment to reducing federal regulations. Additionally, the administration proposed consolidating numerous federal categorical grant programs into block grants, to increase the states' control over their federal funding. Within days of the president's message, however, the administration meekly announced that Stockman had miscalculated the growth in spending for FY 1982 and that perhaps an additional $10 billion in further cuts were needed on top of the $41.4 billion previously outlined.

The immediate reaction to the president's program was generally favorable. House Speaker Thomas "Tip" O'Neill promised the president that "in no way are we going to obstruct you." Senate Minority Leader Robert Byrd also informed Reagan that "our policy is not going to be one of obstruction. Our policy is going to be one of cooperation in reducing federal spending where it can be done equitably and fairly."[7] The public's response was overwhelmingly positive, according to a *Washington Post*/ABC News poll that found Americans believed by a 2 to 1 margin the Reagan program would end inflation. Moreover, 49 percent agreed the food stamp program needed to be trimmed, and 66 percent said the president cared about Americans equally, with only 24 percent saying Reagan favored the rich.[8] Surprisingly, Wall Street exhibited little enthusiasm, as the New York Stock Exchange reported declining stocks outnumbered gaining stocks by a 5 to 2 margin, while the Dow Jones 30 Industrials fell by 13.9 points after Reagan delivered his budget plan.[9] If the Reagan program was intended to alter expectations, it produced only a negative effect in the nation's capital markets, as the fear that deep tax cuts would create huge deficits outweighed any consideration that budget cuts would make up the difference.

On Tuesday, March 10, 1981, the administration delivered its revised budget package to Congress, and quickly the administration received its first victory in the Republican-controlled Senate Budget Committee. The committee approved $36.4 billion in domestic program reductions; within eight days Reagan achieved success in the Democratic House, where the Ways and Means Committee unanimously approved $7.8 billion in social program cuts. Though the administration's budget sailed ahead in Congress, the seams began to unravel in OMB's hastily written budget. The Senate Budget Committee recalculated OMB's economic forecast, questioning its assumptions, and announced that Reagan's budget cuts totaled only $34.1 billion rather than the newly revised $48.6 billion. The committee then based its budget reductions on its own economic estimates instead of depending on the OMB forecast. Furthermore, the Congressional Budget Office reported that OMB underestimated interest rates and unemployment, and projected the deficit to be $80 billion more over the next four years than publicly stated by the administration.

In the wake of the president's success, the Democrats began to respond. The Congressional Black Caucus was the first Democratic group to launch a detailed rebuttal to the Reagan program by presenting its own alternative budget on March 18. The Black Caucus argued that if Reagan was correct in saying that deficits were responsible for the country's economic woes, their proposal would produce a balanced budget sooner than Reagan's, and therefore it deserved more political and public support than the president's. The caucus proposal called for outlays of $721.1 billion and a balanced FY 1982 budget. Their budget plan restored funding for social programs, reduced FY 1982 defense outlays by $2 billion, and still allowed for $56.4 billion in tax reductions. If balanced budgets would truly save the economy, as the president claimed, then the Black Caucus and later other Democratic budgets would supply their own budget balancing plans but without Reagan's programmatic mix.

The Democrats, still dazed at the size of Reagan's electoral margin and fearful that a major political realignment had taken place in 1980, stepped up their assault against the Reagan budget. Then an unexpected event added to Reagan's political momentum. Speaker O'Neill told reporters in mid-March that the president's public support was evaporating, as suggested by the Democrats' mail. Those groups standing to lose federal aid appeared to be organizing, while the Democrats continued to portray the budget cuts to be unfair and the tax cuts simply a sop for the rich. Opposition to the cuts mounted, and the Democrats took solace from a Gallup Poll released in March that indicated Reagan's approval rating stood at 59 percent. Reagan's rating was lower after two months in office than that of any of the preceding six presidents. Although Reagan worked his budget cuts out of the Senate Budget Committee in near record time, the House appeared to be a much more formidable obstacle. But on March 30, John Hinkley shot the president, and Reagan's admirable behavior soon reversed the polls and dampened Democratic spirits.

On April 2, the Senate sent the president a get-well message in the form of a major budget reduction package. By an 88 to 10 margin, the Senate approved a budget reduction measure that included $2.8 billion in spending cuts beyond those requested by the administration. A surprisingly large number of Democrats voted with the Republicans. Among those voting in favor of the $36.9 billion package was Minority Leader Byrd, who observed, "The people want the President to be given a chance with his budget. So I'll vote for it . . . I don't believe they're going to achieve a balanced budget by 1984."[10] By voting for the Republican budget the Democrats wished to appear cooperative rather than obstructionist, and to meet public demands that Reagan's plan be allowed to work. If the program failed, the Democrats intended to let the Republicans take responsibility for the economy. Furthermore, the Democrats suffered from their leadership's inability to produce an alternative budget to the Republican plan. Still, Majority Leader Howard Baker noted, "We're both gambling. It's a high stakes political gamble."[11]

Reagan's victory in the Senate was expected, though it came more quickly than most observers had thought possible. After the Senate acted, the budget battle shifted to the House, where Democrats outnumbered Republicans. The liberal and moderate Democrats on the House Budget Committee reacted much differently than their Senate counterparts. On April 5 the committee voted 17 to 13 to adopt a budget resolution with more social spending and a one year $38 billion tax cut, $16 billion smaller than Reagan's cut for 1982. The Democratic budget totaled $714 billion, substantially larger than Reagan's $695.3 billion request. Moreover, the Democrats' proposed deficit ran nearly half the size contained in Reagan's budget. The Democrats claimed the White House underestimated the inflation rate for 1982, that it would be 10.4 percent rather than 8.3 percent, and thus the Reagan budget actually called for $717.8 billion in outlays. The Democrats therefore contended their budget was smaller than Reagan's and contained only a $25.6 billion deficit instead of the administration's $45 billion figure.

Adopted only six days after Reagan was shot, the Democrats realized their resolution had to contend not only with Republicans and conservative "Boll Weevil" Democrats, but also with national sympathy for the stricken president. To rally support and present a unified front the 242-member Democratic Caucus adopted by voice vote a statement setting out their opposition to the Reagan budget. The statement accepted the idea that deficits were an important factor in driving up interest rates and inflation:

> The causes of high inflation are numerous, most of them experienced by nations throughout the world. Its cures are just as many. There is no single act of government . . . that can stop inflation in its tracks. Its momentum, built into certain wage agreements and pricing policies . . . encouraged by expectations of more inflation to come and worsened by high interest rates and high government deficits, is too strong to be reversed by any one policy. . . . Reducing the Federal deficit is important to bringing down interest rates.[12]

The caucus statement declared the "American government" was neither the enemy of the people nor an economic problem. Although a "national consensus" called for slowing the growth of government, the Democrats opposed a program of "fiscal control that puts the main burden of fighting inflation on the backs of middle- and low-income workers while providing unprecedented benefits for the privileged few." "Tax cuts," the Democrats added, "should be coordinated with spending cuts so as not to increase the deficit."[13]

Democratic unity, however, was not preserved. Democratic Congressman Phil Gramm joined Delbert Latta, the senior Republican on the House Budget Committee, to construct an alternative budget resolution more in line with the Reagan request for $695.3 billion in outlays. In fact, the Gramm-Latta resolution was lower than both the Democratic and White House budgets, as shown in Table 20, though its deficit was higher than the Democratic version as Gramm-Latta included the president's tax cuts. Still, Gramm-Latta projected a balanced FY 1984 budget. On April

Table 20. FY 1982 House Budget Committee resolution and the Gramm-Latta alternative (in billions of dollars)

Program	Actual FY 1981*	Reagan proposed FY 1982	House Budget Committee	Gramm-Latta	House-Senate Conference Commitee
Military	159.0	188.8	188.8	188.8	188.8
International affairs	10.5	11.2	11.2	11.2	11.2
Science, space	6.1	6.9	7.0	6.9	7.0
Energy	7.8	8.7	6.8	4.2	6.0
Natural resources	13.1	11.9	12.3	11.9	12.4
Agriculture	2.1	4.4	5.1	4.4	4.5
Commerce, housing	0.9	3.1	4.3	3.1	4.0
Transportation	19.7	19.9	21.1	19.7	20.4
Community develop.	10.4	8.1	9.5	8.1	8.7
Education, training	29.8	25.8	29.4	25.7	26.8
Health	63.1	73.4	74.4	73.3	73.4
Income security	225.5	241.4	247.6	241.2	239.7
Veterans' benefits	21.7	23.6	24.0	24.0	24.0
Justice	4.4	4.4	4.5	4.4	4.4
General gov't.	4.4	5.0	4.9	5.0	4.9
Fiscal assistance	7.0	6.4	6.1	6.4	6.4
Interest	71.9	82.5	90.1	81.7	85.7
Allowances	0.4	1.8	0.7	0.7	—
Undistributed receipts	−25.8	−32.0	−34.6	−32.0	−32.9
Total outlays	632.4	695.3	713.7	689.2	695.4
Revenues	605.0	650.3	688.9	657.8	657.8
Deficit	−27.4	−45.0	−24.8	−31.4	−37.6

Sources: "Comparison of Budget Proposals," *New York Times*, May 1, 1981; "Comparison of Budget Proposals," *New York Times*, May 7, 1981; "A Comparison of Budget Plans," *New York Times*, May 15, 1981; *Congressional Quarterly Weekly Report*, May 9, 1981, p. 785.

*These numbers are from the FY 1981 Second Budget Resolution; they represent the federal budget as it was known in early 1981.

28, less than a month after his shooting, President Reagan gave a dramatic televised presentation before the Congress to call upon the public to pressure the House into rejecting the Budget Committee's resolution and to adopt the Gramm-Latta alternative. "Let me say that we embrace and fully support that bipartisan substitute," proclaimed the president. "The massive national debt which we accumulated is the result of the Government's high spending diet. Well, it's time to change the diet and to change it in the right way."[14] After a bout of declining public approval, Reagan enjoyed a "second honeymoon," and the Democrats were deluged with telegrams and letters asking them to adopt Gramm-Latta. Speaker O'Neill soberly informed reporters that his mail ran 5 to 1 in favor of Gramm-Latta; a *New York Times*/CBS News poll released on April 30 found Reagan's approval rating stood at 67 percent, an increase of 8 percent from March.

On May 6, the House rejected the Black Caucus budget and another liberal budget offered by Congressman David Obey. The Obey budget increased social spending and deferred personal tax cuts until 1983. First, the Black Caucus budget lost by a 356 to 69 vote, and the Obey budget failed by a 303 to 119 margin. The next day, May 7, the House adopted the Gramm-Latta budget resolution by 253 votes to 176. Not a single Republican voted against Gramm-Latta, while 63 Democrats defected to vote for the conservative budget. All four budgets, the Black Caucus, the Obey budget, Gramm-Latta, and the Budget Committee resolution, proposed balanced budgets no later than FY 1984.

Meanwhile, the administration experienced some unexpected trouble in passing the Senate's budget resolution. Although the Senate accepted the Budget Committee's budget reduction plan, the resolution itself still required approval. The resolution proposed by the Republican majority was stalled in the Budget Committee. In fact, the resolution, which called for $704.1 billion in outlays and a $53.8 billion deficit, was rejected by a 12 to 8 vote. Three staunchly conservative senators, William Armstrong of Colorado, Steven Symms of Idaho, and Charles Grassley of Iowa, joined with the committee's Democratic minority to defeat the resolution, as the three believed its deficits and spending levels were too high. "I'm so committed to a balanced budget," declared Armstrong, "that I am prepared to vote against the defense budget, which I've never done before, and against water projects, something no senator from Colorado has done in 80 years."[15] The nine Democrats on the committee looked on the split in Republican ranks with pleasure, as Senator Daniel Moynihan noted, "The gentlemen on the other side of the table promised us miracles, and now they are encountering reality."[16] Two weeks passed while anxious Republicans searched for new budgetary savings and lower deficits to meet the trio's approval. Finally, on May 12 both the Budget Committee and the full Senate accepted a new resolution, as the Republicans achieved paper savings to appease Armstrong, Symms, and Grassley. The resolution assumed, for example, $20 to $25 billion in unspecified FY 1984 budget cuts, $7 billion from reductions in "waste, fraud, and abuse," and another $5 billion in cuts by strengthening the president's authority to rescind or defer appropriations. "The deficit is still there," declared Moynihan after the vote, "it's merely papered over."[17]

Thus, on May 7 the House adopted a modified version of the Gramm-Latta budget resolution, with FY 1982 outlays set at $689.2 billion and a $38.9 billion deficit. The Senate approved its resolution on May 12, with $700.8 billion in outlays and a $50.5 billion deficit. The two resolutions were then sent to a Senate-House conference committee, where a budget of $695.5 billion with a $37.7 billion deficit was approved. The committee assumed the deficit would be lower than the administration's projected $45 billion deficit, or those in the House and Senate resolutions, because the economy performed remarkably well in the first quarter of 1981, with an average annual 8.4 percent GNP growth rate. On May 20 the House approved the conference budget, and the Senate followed on May 21.

Before adopting the budget resolution, however, the Senate dealt President Reagan an embarrassing bipartisan defeat. On May 20, the Senate voted 96 to 0 to voice its objection in a "sense of the Senate" resolution to Reagan's proposal to cut Social Security. Urged on by David Stockman, only 9 days before Reagan had approved a plan to reduce the minimum Social Security benefit to early retirees, and trim the benefits for those who would retire at age 65. The plan was intended to save $17 billion between FY 1982 and FY 1986, but the proposal was politically imprudent given the immense popular support for Social Security. The long-term significance of the Senate's action was to end any serious discussion during Reagan's first term about cutting Social Security, a very large portion of the government's domestic budget. With defense spending, interest payments on the debt, "safety net" programs, and then Social Security removed from the budgetary chopping block, the budget could only be balanced by raising taxes or making deep cuts in a relatively small number of discretionary domestic programs. Having disposed of the Reagan Social Security proposal, the Senate turned to passing the budget resolution.

The First Concurrent Budget Resolution was a nonbinding measure that identified programmatic reductions only in the most general manner by indicating spending ceilings in the budget's functional areas. The next step in the FY 1982 budget battle called for the authorizing committees in the Congress to make real cuts worth $36 billion in visible programs supported by active constituents and vested interests. Then the cuts would be approved by both houses of Congress in their respective reconciliation bills. The peril of the budgetary process for the conservative budget cutters centered on keeping the still relatively independent congressional committees in line with the resolution's spending targets. The Republican leadership in the Senate maintained discipline over the committees, and on June 12 the Senate approved a reconciliation measure specifying $39.6 billion in cuts.[18]

The House committees also exceeded the resolution's instructions for $36 billion in reductions. The Democrats adopted the strategy of making deep and unrequested reductions to emphasize the extent of the cuts and to build a nationwide base of public opinion to oppose the conservatives. Among these budget reductions was the famed closing of 10,000 post offices. As the House Majority Leader Jim Wright told the Democratic Caucus: "The President is responsible for all these cuts, and now he has the audacity to blame us. It's not the Democrats who would close the 10,000 post offices, it's not the Democrats who would cut back on Meals on Wheels, it's not the Democrats who would cut back on student loans."[19] The Democrats met the resolution's spending targets, but the programmatic mix offered by the Democrats was unacceptable to the White House. In a June press conference Reagan assessed the Democratic budget:

> A month ago, the House of Representatives approved by a 77-vote margin a long overdue and unprecedented budget resolution. . . . And yet there is now clear danger of Congressional backsliding and a return to spending as usual. Some House committees have reported spending cuts they know can't be made; closing, for example, one-third of the nation's post offices. One House committee claims to have achieved savings by eliminating a day-care program to provide suppers. But it also slipped into the change of the law to say that lunches can be served at supper time.[20]

To keep the Democratic spending cuts in line with the president's request, the House conservatives devised their own set of reductions that provided for an additional $2.2 billion in cuts. Sponsored by Democrat Phil Gramm and Republican Delbert Latta, the conservatives' amendment to the main reconciliation package was dubbed "Gramm-Latta II."

To preserve unity among the Boll Weevils and Republicans while keeping the Gram-Latta II package intact, the conservatives sought a single up or down vote on the amendment. The single vote on these cuts endorsed by the president meant the White House needed only to maintain loyalty among the conservative ranks for one big vote, rather than six individual votes desired by the House leadership. For in response to Gramm-Latta II, the Democrats devised a parliamentary tactic approved by the Rules Committee to divide the vote on the conservative proposal into six separate items. But by a 7-vote margin the full House defeated the leadership's rule, adopted the single-vote rule instead, and then approved Gramm-Latta II. The administration received another major victory, in a 217 to 211 vote that cut spending by $5.2 billion in some programs and added $3 billion to others, for a net $2.2 billion in reductions more than were contained in the Democratic plan. The House adopted the full reconciliation bill on the same day, June 26.[21]

The battle over the conservative amendment was so chaotic that copies of Gramm-Latta II were distributed at noon, June 26, the same day as the vote on the amendment. Quite simply, the great majority of House members were only vaguely aware of the numbers they voted for or against. Gramm-Latta II contained no index or sequentially numbered pages, leaving specifications concerning particular programs lost somewhere in the text for only the most diligent observers to locate. The text's individual pages had been quickly photocopied from working drafts, and they still listed unintended and embarrassing bits of information, such as a staff member's name and telephone number. Speaker O'Neill noticed one page with the notation, "Source, Rita Seymour, 225-4844." "Is that part of the permanent record?" O'Neill asked. Replied Delbert Latta, "Maybe that's her golf score," later assuring O'Neill the item would be stricken from the legislation.[22]

Reagan's biggest victory was the product of his renewed popularity, the support of twenty-nine conservative Democrats, and a massive lobbying effort conducted by the White House which included telephone calls and personal meetings with the president, the distribution of presidential cuff links, social invitations to the White House, and tickets to performances at the Kennedy Center. Furthermore, the White House faced what appeared to be a lax Democratic leadership. While the administration worked overtime to gather votes, Tip O'Neill led a congressional junket to New Zealand and Australia. Finally, the strategy to employ the little-used reconciliation process allowed the conservatives to bypass the normal budgetary process of addressing federal programs one by one. Nevertheless, the number of Democratic votes following the president declined from 63 on the budget resolution to 29 on the reconciliation measure.

After a 225-member Senate-House conference committee modified the two reconciliation bills, the Congress sent the 1981 Omnibus Reconciliation Bill to the president for his signature. On August 13, Reagan signed both the budget that provided some $130.5 billion in budget reductions spread over three years and the tax bill that reduced revenues by approximately $787 billion over three years. The president received nearly all his requested budget cuts and more tax reductions than called for in the Program for Economic Recovery, in addition to the bulk of his restructured fiscal assistance and block grants programs. At the same time, despite Wall Street's cool reception to the tax cuts, the economy grew at an improved pace in the third quarter. Yet, as progress in the budget battle repeatedly demonstrated, the conservatives' unity was based not only in their loyalty to the president, but also in their faith in his pledge to balance the budget. This march toward a balanced budget encouraged Boll Weevils to desert Democratic ranks and moderate Gypsy Moth Republicans of the Midwest and Northeast to vote against programs aiding their constituencies. Ronald Reagan's handling of the deficit issue enabled him to achieve the largest federal budget reduction in the nation's history. But events quickly proved that many of the president's supporters kept faith in Reagan's budget proposals only as long as the balanced budget goal seemed obtainable. As a result, Reagan's great political success in August was followed by a more discouraging note as the promised balanced budget vanished.

Within days of Reagan's greatest political victory his aides informed him that the deficit would grow larger than projected and further budget reductions of $10 to $20 billion in the FY 1982 budget were required to prevent the deficit from reaching $60 billion. One cause of the expanding deficit was the country's worsening economic conditions. Though the third quarter in 1981 recorded an average annual GNP growth rate of some 2.5 percent, a significant improvement over the second quarter, the fourth quarter dropped nearly to a minus 6 percent. Unemployment actually decreased in August, but interest rates soared, as the prime rate in July stood at 20.5 percent with home loans edging toward 17 percent. As interest rates advanced, congressional and public pressure on the Federal Reserve to reduce these high rates increased. Chairman Paul Volcker maintained, however, that inflation needed to be defeated, reminding his critics that "turning back the inflationary tide, as we can see, is not a simple painless process, free from the risks and strains of its own."[23] The administration approved of the Fed's tight monetary policy, as Secretary Regan told reporters, "you cannot get inflation under control without having high interest rates."[24] Public opinion appeared to agree with Volcker and Regan's goal. A Common Cause poll of 51,000 of its members, for example, found 73 percent agreeing that a "continued high rate of inflation" was the country's most serious problem; only 24 percent thought unemployment was the worst problem.

By September, high interest rates and a deteriorating economy made any prospect of holding the deficit to $45 billion an impossible task, and the White House began looking for new reductions in the FY 1982 budget. On September 24, Reagan appeared on television and called for an additional $13 billion in cuts and $3 billion in revenue increases to control the deficit. Deferred defense expenditures accounted for $2 billion of the total, and the bulk of the remaining cuts came from a 12 percent across-the-board cut in most nondefense outlays. The tax increase consisted of eliminating "abuses and obsolete incentives" for business that totaled $3 billion in 1982, $8 billion in 1983, and $11 billion in 1984.

An overwhelmingly negative response greeted the president's request.

The Stock Market reacted poorly, the Dow Jones 30 Industrials falling 11.13 points, which continued its decline of some 20 points since April. Republican congressional leadership predicted before Reagan's televised address that the cuts would be refused. Senate Majority Leader Baker told reporters, "At best, it would be a very difficult fight."[25] Meanwhile, the administration seemed confused over its deficit projections, as Commerce Secretary Malcolm Baldridge contradicted the president by saying the deficit could grow to at least $50 billion rather than the $43.1 billion White House target. "Whether it's $42.5 billion, $48.5 billion, or $50 billion doesn't make a difference," said Baldridge.[26] In addition, the public seemed reluctant to embrace the new cuts, as the media highlighted the social consequences of budget reductions already in place. Included in these media reports was the famous story about how new Agriculture Department guidelines listed ketchup and pickle relish as vegetables in school lunches, forcing the embarrassed White House to countermand the order. On September 19, 240,000 people rallied in Washington to protest the Reagan budget cuts in social programs. Public confidence in the administration was falling. A Gallup Poll released on October 8 indicated only 44 percent of the respondents approved of the way Reagan handled the economy. Ironically, the *Wall Street Journal* placed much of the blame for the president's declining support on David Stockman's emphasis on reducing the deficit. Said the *Journal's* editorial, "Mr. Stockman wanted more and bigger cuts, which made the public and the Congress even more doubtful about the administration's confidence in its own programs."[27]

Reagan's new budget package received only limited support in Congress, particularly because defense reductions remained relatively small. "There's great consternation that the President's mix won't work," declared Senate Budget Committee chairman Pete Domenici. "There's an evolving consensus that we need big cuts, but made up differently than what the President had proposed."[28] In addition, the liberal and moderate Gypsy Moth Republicans claimed Reagan violated an earlier promise made to them for their support on previously enacted reductions, that any future cuts would be applied primarily in defense outlays. Noted Congressman Carl Pursell, the Moths' cochairman, "We want to see a *quid pro quo* on cuts in defense, water projects, and tobacco."[29] Reagan finally bowed to congressional pressure and agreed to $5 to $6 billion in cuts, and to $7 to $8 billion in new revenues; later, the president lowered his demand to $3.7 billion in reductions that were included in the third continuing budget resolution.

On October 18, Ronald Reagan for the first time admitted the economy was indeed in a recession. By the end of the month the nation's unemployment rate was 8 percent, the highest level in nearly six years. Hard hit by high interest rates stemming from a monetary policy endorsed by the administration, the economy could only force the government to run deficits, not produce a balanced budget, as the administration soon acknowledged. Later in October, Secretary Regan announced that President Reagan's promise to balance the FY 1984 budget was "not probable."[30] Moreover, Reagan himself reported on November 6 that "a balanced budget has never been an end in itself justifying any means. . . . We never agreed to balance the budget on the backs of the taxpayers the way the last Administration tried to do it."[31] The president was further dismayed by the November release of the *Atlantic Monthly* interview with David Stockman, which referred to "Trojan Horse" and "trickle-down" tax cuts, phony OMB budget figures, and Stockman's early projections that indicated the tax cuts would produce huge budget deficits rather than surpluses.[32]

The battle of the FY 1982 budget came to an end with the approval of four continuing budget resolutions and the second budget resolution. Four continuing resolutions were required to keep the government funded, because by the end of the 1981 fiscal year the Congress had yet to pass a single appropriations bill. Thus, in the interim period before Congress approved the FY 1982 appropriations, the government operated on funding levels carried over from the FY 1981 budget. Congress was forced to adopt a fourth continuing resolution as late as March 1982 to keep the bureaucracy functioning. In a test of will, and perhaps to regain political initiative after the damaging Stockman interview was released, the president did veto the second continuing resolution, leaving the country with the spectacle of the government closing down, as furloughed employees left their jobs for a single working day.[33] The Congress, exhausted by the budget fight, also adopted a binding Second Concurrent Resolution calling for $695.5 billion in outlays and a $37.7 billion deficit, despite everyone's realization the deficit figure was just wishful thinking. Ernest Hollings, senior Democrat on the Senate Budget Committee, claimed the resolution was "just a sham . . . dangerous to the Committee and the process itself."[34] Added Leon Panetta of the House Budget Committee, "What this all comes down to is a bid for time. The battleground is not in this session of Congress, but the battleground is clearly next spring."[35]

By the end of 1981 the president's long and difficult task of separating political symbolism from economics was well under way. On December 7, OMB released figures indicating the deficit would climb to $109 billion in FY 1982. Within days of the OMB announcement, however, Chairman Murray Weidenbaum and William Niskanen of the Council of Economic Advisors reported to a gathering at the American Enterprise Institute in Washington, D.C., that the relationship between deficits and interest rates and inflation had been exaggerated. Weidenbaum, Niskanen, and the administration were subsequently strongly rebuked by conservatives for recanting the economic arguments against deficits. In one of President Reagan's most memorable press conferences, held on December 18, he defended his administration's handling of the budget and his aides' comments. Asked about his campaign pledge to balance the budget, Reagan responded:

> Well, because in the first place, I said what was our goal, not a promise. . . . We did not foresee a recession and I don't think anyone else did. . . . Now, I will be the first to tell you that I think it's highly unlikely the budget could be, now in these new circumstances, . . . balanced by 1984—which was our goal, the target, that we were aiming at. . . . But this is not a case of a broken promise; this is a case of circumstances beyond our control, whose foundation has been laid over the last several decades.[36]

Defending Weidenbaum and Niskanen, Reagan remarked:

> What they were trying to explain was—not that a deficit is all right and not that we shouldn't continue a program to eventually get us back, as I've said, within our means. . . . I think what they're pointing out is—you can balance the budget by robbing the people by imposing a punitive tax system on the people. . . . The only proper way to balance the budget is through control of Government spending.[37]

The *Wall Street Journal* quickly echoed Reagan's theme on the need to distinguish symbolism from economics, as it editorialized on the debate between supply-siders who opposed higher taxes to reduce the deficit and Republican "traditionalists" who endorsed higher taxes:

> In truth, the intra-GOP battle over the deficit is a battle less over economic theory than over political symbols. Some agree that lower spending is the true goal, but argue that the deficit is the club for achieving this. . . . In fact, experience seems to suggest that the deficit is a club to get Republicans to levy taxes to cover Democratic spending programs. If the "Reagan revolution" is not about ending this no-win game for both his party and the nation, it is about nothing at all.[38]

Before Reagan could convince the Republican party to accept his position that deficits were more tolerable than tax increases, however, his budget cutting revolution came to an end.

The Reagan Thermidor: FY 1983

The president's proposed FY 1983 budget with its projection for huge deficits stands as the major turning point in Reagan's relationship with congressional Republicans, thereby signaling the demise of Reagan's revolution. Throughout the battle over the FY 1982 budget, Reagan's conservative forces remained unified despite the budgetary process's confusing and complicated nature; despite an ever-changing set of economic assumptions, budget projections, "magic-asterisk" assumed reductions in future spending, questionable outlay estimates; despite cutting funds in programs aiding their constituents; and despite the exhaustion of it all, in order to achieve a balanced budget. Nevertheless, high interest rates endorsed by the administration and a weak economy had already made a farce of the FY 1982 budget's projected $37.7 billion deficit. If the White House was to maintain conservative unity, somehow, some way, the FY 1983 budget proposal needed to make the balanced budget goal again believeable.

Instead, the FY 1983 budget proposal released on February 6, 1982, called for total federal outlays of $757.6 billion, a 4.5 percent increase over FY 1982, and a $91.5 billion deficit. In addition, the budget outlined some $25.9 billion in social program cuts, while military outlays would increase 18 percent, from $187.5 billion to $221.1 billion in FY 1983. The budget's revenue assumptions preserved the 1981 Economic Recovery Tax Act's revenue reductions, as the president rejected advice offered by members of his staff to raise $45 billion in "sin" taxes. During his January 26 State of the Union Address, Reagan reiterated his opposition to increasing taxes: "Higher taxes would not mean lower deficits. If they did, how would we explain that tax revenues more than doubled just since 1976? Yet in the same six-year period we ran the largest series of deficits in our history. . . . So I will not ask you to try to balance the budget on the backs of the American taxpayer."[39]

The response to the president's budget proposal was a tidal wave of shock and anger at the deficit's size and the magnitude of the defense increase. "When hawks like me are talking about cutting military spending," declared the conservative Republican senator William Armstrong, "you know something is in the wind."[40] Added House Minority Leader Robert Michel, "Most of the members felt that they went along with a precipitious increase in defense spending last year, and that you can't have that two years in a row."[41] After fifty-four freshmen House Republicans met to discuss the budget, Gypsy Moth leader Lawrence DeNardis noted: "The education budget is scheduled for a 30 percent reduction, and at the same time the defense budget is going to be increased 15 percent. That's absolutely indefensible."[42] Within days of the budget's distribution, a delegation of congressional Republican leaders, including Senators Howard Baker and Paul Laxalt, advised the president that the budget could not be approved in its current form. Furthermore, there was little likelihood Congress would consent to more domestic budget reductions. Leaving the meeting, Representative Michel said the deficit caused his colleagues the greatest concern, as the budget contained "figures that strike these members as though they had been pole-axed."[43] Though

Laxalt and the others felt Reagan would compromise on the budget, only two days later Reagan sent a letter to congressional Republicans saying, "Where we have honest difficulties, you can count on me to be a willing listener and a sincere partner. But this is not the time for turning back."[44] Moreover, in a speech before the Indiana legislature presented several days before the meeting, Reagan accused his critics of "theatrics," proclaiming they should "put up or shut up. . . . We have a plan already in place. What do they have? Before the budget came out you could hear the sound of knees jerking all over Washington. . . . Despite all the talk, there is a deafening silence on alternatives."[45]

Congressional support for an alternative budget grew stronger, particularly among disillusioned Senate Republican leaders, including Robert Dole, Finance Committee chairman, and Pete Domenici, Budget Committee chairman. Both Dole and Domenici began to design alternatives to the White House proposal, with each new version calling for major reductions in the president's defense plan, and steady-state social spending. While asking Senate Democrats to join him in making a "midcourse correction," Dole noted, "There seems to be a consensus growing among Republicans that we will have to do something about cutting on the defense side."[46] Dole's Republican colleague Dan Quayle agreed. "We have a $100 billion increase for defense over three years as we're cutting social programs," said Quayle. "That's totally unacceptable."[47] Another Republican senator, Malcolm Wallop, concurred adding that he supported defense reductions while preserving social programs at their current levels since the Reagan budget did "not follow a path toward balance in the forseeable future."[48] Finally, on February 23, a Republican delegation led by Howard Baker and Robert Michel informed Reagan that his budget was "dead" and that he could expect significant cuts in his proposed defense increase.

Reagan also drew fire from the nation's business community for his tax cuts, defense buildup, and the growing deficit. The Business Roundtable called the deficits unacceptable and requested Congress to reduce defense spending. The Roundtable also supported deferring the tax cut and changing the key leasing components in the tax bill. Within a week, the National Association of Manufacturers also urged defense and Social Security reductions. In addition, Arthur Levitt, Jr., chairman of the American Stock Exchange, said the tax cuts were ill-timed and that only 41 percent of 350 Wall Street executives polled approved of Reagan's handling of the economy, as compared to 67 percent in 1981.[49] The source of Wall Street's anxiety was the fear that large deficits would create high interest rates. President Reagan supported Chairman Volcker's tight monetary policy that produced the high interest rates responsible for devastating the economy. On February 18, Volcker met with the president, and Reagan gave what was described as an "unqualified endorsement" of the

Fed's policies. Later, in Reagan's eighth televised press conference he stated, "We also support the Federal Reserve's 1982 monetary growth targets, which are fully consistent with the Administration's economic projections for the coming year."[50] Within a few weeks, David Stockman noted that high deficits, high interest rates, unemployment, and bankruptcies were "all part of the cure, not the problem."[51] Incidentally, though Paul Volcker could always be counted on to attack the government's deficits, he did say in February the deficits might actually aid the economy: "A large deficit in the midst of the recession should be manageable; it indeed provides some support for the economy in a time of stress."[52]

Ronald Reagan argued tenaciously against his critics. To the country's business leaders, Reagan replied, "What we need now is not last-minute haggling or displays of blatant self interest. We need the support that only America's businessmen can give us."[53] In a speech before the Conservative Political Action Committee, Reagan claimed his critics were guilty of "sob sister attempts to portray our desire to get Government spending under control as a hard-hearted attack on the poor people of America. . . . Only here in this city of Oz would a budget this big and this generous be characterized as a miserly attack on the poor."[54] Though Reagan's defiant speeches focused on the Democrats, he no doubt also had several Republicans in mind. In another speech, Reagan called his own party's "so-called alternatives" designed in the Senate "political documents designed for saving certain legislators' political hides rather than saving the economy."[55] Elsewhere, Reagan proclaimed: "No one sympathizes more with the idea of a balanced budget than I do. . . . The deficits we propose are much larger than I would like, *but they're a necessary evil in the real world today*. [emphasis added]."[56] Whether Reagan considered his deficits "necessary evil" ones or not, the Senate served formal notice on the president that his budget was indeed dead. On March 30 the Budget Committee voted 16 to 1 to reject OMB's economic forecasts and adopted the Congressional Budget Office's more pessimistic projections, signaling the committee's intent to draft its own budget.

The president was backed into a corner and in order to retain some influence over the budget Reagan authorized Donald Regan, David Stockman, and White House Chief of Staff James Baker to meet with Senate Republicans to design a new budget to reduce the deficit. Toward the end of March the White House budget team had come close to agreeing with the Senate's leadership over a revised budget package. The plan called for $135 billion in tax increases spread over three years, $35 billion in defense reductions also divided over three years, and restraint in Social Security spending. After finding some basis for compromise with the Senate, the administration next attempted to reach an accord with the Democratic leadership in the House, which included James Jones, Budget

Committee chair; Dan Rostenkowski, Ways and Means chair; and Richard Bolling, chairman of the Rules Committee. Eventually the full White House-Senate-House negotiation team was labeled the "Gang of Seventeen." Though Stockman, Baker, and Regan agreed with the Democrats that revenue enhancement was necessary to stem the deficit—then estimated to soar to $180 billion in FY 1983—the type of taxes, their size, and what trade-off the Democrats would make to induce the president into accepting the taxes remained points of contention. The House leadership, for example, believed consensus existed within the Congress for repealing the third year of the personal income tax cut. Furthermore, while the Republicans were willing to increase revenues by $25 billion in 1983, Rostenkowski wanted $35 billion.

Though Reagan pledged "to go the extra mile" to achieve an agreement with the Democrats, by the end of April no agreement was in sight. In a desperate attempt to resolve their differences, Speaker Tip O'Neill met with President Reagan on April 28 to work out the trade-offs that had been under discussion for the past four weeks. O'Neill and Reagan started out with similar deficit reduction targets. If no reductions in the deficit were to take place, it would reach $182 billion in FY 1983. To bring the deficit to the $105 to $110 billion range in FY 1983, at least $72 to $77 billion in tax increases and spending reductions were needed. Reagan offered to split the difference in spending cuts and tax increases, which reduced defense spending by $28 billion over three years. In exchange, Reagan asked for a three-month delay in the cost of living adjustment for Social Security and similar benefit programs. "That, for all practical purposes," Richard Bolling later reported, "was not a deal at all."[57] The Democrats were not about to reduce Social Security benefits after the Senate had unamiously defeated a proposal made by the president in 1981 to reduce benefits. Moreover, the Democrats argued that they held the political high ground since their budget plan lowered the deficit to $30 billion in FY 1985 while the president's deficit stood at $38 billion.[58] The conference failed, the Gang of Seventeen disbanded, and with the deadline for the first budget resolution set for May 15, the Congress seemed nowhere near ready to meet their budgetary responsibilities.

In the Senate, however, Budget Committee chairman Pete Domenici quickly produced yet another budget, this one sharply at odds with the administration's firm position on delaying the third-year personal income tax cut. Domenici's FY 1983 budget called for $30 billion in tax increases, a $6 billion cut in domestic discretionary spending, $7 billion in savings from frozen federal salaries, a $5 billion cut in defense outlays, and a cost of living adjustment in entitlement programs, including Social Security, that added another $15 billion in savings. Three-year savings totaled to $228 billion in reduced outlays and $125 billion in tax increases. The White House objected strenuously to changes in the tax cut and sought more permanent entitlement reductions. On May 5 the Budget Committee voted to accept a modified version of Domenici's plan as its recommended first budget resolution. To win the president's support, the committee kept the personal income tax in place, while providing for $95 billion in new revenues collected over three years. Moreover, Domenici withdrew his suggestion for a freeze on entitlement cost of living adjustments in return for an unspecified three-year cut in Social Security. In addition, the committee voted 20 to 0 to reject the FY 1983 Reagan budget proposal.

After the committee reported its resolution to the full Senate, however, the fifty-four member Republican Caucus quickly rejected the Social Security cut and increased domestic discretionary spending by $3 billion to appease the moderate Gypsy Moths. With the economy deep in recession during an election year, the jittery Republicans had no intention of adding Social Security cuts to their political burdens. Finally, their election fears calmed, the Senate voted 49 to 43 to pass its version of the first budget resolution. The resolution included $784 billion in outlays, a $115.8 billion deficit, and $21.2 billion in new, unspecified taxes for the fiscal year. The personal income tax cut's third year remained intact.

Meanwhile, no less than nine alternative budget resolutions were under review in the House of Representatives. Between May 24 and May 27, the House rejected seven different budgets and most of sixty-eight other budget amendments. The slaughter began on May 24, when three liberal budgets suffered defeat. The first to fall was George Miller's "pay-as-you-go" plan, which required equal spending cuts and new taxes to meet all outlays made above the FY 1982 level. Also rejected was David Obey's budget calling for a three-year $233 billion tax increase, versus the House Budget Committee's recommended $147 billion increase and the $95 billion addition provided for in the Senate resolution. A third liberal budget offered by the Black Caucus, which projected a balanced FY 1986 budget by raising taxes, cutting defense, and increasing social spending, was also defeated. On Wednesday, May 26, the House rejected a fourth proposal made by John Rousselot and his conservative coalition. The conservative budget provided for a balanced FY 1983 budget cutting domestic social spending $113.9 billion in the fiscal year. Three budgets remained, including one designed by Minority Leader Michel and supported by the president, the Budget Committee's, and a third authorized by a "moderate bipartisan" coalition.[59] On Thursday, the frustrated and divided House surprisingly rejected all three budgets. Michel's defeated budget represented President Reagan's first budgetary defeat in the House.

Republican and Democratic House leaders immediately went to work writing new budget proposals in early June. There would be only two budget packages considered this time, one each offered by the two parties, both versions attempting to keep the deficit as close as possible to the $100 billion mark for FY 1983. With a balanced FY 1984 budget an impossible goal, the $100 billion deficit for FY 1983 temporarily assumed the status of responsible fiscal policy. Maliciously, the Democratic leadership introduced a third budget, the newly revised White House budget with its $132 billion deficit to embarrass Reagan and the Republicans. The House Republicans, who avoided the president's budget, instead endorsed their own proposal with its lower deficit, and subsequently the Reagan budget never came to a vote. On June 10 the House finally adopted its first budget resolution by accepting the Republican budget. The administration obtained another important victory on a 219 to 206 vote, as 46 Democrats supported the Republican resolution containing a fanciful $99.3 billion deficit.[60]

Later, on June 22 and 23, the House and Senate voted to accept the conference committee's recommended budget resolution with its $103.9 billion deficit. The resolution reduced the president's defense proposal by $7.6 billion, thereby allowing for a 7 percent increase over FY 1982 instead of Reagan's proposed 18 percent increase. In addition, the resolution provided for a three-year $98.3 billion revenue increase, with $20.9 billion in new taxes taking effect in FY 1983. The resolution's budgetary ceilings were made binding, and thus there would be no need for a second resolution. Before the Congress even voted to adopt the First Concurrent Budget Resolution, however, the Congressional Budget Office found it contained higher spending and larger deficits than projected. Rather than $769.8 billion in outlays, CBO claimed the real figure stood at $775.5 billion, with a $116.4 billion deficit. The new resolution, moreover, included plans to reduce the FY 1983 deficit by $76.8 billion from its latest estimated $180.7 billion level, as part of a three-year $378.5 billion deficit reduction plan. Nevertheless, the resolution assumed budgetary savings Congress had no power to control, including $14.5 billion in lower interest payments and $13 billion in "management savings." Thus, much of the deficit reduction package, like many to come in the next two years, consisted of "soft" numbers lying outside the span of congressional authority. The reconciliation instructions actually incorporated into the resolution specified just $6.7 billion in FY 1983 outlay savings, compared to the Reagan February request for $25.9 billion in cuts. The final reconciliation legislation, the 1982 Omnibus Reconciliation Act and the 1982 Tax Equity and Fiscal Responsibility Act passed by Congress in mid-August, provided for $30.8 billion in budgetary savings to be achieved over three years. Together, the two measures were expected to reduce the FY 1983–85 deficits by $129.1 billion.

Finally, because Congress delayed approving the reconciliation legislation until August, only one of thirteen appropriations bills had made its way through Congress by October 1, the start of the new fiscal year. So on the very first day of FY 1983 the Congress at last adopted a continuing budget resolution to fund the government. When that resolution expired on December 17, only two more bills had become law, forcing Congress to pass a second continuing resolution that extended funding through the rest of FY 1983. Congress approved the legislation on December 20 and the president signed the measure on December 21, several days after the first continuing resolution expired, leaving most government agencies technically broke.

Two other budget-related events highlighted President Reagan's mixed success in 1982. To meet the expected call for new taxes in the first budget resolution, Senator Robert Dole had his Finance Committee hard at work designing a tax bill that would eventually raise nearly $244 billion in revenues divided over six years. On July 23 the full Senate approved Dole's recommended taxes, thereby recovering approximately a third of the estimated $787 billion in revenues lost in the 1981 Economic Recovery Tax Act.[61] Noted Dole after the Senate voted 50 to 47 to pass the legislation, "I talked to the President and he's very pleased with the bill."[62] Dole was quickly subjected to intense criticism from the supply-side faction in the Republican party and from those conservatives who simply disliked taxes, including Representative Jack Kemp, and the *Wall Street Journal*.[63] Responding to Kemp's censure, Dole commented that "maybe we went too far last year with some of Mr. Kemp's ideas. I never really understood all that supply-side business."[64] "We hear this sort of argument," Kemp rejoined: "To revive the economy, we have to get interest rates down. To lower interest rates, we have to reduce the deficit. To reduce the deficit we have to raise taxes. . . . The tax increase will only boost the deficit. It's a tax on the type of savings and investment necessary to get the country moving again."[65] A *Wall Street Journal* editorial simply pointed out the tax increase was "an exercise in economic idiocy. Every school child knows you don't raise taxes in recession unless you want to make it worse."[66] Although the tax bill passed in the Senate, Kemp vowed to fight the president and the measure tooth and nail in the House.

The tax bill did in fact pass in the Senate with President Reagan's blessing. Reagan endorsed the new taxes, though only after the Senate's leadership threatened to eliminate the third year of the personal income tax reduction and stall Senate action on the first budget resolution. The White House staff, principally David Stockman and James Baker, also convinced Reagan the tax bill consisted of "reforms" and closed loopholes rather than established new taxes. Furthermore, the 1981 Economic Recovery Tax Act's final version contained significantly larger tax reductions than the administration originally requested, thereby leaving Reagan some ideological maneuvering room to raise taxes when defending against the charge that he had revoked his conservative position on taxation.

Although the Senate approved the tax bill, the House of Representatives, the constitutionally authorized body responsible for originating revenue measures, refused to propose any tax increase. To avoid the implication that they supported an election year tax bill, the House Democratic leadership instead formed a delegation to meet with the Senate's representatives in a conference committee to consider the Senate's tax legislation. By mid-August the committee-approved bill was due for a vote in the House, where Jack Kemp and some 100 Republicans pledged to defeat the measure. The Democrats, in turn, also refused to support new taxes unless the president personally worked for the tax bill's success. "I want him to use that smiley countenance, that sweet-talking voice of his," Speaker O'Neill declared, "and be as hard-knuckled with his Republicans as he has been along the line."[67] Reagan let loose the heavy artillery on his conservative opposition, as the White House and House Republican leaders buttonholed their members to support the bill. On August 13 the president appeared on television, claiming "this bill is 80 percent tax reform, not tax increases," as he asked the public to encourage Congress to pass the tax measure.[68] Though 123 Democrats voted with 103 Republicans to approve the tax bill, the House leadership attempted to make the legislation appear Republican in design. The media immediately speculated that Reagan was becoming a pragmatic centrist who risked the wrath of his hard-core conservative followers, and who had split the Republican party with the tax bill. Gleefully observing the Republican division, Democratic Congressman Henry Reuss editorialized in the *New York Times*: "Reaganomics—a combination of Representative Jack Kemp's supply-side tax reductions to stimulate growth, and a super-tight monetarist Federal Reserve policy to fight inflation—is no more. Supply-side economics has come un-Kempt. In the titanic struggle between The Great Communicator and The Great Supply-Sider, President Reagan has prevailed, and taxes will be raised."[69] Reagan soon signed into law the 1982 Tax Equity and Fiscal Responsibility Act.

In the second budget issue, as the 1982 fiscal year came to an end, Congress acted to pass a supplemental appropriations bill to fund selected FY 1982 programs through the rest of the year. Twice, in June and July, Congress sent supplementals to Reagan for his approval, only to have the president veto them, as Reagan declared Congress was engaging in its "old spendthrift habits." After twice failing to get the supplemental approved, Congress gave the president nearly everything he requested in the bill, including $5 billion for military pay raises and $350 million for his recently proposed economic assistance package, the Caribbean Basin Initiative. Furthermore, the $14.1 billion supplemental was smaller by some $1.5 billion than the maximum level previously agreed to by the administration. Congress, however, had also cut some $2 billion in defense spending and added $500 million to domestic programs. Reagan announced the supplemental was a "budget-buster," and promptly vetoed the bill.

Though David Stockman, who recommended the veto, and others in the White House were confident the president's action would be upheld, bipartisan activity began immediately to override the veto. With the economy suffering from a 9.8 percent unemployment rate during an election year, many Republicans anxiously sought to distance themselves from the administration and prove they were not "Reagan's Robots," as the Democrats charged. The House voted 301 to 117 on September 9 to override the veto, with 81 Republicans joining the Democrats. The next day the Senate surprisingly banded together with the House to override, as 21 Republicans voted against the president in a 60 to 30 vote. Among the Republican defectors were conservatives James Abdnor and Larry Pressler from South Dakota, and Charles Grassley and Roger Jepsen from Iowa. Reacting to his defeat, Reagan told reporters, "I'm not angry, I'm just terribly, terribly hurt."[70] Reagan had experienced his worst budgetary defeat, and with the 1982 elections just two months away his conservative coalition appeared hopelessly divided.

The Democratic Resurgence: FY 1984

Ronald Reagan's political difficulties continued into the new year, 1983. The November 1982 election allowed the Democratic leadership to expand its control over the House of Representatives, as twenty-six new Democrats—an estimated net loss of twenty-four conservative votes— were sent to Congress. In Illinois the House minority leader, Republican Robert Michel, won reelection by only 4 percent and in his victory speech he tearfully promised his district that he had "some things to tell in Washington about adjusting . . . the direction in which we've been going."[71] The Republicans maintained control over the Senate, but just barely as four Republicans won reelection by the slimmest of margins. The Democrats also won seven governorships and took command over thirty-four state legislatures. Considering the recession's severe effect on the country the Republicans nevertheless did remarkably well, but the election destroyed the president's conservative working majority in the House, leaving the prospect for deeper reductions in social and domestic federal spending highly unlikely.

With the newly released unemployment figures for December indicating 10.8 percent of the labor force was unemployed, added to the election results, even conservative commentators pronounced Reaganomics dead. "The election of 1980," wrote Irving Kristol,

> for the first time provided signs that a new Republican Party might be emerging. Ronald Reagan was anything but a typical Republican candidate, and never earned the favor of the Republican establishment. . . . There are, it turns out—perhaps there always have been—two Ronald Reagans. The presidential Ronald Reagan is quite different from the campaigning Ronald Reagan. . . . So the administration bumbles along in foreign policy, in social policy, in economic policy, resembling more and more the caricature of Republicans in liberal cartoons.[72]

"I think it's important that Congress modify or in some cases abandon Reaganomics in order to save Reaganology," added Kevin Phillips. "[Walter] Heller suggests that Reaganomics has been a flop, and I agree: You cannot run—you cannot rebuild—a huge and complex economy like ours with naive tax cuts and antigovernment rhetoric. . . . 'Reaganology' probably sums up why this commentator, for one, voted for Ronald Reagan back in 1980. It certainly wasn't because I believed in his Calvin Coolidge-style economic programs—or that I ever believed they would work."[73] Referring to unnamed White House staff who told reporters that Reagan was inflexible, rigid, and simple-minded on economic as well as all policy matters, William Safire sadly observed: "The breaking of the President is merrily under way. Mr. Reagan's split staff buttonholes reporters to portray him as unwilling to listen to reason, and what Mr. Eisenhower called 'sensation-seeking columnists' berate him for not abandoning the principles on which he was elected. . . . He should stop pretending the press is making up its own leaks and start to decide which of the two White House staffs represents him."[74]

Finally, David Broder, national correspondent for the *Washington Post*, declared that Reaganomics had been only a brief and passing phase in American politics: "What we are witnessing this January is not the midpoint in the Reagan presidency, but its phase-out. 'Reaganism,' it is becoming increasingly clear, was a one-year phenomenon, lasting from his nomination in the summer of 1980 to the passage of his budget and tax bills in summer, 1981. What has been occurring ever since is an accelerating retreat from Reaganism, a process in which he is more spectator than leader."[75] Though Reaganomics, Reaganology, and Reaganism were pronounced dead, Ronald Reagan's personal political fortunes were silently rising.

Slowly, the economy recovered from the recession. From peak to trough the recession lasted sixteen months, tied for the second-longest recession since the Great Depression.[76] The low point was November 1982, and finally in February 1983 the recovery took hold. Spurred by lower interest rates, unemployment dropped to less than 10 percent for the first time since September, while housing starts rose 35.9 percent. With inflation growing at less than 4 percent on an annual basis the Federal Reserve relaxed its grip on the money supply, and the prime rate fell to 11 percent in January, the lowest rate since August 1980, and to 10.5 percent in February. As the recovery's momentum worked in Reagan's favor, the president had the opportunity to regain his influence over the budget, but an unrealistic FY 1984 budget proposal, reinvigorated Democratic leadership in the House, and an endless stream of projected deficits, doomed much of the administration's budget plan.

Public pressure on the White House to cut defense spending and to reduce the deficit continued to build in early 1983. In January, Paul Laxalt, Reagan's closest friend and ally in the Senate, warned the president to lower his defense spending in the coming budget proposal or face overwhelming opposition in Congress. "Those numbers are a little terrifying," Laxalt told reporters after his meeting with Reagan.[77] Business leaders continued to warn Reagan the deficits were too large and defense spending needed trimming. Arthur Levitt, Jr., chairman of the American Business Conference and the American Stock Exchange, declared "the specter of expanding deficits of gargantuan proportions threatens to cut off the recovery."[78] Leaders of two other business groups, the National Association of Manufacturers (NAM) and the National Federation of Independent Business, agreed with Levitt's concerns. The NAM urged the president to make budget reductions of at least $18 to $23 billion in federal spending, with half coming from the defense side of the budget.[79] Meanwhile, a *New York Times*/CBS News poll found 63 percent of respondents favoring a reduction in the defense buildup to cut the deficit, 62 percent willing to eliminate the third year of the tax cut scheduled to take effect in July, 42 percent supporting reduced Social Security cost of living adjustments, with only 29 percent endorsing budget cuts in programs for the poor.[80]

The pressure appeared to have some effect on the administration. Defense Secretary Caspar Weinberger finally agreed during the White House budget negotiations to reduce the Defense Department's FY 1984 proposal by $8 billion. "In response to economic problems we have agreed before, as we agree now," said Weinberger, "to modifications in our original program to rearm America."[81] In addition, rumors abounded that Reagan had accepted some form of new taxation to cut the deficit. Reagan indeed acknowledged the need for imposing a "trigger" tax that would take effect when the deficit exceeded some yet unspecified number in the budget's outyears, FY 1986–88. The president's decision to accept the trigger tax came about largely through the urging of Secretary of State George Shultz, who informed Reagan the deficits could extend the recession and prevent economic recovery. During November and

December 1982, the White House economic and budget team—consisting principally of David Stockman, James Baker, Donald Regan, Edwin Meese, and the new chairman of the Council of Economic Advisors Martin Feldstein—had arrived at the conclusion that new taxes were required to reduce the growing deficit. After gaining Weinberger's reluctant agreement to reduce his defense proposal, the group convinced Shultz to act as point man with the president to press the argument for new taxes and defense cuts. On January 3 the group presented Reagan with their new economic projections, indicating his options and their economic consequences. Within five minutes of examining the deficit estimate, Reagan told his advisers, "I can't go to the country with these deficits," and he soon agreed to the group's idea for a trigger tax and the defense cuts.[82]

On January 25, 1983, the president outlined his new budget package in his State of the Union Address. To restrict the deficit's growth, Reagan proposed a four point program. First, most domestic spending would be frozen in constant dollars. Second, Reagan indicated he would propose to Congress "specific measures" to control entitlement programs. "They are," Reagan said, "the largest, single cause of the built-in or 'structural' deficit problem."[83] Third, Reagan announced the administration would seek $55 billion in defense outlay savings, divided over a five-year period.[84] Last, the president proposed that a trigger tax no larger than 1 percent of the GNP begin in FY 1986. "It would last no more than three years," stated Reagan, "and would start only if the Congress has first approved our spending freeze and budget control program."[85] Reagan added that the trigger tax would have no effect on the third year of the tax cut or tax indexing. Despite Reagan's willingness to implement the trigger tax, he refused to blame either the tax cuts or the defense increase for the deficit: "Let us be clear about where the deficit problem comes from. Contrary to the drumbeat we have been hearing for the last few months, the deficits we face are not rooted in defense spending. . . . Nor is the deficit, as some would have it, rooted in tax cuts. . . . The fact is, our deficits come from the uncontrolled growth of the budget for domestic spending."[86]

The budget itself called for $848.5 billion in outlays, and a $188.8 billion deficit. Total outlays would increase $43.5 billion above FY 1983, including $30 billion for defense. Even after Weinberger's $8 billion cut the defense budget would grow by 14 percent. Meanwhile, $19 billion in savings would be derived from frozen domestic programs, with an additional $19 billion in savings achieved from "structural reforms" in such social programs as veterans' benefits and health care. With all the cuts and contingency tax adopted, the projected out-year deficits stood at $195 billion in FY 1985 and $148 billion in FY 1986, trailing down to $117 billion in FY 1988. Without the reductions and the tax, the administration's economic forecast indicated the deficit could grow to $253 billion in FY 1985, $271 billion in FY 1986, and $300 billion in FY 1988. The Reagan FY 1984 budget proposal is outlined in Table 21.

The public debate over the deficit's economic consequences continued. In January, a group of 500 business, government, and academic leaders, led by 6 former cabinet secretaries including 5 treasury secretaries, signed a letter calling for significant reductions in the deficit. Commonly called the Peterson letter, after Nixon's commerce secretary Peter Peterson, the document stated, "Our principal concern is not today's deficit, which is obviously in part a result of today's recession. The huge deficits in prospect for the mid and late 1980s are different. They are largely the result of embedded Federal policies, not abnormal economic conditions, and they are a primary cause of today's continuing economic distress."[87] The group sought to reduce the FY 1985 deficit to $75 billion, by cutting $25 billion from defense, $60 billion in other spending, and by increasing taxes $60 billion.

Even within the group that signed the "Bipartisan Budget Appeal," however, divisions occurred over what exactly the deficits would do to the economy, and what measures should be taken to reduce the deficit's size. Said Alfred Kahn, who had signed the letter: "Only a few dupes like me let themselves be coopted into supporting Peterson's attempt to substitute Herbert Hooverism for Reaganomics; most liberal economists saw the trap in time to avoid it. . . . The economy badly needs a stimulus these days; whether the deficit, we ought to let the tax cut go into effect, although I'd like to see some limit on the benefits to the wealthy."[88]

Another liberal economist, Lester Thurow, agreed with Kahn and added, "I regret that my name was associated with an advertisement that has come to be seen as a simple plea for a balanced budget as a cure for our economic problems—even if a close reading of that advertisement reveals a more sophisticated view."[89] Despite the divisions that existed over the matter of deficit spending even among those who signed the "Bipartisan Appeal," a consensus was forming among economists that although deficits might harm the economy in some budgetary out-year, during the recession they were of greater benefit than harm.

While economists continued to assess the size and influence of the deficits on the economy, the House of Representatives produced the first legislative response to Reagan's budget. With the 1982 elections restoring to the House leadership much of the power it had lost in 1980, the Democrats successfully adopted their first budget resolution since Ronald Reagan became president. First, the House Budget Committee approved a resolution that raised defense spending only 4 percent in real terms, versus Reagan's 10 percent, while increasing taxes by $30 billion from unspecified sources. The resolution, adopted by the committee on March 14, called for total spending of $864 billion compared to the

Table 21. FY 1984 Reagan budget proposal (in billions of dollars)

Program	FY 1981 actual	Carter FY 1982 proposal	Reagan FY 1982 proposal	FY 1982 actual	Reagan FY 1983 proposal	FY 1983 estimated*	Reagan FY 1984 proposal
Defense	159.8	184.4	188.8	187.4	221.1	214.8	245.3
International affairs	11.1	12.2	11.2	10.0	12.0	11.9	13.2
Science, space	6.4	7.6	6.9	7.1	7.6	7.8	8.2
Energy	10.3	12.0	8.7	4.7	4.2	4.5	3.3
Natural resources	13.5	14.0	11.9	12.9	9.9	12.1	9.8
Agriculture	5.6	4.8	4.4	14.9	4.5	21.1	12.1
Commerce, housing	3.9	8.1	3.1	3.9	1.6	1.9	0.4
Transportation	23.4	21.6	19.9	20.6	19.6	21.9	25.1
Community develop.	9.4	9.1	8.1	7.2	7.3	7.4	7.0
Education, training	31.4	34.5	25.8	26.3	21.6	26.7	25.3
Health	66.0	74.6	73.4	74.0	78.1	82.4	90.6
Income security	225.1	255.0	241.4	248.3	261.7	282.5	282.4
Veterans' benefits	23.0	24.5	23.6	24.0	24.4	24.4	25.7
Justice	4.7	4.9	4.4	4.7	4.6	5.3	5.5
General gov't.	4.6	5.2	5.0	4.7	5.0	5.3	5.5
Fiscal assistance	6.9	6.9	6.4	6.4	6.7	6.4	7.0
Interest	82.5	89.9	82.5	84.5	112.5	88.9	103.2
Allowances	—	1.9	1.8	—	—	—	—
Contingencies	—	—	—	—	-2.0	—	—
Offsetting receipts	-30.3	-31.9	-32.0	-13.2	-43.5	-20.4	-22.0
Total outlays	657.2	739.3	695.3	728.4	757.6	805.2	848.5
Revenues	599.3	711.8	650.3	617.8	666.1	597.5	659.7
Deficit	-57.9	-27.5	-45.0	-110.6	-91.5	-207.7	-188.8

Source: *San Francisco Examiner*, January 31, 1983.
*January 1983 estimate.

administration's $848 billion, and it included a deficit of $174 billion. The president quickly counterattacked, declaring in some of his most aggressive language:

> Clearly, this partisan Democrat budget is a dagger aimed straight at the heart of America's [defense] rebuilding program. . . . Nor would this tremendous tax increase reduce the deficit. To reduce the deficit, we don't want or need higher taxes. We need economic growth. . . . But the Democratic budget would cripple our defense budget authority request. . . . Nothing could bring greater joy to the Kremlin than seeing the United States abandon its defense rebuilding program after barely one year.[90]

Despite the president's comments, the House approved the resolution by a vote of 229 to 196 on March 23. Though 36 Democrats voted with the Republicans, 4 Republicans voted with the Democrats. The Republicans offered neither their own alternative resolution nor Reagan's budget plan. "The President's budget has been rejected," observed happy Democrat Leon Panetta. "It wasn't presented as an alternative here. It wasn't presented as an alternative in committee."[91]

The president's conservative coalition in the House seemed impotent to press the administration's budget plans—only twenty-two full-fledged Boll Weevils voted against the Democratic resolution—so if Ronald Reagan was to experience a significant budget victory it would have to be in the Senate. In the Senate too, however, the White House budget came under fire. In February hearings before the Appropriations Committee, for example, David Stockman was berated by conservative North Dakota Senator Mark Andrews on the administration's intention to cut more funds from child nutrition and food stamps. "Of all the dumb ways to save money," Andrews remarked, "not feeding kids is the dumbest. . . . Damn it, we've been in office two years! It's time we start cleaning up those programs and not point our finger. Don't sit there and say the need isn't there. The need is there." Andrews noted that he had seen people "scrounging around in dumpsters" searching for food.[92] Aside from a general unwillingness on the part of many Republicans to make further deep cuts in domestic spending, the administration was confronted by the Budget Committee's chair Pete Domenici, who insisted on increasing defense spending in real terms by no more than 5 percent for five years.

Domenici's persistence in reducing the Reagan defense increase by half forced the White House to concede the issue. Reported White House spokesman Larry Speakes, "I think the president is going to push for adequate spending levels and will work with the committee to come out as close to his figures as he can."[93] On April 7 the Budget Committee voted to approve a resolution calling for the 5 percent increase, setting defense outlays at $240 billion, compared to $235.4 billion in the House resolution, and the $245.3 billion requested in the Reagan budget. More significantly, the Senate resolution reduced defense budget authority from Reagan's $280.5 billion to $267 billion. Furthermore, on April 13 the committee completed a first draft of the full resolution that included total spending levels $8 billion higher than the administration's.

Despite the apparent agreement within the committee, during the following five weeks the issue of taxation produced a state of budgetary confusion rivaling the chaos that accompanied the adoption of the 1982 House resolution. While the committee's resolution was being drafted, its Democratic members persistently demanded that Domenici and the Republicans raise taxes to reduce the deficit. Domenici refused to accept the Democrats' tax proposals, claiming that "our job is to reduce this deficit as much as we can on the expenditure side."[94] Nevertheless, on April 21 the Budget Committee approved a final budget plan that included $30 billion in new taxes for FY 1984, leading to a $51.9 billion increase in FY 1988, plus total spending of $848.8 billion, and a deficit of $162.1 billion in FY 1988. The Republicans on the committee were so divided over whether to raise taxes, and if so by how much, that in order to report any resolution to the Senate, Domenici and three other Republicans voted with the Democrats to approve the tax increases. Domenici called the vote a tactical necessity, saying, "There was little chance of getting a solid Republican budget resolution. I will work with the White House and with Republican leaders in the Senate to try to put together a package more to the liking of the president."[95]

Following the Easter recess, the Senate began debate over the budget resolution, with taxation serving as the primary source of dissention. Some Republicans, like William Armstrong, Orrin Hatch, and Steven Symms, objected to any new taxes, contending that new revenues would only stimulate new spending. Other Republicans, including Mark Andrews, argued new revenues were needed to reduce the deficit, and five Republicans led by Mark Hatfield and John Chafee had sent a letter to Reagan calling for the repeal of the third year of the 1981 tax cut. A third group of Republican senators following the suggestions of Pete Domenici favored minor tax increases in FY 1984 to be joined by larger tax levies when the economy improved. The Democrats, meanwhile, continued to push for the $30 billion in new taxes. Declared Lawton Chiles, senior Democrat on the Budget Committee, "The central issue before the Senate in this budget debate is interest rates . . . we've got to cut Federal deficits."[96] The Democratic leadership remained insistent that deficits created high interest rates and otherwise weakened the economy; they were willing to raise taxes despite the fact that economic recovery was in an embryonic stage.

After several days of debate without a consensus forming around any specific plan, the Senate considered six separate budget resolutions on May 11. The first resolution was offered by Howard Baker and Pete

Domenici. Their proposal called for revenue increases of $2.6 billion in FY 1984 and $5.7 billion in FY 1985. In addition, defense outlays were increased by 7.5 percent in real terms while the deficit was estimated to be $192.4 billion. A second budget, supported by a group of moderate Republicans organized by the "Gang of Five," raised taxes by $14 billion by placing a $300 cap on the third year of the tax cut and by limiting the cut to individuals earning $50,000 or less. The Gang of Five, consisting of Senators John Chafee, Mark Hatfield, Lowell Weicker, Robert Stafford, and Charles Mathias, also endorsed a 6 percent real gain in defense spending. The majority of Democrats supported a third budget, the original Senate Budget Committee resolution. On May 11 the Senate defeated the Republican leadership budget 52 to 48, and then the moderate Republican budget 53 to 46. Besides these two Republican budgets, the Senate also rejected four other budgets. These included one designed by Orrin Hatch which kept the tax cut intact, raised defense spending, and cut domestic spending; Ernest Holling's proposal for a freeze on all domestic spending while increasing defense by 3 percent; a conservative Democrat budget offered by J. Bennett Johnston which held defense to 5 percent, domestic spending to 2 percent, and increased taxes after 1985; and a fourth budget proposed by Republican Charles Grassley which froze both defense and domestic spending, while keeping the tax cuts intact. Then, without considering the Budget Committee's resolution, the Senate by voice vote ordered the committee to design a new resolution.

In the days following the defeat of the six budgets, the Budget Committee labored over a new resolution, while the political rhetoric offered by all parties became increasingly tense. The Democrats continued to defend tax increases by pointing to the growing deficit. "We Democrats have learned a little by our past errors," said Lawton Chiles. "We used to think we could spend our way to prosperity."[97] Though the Democratic resolution raised taxes, it still included more domestic spending than contained in the original Reagan budget. The president, meanwhile, attacked both Democrats and Republicans alike for threatening to increase taxes and domestic spending: "They've got a credit card that's run out of credit and are asking the American people to raise the limit. We must answer with one word, an overwhelming, unequivocal 'no.' . . . When you clear away the rhetoric, the issue is quite simple: Deficits are the symptom. The disease is uncontrolled spending and the cause is an addiction to Big Government."[98] Reagan compared the Congress to "deficit doctors" who were "getting ready to operate on your wallet."[99] Reagan's comments appeared to antagonize the Democrats rather than to unite them behind the president. "I'm not in a very bipartisan mood," responded Democratic Senator James Sasser after Reagan had made his statement. "I think we're going to need some silence at least from the administration."[100]

On May 18 the Senate Budget Committee sent to the full Senate yet another resolution, this version advocating an $8 billion tax hike, with the defense increase set at 7.1 percent. A product of the Democratic minority and a handful of Republicans, Majority Leader Baker immediately refused to support any resolution not approved by the majority of Republicans serving on the committee. Consequently, the resolution failed by a 56 to 43 vote. On the same day the Senate rejected still another splinter-group budget that contained a moderate tax increase, this resolution was defeated by a vote of 52 to 48. Finally, after rejecting eight different resolutions, the Senate adopted a budget plan on May 19 that would raise taxes by $9.9 billion in FY 1984 and by a total of $73 billion over three years. Defense spending was set to grow at 6 percent, versus the 4 percent in the House budget and the 10 percent in the president's request. The resolution was immediately interpreted as a major defeat for President Reagan. White House spokesman Larry Speakes added to that impression by telling reporters, "The budget is off target in all three areas. Defense is too low, taxes are too high, and domestic spending is too high."[101] On the other hand, Democratic Minority Leader Robert Byrd called the budget "a victory for moderate Republicans and Democrats who believe the deficit ought to be lower."[102] "The President can't completely have his way in the United States Senate now," added Lawton Chiles. "He does need to consult with both sides."[103] The Reagan budget projected the FY 1984 deficit to be $188.8 billion; the House resolution's deficit stood at $174.5 billion; and the Senate deficit was estimated to be $178.6 billion.

After the Senate-House Conference Committee approved its version of the budget resolution on June 20, both the House and Senate voted on June 23 to adopt the First Budget Resolution. The agreement set outlays at $849.5 billion, just $1 billion higher than Reagan's January budget, in addition to increasing taxes by $12 billion while holding the defense increase to 5 percent in real terms. Furthermore, the reconciliation instructions in the resolution required $2.8 billion in budget reductions in FY 1984, for a three-year total extending through FY 1986 of $12.3 billion. The resolution also contained provisions that made its spending ceilings binding, eliminating the need for a second budget resolution. In light of the strengthening economy, new budget estimates projected the deficit to reach $169.9 billion. The economy had improved rapidly since the recovery took hold in February, as the average annual GNP growth rate in the second quarter rose to 6.6 percent. With the resolution adopted, the Congress went to work on the thirteen appropriations bills.

The adoption of the FY 1984 appropriations bills that did make their way through Congress signaled that the administration was no longer able to order deep reductions in domestic spending, although the threat of a presidential veto held federal spending very close to the White House's budgetary recommendations. After Congress had approved its resolution, President Reagan declared, "The last thing we need is more taxes for more spending. If they can't get that through their heads, then I am prepared to veto their budget-busting bills again and again and again."[104] Reagan's threat worked. By October he had yet to veto any of the five appropriations bills sent to him, as each was no more than $600 million above his January request.[105] When asked whether Congress and the Democrats were staying within the limits outlined by the White House, Speaker O'Neill replied, "The answer is yes. There's no sense in sending things over there and having them vetoed."[106] Concurred Jim Wright, "At one time the President was desperately looking for a bill to veto, but he's now more or less changed his view."[107] "There is a kind of movement on both sides," Democratic House Whip Thomas Foley added, "to avoid unnecessary confrontation."[108] In one example, House negotiators in the conference committee created to review the transportation appropriations bill agreed to $368 million less spending than contained in the House version of the bill to avoid conflict with the president. The Democrats had little interest in providing Ronald Reagan with the budgetary vehicle that might label them as big spenders in the upcoming election year.

Despite the president's signing of four appropriations bills before the beginning of the new fiscal year, the government was once again forced to operate on a continuing resolution. The First Continuing Resolution was quickly approved, extending through November 10. By that date, however, a second continuing resolution was required to fund the agencies covered by the five bills yet to make their way through the legislative process. Gaining approval for the second resolution proved to be more difficult than the first. Though the measure passed in the Senate, the House rejected it as seventy-seven mostly first-term Democrats joined with Republicans to protest against the deficit. Congressman Jim Bates declared the Democrats acted to defeat the bill "because many of us in the freshman class wanted to send a message to the leadership that we have to do something about deficits."[109] The resolution's rejection, the first defeat of a continuing resolution since 1967, was viewed as a direct assault on Speaker O'Neill. Incensed, the House leadership quickly restored order in the Democratic ranks and passed the resolution. President Reagan signed the Second Continuing Resolution on November 14, three days after some federal agencies technically ran out of funds. On a final budget note, the House approved its version of the reconciliation bill on October 23. The House accepted only $10.3 billion of the three-year $12.3 billion in savings called for by the First Budget Resolution. The Senate did not pass its reconciliation bill until April 5, 1984, and then for only $8.2 billion in savings spread over three years. Both reconciliation bills achieved their savings primarily through cost of living adjustments and by limiting federal pay raises.

The House leadership's budgetary "resurgence" following the Democratic gains made in the 1982 election produced important but limited budget victories. For example, the House budget resolution with its 4 percent real growth in defense aided congressional efforts to restrain the president's defense budget. In addition, there would be no deep cuts in domestic spending in FY 1984, as the reconciliation legislation produced only some $2 billion in savings for FY 1984, compared to the administration's proposed $38 billion gained from frozen budgets and structural reforms. Still the Democrats made no serious effort to promote significant new federal programs or to rebuild those trimmed since 1981. The Democrats were boxed in not only by their fear of the president's veto, but also by their own rhetoric over the deficit. After blaming deficits for every political and economic evil under the sun, the Democrats could not very well propose new social programs that would label them as budget-busters, as Reagan promised he would do. Moreover, the Democrats were constrained on the revenue side, as they sought to avoid being called the party of tax-tax-spend-spend. Neither the Democrats nor the Republicans passed the necessary legislation providing the revenues called for by the budget resolution. The Democrats refused to be the first to approve new taxes, Tip O'Neill said, for taxes "would have to come from the President or the Republican Party."[110] Thus, both political parties refrained from making major reductions in the deficit, and the nation's press intensified its attacks on the "do-nothing" Congress and chief executive.

The Democrats were also limited in any efforts they might make to increase large-scale domestic spending by their plans to use the deficit as the major campaign issue for 1984. Though public opinion changed in 1984, polls taken in 1983 implied that such a strategy might prove to be rewarding. A January *New York Times*/CBS News Poll found 63 percent of respondents willing to cut defense spending to reduce the deficit and 62 percent favoring eliminating the third year of the tax cut. In August, a Harris Poll found a 59 percent majority agreeing with the statement that Reagan did not deserve reelection "on the basis of his record on balancing the federal budget," with 63 percent agreeing that Reagan had "gone back on his campaign promises when his budgets have produced federal deficits." In September the Democrats began running radio commercials attacking the "Republican deficits" as part of their planned thirteen-month election campaign leading to November 1984. To the sound of dripping water, one commercial pointed out that Republicans had long blamed the Democrats for budgetary red ink, but, as the dripping became a torrent, the announcer declared the Republican tax cuts and defense spending had created the huge new deficits. Congressman Tony Coelho, chair of the House Democratic Congressional Campaign Committee, predicted that "when we talk about mortgaging the future of your kids—that sells."[111] Coelho and his fellow Democrats were certain they could profit politically at the expense of Reagan and his deficit spending.

While the deficit issue restrained the Democrats' resurgence but persuaded them they could capitalize on the matter, the issue worked to divide the White House. Since 1981 David Stockman had been under attack from supply-siders who claimed that Stockman's emphasis on cutting deficits only justified high tax rates, which of course the supply-siders regarded as an anathema. This conflict was an old story by 1983, when the debate over the deficits' effect on the economy between Donald Regan and Martin Feldstein again made the White House gossip on this matter interesting. As noted in Chapter 7, the president received competing advice from his two top economic advisers on the issue of deficit spending. Feldstein, chairman of the Council of Economic Advisors, argued that deficits caused high interest rates: "The reason for the very high level on the long-term real interest rates is undoubtedly the unprecedented level of the budget deficits."[112] Immediately responding to Feldstein's comments made before the U.S. Chamber of Commerce, Regan replied, "Economists who continue to claim that deficits make for high interest rates should climb down from their celestial observatories and acquaint themselves with terrestrial facts."[113]

Since 1982, both the president and the treasury secretary had argued the deficits were not the cause of high interest rates, as they no longer worried about the charge that deficits caused inflation, for the recession and a tight monetary policy chopped inflation rates in half. In May 1983, for example, the Treasury released what is perhaps the most interesting document of Ronald Reagan's first term. In preparation for the Williamsburg economic summit of Western leaders, the administration anticipated their criticism of the president's deficits as the source of high interest rates and the worldwide recession. The report examined the economic relationship between deficits and interest rates and concluded that the connection between large federal deficits and high interest rates was ambiguous. "Attempts to resolve the ambiguity by appealing to historical data have revealed no conclusive evidence to support the assertion that large deficits cause high interest rates."[114]

In November, however, Feldstein contradicted two fundamental assumptions made by the president, namely, that military spending had not caused the deficits and that tax increases would not be needed to reduce the deficits. Feldstein instead reported to the Congress that he found the deficits to be linked to the tax cuts, defense increases, and larger interest payments, while the reduction in domestic spending had been "quite dramatic." Economic growth alone, he further observed, would not be sufficient to reduce the deficit to acceptable levels; to accomplish this task new taxes were required. Feldstein did add that although "the near-term deficits (those of 1983 and 1984) probably have a positive impact on the pace of recovery," future deficit spending "weakens that pace of recovery now."[115] Feldstein was quickly and openly ridiculed by White House spokesman Larry Speakes, who purposely mispronounced Feldstein's name and strongly suggested he would be asked to resign unless he became less vocal in his disagreements with the president and treasury secretary.

FY 1985: The Election Year Deficit "Down payment"

President Reagan's 1984 State of the Union Address delivered on January 25 called for a bipartisan "down payment" to reduce the budget deficit by $100 billion over three years. Though the address was somewhat vague about how the down payment would be structured, Reagan suggested that a bipartisan congressional committee could be brought together to form a package from "the less contentious spending cuts," the closing of "certain tax loopholes," and savings derived from recommendations offered by the Grace Commission, the president's task force organized to propose administrative efficiencies and the elimination of waste. On the matter of large-scale taxation, Reagan commented:

> Now we know deficits are a cause for worry. But there is a difference of opinion as to whether taxes should be increased, spending cut, or some of both. Fear is expressed that Government borrowing to fund the deficit could inhibit the economic recovery by taking capital needed for business and industrial expansion. I think that debate is missing an important point. Whether Government borrows or increases taxes, it will be taking the same amount of money from the private sector, and either way, it's too much. Simple fairness dictates Government must not raise taxes on families struggling to pay their bills.[116]

The proper way to reduce the deficit from the president's perspective, of course, was to reduce social and domestic spending.

The State of the Union Address was but another declaration of Reagan's unwillingness to increase taxes by any great amount to trim the deficit. The president certainly had been urged from within the administration to raise taxes. Martin Feldstein again endorsed higher taxes in a January 2 memo to Reagan. Feldstein called for new taxes in the range of $50 billion a year for three years, otherwise the country would experience deficits of "at least $170 billion in every year between now and 1989," even if Reagan received "all of the spending cuts that we are asking for."[117] David Stockman also pushed for additional taxes. Stockman argued that "there are a lot of dreamers, including [some] in the administration," who believed a second Reagan administration would be able to convince Congress to make major reductions in domestic spending.[118] However, continued Stockman, "The point is that we have knocked on all those doors for three years and three budget rounds, and the result is, people want to have mass-transit subsidies and middle-class subsidies for education. And the agriculture sector wants all those benefits. I can't foresee that at any time in this decade we will have the kind of people in Congress who will abolish those things. Now we have to figure out how to pay our bills."[119] Stockman added that there was little "fraud, waste, and abuse" left to cut. "In fact, nearly every stone has been turned over."[120]

Congressional Democrats greeted the president's bipartisan request with caution. Speaker O'Neill replied to the idea of a bipartisan commission by saying, "I am determined that the commission not become a public relations ploy to take the heat off those properly responsible for Government policy. It is the President who submits the budget. It is the President who has recommended the sky-rocketing deficits of the past three years."[121] The Democrats arranged to have Congressman Jim Wright and Senator Daniel Inouye of Hawaii meet with the Republican delegates to the commission. Nevertheless, the Democrats' principal concern about the commission was that any serious bipartisan action might defuse their primary political weapon in 1984, namely, their claim that Republican policies were unfair and created huge deficits that threatened the economy. Democratic congressman Les Aspin summarized the matter by saying, "The question is, how do we negotiate in good faith and keep the issue alive in November?"[122] Observed one aide to a Republican congressional leader: "It's a good way for the White House to put a decent face on a big problem. . . . By tossing out the idea of a bipartisan task force, they really co-opt Speaker O'Neill and Senator Byrd. They can't afford to refuse the invitation and so the White House gets them to share the blame for the deficits."[123]

The FY 1985 budget released on February 1 included $925.5 billion in outlays, a $180.4 billion deficit, and a real defense increase of 9.5 percent. The budget proposed relatively few domestic spending cuts. Although revenues were to be increased by $33 billion over three years, the election year budget contained only $26 billion in cuts in the same three years. A Republican aide pointed out that in past budgets the administration demanded a 3 to 1 rate of cuts to tax increases, as compared to FY 1985. Perhaps the most startling budgetary item was the rapid buildup of interest payments on the debt. Payments for FY 1985 were projected to be $116.1 billion, as shown in Table 22, or 12.5 cents of every dollar in the budget.

The budget received its by-now-standard Democratic attack on defense spending and the deficit. Senator Sam Nunn stated flatly, "The level of defense spending that is being proposed today will be reduced. The question is not whether it will be reduced but when and how much."[124] Conservative Democrat John Stennis told reporters, "When you passed

Table 22. FY 1985 Reagan budget proposal (in billions of dollars)

Outlays by function	FY 1982 actual	FY 1983 actual	FY 1984 estimate*	Reagan FY 1985 proposal
International affairs	10.1	9.0	13.5	17.5
Science, space	7.1	7.7	8.3	8.8
Energy	4.7	4.0	3.5	3.1
Defense	187.4	210.5	237.5	272.0
Natural resources	12.9	12.7	12.3	11.3
Agriculture	14.9	22.2	10.7	14.3
Commerce, housing	3.9	4.4	3.8	1.1
Transportation	20.6	21.4	26.1	27.1
Community develop.	7.2	6.9	7.6	7.6
Education, training	26.3	26.6	28.7	27.9
Health	27.4	28.7	30.7	32.9
Social security & medicare	202.5	223.3	240.2	260.3
Income security	92.1	106.2	96.0	114.4
Veterans' benefits	24.0	24.8	25.8	26.7
Justice	4.7	5.1	6.0	6.1
General gov't.	4.4	4.8	5.7	5.7
Fiscal assistance	6.4	6.5	6.7	6.7
Interest	84.7	89.8	108.2	116.1
Allowances	—	—	—	0.9
Offsetting receipts	−13.2	−18.6	−17.5	−35.3
Total	728.4	796.0	853.8	925.5
Receipts by source				
Individual income tax	297.7	288.9	293.3	328.4
Corporate income tax	49.2	37.0	66.6	76.5
Social security tax	201.5	209.0	239.5	270.7
Excise tax	36.3	35.3	38.2	38.4
Other	33.1	30.4	32.5	31.0
Total	617.8	600.6	670.1	745.0
Deficit	−110.6	−195.4	−183.7	−180.4

Source: "Comparing the Budgets," *San Francisco Chronicle*, February 2, 1984.
*February 1984 estimate.

that $300 billion mark [in defense spending], you left me somewhere out there in a void."[125] Added Lawton Chiles, ranking Democrat on the Senate Budget Committee, "We just need a new budget. A $100 billion [down payment] doesn't approach the problem when you look at the figures just out today from the Congressional Budget Office, you see those deficits are really soaring."[126] The CBO estimates Chiles referred to indicated that the White House figures greatly underestimated the deficit. The CBO projected the FY 1987 deficit to be $248 billion instead of OMB's $123 billion.

While the Democrats berated his budget, the president received little comfort from his chairman of the Council of Economic Advisors. When asked whether the $100 billion down payment would reduce future deficits, Feldstein replied, "Sort of approximately almost maybe yes."[127] Feldstein's comment was mild compared to his earlier testimony presented on Capitol Hill, where he told congressmen, "The budget is not what we want to see happen in 1985. We're going to have to have additional tax revenues, we're going to have to trim back on the size of the defense authorization, and we're going to have domestic spending cuts."[128] David Stockman disagreed with Feldstein, arguing that increasing the down payment more than $100 billion would divide the Congress and limit the president's interest in such a proposal. "I think we all ought to recognize," said Stockman, "that we've gone through one year of complete stalemate where we talked huge plans back and forth that reflect the various philosophical and political positions that are represented in the Congress and the country, and when we dealt with those big plans and those sweeping numbers, we couldn't come to agreement."[129]

The Council of Economic Advisors' annual report was more pessimistic than the OMB budget—the Democrats employed it to attack the Reagan economic program—and it contained Feldstein's fears about the deficit driving up interest rates, contradicting Donald Regan's position on the issue. The treasury secretary struck back, telling the Senate Budget Committee that with the exception of the president's economic statement contained in the report, "As far as I'm concerned, you can throw the rest away."[130]

Talks between the Republican and Democratic delegates to the bipartisan commission began on February 8. The initial meeting the party leaders quickly fell apart, however, becoming a "charade" in the words of Democratic senator J. Bennett Johnston, as the Democrats discovered that the list of budgetary and tax changes proposed by Howard Baker were already included in the president's budget proposal.[131] Even if all the items were approved the deficit would still reach $180 billion in FY 1985, but the Democrats were seeking to cut that figure by $30 billion. Other commission gatherings were equally unproductive. Neither the Republicans, Democrats, nor White House officials could agree on taxes, defense spending, or funds for domestic programs. At the February 24 meeting, for example, Pete Domenici proposed to reduce the defense increase in a manner that cut $45 billion over three years from the president's budget. The president rejected this plan, as well as Democratically sponsored tax increases. By the first week in March the bipartisan group had met only three times, and with no effect.

Without producing any budgetary substance, the meetings simply provided another occasion for bickering between the Republicans and Democrats. After the president told reporters the Democrats had "begged away" from participating in the talks, Tip O'Neill responded by declaring, "The President is absolutely trying to play politics with this. . . . This is positively fraud on his part."[132] Two weeks later Reagan expressed his doubts about the sincerity of the Democrats' concern over the deficits: "I am a little struck by these born-again budget balancers, who for 40 out of the last 44 years have controlled both houses of Congress and who have religiously had a policy of deficit spending and never raised their voices about it."[133] Rejoined O'Neill, "On the campaign trail, the President condems deficits. Here in Washington, he defends them."[134]

Indeed, there was legitimacy to O'Neill's charge that the Republicans were defending their deficit. As "pessimists" chimed in that large-scale deficit spending would derail the economic recovery, Donald Regan countered, "I wish those economists would sit back and relax. This will be one of the greatest recoveries in history."[135] Meanwhile, in the Congress, the Joint Economic Committee issued its March analysis of the president's 1984 Economic Report. The Republican section of the analysis stated, "We believe that the near-term effects of deficits are not of immediate crisis proportions," pointing out these deficits were a consequence of "cyclical factors."[136] The Republicans even added a table comparing the cyclical to the structural deficit, claiming the structural deficit had declined from $55 billion in 1980 to $48 billion in 1982. Meanwhile, the cyclical deficit climbed at a much faster pace, only to be outdistanced again by the structural component after FY 1984.[137] To reduce the growing structural deficit, however, the Republicans cautioned that "there should be no attempt at drastic quick fixes. . . . The markets are not calling for a balanced budget this year or next, but we should be moving in that direction."[138] The Republican position on deficit spending had evolved during the Reagan presidency to the point where they were willing to argue the budget should be balanced not for some intrinsic political value, but in a Keynesian fashion to meet economic conditions, if not to appease the financial markets.

With the bipartisan commission locked in stalemate, the finance and budget committees in the Senate and the House Ways and Means Committee were hard at work designing their own deficit reduction measures. On March 1 the Ways and Means Committee approved a $49.2 billion tax increase spread over four years. Without touching the personal income tax cut, the committee raised taxes on liquor, cigarettes, interest income, and telephone service, among other items. In the Senate, the Finance Committee approved its own tax package on March 23, which consisted of $48 billion in tax hikes for the same period. In addition, the Finance Committee agreed to $25.8 billion in budgetary savings. Furthermore, the president himself gave up on the bipartisan approach, remarking on March 13 that he had "lost faith in the bipartisan" commission, and would work through Republican leadership in the Congress.[139] Two days later Reagan reached an agreement with Senate Republicans; he would reduce defense spending by $57 billion over three years if the FY 1985 defense increase was set at 7.8 percent in real terms and treated as a budgetary floor rather than a ceiling when negotiating with the Democrats. The Republican deficit reduction plan finally fashioned from Senate committee decisions, and from Senate leadership compromises made with the White House, would produce a $149 billion reduction in the deficit, as shown in Table 23. While the growth in the defense budget would fall $41 billion, taxes would be raised by $45 billion, and domestic spending reduced by $43.2 billion through cost of living freezes and entitlement "reforms." When asked whether the Democrats would support the plan, Reagan replied, "Why shouldn't they? They have been complaining they want the deficits reduced. After 50 years of raising the deficits, here is a chance to go the other way."[140]

Table 23. House and Senate deficit reduction packages, March 21, 1984 (in billions of dollars)

	FY	House	Senate & Reagan
Tax increase	1985	9.5	10.0
	1986	17.3	15.0
	1987	22.0	20.0
		48.8	45.0
Entitlement cuts	1985	1.9	5.0
	1986	3.6	10.0
	1987	5.3	15.0
		10.8	30.0*
Defense cuts	1985	16.1	6.0
	1986	34.8	16.0
	1987	44.7	19.0
		95.6	41.0
Other domestic	1985	0.5	3.0
	1986	1.6	4.0
	1987	2.9	6.0
		5.0	13.0
Grace Commission savings	1985	1.7	
	1986	0.2	
	1987	0.1	
		2.0	
Interest savings	1985	1.7	2.0
	1986	6.4	6.0
	1987	14.0	12.0
		22.1	20.0
Totals	1985	31.4	26.0
	1986	63.9	51.0
	1987	89.0	72.0
		184.3	149.0

Source: "Two Plans for a Tighter Budget," *New York Times*, March 23, 1984.

*Includes $3.1 billion in Grace Commission recommended entitlement savings.

The House Democratic leadership gathered together on March 20 and agreed to support their own deficit reduction measure. The plan sought to reduce deficits by $184 billion over three years, in contrast to the Republicans' $149 billion cut. The centerpiece of the Democratic package was a ceiling placed on most domestic expenditure increases of 3.5 percent, or 1.5 percent less than the expected rate of inflation. However, cost of living adjustments for most welfare programs and Social Security would be adjusted for the full effects of inflation. Defense spending was set to grow by 3.5 percent in real terms. Moreover, the Democrats agreed in principle to a "pay-as-you-go" provision pushed by liberals led by Californian George Miller, which allowed federal spending to grow by more than the 3.5 percent in the restricted domestic programs if taxes were raised to compensate for the difference. The House Budget Committee essentially ratified the leadership's plan in a 19 to 9 partisan vote taken on March 28. The House began debate over the first budget resolution on April 4 and quickly disposed of seven alternatives to the Budget Committee's recommendation. The Republican budget receiving the most support reduced the deficit by $204.9 billion over three years; the liberal Democratic Study Group went further, cutting the deficit by $261.5 billion. These various alternatives were defeated one after another, with the Budget Committee version winning by 250 votes to 168, supported by only 21 Republicans. The First Budget Resolution passed April 5. Just six days later the House approved the $49.2 billion tax bill by the huge vote of 318 to 97. On April 12 the House passed its reconciliation bill with its three-year $3.9 billion cut in entitlements. After including these cuts in the tax bill, the measure was sent to the Senate.

The Senate leadership and the White House had agreed to a budget reduction package in March that was labeled the "Rose Garden" plan. The Republicans decided that before they would adopt their own budget resolution in the Senate, they would first consider the House bill with its budget cuts and tax increases. After spending four weeks debating the numerous alternatives offered by moderate Republicans and the Democrats, the Senate passed its version of the House tax bill, H.R. 4170, substituting the entire Rose Garden package for the Democratic provisions. (On the following day, May 18, the Senate then adopted the House budget resolution as its own, once again after altering the language in favor of the Rose Garden plan.) The Republicans' deficit reduction program at first glance appeared nearly identical to the House plan, as both versions of H.R. 4170 called for approximately $50 billion in new taxes spread over three years. The Democrats employed the House budget resolution to spell out their deficit reduction program, but the Republicans had inserted their plan in both the Senate resolution and in an actual piece of legislation, H.R. 4170. By following this procedure the Republicans understood that any spending ceilings included in this bill would become a part of law once signed by the president, whereas the House budget resolution merely set nonbinding spending targets. Thus, the Republicans added budgetary "caps" to their version of H.R. 4170, one imposed on domestic, the other on defense spending. These three-year budgetary caps, or ceilings, were put in place to guarantee that spending reductions would indeed occur. The spending caps proved to be a major source of contention. "The President won't sign it without the caps," declared Howard Baker. "I'm not going to support it without the caps, and I have requested our conferees to stand by the caps."[141] Nevertheless, countered James Jones of the House Budget Committee, "The caps will not be agreed to because the Senate ultimately has to come down on defense and both sides will recognize that a cap is not enforceable in the next Congress."[142]

The Conference Committee created to work out the differences in H.R. 4170 began its task on June 6. The committee quickly agreed on the tax provisions in the bill, and by June 8 it had adopted $40 billion in revenue increases. After this initial success the conference stalled because the House Democrats refused to accept the spending caps. In mid-June the Senate leadership reached a compromise with the Democrats by making the caps a nonbinding spending ceiling. The committee substituted "sense" language for the caps, as each branch of Congress expressed a "sense of the Senate" or "sense of the House" message in H.R. 4170 to reflect the goals of the competing deficit reduction plans. With the spending cap issue set aside, the committee made progress on the rest of its agenda. By June 22 the conferees agreed to $11 billion in budget cuts, with $3 billion recommended by the president's Grace Commission and another $8 billion in savings gained from welfare and health programs. Altogether, the conference agreed on June 23 to a total of $61 billion in tax increases and budgetary savings, making this the first installment on the three-year down payment to reduce the government's deficits. On June 27 both the House and the Senate voted to accept the conference report, but in the process the Congress raised the deficit reduction total to $63 billion.

Although President Reagan signed the 1984 Deficit Reduction Act, this legislation did not constitute a budget resolution, and Congress still had to set spending ceilings for the defense budget and most domestic programs. Through mid-July the Conference Committee established to review the two budget resolutions was hopelessly stuck on the defense budget. With its planned 7 percent real growth for defense, the Senate resolution called for military spending of $299 billion in budget authority. The House resolution, however, contained only $285.7 billion for a 3.5 percent real gain. As the conference dragged on, the House voted to waive the need for a resolution, and began to work on the various appropriations bills in late May. In the Senate, Pete Domenici attempted to secure the same waiver, but his act touched off a three-day filibuster led by Democrat Lawton Chiles, the senior minority member of the Budget Committee. "Someday I want to be chairman of the Budget Committee," declared Chiles, "and there ain't going to be nothing to be chairman of. I'm not responsible for what they do in the House, and thank God I'm not."[143] Chiles filibustered in order to force the Senate to follow the normal budgetary process of first approving a budget resolution before considering the individual appropriations bills. Though the Senate invoked cloture to cut off Chiles's filibuster, he had delayed action on the appropriations bills by a week and he threatened to renew the filibuster unless the Senate agreed to a resolution. The resolution, of course, was stalled by the defense budget. To reach a compromise between the Senate and House, Chiles recommended to Howard Baker that Baker meet with Tip O'Neill to settle their differences on the matter. The Baker-O'Neill conference succeeded, as the Republicans and Democrats split their defense increases and agreed to a 5 percent real growth in military spending. The Senate passed the conference report on September 26, and the House approved the First Budget Resolution on October 1, the first day of the new 1985 fiscal year.

The beginning of the fiscal year did not take place until Congress experienced what had by now become a typical, last-minute, frantic rush to fund the government. Having failed to approve a budget resolution to guide its budgetary deliberations, and distracted by the events common to an election year, Congress had passed only four of the thirteen appropriations bills by October 1. Consequently, the Congress passed three continuing resolutions within a week's time to fund the agencies and programs covered in the nine other bills. Extended to run the full twelve months of the fiscal year, the third and final continuing resolution was not approved in time to prevent the one-day furlough of 500,000 federal workers. Once again confusion reigned as the huge budget package was pieced together with a string of unrelated legislation. "I haven't been able to find anybody who can tell me what the level of appropriations in this bill is," said the frustrated Republican congressman William Dannemeyer. "I don't think anybody knows. Something is seriously wrong with the process under which we and the other bodies are working."[144] Both houses of Congress overwhelmingly approved the continuing resolution, signaling their impatience to move on to the election at hand.

Appendix 3

Federal Receipts, Expenditures, Surpluses, Deficits, and Debt, 1789–1984

Summary of Federal Finances, 1789–1984

Fiscal year	Budget receipts	Budget expenditures	Surplus or deficit	Total gross debt
1789–91	$ 4,419*	$ 4,269*	$ 150*	$ 77,228*
1792	3,670	5,080	−1,410	80,359
1793	4,653	4,482	171	78,427
1794	5,432	6,991	−1,559	80,748
1795	6,115	7,540	−1,425	83,762
1796	8,378	5,727	2,651	82,064
1797	8,689	6,134	2,555	79,229
1798	7,900	7,677	224	78,409
1799	7,547	9,666	−2,120	82,976
1800	10,849	10,786	63	83,038
1801	12,935	9,395	3,541	80,713
1802	14,996	7,862	7,134	77,055
1803	11,064	7,852	3,212	86,427
1804	11,826	8,719	3,107	82,312
1805	13,561	10,506	3,054	75,723
1806	15,560	9,804	5,756	69,218
1807	16,398	8,354	8,044	65,196
1808	17,061	9,932	7,128	57,023
1809	7,773	10,281	−2,507	53,173
1810	9,384	8,157	1,228	48,006
1811	14,424	8,058	6,365	45,210
1812	9,801	20,281	−10,480	55,963
1813	14,340	31,682	−17,341	81,488
1814	11,182	34,721	−23,539	99,834
1815	15,729	32,708	−16,979	127,335

Fiscal year	Budget receipts	Budget expenditures	Surplus or deficit	Total gross debt
1816	47,678	30,587	17,091	123,492
1817	33,099	21,844	11,255	103,467
1818	21,585	19,825	1,760	95,530
1819	24,603	21,464	3,140	91,016
1820	17,881	18,261	−380	89,987
1821	14,573	15,811	−1,237	93,547
1822	20,232	15,000	5,232	90,876
1823	20,541	14,707	5,834	90,270
1824	19,381	20,327	−945	83,788
1825	21,841	15,857	5,984	81,054
1826	25,260	17,036	8,225	73,987
1827	22,966	16,139	6,827	67,475
1828	24,764	16,395	8,369	58,421
1829	24,828	15,203	9,624	48,565
1830	24,844	15,143	9,701	39,123
1831	28,527	15,248	13,279	24,322
1832	31,866	17,289	14,577	7,012
1833	33,948	23,018	10,931	4,760
1834	21,792	18,628	3,164	38
1835	35,430	17,573	17,857	38
1836	50,827	30,868	19,959	337
1837	24,954	37,243	−12,289	3,308
1838	26,303	33,865	−7,562	10,434
1839	31,483	26,899	4,584	3,573
1840	19,480	24,318	−4,837	5,251
1841	16,860	26,566	−9,706	13,594
1842	19,976	25,206	−5,230	20,201
1843	8,303	11,858	−3,555	32,743
1844	29,321	22,338	6,984	23,462
1845	29,970	22,937	7,033	15,925
1846	29,700	27,767	1,933	15,550
1847	26,496	57,281	−30,786	38,827
1848	35,736	45,377	−9,641	47,045
1849	31,208	45,052	−13,844	63,062
1850	43,603	39,543	4,060	63,453
1851	52,559	47,709	4,850	68,305
1852	49,847	44,195	5,652	66,199
1853	61,587	48,184	13,403	59,805
1854	73,800	58,045	15,755	42,244
1855	65,351	59,743	5,608	35,588
1856	74,057	69,571	4,486	31,974
1857	68,965	67,796	1,170	28,701
1858	46,655	74,185	−27,530	44,913
1859	53,486	69,071	−15,585	58,498
1860	56,065	63,131	−7,066	64,844
1861	41,510	66,547	−25,037	90,582
1862	51,987	474,762	−422,774	524,178
1863	112,697	714,741	−602,043	1,119,774
1864	264,627	865,323	−600,696	1,815,831
1865	333,715	1,297,555	−963,841	2,677,929
1866	558,033	520,809	37,223	2,755,764
1867	490,634	357,543	133,091	2,650,168

Fiscal year	Budget receipts	Budget expenditures	Surplus or deficit	Total gross debt
1868	405,638	377,340	28,298	2,583,446
1869	370,944	322,865	48,078	2,545,111
1870	411,255	309,654	101,602	2,436,453
1871	383,324	292,177	91,147	2,322,052
1872	374,107	277,518	96,589	2,209,991
1873	333,738	290,345	43,393	2,151,210
1874	304,979	302,634	2,345	2,159,933
1875	288,000	274,623	13,377	2,156,277
1876	294,096	265,101	28,995	2,130,846
1877	281,406	241,334	40,072	2,107,760
1878	257,764	236,964	20,800	2,159,418
1879	273,827	266,948	6,879	2,298,913
1880	333,527	267,643	65,884	2,090,909
1881	360,782	260,713	100,069	2,019,286
1882	403,525	257,981	145,544	1,856,916
1883	398,288	265,408	132,879	1,721,959
1884	348,520	244,126	104,394	1,625,307
1885	323,691	260,227	63,464	1,578,551
1886	336,440	242,483	93,957	1,555,660
1887	371,403	267,932	103,471	1,465,485
1888	379,266	267,925	111,341	1,384,632
1889	387,050	299,289	87,761	1,249,471
1890	403,081	318,041	85,040	1,122,397
1891	392,612	365,774	26,839	1,005,807
1892	354,938	345,023	9,914	968,219
1893	385,820	383,478	2,342	961,432
1894	306,355	367,525	−61,170	1,016,898
1895	324,729	356,195	−31,466	1,096,913
1896	338,142	352,179	−14,037	1,222,729
1897	347,722	365,774	−18,052	1,226,794
1898	405,321	443,369	−38,047	1,232,743
1899	515,961	605,072	−89,112	1,436,701
1900	567,241	520,861	46,380	1,263,417
1901	587,685	524,617	63,068	1,221,572
1902	562,478	485,234	77,244	1,178,031
1903	561,881	517,006	44,875	1,159,406
1904	541,087	583,660	−42,573	1,136,259
1905	544,275	567,279	−23,004	1,132,357
1906	594,984	570,202	24,782	1,142,523
1907	665,860	579,129	86,732	1,147,178
1908	601,862	659,196	−57,334	1,177,690
1909	604,320	693,744	−89,423	1,148,315
1910	675,512	693,617	−18,105	1,146,940
1911	701,833	691,202	10,631	1,153,985
1912	692,609	689,881	2,728	1,193,839
1913	724,111	724,512	−401	1,193,048
1914	734,673	735,081	−408	1,188,235
1915	697,911	760,587	−62,676	1,191,264
1916	782,535	734,056	48,478	1,225,146
1917	1,124,325	1,977,682	−853,357	2,975,619
1918	3,664,583	12,696,702	−9,032,120	12,455,225
1919	5,152,257	18,514,880	−13,362,623	25,484,506

Fiscal year	Budget receipts	Budget expenditures	Surplus or deficit	Total gross debt
1920	6,694,565	6,403,344	291,222	24,229,321
1921	5,624,933	5,115,928	509,005	23,977,451
1922	4,109,104	3,372,608	736,496	22,963,382
1923	4,007,135	3,294,628	712,508	22,349,707
1924	4,012,045	3,048,678	963,367	21,250,813
1925	3,780,149	3,063,105	717,043	20,516,194
1926	3,962,756	3,097,612	865,144	19,643,216
1927	4,129,394	2,974,030	1,155,365	18,511,907
1928	4,042,348	3,103,265	939,083	17,604,293
1929	4,033,250	3,298,859	734,391	16,931,088
1930	4,177,942	3,440,269	737,673	16,185,310
1931	3,115,557	3,577,434	−461,877	16,801,281
1932	1,923,913	4,659,203	−2,735,290	19,487,002
1933	2,021,213	4,622,865	−2,601,652	22,538,673
1934	3,064,268	6,693,900	−3,629,632	27,053,141
1935	3,729,914	6,520,966	−2,791,052	28,700,893
1936	4,068,937	8,493,486	−4,424,549	33,778,543
1937	4,978,601	7,756,021	−2,777,421	36,424,614
1938	5,615,221	6,791,838	−1,176,617	37,164,740
1939	4,996,300	8,858,458	−3,862,158	40,439,532
1940	5,144,013	9,062,032	−3,918,019	42,967,531
1941	7,102,931	13,262,204	−6,159,272	48,961,444
1942	14,350**	35,114**	−20,764**	72.4†
1943	23,649	78,533	−54,884	136.7
1944	44,276	91,280	−47,004	201.0
1945	45,216	92,690	−47,474	258.7
1946	39,327	55,183	−15,856	269.4
1947	38,394	34,532	3,862	258.3
1948	41,774	29,773	12,001	252.3
1949	39,437	38,834	603	252.8
1950	39,485	42,597	−3,122	257.4
1951	51,646	45,546	6,100	255.2
1952	66,204	67,721	−1,517	259.1
1953	69,574	76,107	−6,533	266.1
1954	69,719	70,890	−1,170	270.8
1955	65,469	68,509	−3,041	274.4
1956	74,547	70,460	4,087	272.8
1957	79,990	76,741	3,249	272.4
1958	79,636	82,575	−2,939	279.7
1959	79,249	92,104	−12,855	287.8
1960	92,492	92,223	269	290.9
1961	94,389	97,795	−3,406	292.9
1962	99,676	106,813	−7,137	303.3
1963	106,560	111,311	−4,751	310.8
1964	112,662	118,584	−5,922	316.8
1965	116,833	118,430	−1,596	323.2
1966	130,856	134,652	−3,796	329.5
1967	148,906	157,608	−8,702	341.3
1968	152,973	178,134	−25,161	369.8
1969	186,882	183,645	3,236	367.1
1970	192,807	195,652	−2,845	382.6
1971	187,139	210,172	−23,033	409.5

Fiscal year	Budget receipts	Budget expenditures	Surplus or deficit	Total gross debt
1972	207,309	230,681	−23,373	437.3
1973	230,799	245,647	−14,849	468.4
1974	263,224	267,912	−4,688	486.2
1975	279,090	324,245	−45,154	544.1
1976	298,060	364,473	−66,413	631.9
1977††	436,791	494,694	−57,904	709.1
1978	399,561	448,368	−48,807	780.4
1979	463,302	490,997	−27,694	833.8
1980	517,112	576,675	−59,563	914.3
1981	599,272	657,204	−57,932	1,003.9
1982	617,766	728,375	−110,609	1,147.0
1983	600,562	795,969	−195,407	1,381.9
1984	666,457	841,815	−175,358	1,576.7

Sources: 1789–1941: *Historical Statistics of the United States: Colonial Times to 1957*, U.S. Bureau of the Census, 1960. 1942–83: *Budget of the United States Government, FY 1986*.
*In thousands of dollars.
**In millions of dollars.
†In billions of dollars.
††Includes transition quarter data.
Note: Data for 1789–1939 are for the administrative budget; data for 1940 and all following years are for the unified budget.

Notes

Chapter 1. Balanced Budgets and Symbolic Politics

1. In 1979, according to Paul McCracken, "deficits were equal to 8% or so of GNP for Belgium and Italy, and in the 3%-to-5% zone for the Netherlands, Germany, Sweden, the U.K. and even Japan (though Japan's high savings rate makes large government deficits more easily financed)." At the same time the federal deficit was 2.1 percent of GNP. Paul W. McCracken, "Economic Policy in the U.S.: Chapter Two," *Wall Street Journal*, August 27, 1981. For more cross-national data, see *Balancing the Federal Budget and Limiting Federal Spending Constitutional and Statutory Approaches*, The Congressional Budget Office (Washington, D.C.: GPO, 1982), esp. pp. 13–22.

2. In the case of Japan, between 1970 and 1980 the average Japanese general account deficit as a proportion of nominal GNP was 3.7 percent, while the average deficit equaled 24.7 percent of the total Japanese budget. In contrast, the deficit of the U.S. government averaged 2.1 percent of GNP and constituted an average of 9.7 percent of total federal outlays during this same period. For Japanese data, see *Industrial Policy: Japan's Flexible Approach*, U.S. General Accounting Office (Washington, D.C.: GPO, June 23, 1982), Report no. GAD/ID-82-32, p. 21. On the Japanese budget and budgetary politics, see John Creighton Campbell, *Contemporary Japanese Budget Politics* (Berkeley, Calif., 1977).

3. Herbert Stein, *The Fiscal Revolution in America* (Chicago, 1969), p. 16.

4. Carolyn Webber, "Development of Ideas about Balanced Budgets," in Aaron B. Wildavsky, *How to Limit Government Spending* (Berkeley, Calif., 1980), pp. 163–80.

5. For a comparative perspective on debt loads, see R. Dudley Baxter, *National Debts* (London, 1871), esp. Figure 1.

6. "But Mr. Suzuki, Your Big Budget Deficit Is Far Too Small," *The Economist*, October 23, 1982.

7. Senator Alan Cranston, Democratic minority whip, made this statement as part of the argument against a balanced budget amendment in 1982. Alan Cranston, "Is a Balanced Budget Constitutional Amendment Necessary?" *San Francisco Examiner*, July 26, 1982.

8. Thomas J. Anton, "Roles and Symbols in the Determination of State Expenditures," *Midwest Journal of Political Science* 11 (February 1967): 40.
9. Ibid.
10. This definition of symbolism is derived from a number of sources, including Edward Sapir, "Symbolism," in *The Encyclopedia of the Social Sciences* (New York, 1934), pp. 492–95; Murray Edelman, *The Symbolic Uses of Politics* (Urbana, 1980), pp. 6–21; Hanna Fenichel Pitkin, *The Concept of Representation* (Berkeley, Calif., 1967), chap. 5; and Ronald D. Brunner, "Book Review," *Political Psychology* 5 (1984): 109–10. The definition employed in this book attempts to take into account the dual definitions of symbolism mentioned by Sapir, Edelman, and others. Balanced budgets act as condensation symbols, in that they evoke an emotional response. They also act as a referential symbol, because balanced budgets refer to "objective elements in objects or situations," as Edelman notes (p. 6). These two notions of symbolism are not mutually incompatible, however, and they often operate at the same time. Such is the situation that applies to the balanced budget idea.
11. Aaron Wildavsky, "The Once and Future School of Public Policy," *Public Interest* 79 (Spring 1985): 40–41. Also see Aaron Wildavsky's "The Budget as New Social Contract," *Journal of Contemporary Studies* 5 (Spring 1982): 3–19, and his "Budgeting as Compromises among Social Orders," in Michael J. Boskin and Aaron Wildavsky, eds., *The Federal Budget: Economics and Politics* (San Francisco, 1982), pp. 21–37.
12. This is how Robert Dallek views Reagan's symbolism: "Some of the most significant forces influencing the Reagan movement are nonrational. While Reaganites may be seen in part as practitioners of traditional politics . . . they should also be viewed as caught up in symbolic politics: their public goals satisfy psychological needs as much as material needs." Dallek continues, "Reagan's policies are less a response to actual problems at home and abroad than a means of restoring traditional values to the center of American life and boosting the self-esteem of Reaganites." Rather than being an expression of public policy and political ideology, Dallek's understanding of symbolism is largely one of manipulation and is based on psychological need. Robert Dallek, *Ronald Reagan: The Politics of Symbolism* (Cambridge, Mass., 1984), pp. viii–ix; also see pp. 72–73. Also see Murray Edelman, "Political Language and Political Reality," *PS* (Winter 1985): 10–19, and Edelman's *Political Language* (New York, 1977). Edelman correctly points out that political language can be used to justify public policies, to convey a sense of future possibilities, and to mobilize supporters. He shares Dallek's thinking that language should be regarded cynically, and thus he subtitled *Political Language*, "Words that Succeed and Policies that Fail." Contrary to Dallek and Edelman, I consider language to be a valuable guide to understanding public policy and find a high degree of correspondence between the two, rather than regarding language as primarily employed to deceive the public.
13. Louis Hartz, *The Liberal Tradition in America* (New York, 1955); Charles Beard and Mary Beard, *The Rise of American Civilization* (New York, 1959); Arthur M. Schlesinger, Jr., *The Crisis of the Old Order, 1919–1933* (Boston, 1957); Bruce Palmer, *"Man over Money": The Southern Populist Critique of American Capitalism* (Chapel Hill, N.C., 1980); R. Jeffrey Lustig, *Corporate Liberalism* (Berkeley, Calif., 1982); and Leonard D. White's trilogy, *The Federalists: A Study in Administrative History, 1789–1801* (New York, 1965), *The Jeffersonians: A Study in Administrative History, 1801–1829* (New York, 1965), and *The Jacksonians: A Study in Administrative History, 1829–1861* (New York, 1965).
14. Leslie Lipson, *The Democratic Civilization* (Oxford, 1964), p. 216.
15. Some writers suggest that Americans have always been united in their opposition to federal deficits and debt. Alvin Rabushka contends, for example, that Jefferson and Hamilton agreed on the matter of deficits and debt: "Alexander Hamilton strongly urged the repayment of national debt." As shown in Chapter 4, Jefferson would disagree with Rabushka on this interpretation of American history. See Alvin Rabushka, *A Compelling Case for a Constitutional Amendment to Balance the Budget and Limit Taxes* (Washington D.C., 1982), p. 7.

16. Such a division of American history into what he calls the "nineteeth-century ideal" and the world of the New Deal and beyond is made by Theodore J. Lowi, in *The End of Liberalism* (New York, 1979), p. 300.

Chapter 2. The Economics of Deficit Spending

1. "Prosperity without Inflation: Interviews with Four Nobel Prize Winners," *U.S. News & World Report*, December 15, 1980, pp. 50–54.
2. The unified budget is employed throughout unless otherwise noted. To compare the unified budget deficit to the national income products account, the full-employment, and the standardized deficits, see *Understanding Fiscal Policy* (Washington, D.C.: Congressional Budget Office, April 1978), pp. 30–37.
3. One of the best pre-Reagan studies of deficit spending's economic effects is Herbert Stein's "Balancing the Budget," in W. Fellner, ed., *Contemporary Economic Problems, 1979* (Washington, D.C., 1979). Stein pointed out that the "deliberate creation of larger and more durable deficits in the recessions of the 1970s, and the dissipation of the surplus during the early 1960s, had several causes." Stein says that the "impatience to regain what was regarded as high employment was great. The inflationary consequences of rapid recovery were considered to be slight. The difficulty of undoing expenditure increases, adopted as temporary stimuli, when recovery was achieved was underestimated. Too much reliance was placed on the long-run growth of revenue to balance expenditure increases made in recessions, without appreciating how many other claims there would be on that future revenue. Finally, slight, and mainly rhetorical, value was attached to achieving a balanced budget or a surplus" (p. 211).
4. On these and other reasons for the deficits of this time, see "Joblessness in Wrecking U.S. Budget," *San Francisco Chronicle*, July 11, 1980; "$59 Billion Federal Deficit for Year," *San Francisco Examiner*, October 30, 1980; "Costly St. Helens Cleanup," *San Francisco Examiner*, August 21, 1981; "Second-Biggest Federal Deficit," *San Francisco Chronicle*, October 30, 1980; and "$30 Billion Deficit in Carter Budget," *Oakland Tribune*, July 21, 1980.
5. Gregory B. Mills and John L. Palmer, *The Deficit Dilemma: Budget Policy in the Reagan Era* (Washington, D.C., 1984), p. 32.
6. Benjamin M. Friedman, "Testimony before the United States Senate Committee on Finance," December 12, 1983, *Deficit Reduction Proposals, Hearings before the Committee on Finance, United States Senate* (Washington, D.C.: GPO, 1984), pp. 58–59.
7. Allan H. Meltzer, "Closing the Deficit: December 12, 1983," in ibid., p. 101.
8. "A Program for Economic Recovery" (Washington, D.C.: GPO, 1981), p. 34/12. Each page of the "Program" has two numbers, one at the top and another at the bottom of the page.
9. Ibid., p. 53/1.
10. Walter B. Wriston was interviewed on "Meet the Press," June 28, 1981.
11. Otto Eckstein and Christopher Probyn, "Do Budget Deficits Matter?" *Data Resources U.S. Review* (December 1981): 1.12.
12. Stephen Brooks, "A Balanced Budget, 1972–1978: What Would Have Happened?" in Allan R. Sanderson, ed., *D.R.I. Readings in Macroeconomics* (New York, 1981), p. 244.
13. Ibid., p. 251.
14. George Guess and Kenneth Koford, "Inflation, Recession and the Federal Budget Deficit (or, Blaming Economic Problems on a Statistical Mirage)," *Policy Sciences* 17 (1984): 399.
15. See, for example, "Conflict Looming over a U.S. View on Aid for States," *New York Times*, November 24, 1984, where federal aid was estimated at $150 billion.
16. Lester C. Thurow, *The Zero-Sum Society* (New York, 1980), p. 74.
17. Ibid.
18. Personal communication with the Office of Management and Budget, November 8, 1984.
19. Consider Paul Volcker's statement in October 1984: "We're becoming a debtor country.

We're borrowing abroad at the rate of $80 billion to $90 billion. We are directly or indirectly financing that budget deficit from abroad." Volcker estimated foreign lenders held $174 billion in federal securities. "U.S. about to Join the Debtor States," *Los Angeles Times*, October 12, 1984.

20. "Will Interest Rates Come Down? Interview with Walter B. Wriston, Chairman, Citicorp," *U.S. News & World Report* (May 31, 1982): 26.

21. "Two Economists Speak Out," *Newsweek* (September 21, 1981): 39.

22. James L. Pierce, "Interest Rates and Their Prospects in the Recovery," *Brookings Papers on Economic Activity* (1975): 102.

23. The development of Federal Reserve policy may best be understood by reviewing the *Federal Reserve Bulletin*, especially February 1979, pp. 118–30; August 1979, pp. 591–602; February 1980, pp. 127–48; and March 1980, pp. 177–89.

24. Paul Volcker was interviewed on "MacNeil-Lehrer Report," August 20, 1981, Show no. 7039, Library no. 1539, pp. 3, 4. Volcker was also interviewed on "Issues and Answers," August 30, 1981.

25. Economist Mickey Levy analyzed data from 1952 through 1978, and concluded that the "empirical results show that during the post-Accord period the Federal Reserve has tended to expand the monetary base in response to increases in inflationary expectations and government deficits and . . . has tended to accommodate its own previous actions rather than abruptly change policy." See Levy, "Factors Affecting Monetary Policy in an Era of Inflation," *Journal of Monetary Economics* 8 (1981): 367. Levy's results led him to mispredict the Federal Reserve's behavior in the next year, however, as he also wrote: "Based on this model, we can expect continued rapid growth of the monetary base" (p. 368). While the deficit grew to its highest levels the Federal Reserve restrained the money supply.

26. Robert Aaron Gordon, *Economic Instability & Growth* (New York, 1974), p. 176.

27. Commenting on fears that this monetary expansion would produce inflation, particularly in light of Milton Friedman's statement that "inflation is always and everywhere a monetary phenomenon," economist Robert J. Gordon had this to say about the economy of 1974: "But excessive monetary growth is not necessary for inflation, because inflation can be caused without any change in the rate of monetary growth. Only one example is necessary to contradict a generalization as sweeping as Friedman's: the unusual 1974 events in which inflation accelerated without any similar previous acceleration in monetary growth." Robert J. Gordon, *Macroeconomics* (Boston, 1978), pp. 239–40.

28. Alan S. Blinder is quoted in A. F. Ehrbar, "Monetization of Deficits," *National Bureau of Economic Research Digest* (May 1983): 2.

29. Lindley H. Clark, Jr., reviewed this period and wrote: "In early 1973 the Fed tightened up to fight rising inflation. In 1977 the economy seemed to be weakening, inflation was still fairly low and the Fed embarked on an expansionary policy. In 1981 the Reagan administration said it wanted a reduction in the growth rate of the money supply, and that's what it got, although the slowdown was more abrupt than the administration asked." See "What Will the Fed Do after the Election?" *Wall Street Journal*, November 5, 1984.

30. "Tobin Says Fed Imperils Recovery," *New York Times*, February 25, 1982.

31. Clark, "What Will the Fed Do after the Election?" Clark noted in early November: "If those forecasts are anywhere near the mark, there is no reason at all to expect the Fed to ease policy in the coming year, pouring more funds into the economy. If there is any significant change, the Fed's history in post-election years suggests it's more likely to be in the direction of restraint. No Federal Reserve officials have said that they regard a 5%-and-rising inflation to be acceptable."

32. "Vice Chairman of Fed Is Critical of Tight Rein," *New York Times*, May 4, 1984.

33. "Fed Vice Chairman Says Policy Is Steady, but Some Accommodation Is Appropriate," *Wall Street Journal*, November 7, 1984.

34. Meltzer, "Closing the Deficit," p. 101.

35. Brian Motley, "Real Interest Rates, Money and Government Deficits," Federal Reserve Bank of San Francisco *Economic Review* (Summer 1983): 31, 43.
36. "Wall Street Jitters," *MacNeil-Lehrer Report*, May 8, 1981, Show no. 6225, Transcript no. 1465, pp. 1–2.
37. V. Vance Roley, "The Financing of Federal Deficits: An Analysis of Crowding Out," Federal Reserve Bank of Kansas City *Economic Review* (July–August 1981): 24.
38. Benjamin M. Friedman, "Crowding Out or Crowding In? Economic Consequences of Financing Government Deficits," *Brookings Papers on Economic Activity* 3 (1978): 596–97.
39. According to Friedman: "The 'crowding out' aspects of debt-financed fiscal policy have undergone substantial analysis in the academic literature and have received widespread attention in the financial press and, more generally, among the government and business communities. Discussion along these lines abated somewhat after interest rates on private borrowing failed to rise during 1975 and 1976, but debate has recently intensified . . . because the deficit has remained large and fixed investment has been slow to regain vigor during the subsequent recovery" (ibid., 596). An interesting review of this research conducted before 1975 is "Crowding Out and Its Critics," by Keith M. Carlson and Roger W. Spencer, in Federal Reserve Bank of St. Louis *Review* (December 1975). Carlson and Spencer summarized both theoretical and empirical studies, and concluded that the empirical literature "has taken the form of simulations of Government actions and has yielded results that show signs of being consistent with the crowding-out hypothesis. This crowding out tends to be very slow in developing, however, and occurs in real rather than nominal terms" (p. 15). This review did not distinguish between portfolio and transaction crowding out, and was written before Friedman made his important contribution to this area of research.
40. Friedman, "Crowding Out or Crowding In?" p. 607.
41. Ibid., pp. 640–41.
42. Ibid., p. 640.
43. Ibid.
44. Roley, "The Financing of Federal Deficits," p. 29.
45. Ibid., p. 28.
46. Ibid.
47. Ibid.
48. James Tobin, "A Keynesian View of the Budget Deficit," *California Management Review* 26 (Winter 1984): 11.
49. Friedman, "Testimony before the United States Senate Committee on Finance," p. 70.
50. Lawrence Klein, "The Deficit and Economic Performance," *Deficit Reduction Proposals, Hearings before the Committee on Finance, United States Senate*, p. 94.
51. "A Debt of $1 Trillion: Its Effect on Economy," *New York Times*, September 30, 1981.
52. David J. Ott and Attiat F. Ott, *Federal Budget Policy* (Washington, D.C., 1977), p. 120.
53. Robert Eisner and Paul J. Pieper, "A New View of the Federal Debt and Budget Deficits," *American Economic Review* 74 (March 1984): 23.
54. "A Debt of $1 Trillion: Its Effect on Economy," *New York Times*, September 30, 1981.
55. William Cates, *Where Is the Free Lunch?? The Voter's Guide to Government Economic Policy* (New York, 1980), p. 35.
56. Ibid., p. 35.
57. "U.S. Debt Interest Wipes Out Saving," *New York Times*, February 4, 1984.
58. "Program for Economic Recovery," pp. 46/24, 34/12.
59. Ibid., pp. 23/1–24/2.
60. The macroeconomic theory described here is based on Robert J. Gordon, *Macroeconomics*.
61. Mark Willes, " 'Rational Expectations' as a Counterrevolution," in Daniel Bell and Irving Kristol, eds., *The Crisis in Economic Theory* (New York, 1981), p. 82.
62. Daniel Bell, "Models and Reality in Economic Discourse," in ibid., p. 64.
63. Willes, " 'Rational Expectations,' " p. 85.

64. Thomas J. Sargent, "Stopping Moderate Inflation: The Methods of Poincaré and Thatcher," in Rudiger Dornbusch and Mario Henrique Simonsen, eds., *Inflation, Debt, and Indexation*, (Cambridge: MIT Press, 1983), pp. 54–55.

65. Willes, "'Rational Expectations,'" pp. 87, 92.

66. "Program for Economic Recovery," p. 46/24.

67. Willes, "'Rational Expectations,'" p. 93, and "Program for Economic Recovery," p. 23/1.

68. Sargent, "Stopping Moderate Inflation," p. 6.

69. Ibid., p. 4.

70. Thomas J. Sargent, "The Ends of Four Big Inflations," Working Paper 158, Federal Reserve Bank of Minneapolis, revised May 1981, p. 2.

71. Robert Heilbroner observed in 1984: "One difference is that there has never been a default on any item of the federal government's obligation; that is why the credit rating of the government is the standard against which all others are measured." See "Reflections: The Deficit," *New Yorker* (July 30, 1984): 50.

72. The literature here is vast. Begin with Herbert Simon, *Administrative Behavior* (New York, 1967); David Braybrooke and Charles Lindblom, *A Strategy of Decision* (New York, 1970); and Harvey Leibenstein, "Microeconomics and X-Efficiency Theory," in Bell and Kristol, eds. *The Crisis in Economic Theory*. In addition, for an interesting criticism of the rational economics model, see Robert J. Gordon, "'Credibility' vs. 'Mainstream': Two Views of the Inflation Process," in *Inflation: Prospects and Remedies*, Center for National Policy, Washington, D.C., no. 10, 1983.

73. Isabel V. Sawhill, "Economic Policy," in John L. Palmer and Isabel V. Sawhill, eds., *The Reagan Experiment* (Washington, D.C., 1982), p. 54.

74. "Prepared Statement of Dr. Isabel V. Sawhill," *Budget Policies to Restore Growth, Jobs, and Equity: Hearings before the Committee on the Budget, House of Representatives* (Washington, D.C.: GPO, February 8 and 10, 1983), p. 8.

75. Isabel V. Sawhill and Charles F. Stone, "The Economy, the Key to Success," in John L. Palmer and Isabel V. Sawhill, eds., *The Reagan Record* (Washington, D.C., 1984), p. 92.

76. In July 1982, Wharton Econometric Forecasting Associates provided Senator Daniel P. Moynihan with analyses that simulated the effect on the economy produced by a balanced budget in the manner designed by S.J. Res. 58, the balanced budget amendment passed by the Senate in 1982, in conjunction with the tax and spending program approved in July 1981. The data reported here are from the summary sheet "Summary of Economic Impact of S.J. Res. 58, Analysis Prepared by Wharton Econometric Forecasting Associates." The "Summary" was distributed at the time the amendment was debated in the Senate.

77. "What Went Wrong with 'Supply Side' Economics," *U.S. News & World Report* (January 18, 1982): 36.

78. Friedman, "Testimony before the United States Senate Committee on Finance," p. 66.

79. Sawhill and Stone concurred with Friedman, but were still uncertain about how the government's fiscal policy would influence the economy in the budget's out-years: "In summary, Reagan tax policies have stimulated investment demand, but the budget deficits threaten to absorb so much saving that the net effect of Reagan policies could easily be negative. Translating the effect on capital formation . . . into effects on economic growth, we estimate that the net effect . . . could be to lower output by as much as 2.8 percent in 1990 or to raise it by as much as 1.2 percent." Sawhill and Stone, "The Economy," p. 99. Allan Meltzer also worried about the effects of the deficits on capital markets and interest rates, noting that "real interest rates raises costs for all borrowers. The Federal government, as a major debtor, cannot avoid these costs. . . . A fiscal policy that requires the debt to grow without limit cannot continue. A policy of this kind is infeasible." Meltzer, "Closing the Deficit," p. 103.

80. Herbert Stein, "Controlling the Budget Deficit: If Not Now, When? If Not Us, Who?" *Deficit Reduction Proposals, Hearing before the Committee on Finance, United States Senate*, p. 156.

81. Klein, "The Deficit and Economic Performance," pp. 94–95.
82. *The UCLA National Business Forecast*, UCLA Business Forecasting Project, Graduate School of Management, September 1984, p. 1.
83. Tobin, "A Keynesian View of the Budget Deficit," pp. 12–13.
84. "Reagan: 'I'm Not in a Compromising Mood,'" *Newsweek* (November 26, 1984): 39.
85. Albert T. Sommers, "Statement of Dr. Albert T. Sommers, Vice President and Chief Economist, the Conference Board," *Budget Policies to Restore Growth, Jobs, and Equity: Hearings before the Committee on the Budget, House of Representatives* (Washington, D.C.: GPO, February 8 and 10, 1983), p. 19.
86. Paul McCracken, "Prepared Statement of Dr. Paul W. McCracken," in ibid., p. 152.
87. Stein, "Controlling the Budget Deficit," pp. 160–61.
88. In the fight against a constitutional amendment requiring balanced federal budgets, 172 economists, including 6 Nobel Prize winners, presented a petition to Congress voicing their opposition to the amendment. See for example, "Economists Call Plan Unworkable: Balanced Budget Amendment Decried," *Washington Post*, July 28, 1982.

Chapter 3. Colonial Deficits, Constitutional Restrictions, and the Rise of Hamiltonian Government

1. Joseph Dorfman, *The Economic Mind in American Civilization, 1601–1865* (New York, 1953), 1:14.
2. Gary B. Nash, *The Urban Crucible: Social Change, Political Consciousness, and the Origins of the American Revolution* (Cambridge, Mass., 1979), p. 71.
3. Ibid., p. 60. Nash made this observation about New York's colonial tax base: "By employing the reverse of the modern-day graduated income tax, the assessors placed the heaviest proportionate tax burden on the lower and middle classes and the lightest proportionate burden on those at the top," p. 71.
4. Ibid., p. 61
5. Ibid., pp. 62, 225, 253.
6. Ibid., p. 138.
7. Ibid., p. 119.
8. Ibid., p. 120.
9. Dorfman, *The Economic Mind in American Civilization*, p. 145.
10. Nash, *The Urban Crucible*, p. 125.
11. Dorfman, *The Economic Mind in American Civilization*, p. 168.
12. Ibid., pp. 167–68.
13. Ibid., pp. 142, 135.
14. Ibid., p. 154.
15. Ibid.
16. Nash, *The Urban Crucible*, pp. 256, 317.
17. Ibid., pp. 143, 86, 87.
18. Ibid., p. 175.
19. Dorfman, *The Economic Mind in American Civilization*, p. 142.
20. Nash, *The Urban Crucible*, p. 137.
21. Dorfman, *The Economic Mind in American Civilization*, pp. 149–50, and Nash, *The Urban Crucible*, 212–13.
22. Nash, *The Urban Crucible*, pp. 225–26.
23. Ibid., pp. 149, 150, 151.
24. Benjamin Franklin, *A Modest Enquiry into the Nature and Necessity of a Paper Currency*, in Clarence L. Ver Steeg and Richard Hofstadter, eds., *Great Issues in American History* (New York, 1969), p. 174.
25. Dorfman, *The Economic Mind in American Civilization*, p. 188.
26. Nash, *The Urban Crucible*, p. 286.
27. Davis Rich Dewey, *Financial History of the United States* (New York, 1920), p. 30.
28. Ibid., pp. 23–24, 30.

29. Ibid., p. 30.
30. E. James Ferguson, *The Power of the Purse* (Chapel Hill, N.C., 1961), pp. 18–19.
31. John Watts Kearny, *Sketch of American Finances: 1789–1835* (New York, 1887), p. 3.
32. Ferguson, *The Power of the Purse*, p. 26.
33. Ibid., pp. 29–30; and Don Higginbotham, *The War of American Independence* (Bloomington, Ind., 1977), pp. 289–90.
34. Ferguson, *The Power of the Purse*, p. 37.
35. Higginbotham, *The War of American Independence*, p. 290, and Ferguson, *The Power of the Purse*, p. 39.
36. Kearny, *Sketch of American Finances*, pp. 4, 7.
37. Higginbotham, *The War of American Independence*, p. 289.
38. Albert Bolles, *The Financial History of the United States, from 1774 to 1789: Embracing the Period of the American Revolution* (New York, 1879), pp. 215–16.
39. Ibid., pp. 212–13.
40. Higginbotham, *The War of American Independence*, p. 293.
41. Ibid.
42. In 1879 economic historian Albert Bolles criticized the decision of Congress to issue paper money, saying, "In thus issuing paper money, it has been affirmed that Congress committed two capital errors: first, in issuing any bills whatever; and secondly, in not taxing the Colonies immediately to redeem them." Bolles, *The Financial History of the United States*, p. 33. Bolles was a "hard-money" man who wrote in the midst of the debate over silver specie. In 1961, Ferguson noted that the conception of Revolutionary finance was "until recently based on the writings of nineteenth-century scholars . . . engaged in the defense of sound money against silverites and inflationists. Because the keystone of public finance in early America was fiat money, they enlarged upon its failures as an object lesson for their own generation." He says that, in their view, the "same obsession with paper money was the primary source of national difficulties in the 'critical period' of the Confederation. The denouement was the rise of the Federalists and Alexander Hamilton, who rescued the country from its errors." See Ferguson, *The Power of the Purse*, p. xiv. Ferguson's comments hold true for Bolles's interpretation of paper money in American history.
43. Jackson Turner Main, *Political Parties before the Constitution* (New York, 1974), p. 86.
44. Ibid., p. 48.
45. Higginbotham, *The War of American Independence*, p. 294.
46. Bolles, *The Financial History of the United States*, p. 280.
47. Edward Conrad Smith, ed., *The Constitution of the United States* (New York, 1972), p. 5.
48. Ibid., p. 35.
49. Ibid., p. 39.
50. Higginbotham, *The War of American Independence*, pp. 296, 438.
51. Ferguson, *The Power of the Purse*, p. 143.
52. Higginbotham, *The War of American Independence*, p. 297.
53. Bolles, *The Financial History of the United States*, p. 286.
54. Ferguson, *The Power of the Purse*, p. 143. Ferguson also observed: "New delegates altered the composition of Congress. The Adams-Lee alliance was fractured at the northern end by the advent of Oliver Wolcott of Connecticut, John Sullivan of New Hampshire, and Ezekiel Cornell and James Mitchell Varnum of Rhode Island. Richard Henry Lee left Congress and the Virginia delegation was guided until 1783 by Theodorick Blank, Joseph Jones, and James Madison, who joined with Daniel Carroll and John Hanson of Maryland to give the southern states a conservative representation," p. 113.
55. Ibid., p. 142.
56. Main, *Political Parties before the Constitution*, p. 51.
57. Ibid., pp. 326–331. The seven states in Main's Study were Massachusetts, New York, New Jersey, Pennsylvania, Maryland, Virginia, and South Carolina.

58. Ibid., p. 63.
59. Bolles, *The Financial History of the United States,* pp. 349–50.
60. Ibid., p. 348.
61. *The Federalist Papers* (New York, 1961), no. 30, pp. 188–89.
62. Smith, *The Constitution of the United States,* p. 35.
63. *The Federalist Papers,* no. 21, pp. 141–42, 138.
64. Ibid., no. 30, p. 189.
65. Ibid., no. 34, pp. 205, 206–7.
66. Ibid., pp. 209–10.
67. Ibid., no. 44, p. 281.
68. Ibid., pp. 281–82.
69. Ibid., no. 31, pp. 194–95.
70. Ibid., no. 30, p. 190.
71. Ibid., no. 31, p. 195.
72. Ibid., p. 196; no. 33, p. 202.
73. Ibid., no. 32, p. 197.
74. Ibid., no. 33, p. 203.
75. Jonathan Elliot, ed., *Debates on the Adoption of the Federal Constitution* in the Convention Held at Philadelphia, in 1787; with a Diary of the Debates of the Congress of the Convention; as Reported by James Madison, a Member and Deputy from Virginia (Philadelphia, 1845), 5:378.
76. James Madison, *The Journal of the Debates which* Framed the Constitution of the United States: May–September, 1787, Gaillard Hunt, ed. (New York, 1908), 2:181–83. The members of the Constitutional Convention participating in the debate on bills of credit were Nathaniel Gorham (Mass.); Gouverneur Morris (Pa.); George Mason (Va.); James Mercer (Md.); Oliver Ellsworth (Conn.); Edmund Randolph (Va.); George Read (Del.); John Langdon (N.H.); James Wilson (Pa.); Pierce Butler (S.C.); and Madison.
77. The debate at the convention over the use of federal bills of credit was later subjected to some interpretation as to the convention's intent on this matter. Words and deeds support the interpretation provided in this chapter. For example, Davis Dewey presented additional insight on the issue in his *Financial History of the United States,* p. 69:

> The question was thus left in such a doubtful form that it is difficult now to decide whether the convention intended to deny absolutely to Congress the right to emit bills of credit under any circumstances whatever. Mr. Bancroft, an authority on the history of the Constitution, declares that the refusal is so clear that according to all rules by which public documents are interpreted the prohibition should not even be treated as questionable; he cites in proof the statement just quoted from the debates and makes a striking argument in support of this conclusion. . . . Doubt is raised when it is remembered that the discussion in the convention was over the clause making a positive grant of power to Congress rather than over an express denial. Hamilton . . . appears to have felt that the prohibition was not literally complete. "The emitting of paper money by the authority of government is wisely prohibited to the individual States by the national Constitution; and the spirit of that prohibition ought not to be disregarded by the government of the United States. The wisdom of the Government will be shown in never trusting itself with the use of so seducing and dangerous an expedient." It is also difficult to believe that the issue of treasury notes in 1812, although not payable on demand or legal tender, would have been so easily accomplished if the framers of the Constitution who were still influential in public affairs had been confident in their conviction that the Constitution had absolutely taken away the right of emission of bills of credit. . . . The subsequent action of Congress from 1812 to 1860 in repeatedly authorizing bills of credit, and from 1862 to the present day in emitting legal tenders, affords a striking example of the ease with which the Constitution has been adjusted, if not strained, in order to meet real or fanciful emergencies.

Later, Charles Warren clarified the issue further by noting that despite this action by the convention on August 16, "it was held, many years later, by the Supreme Court of the

United States that under the Necessary and Proper Clause of the Constitution, the power to emit bills of credit and also the power to make them legal tender in payment of private debts were to be implied from the express power 'to borrow money,' such subsidiary powers being deemed to be appropriate means to carry out that end." Warren, *The Making of the Constitution* (Boston, 1928), p. 696.

78. Elliot, *Debates*, 5:381.
79. Madison, *Journal*, 2:262.
80. Morton Borden, ed., *The Antifederalist Papers* (East Lansing, Mich., 1965), pp. 31–32. Other Anti-Federalist works may be found in Cecelia Kenyon, ed., *The Antifederalists* (New York, 1966).
81. Elliot, *Debates*, 4:169.
82. Ibid., 3:471.
83. Said Beard, "Two small clauses embody the chief demands of personality against agrarianism: the emission of paper money is prohibited and the states are forbidden to impair the obligation of contract. The first of these means a return to specie basis. . . . The Shays and their paper money legions, who assaulted the vested rights of personalty by the process of legislative depreciation, are now subdued forever, and money lenders and security holders may be sure of their operations." Charles Beard, *An Economic Interpretation of the Constitution of the United States* (New York, 1960), pp. 178–79. Some interesting objections to Beard's thesis are raised in Leonard W. Levy, ed., *Essays on the Making of the Constitution* (New York, 1969).
84. Elliot, *Debates*, 3:471.
85. Herbert Storing, *What the Anti-Federalists Were For* (Chicago, 1981), p. 42. Jackson Turner Main noted, "In most of the states the Federalists accused their opponents of being motivated by a desire for paper money." *The Anti-Federalists: Critics of the Constitution: 1781–1788* (Chapel Hill, N.C., 1961), p. 167.
86. Elliot, *Debates*, 1:330. Rhode Island's statement is on p. 336.

Chapter 4. Creating a Symbol: Balanced Budgets and the Concept of Corruption

1. Albert Bolles, *The Financial History of the United States, from 1789 to 1860* (New York, 1883), p. 127. This is the second volume of Bolles's three-volume history, and will be noted as vol. 2 in subsequent notes.
2. See Appendix 3 for data on federal revenues, expenditures, deficits, and debts.
3. Jacob E. Cooke, ed., *The Reports of Alexander Hamilton* (New York, 1964), p. 2.
4. Ibid., pp. 2, 5, 6.
5. Ibid., pp. 6–7.
6. Several good summaries of Hamilton's programs are available, including Kearny's *Sketch of American Finances*, and William J. Schultz and M. R. Caine's "Federalist Finance," in George R. Taylor, ed., *Hamilton and the National Debt* (Boston, 1950), pp. 1–8, in addition to Cooke, *The Reports of Alexander Hamilton*, p. 2.
7. Cooke, ed., *The Reports of Alexander Hamilton*, pp. 13, 14.
8. Kearny, *Sketch of American Finances*, pp. 23–24.
9. Cooke, ed., *The Reports of Alexander Hamilton*, pp. 8, 11.
10. Ibid., p. xvi. This quotation comes from Hamilton's letter to Robert Morris, April 30, 1781.
11. Ibid., p. xix.
12. Adrienne Koch and William Peder, eds., *The Life and Selected Writings of Thomas Jefferson* (New York, 1944), p. 124.
13. Cooke, ed., *The Reports of Alexander Hamilton*, p. xix.
14. Koch and Peder, eds., *Life and Writings of Jefferson*, p. 123.
15. Ibid., p. 127.
16. Ibid., pp. 120, 121.
17. Ibid., pp. 129, 124, 125.

18. See Leo Marx, *The Machine in the Garden* (New York, 1964), on the imagery of the machine and the engine in American thought.
19. The idea of corruption is most fully explored in Lance Banning, *The Jeffersonian Persuasion* (Ithaca, N.Y., 1978); Drew R. McCoy, *The Elusive Republic: Political Economy in Jeffersonian America* (New York, 1980); Gordon S. Wood, *The Creation of the American Republic, 1776–1787* (New York, 1969); and J. G. A. Pocock, *The Machiavellian Moment: Florentine Political Thought and the Atlantic Republican Tradition* (Princeton, N.J., 1975).
20. The term "corruption" was widely, but specifically, used during this period. Hamilton, for example, defended the Constitution at the New York ratification convention against defenders of the Articles of Confederation by claiming that "it would be easy, in comparing the two Constitutions, to prove that the chances of corruption under the new are much fewer than those to which the old is exposed." Elliot, ed., *Debates*, 2: p. 263.
21. Banning, *The Jeffersonian Persuasion*, pp. 43, 56. An excellent review of the English treasury system at that time can be found in J. E. D. Binney, *British Public Finance and Administration, 1774–92* (London, 1958), and P. G. M. Dickson,*The Financial Revolution in England: A Study in the Development of Public Credit, 1688–1756* (New York, 1967).
22. Banning, *The Jeffersonian Persuasion*, p. 59.
23. Koch and Peder, eds., *Life and Writings of Jefferson*, p. 126.
24. Hamilton wrote in *Federalist Paper* no. 13, "If the States are united under one government, there will be but one national civil list to support." *The Federalist Papers*, p. 97.
25. Koch and Peder, eds., *Life and Writings of Jefferson*, p. 123.
26. McCoy, *The Ellusive Republic*, p. 12.
27. Koch and Peder, eds., *Life and Writings of Jefferson*, p. 441.
28. Jefferson believed the Louisiana Purchase was crucial to ensure the agrarian nature of American society. Interestingly enough, the terms of the debt instruments that financed the purchase effectively delayed the first major payments until after Jefferson's presidency, enabling him to balance his budgets. On the importance of the purchase to the concept of corruption, see McCoy, *The Elusive Republic*, esp. chap. 8.
29. The differences between the Federalists and the Jeffersonians on matters of military strategy and finance are outlined in Russell F. Weigley, *The American Way of War* (Bloomington, Ind., 1975), chap. 3.
30. Bolles, *The Financial History of the United States*, 2:219.
31. Ibid., 2:225.
32. Ibid., 2:236.
33. Ibid., 2:250.
34. On the number of banks, see Robert V. Remini, *Andrew Jackson and the Bank War* (New York, 1967), p. 26.
35. T. H. Greene and T. H. Grose, eds., *Essays: Moral, Political and Literary by David Hume* (London, 1875), pp. 363–64.
36. Adam Smith, *The Wealth of Nations* (London, 1981), p. 419.
37. Cooke, ed., *The Reports of Alexander Hamilton*, pp. 61–63.
38. Dewey, *Financial History of the United States*, p. 149.
39. Clay's estimate may have been on the high side. Davis Dewey noted in 1920 that "the State banks reduced their note issues from $100,000,000 in 1817 to $45,000,000 in 1818." Ibid., p. 166.
40. Ibid., p. 167. Dewey wrote that between 1817 and 1819 the federal government redeemed $32 million of the debt, which is approximately 40 percent of federal revenues produced during that period.
41. T. H. Greer, "The Depression of 1819–1821," Ph.D. dissertation, University of California, Berkeley, 1938, p. 152.
42. John Spencer Basset, *The Life of Andrew Jackson* (New York, 1967), p. 428.
43. Lewis Kimmel, *Federal Budget and Fiscal Policy: 1789–1958* (Washington, D.C., 1959), pp. 20, 22, 23.

44. On this period in Jackson's life, see Remini, *Andrew Jackson and the Bank War*, pp. 17–23.

45. Joseph Blau, ed., *Social Theories of Jacksonian Democracy* (New York, 1954), pp. 184, 188.

46. Robert V. Remini, *Andrew Jackson and the Course of American Freedom 1822–1832* (New York, 1981), 2:34.

47. Kimmel, *Federal Budget and Fiscal Policy*, p. 19.

48. Blau, *Social Theories of Jacksonian Democracy*, pp. 14–15.

49. Ibid., pp. 13, 14.

50. Remini, *Andrew Jackson and the Bank War*, pp. 44, 166. For more on the notion of corruption in Jacksonian America, see Rush Welter, *The Mind of America, 1820–1860* (New York, 1975), pp. 172–73.

51. The Bank War and the Jacksonian era are widely debated by historians. Some of the more important books on the subject, in addition to those previously mentioned, include: Arthur M. Schlesinger, Jr., *The Age of Jackson* (Boston, 1945); Bray Hammond, *Banks and Politics in America from the Revolution to the Civil War* (Princeton, N.J., 1957); John McFaul, *The Politics of Jacksonian Finance* (Ithaca, N.Y., 1972); Peter Temin, *The Jacksonian Economy* (New York, 1969); and Marvin Meyer, *The Jacksonian Persuasion: Politics and Beliefs* (Stanford, Calif., 1957).

52. A fine review of the positions taken by American and European economists is contained in Kimmel, *Federal Budget and Fiscal Policy*, pp. 37–55. Kimmel neglected to mention the crucial influence David Hume had on Alexander Hamilton, however. Also see Jesse Burkhead, "The Balanced Budget," in Arthur Smithies and J. Keith Butters, eds., *American Economic Association Readings in Fiscal Policy* (New York, 1955), 3:3–27.

53. Paul Leicester Ford, ed., *The Works of Thomas Jefferson* (New York, 1887), 8:481. I thank James D. Davidson for providing the date of Jefferson's letter.

54. Saul K. Padover, *the Complete Jefferson* (New York, 1943), p. 274.

55. Bolles, *The Financial History of the United States*, 2:237. On Jefferson's position on manufacturing, see his 1816 letter to Benjamin Austin, in John S. Pancake, ed., *Thomas Jefferson: Revolutionary Philosopher, A Selection of Writings* (Woodbury, N.Y., 1976), pp. 113–16.

56. B. U. Ratchford, *American State Debts* (Durham, N.C., 1941), pp. 77, 73, 74.

57. Reginald C. McGrane, *Foreign Bondholders and American State Debts* (New York, 1935), p. 5.

58. Henry C. Adams, *Public Debts: An Essay in the Science of Finance* (New York, 1887), p. 321.

59. Ratchford, *American State Debts*, p. 81.

60. Samuel H. Beer, "The Idea of the Nation," *New Republic* (July 19, 26, 1982): 26.

61. William Letwin, ed., *A Documentary History of American Economic Policy Since 1789* (New York, 1972), p. 63.

62. Ibid., p. 64.

63. Daniel Walker Howe, *The Political Culture of the American Whigs* (Chicago, 1979), p. 36.

64. Jackson's opposition to the Whig's program for internal improvements was part politics and part political philosophy. Glyndon G. Van Deusen noted that his veto was "largely political, for Jackson signed some internal improvements bills fully as local as the Maysville Road. It was a slap at Clay, who had energetically pushed the Maysville Road, and at the American System. . . . It also served notice that, in Jackson's opinion, the construction of roads and canals lay more within the province of the states than of the nation. Jefferson's belief in limiting the scope of action of the national government was now to be one of the tenets of Jacksonian Democracy." See Van Deusen, *The Jacksonian Era, 1828–1848* (New York, 1959), p. 52.

65. Dewey, *Financial History of the United States*, p. 225.

66. Richard K. Crallé, ed., *Reports and Public Letters of John C. Calhoun* (New York, 1968), 3:429.

67. Dewey, *Financial History of the United States*, pp. 229–30.
68. Ratchford, *American State Debts*, pp. 86, 98–99.
69. Ibid., pp. 100–102. Also see Dewey, *Financial History of the United States*, pp. 243–46.
70. Crallé, *Reports and Letters of Calhoun*, pp. 439, 438.
71. Ibid., pp. 427, 428.
72. Ibid., pp. 427, 428.
73. Blau, *Social Theories of Jacksonian Democracy*, pp. 10, 11.
74. Ibid., p. 11.
75. Van Deusen, *The Jacksonian Era*, p. 11.
76. The debate over the federal budget surplus involved a conflict of philosophies between the Whigs and the Jacksonians, but it was also a matter of hard-core politics. Van Deusen observed that the "surplus was largely paper, but the states yearned for it and the politicians longed to satisfy their yearnings." In June 1836, "with the blessing of both the administration and the Whigs, Congress passed a bill which distributed all of the surplus over $5 million to the states," in proportion to their congressional representatives. According to Van Deusen, "This porkbarrel legislation stimulated an already unhealthy inflation. Clay supported it against his better judgement. The administration claimed credit for its passage, only to be critical of it after the election was over. It was a voters' market in a presidential year, and the surplus was the lure." Ibid., p. 107. The Whigs eventually supported the distribution of the surplus to the states because they realized Jackson would prevent the federally funded internal improvements they desired. With these additional funds and bank loans, the states could carry out those projects so dear to the Whigs. Jackson opposed the surplus in part because they allowed the Whigs to achieve a potentially great political victory.
77. C. Gordon Post, ed., *A Disquisition on Government and Selections from the Discourse, by John C. Calhoun* (New York, 1953), pp. 38, 33.
78. Ibid., pp. 39–40.
79. A. James Heins, *Constitutional Restrictions against State Debts* (Madison, Wis., 1963), p. 115.
80. Ratchford, *American State Debts*, p. 122.
81. Blau, *Social Theories of Jacksonian Democracy*, pp. 11, 18.

Chapter 5. Distorting a Symbol: Republican Party Government, 1860–1932

1. Hartz, *The Liberal Tradition in America*, p. 203.
2. Ibid., p. 215. Important studies on the tariff during this period include F. W. Taussig, *The History of the Tariff, 1860–1883* (New York, 1885), and F. W. Taussig, *The Tariff History of the United States* (New York, 1923).
3. Howe, *The Political Culture of the American Whigs*, p. 265.
4. For the Free Soiler influence on Lincoln and the Republicans, see Eric Foner, *Free Soil, Free Labor, Free Men* (Oxford, 1979), chaps. 1 and 5.
5. Robert P. Sharkey, *Money, Class, and Party: An Economic Study of Civil War and Reconstruction* (Baltimore, 1967), p. 22.
6. Ibid., pp. 19–20.
7. Robert T. Patterson, *Federal Debt Management Policies, 1865–1879* (Durham, N.C., 1954), p. 28.
8. Sharkey, *Money, Class, and Party*, p. 81.
9. Ibid., pp. 224–25.
10. Ibid., p. 225.
11. Morton Keller, *Affairs of State: Public Life in Late Nineteenth Century America* (Cambridge, Mass., 1977), pp. 4, 39.
12. Ibid., p. 4.
13. Patterson, *Federal Debt Management Policies*, p. 54.
14. Ibid., p. 56.
15. Ibid., p. 57.

16. Ibid., p. 55.

17. Ibid., p. 57.

18. Roy P. Basler, ed., *The Collected Works of Abraham Lincoln* (New Brunswick, N.J., 1953), 8:142–43.

19. Patterson, *Federal Debt Management Policies,* pp. 56–57.

20. Ibid., p. 53.

21. Samuel Wilkeson, *How Our National Debt May Be a National Blessing* (Philadelphia, 1865), p. 3.

22. Ibid., p. 4.

23. Ibid., p. 6.

24. Ibid., p. 5.

25. Higginbotham, *The War of American Independence,* p. 297.

26. Wilkeson, *How Our National Debt May Be a National Blessing,* p. 6.

27. Ibid., pp. 6–7.

28. Ibid., pp. 7, 8.

29. Ibid., p. 10.

30. Consider inflation first. According to data supplied by Milton Friedman and Anna Schwartz, both the wholesale and implicit price indexes declined greatly after the Civil War and never reached similar levels until 1916. For example, they write, "Wholesale prices more than doubled during the Civil War and then fell irregularly over the next fifteen years to their initial levels." Friedman and Schwartz, *A Monetary History of the United States, 1867–1960* (Princeton, N.J., 1963), p. 85. See especially Chart 62 on p. 678. As for interest payments on the debt, the expenditure numbers provided here in this chapter exclude debt payments. Nevertheless, interest payments declined over the years as the debt was retired. In 1868 these payments totaled $140 million, but by 1877 they fell to $97 million. See Dewey, *Financial History of the United States,* p. 399. The point here is that both inflation and debt payments declined while federal expenditures grew.

31. For river and harbor expenditures in 1850–60 see Dewey, *Financial History of the United States,* p. 268; for 1869–79 see p. 400; for 1880–90 see p. 427; and for 1831–60 see p. 268.

32. Alexander Dana Noyes, *Forty Years of American Finance* (New York, 1909), p. 90.

33. Ibid., p. 90.

34. Keller, *Affairs of State,* p. 382.

35. Carter Goodrich, *Government Promotion of American Canals and Railroads, 1800–1890* (New York, 1960), p. 268.

36. Ibid., p. 269.

37. For the 1878 pension expenditure level see Dewey, *Financial History of the United States,* p. 399; for 1893 see p. 428. The budget percentages are provided by Keller, *Affairs of State,* p. 311.

38. Keller, *Affairs of State,* p. 311.

39. Ibid., p. 381.

40. Ibid., p. 312.

41. Ibid.

42. Charles Haines Stewart III, "The Politics of Structural Reform: Reforming Budgetary Structure in the House, 1861–1921," Ph.D. dissertation, Stanford University, 1985, p. 121.

43. Keller, *Affairs of State,* p. 310.

44. Ratchford, *American State Debts,* p. 161.

45. Ibid., p. 183.

46. Kenneth Stampp, *The Era of Reconstruction, 1865–1877* (New York, 1965), p. 183. Also see Mark W. Summers, *Railroads, Reconstruction, and the Gospel of Prosperity* (Princeton, N.J., 1984).

47. William Thomas Wander, "Patterns of Change in the Congressional Budget Process, 1865–1974," Paper, American Political Science Association, September 6, 1981, p. 7.

48. Stewart, "The Politics of Structural Reform," esp. chap. 5. Stewart's research on the budgetary process of this period makes a significant contribution in its description of the Democrats' role in fragmenting the Appropriations Committee's powers.
49. John H. Reagan, *Memoirs* (New York, 1906), p. 248.
50. Stewart, "The Politics of Structural Reform," p. 172.
51. Louis Fisher, *Presidential Spending Power* (Princeton, N.J., 1975), p. 23. Also see Dennis Ippolito, *Congressional Spending Power* (Ithaca, N.Y., 1981), chap. 2.
52. Keller, *Affairs of State*, pp. 309–10.
53. Albert S. Bolles, *The Financial History of the United States, From 1861 to 1885* (New York, 1886), 3:552–53. This is Bolles's third volume.
54. "Balanced Budget-Tax Limitation Constitutional Amendment," Report of the Committee on the Judiciary, U.S. Senate, July 10, 1981 (Washington D.C.: GPO, 1981), p. 21.
55. Consider Louis Fisher's comment about tariffs: "Prior revenues had come from a system of indirect taxation that the ordinary taxpayer did not see or feel (revenue from tariff duties, taxes on tobacco, or liquor, etc.)." Fisher, *Presidential Spending Power*, p. 30. Tariffs, however, were one of the major political issues of American politics.
56. Baxter, *National Debts*, p. 31.
57. "Refunding the National Debt," Statements before the Committee on Finance, US Senate, January 25, 1881, p. 13.
58. Noyes, *Forty Years of American Finance*, pp. 125–26.
59. Ibid., pp. 187–88.
60. Ibid., p. 137.
61. Matthew Josephson, *The Politicos, 1865–1896* (New York, 1966), pp. 460–61.
62. Alvin M. Josephy, Jr., *On the Hill: A History of the American Congress* (New York, 1979), p. 263.
63. Edwin R. A. Seligman, *The Income Tax: A Study of the History, Theory, and Practice of Income Taxation at Home and Abroad* (New York, 1911), p. 495.
64. Dewey, *Financial History of the United States*, pp. 456–57.
65. Seligman, *The Income Tax*, pp. 506–7.
66. In 1895 the Supreme Court in *Pollack* v. *Farmers' Loan and Trust Company* declared unconstitutional the federal income tax established in the 1894 Gorman-Wilson Tariff Act. The Court ruled in a 5 to 4 decision that the tax was an unlawful attack upon private property rights, and it violated Article 1, Section 9, of the Constitution which declared there shall be no direct tax "laid unless in proportion to the census." The federal government was said to violate the Constitution because it did not apportion the tax among the states on the basis of the census, and instead looked to income for setting the levy. Furthermore, the Court ruled that taxing income was the same as taxing property, which the Court considered a "direct tax," and was therefore illegal.
67. Noyes, *Forty Years of American Finance*, p. 269.
68. Ibid., p. 269.
69. Dewey, *Financial History of the United States*, p. 487.
70. Arthur S. Link, *Woodrow Wilson and the Progressive Era* (New York, 1963), p. 45. See also Robert Craig West, *Banking Reform and the Federal Reserve, 1863–1923* (Ithaca, N.Y., 1977).
71. Link, *Woodrow Wilson and the Progressive Era*, pp. 35–36.
72. Charles Beard and Mary Beard, *The Rise of American Civilization: Vol. II, The Industrial Era* (New York, 1962), p. 344.
73. These federal regulations deserve some mention because, in addition to tariffs and growing federal expenditures, they demonstrate the national government's expanding economic authority which developed under Republican party government. Historians agree that a diverse array of interests supported the creation of regulatory agencies such as the Interstate Commerce Commission and the Federal Trade Commission. Federal regulation of the nation's railroad system, for example, was encouraged by farmers and other small shippers who were concerned about transporting their goods

to market at reasonable rates. Also, Progressive Republicans and Democrats sought to bring economic order to a greatly expanding railroad system, but one that was in a state of chaos due to business practices that were perceived to be unfair and economically destabilizing. The major railroads also looked to federal regulations for relief from state regulation and from economic competition. "Consciously or operationally," noted historian Gabriel Kolko, "most railroad leaders increasingly relied on a Hamiltonian conception of the national government. They saw in certain forms of federal regulation of railroads the solution to their many economic problems as well as the redirection of public reform sentiments toward safer outlets." *Railroads and Regulations, 1877–1916* (New York, 1970), p. 5. Added political scientist Stephen Skowronek: "Thus, whereas the railroads sought to escape competition, and still others sought relief from some particular effect of competition. . . . Each aggrieved party appealed to the national government to make good through legislation the deficiencies it perceived in the workings of the natural laws" of laissez faire. *Building a New American State: The Expansion of National Administrative Capacities* (Cambridge, England, 1982), p. 125. Also see Kolko's *The Triumph of Conservatism* (New York, 1963).

74. Keller, *Affairs of State*, pp. 115–16. See especially Keller's table on p. 116 for a list of debt in selected cities from 1860 to 1875.

75. On municipal reform see Martin J. Schiesl, *The Politics of Efficiency* (Berkeley, Calif., 1977). Schiesl writes: "To those officials who answered to party bosses, the increasing taxes were an inevitable outgrowth of a budget process enabling them to raise the salaries of political appointees and increase the number of jobs in machine administrations. But urban taxpayers confident that these practices could be replaced by new standards and controls" (p. 88).

76. Skowronek, *Building a New American State*, p. 188.

77. Frank Goodnow, *Politics and Administration* (New York, 1967), pp. 129–30.

78. Skowronek, *Building a New American State*, p. 188.

79. Ibid.

80. Donald Frederick King, "From Redistributive to Hegemonic Logic: The Transformation of American Tax Politics, 1894–1963," *Politics & Society* 12 (1983): 16.

81. Dewey, *Financial History of the United States*, p. 486.

82. King, "From Redistribution to Hegemonic Logic," p. 24.

83. Theodore Roosevelt, *An Autobiography* (New York, 1921), p. 369.

84. For Roosevelt's position on the tariff see, for example, his Second Annual Message of December 2, 1902. See his Eighth Annual Message, December 8, 1908, for a statement on internal improvements. Both are in Gilbert Black, ed., *Theodore Roosevelt, 1858–1919* (Dobbs Ferry, N.Y., 1969).

85. Skowronek, *Building a New American State*, p. 132. On the politics of the American Economic Association see Sidney Fine, *Laissez Faire and the General-Welfare State* (Ann Arbor, Mich., 1964), chap. 7.

86. For example, Kimmel, *Federal Budget and Fiscal Policy*, pp. 89–98.

87. John D. Hicks, *Republican Ascendancy, 1921–1933* (New York, 1963), p. 53.

88. "Wholesale prices changed in 1923–29 at a rate 2.5 percentage less than in 1903–13, and implicit prices at a rate 2.1 percentage points less." Friedman and Schwartz, *A Monetary History of the United States*, p. 242. Also see Chart 16, p. 197. The chart shows both the wholesale and implicit price levels for the 1920s fell significantly below their World War I and prewar levels. Thus, the rate of federal expenditures during the Harding, Coolidge, and Hoover years not only grew faster than the rate of inflation, they were made in dollars worth more than in the preceding decade.

89. On the Sherman Antitrust Act see William Letwin, *Law and Economic Policy in America: The Evolution of the Sherman Antitrust Act* (Chicago, 1981).

90. Hicks, *Republican Ascendancy*, pp. 64–67.

91. Ibid., pp. 66–67.

92. Schlesinger, *The Crisis of the Old Order*, p. 19. Historians and political scientists still debate over whether Wilson should properly be classified as a Hamiltonian or Jefferso-

nian. Schlesinger clearly believed Theodore Roosevelt was Hamiltonian and Wilson was Jeffersonian. Schlesinger wrote that Roosevelt "was fortified by the conviction that he was restoring an older tradition of national purpose—the tradition of the Federalists." By comparison, "For Wilson, Jefferson had been a faith" (p. 30 and 33). Certainly there were important differences between Democratic policies made during the Wilson years and those of the Progressive Republicans. Wilson supported a decentralized central banking system through the Federal Reserve Act, whereas the Republicans favored the more centralizing Aldrich Plan. Wilson fought for low tariffs in opposition to the Republicans. Both tariffs and banking were indeed key issues dividing the Hamiltonians and Jeffersonians. But Wilson also endorsed federal regulations that strengthened federal authority at the expense of state regulation. Stephen Skowronek noted, "The Transportation Act of 1920 framed a new order in the relations between state and society in industrial America. . . . Nationalism superseded localism; system superseded fragmentation." *Building a New American State*, p. 283. Wilson's notion of regulation included guaranteed returns for the railroads. After examining Wilson's administration, R. Jeffrey Lustig said, "It would be wrong, that is, to see him as a modern Jeffersonian. Certainly the tenor of his career prior to the campaign of 1921 had always been closer to Hamilton's thinking than to Jefferson's." *Corporate Liberalism*, p. 205.

93. David Burner, *The Politics of Provincialism: The Democratic Party in Transition, 1918–1932* (New York, 1975), p. 161.
94. Ibid., p. 165.
95. Ibid., p. 166.
96. Ibid., p. 174. The Democrats' attempt to woo big business was also reflected in their choice of candidates. "So John W. Davis, counsel to J. P. Morgan, was nominated as the Democratic presidential candidate in 1924, and the party's national committee fell under the control of men who were as much a part of the world of big business and high finances as were the Republican leaders themselves." James L. Sundquist, *Dymanics of the Party System* (Washington, D.C., 1973), p. 167.
97. Hartz, *The Liberal Tradition in America*, p. 216.
98. Robert A. Pastor, *Congress and the Politics of U.S. Foreign Economic Policy* (Berkeley, Calif., 1982), p. 79.
99. Ibid., p. 83.
100. Ibid., p. 79.
101. Stein, *The Fiscal Revolution in America*, p. 83.
102. Sharkey, *Money, Class, and Party*, p. 81. Also see Walter T. K. Nugent, *The Money Question During Reconstruction* (New York, 1967).
103. Sharkey, *Money, Class, and Party*, p. 195.
104. Ibid., pp. 99–100.
105. William S. McFeely, *Grant* (New York, 1982), p. 276.
106. Sharkey, *Money, Class, and Party*, p. 140.
107. Ibid., p. 218.
108. Ibid., p. 195.
109. Friedman and Schwartz, *A Monetary History of the United States*, p. 86.
110. Labor sought not only an increase in greenbacks, but also federally financed jobs. These workers were motivated neither by the political analysis of capitalism offered by the socialist groups of the day nor by a desire to receive charity. Instead, the workers recognized that the panic began in the banking system and that their unemployment was caused by forces outside of their control. Gutman notes, "The labor leaders, antimonopolists, and currency reformers who supported the demand for public works were steeped in pre-Civil War reform ideology. Socialism made no sense to them. Their plea for public works rested on a belief in 'equal rights,' rather than a theory of exploitation." Gutman says they believed that "bankers and speculators perverted the republican governmental structure . . . because irresponsible and venal public officials granted 'special privileges' to the 'Moneyocracy' at the expense of the 'producing

classes.' The unholy alliance between government and the financial classes deprived workers of their 'natural rights' and also caused the economic crisis. Non-socialist speaker after speaker at the unemployment meetings blamed the depression on the power granted the financial community by the government." See Herbert Gutman, "The Failure of the Movement by the Unemployed for Public Works in 1873," *Political Science Quarterly* 80 (June 1965): 268. President Grant responded to these cries for public works by endorsing federal jobs projects, but he was soon dissuaded from this idea and the workers failed to gain their federally funded jobs. See also Samuel Rezneck, "Distress Relief, and the Discontent in the United States During the Depression of 1873–78," *Journal of Political Economy* 58 (December 1950): 494–512.

111. Friedman and Schwartz, *A Monetary History of the United States*, p. 32.
112. In 1870 some 51.6 percent of the population "gainfully employed" worked in agriculture, 48.8 percent in 1880, 42.5 percent in 1890, and only 37.7 percent in 1900. Grant McConnell, *The Decline of Agrarian Democracy* (New York, 1977), p. 198.
113. Palmer, "Man over Money," pp. 37–38.
114. Ibid., p. 121.
115. Ibid., chap. 8. See also Lawrence Goodwyn, *The Populist Moment* (Oxford, 1978), chap. 4.
116. Palmer, "Man over Money," p. 106.
117. The controversy over silver can be summarized by referring to a few key pieces of federal legislation that influenced silver's use as a currency. The year 1873 was notable not only for the 1873 panic, but also for the "Crime of 1873," when federal legislation ordered the Treasury to discontinue minting the 412.5 grain silver dollar. The dollar actually ceased circulation in 1836 as silver's mint price was lower than its price on the open market, and therefore miners found selling silver to the government unprofitable. The silver supply grew rapidly after 1872, however, due to extensive mining and the discovery of new silver fields. This growing silver supply depressed the market price for silver, and now miners found selling silver to the Treasury to be profitable under the old purchasing rule, but the 1873 legislation limited the Treasury's need for silver as specie. The miners demanded that the government buy their silver, in effect subsidizing their mining operations, while other Americans thought silver currency would ease their financial difficulties by expanding the money supply. Congress responded, somewhat, to these demands by passing the Bland-Allison Act in 1878, thereby providing for the purchase of some 2 million ounces of silver a month, but the law did not permit unlimited silver coinage as the silver forces desired. The miners and debtors increased their pressure on Congress, and in 1890, as an offering to rural America to enhance the acceptability of the 1890 McKinley Tariff, the Republicans supported the Sherman Silver Purchase Act. The act more than doubled the Treasury's silver purchase to a monthly 4.5 million ounces. But in 1893 the Republicans repealed the Sherman Act. "The repeal in 1893 of the purchase clause . . . and the money panic of that year both seemed further evidence to the Populists of what they regarded as a betrayal of agrarian debtors to mortgage holders in the East." Friedman and Schwartz, *A Monetary History of the United States*, p. 116.
118. The 1886 Harrison Act controlled territorial debt in several ways. Section 2 of the act declared that no territory could "loan its credit" or "borrow any money" on behalf of any business or company. Section 3 prevented any territorial legislation from authorizing debt, except "to meet a casual deficit in the revenues, to pay the interest upon the Territorial debt, to surpress insurrections, or to provide for the public defense." Finally, Section 4 ordered that no territorial legislature or local government in the territories could incur debt "exceeding four per centum on the value of taxable property." Act of July 30, 1886, Ch. 818, 24 Stat. 170.
119. Dewey, *Financial History of the United States*, p. 459.
120. Palmer, "Man over Money," p. 104.
121. "The result was a paradox and a tragedy; everything Populism sought to avoid came about. Repudiating free silver for more radical demands, it was forced to support a

silver crusade. Trying to remain independent and avoid extinction, it became absorbed by the Democratic party and was destroyed. Having grave reservations on Bryan, it formed the backbone of his following." Norman Pollack, *The Populist Response to Industrial America* (Cambridge, Mass., 1976), p. 103.

122. Friedman and Schwartz, *A Monetary History of the United States*, p. 91.
123. McConnell, *The Decline of Agrarian Democracy*, p. 11.
124. "The keynote was no longer the universality of labor or of the farming interest, but the special crop, the special skill, the special problem, the particular region, and above all a particular stratum of the farming population." Richard Hofstadter, *The Age of Reform* (New York, 1955), p. 123.
125. This attitude is particularly evident in Palmer, *"Man over Money,"* and Goodwyn, *The Populist Moment.*
126. Pollack, *The Populist Response to Industrial America*, p. 88.
127. Other legislation included the Meat Inspection Act (1907); the Grain Standards Act (1916); the Cotton Futures Act (1916); the Rural Post Roads Act (1916); and the Warehouse Act (1916). "What is most impressive is the contrast between the periods before and after 1900." Hofstadter, *The Age of Reform*, pp. 117–18.
128. "The idea in its essentials was to obtain a government guaranty of prices of farm products. This was to be founded on the one method of government interference with the price mechanism that had the approval of tradition, the tariff. To 'make the tariff work' for agriculture, farm surpluses were to be exported at world prices, while domestic prices were to be maintained at an acceptable level. The inevitable losses in such an operation were to be met by one of varying schemes for scrip, debentures, or domestic allotments. The scrip and domestic allotment plans put levies on the marketed units; the debenture plan relied on customs revenue." McConnell, *The Decline of Agrarian Democracy*, p. 63.

Chapter 6. Transforming a Symbol: Democratic Party Government, 1932–1980

1. Elliot Roosevelt, ed., *F.D.R.: His Personal Letters, 1905–1928* (New York, 1948), p. 629.
2. Samuel Rosenman, ed., *The Public Papers of Franklin Delano Roosevelt*: Vol. 1, *The Genius of the New Deal, 1928–1932* (New York, 1938), pp. 746, 628.
3. Ibid., p. 746.
4. Ibid., pp. 746, 748.
5. Ibid., pp. 632, 751–52.
6. Ibid., pp. 745, 638.
7. Ibid., p. 749.
8. John G. Cawelti, *Apostles of the Self-Made Man: Changing Concepts of Success in America* (Chicago, 1965), p. 26.
9. Bell, "Models and Reality in Economic Discourse," p. 48.
10. John Maynard Keynes, *The General Theory of Employment, Interest, and Money* (New York, 1964), pp. 127, 128–29.
11. Herbert Hoover, *The Memoirs of Herbert Hoover: The Great Depression, 1929–1941,* (New York, 1952), pp. 313, 311.
12. "Hoover Attacks the Deficits," *New York Times*, April 10, 1983.
13. Stein, *The Fiscal Revolution in America*, p. 27.
14. Stein summarized Hoover's attitudes toward budget balancing at this time by noting: "Certainly Hoover believed in balancing the budget. Possibly he would have recommended a tax increase rather than project a budget deficit for three fiscal years in a row. But Hoover also believed in recovery and in his own reelection and . . . the idea of budget-balancing did not compel him to raise taxes when he did." Ibid., p. 35.
15. Ibid., p. 24.
16. William E. Leuchtenburg, *Franklin D. Roosevelt and the New Deal 1932–1940* (New York, 1963), pp. 45, 37, 48, 91.

17. Ibid., p. 244.
18. Stein, *The Fiscal Revolution in America*, p. 98.
19. Ibid., p. 97.
20. Leuchtenburg, *Franklin D. Roosevelt and the New Deal*, p. 264.
21. James MacGregor Burns, *Roosevelt: The Lion and the Fox* (New York, 1956), p. 335.
22. Rosenman, *The Public Papers of Franklin Delano Roosevelt*, p. 812.
23. Stein, *The Fiscal Revolution in America*, pp. 117–18.
24. "Creating Dictators," *New York Times*, April 10, 1983.
25. B. C. Forbes quoted in Roy Helton, "Must America Go Fascist? Debt Threatens Democracy," *Harper's Magazine* 179, (June 1939): 3.
26. E. Francis Brown, "The American Road to Fascism," *Current History* (July 1933): 397. Also see "Need the New Deal Be Fascist?" *The Nation*, January 9, 1935, p. 33.
27. Hoover, *Memoirs*, p. vii. Hoover's memoirs include a number of surprisingly vicious attacks on Roosevelt and the New Deal: "Although Roosevelt had denied any such intent during the campaign of 1932, he stepped as soon as possible into managed currency, the power to create fiat money, and the abandonment of the convertible gold standard just as I had forecast. In every case, that was the first step toward fascism, communism, socialism, stateism, planned economy, or whatever name collectivism happens to be using at the moment" (p. 390). In another instance Hoover wrote, "Along with currency manipulation, the New Deal introduced to Americans the spectacle of Fascist dictation to business, labor and agriculture" (p. 408).
28. Helton, "Must America Go Fascist?" p. 7.
29. Ibid.
30. William Hamovitch, ed., *The Federal Deficit: Fiscal Imprudence or Policy Weapon?* (Boston, 1965), pp. 111–12.
31. Hoover, *Memoirs*, p. 390.
32. Stein, *The Fiscal Revolution in America*, pp. 298–99.
33. Eccles wrote, "If for any reason we get out of balance again and unemployment starts to develop, surplus Federal revenue should be promptly diverted into the spending stream and away from the stream of the reduction of Federal debt. If that is not sufficient to meet the unemployment situation and stop credit contraction in its inception, we should be ready to incur a budgetary deficit. . . . The Government must be looked upon as a compensatory agency . . . to do just the opposite to what private business and individuals do. The latter are necessarily motivated by the desire for profit. The former must be motivated by social obligation." From a speech, "Compensatory Action and the Role of Government," November 13, 1936, in Rudolph L. Weissman, ed., *Economic Balance and a Balanced Budget: Public Papers of Marriner S. Eccles* (New York, 1940), p. 63.
34. Walter W. Heller, *New Dimensions of Political Economy* (Cambridge, Mass., 1967), p. 27.
35. Stein, *The Fiscal Revolution in America*, p. 367.
36. Nixon wrote in *Six Crises:* "Unfortunately, Arthur Burns turned out to be a good prophet. The bottom of the 1960 dip did come in October and the economy started to move up again in November—after it was too late to affect the election returns. In October, usually a month of rising employment, the jobless rolls increased by 452,000. All the speeches, television broadcasts, and precinct work in the world could not counteract that one hard fact." Richard M. Nixon, *Six Crises* (Garden City, New York, 1962), pp. 310–11.
37. Heller, *New Dimensions of Political Economy*, p. 30, 31, 32.
38. Arthur M. Okun, *The Political Economy of Prosperity* (New York, 1970), p. 45.
39. Ibid., p. 47.
40. Heller, *New Directions of Political Economy*, p. 113.
41. Ibid., p. 26.
42. James L. Sundquist, *Politics and Policy: The Eisenhower, Kennedy, and Johnson Years* (Washington, D.C., 1968), pp. 46–47.
43. Heller, *New Directions of Political Economy*, p. 29.

44. Stein, *The Fiscal Revolution in America*, p. 402.

45. Edwin L. Dale, "When Will It Be Safe to Balance the Budget?" *American Fiscal and Monetary Policy*, ed. Harold Wolozin (Chicago, 1970), p. 112.

46. Stein, *The Fiscal Revolution in America*, p. 353.

47. Okun, *The Political Economy of Prosperity*, p. 59.

48. Phillip Cagan, *Persistent Inflation: Historical and Policy Essays* (New York, 1979), p. 105.

49. Okun, *The Political Economy of Prosperity*, pp. 71–72.

50. Ibid., p. 79.

51. Cagan, *Persistent Inflation*, pp. 109, 113, 116.

52. Arthur Okun wrote that "economists cannot feel proud of their diagnostic or predictive performance during the second half of 1965. To be sure, no one could have foreseen the upsurge before the Vietnam supplemental budget was announced. It is neither surprising nor embarrassing that the profession was, to the best of my knowledge, unanimous as of midyear that the second half of 1965 would witness moderation from the brisk advance of the first half. What is disappointing, however, is that we took so long to recognize the full significance of emerging developments." Okun, *The Political Economy of Prosperity*, pp. 67–68.

53. *Economic Report of the President* (Washington D.C.: GPO, 1970), p. 8.

54. Rowland Evans, Jr., and Robert D. Novak, *Nixon in the White House: The Frustration of Power* (New York, 1971), p. 187.

55. *Economic Report of the President* (Washington, D.C.: GPO, 1971), p. 6.

56. *The United States Budget in Brief, Fiscal Year 1974* (Washington, D.C.: GPO, 1973), p. 6.

57. Louis Fisher writes that after Nixon inherited the Great Society programs of Lyndon Johnson, he "relied on impoundment to move toward his own priorities. . . . after less than a year in office President Nixon announced plans to reduce research health grants, Model Cities funds, and grants for urban renewal. Critics noted that the cutbacks were made at the same time that the Administration was sponsoring such costly projects as the supersonic transport, a manned landing on Mars, general revenue sharing, a larger Merchant Marine fleet, and the Safeguard ABM system." Fisher notes that such cuts were made "in the name of fiscal integrity," but in fact "were part of a redistribution of Federal funds from Democratic programs to those supported by the Nixon Administration." Fisher, *Presidential Spending Power* (Princeton, N.J., 1975), p. 169.

58. *The United States Budget in Brief, Fiscal Year 1974*, pp. 6–7.

59. *The Budget of the United States Government, Fiscal Year 1976* (Washington, D.C.: GPO, 1975), pp. 4, 19.

60. *The 1976 Joint Economic Report* (Washington, D.C.: GPO, 1976), p. 7.

61. Friedman, "Crowding Out or Crowding In?" p. 596.

62. See, for example, Ippolito, *Congressional Spending Power*, chap. 3.

63. Allen Schick, *Congress and Money* (Washington, D.C., 1980), p. 351.

64. Paul E. Peterson, "The New Politics of Deficits," in John E. Chubb and Paul E. Peterson, eds., *The New Direction in American Politics* (Washington, D.C., 1985), p. 375.

65. On the tariff issue see Pastor, *Congress and the Politics of U.S. Foreign Economic Policy*, and Robert Dallek, *Franklin D. Roosevelt and American Foreign Policy, 1932–1945* (New York, 1979).

66. A good summary of role banks play in the current economy, in addition to a brief description of New Deal banking regulations, is in Anthony Sampson, *The Money Lenders: The People and Politics of the World Banking Crisis* (New York, 1981).

67. Ibid., p. 172.

68. For a good description of Proposition 13 and related events, see David O. Sears and Jack Citrin, *Tax Revolt: Something for Nothing in California* (Cambridge, Mass., 1982), esp. chap. 8.

69. "A Constitutional Ban on Red Ink?" *U.S. News & World Report* (January 29, 1979): 27.

70. Morris P. Fiorina, *Congress, Keystone of the Washington Establishment* (New Haven, Conn., 1979), pp. 71, 70.
71. James M. Buchanan and Richard E. Wagner, *Democracy in Deficit: The Political Legacy of Lord Keynes* (New York, 1977), pp. 167, 170–71. Also see Buchanan and Wagner, *Fiscal Responsibility in Constitutional Democracy* (Boston, 1978), and Buchanan, *Public Principles of Public Debt* (Homewood, Ill., 1958). Richard Rose and Guy Peters argue along the same lines in *Can Government Go Bankrupt?* (New York, 1978). Rose and Peters write that economic bankruptcy goes hand in hand with what they call "political bankruptcy," though they are vague about what political bankruptcy is. Somehow, this bankruptcy is tied to declining political authority, "civic indifference," and citizen unwillingness to pay taxes. They also note that "government goes on—but not as before," to leave the idea of political bankruptcy cloudy for its measurable influence on regime loyalty.
72. For a debate over the economic validity of Buchanan and Wagner's research, see Karl Brunner, ed., "Keynesian Policies, the Drift into Permanent Deficits and the Growth of Government: A Symposium," *Journal of Monetary Economics* 4 (1978): 569–636.
73. Manuel Castells, *The Economic Crisis and American Society* (Princeton, N.J., 1980), p. 104. Also see James O'Connor, *The Fiscal Crisis of the State* (New York, 1973), and Ernest Mandel, *Late Capitalism* (London, 1975), especially chap. 13.
74. *The Presidential Campaign 1976*, vol. 1, pt. 1: *Jimmy Carter* (Washington, D.C.: GPO, 1978), p. 146.
75. *The Presidential Campaign 1976*, vol. 1, pt. 2: *Jimmy Carter* (Washington, D.C.: GPO, 1978), pp. 749, 755.
76. *Public Papers of the Presidents of the United States: Jimmy Carter, 1977*, 2 vols., (Washington, D.C.: GPO, 1978), 1:497, 890.
77. Ibid., 2:2194.
78. *Public Papers of the Presidents of the United States: Jimmy Carter, 1978* (Washington, D.C.: GPO, 1979), 2:1894.
79. For the $55.4 billion figure, see Charles A. Waite and Joseph C. Wakefield, "Federal Fiscal Programs," *Survey of Current Business* (February 1980): Table 2, p. 13. In August 1983, the high-employment deficit was reestimated to be $3.2 billion, in Joseph C. Wakefield, "Federal Budget Developments," *Survey of Current Business* (August 1983): Table 6, p. 13.
80. Interview with Charles Schultze, Stanford University, October 7, 1982.
81. Jimmy Carter, *Keeping Faith: Memoirs of a President* (New York, 1982), pp. 76–77.
82. Interview with Charles Schultze, October 7, 1982.
83. Telephone interview with Stuart Eizenstat, Berkeley, California, December 2, 1981.
84. "Statement of Alice M. Rivlin, Director, Congressional Budget Office, before the Subcommittee on Employment Opportunities, Committee on Education and Labor, U.S. House of Representatives," February 13, 1979, p. 3.
85. Interview with Charles Schultze, October 7, 1982.
86. Interview with James McIntyre, Jr., Washington, D.C. November 18, 1982.
87. Bruce K. MacLaury, "Which Way to a Balanced Budget?" *Brookings, the Brookings Bulletin* 16 (Summer 1979): 1.
88. *Democratic Congressional Views:* Democratic Congressional Campaign Committee (Washington, D.C., August 1980), p. 4.
89. Carter, *Keeping Faith*, p. 527.
90. James McIntyre noted, "Obviously, as you raise gasoline prices you will have a onetime increase in the inflation rate." Interview, November 18, 1982.
91. "The 1980 Democratic National Platform" (Washington, D.C.: Democratic National Committee, 1980), p. 2. The AFL-CIO also opposed a budget balancing amendment at both the Democratic and Republican national conventions. "Statutory or constitutional measures that arbitrarily and mechanistically limit the government budgeting process prevent the people's representatives from adopting a prudent, flexible budget based on actual economic and international conditions." "The AFL-CIO Platform

Proposals, Presented to the Democratic and Republican National Conventions 1980"
(Washington, D.C.: American Federation of Labor and Congress of Industrial Organization, 1980), p. 18.

92. "The 1980 Democratic National Platform," p. 3. Compare the Democrats' platform
statement on the benign effect of the deficit to this statement by Jimmy Carter in his
memoirs: "I had inherited the largest deficit in history—more than $66 billion—and it
was important to me to stop the constantly escalating federal expenditures that tended
to drive up interest rates and were one of the root causes of inflation and unemployment. As measured in real or constant valued dollars, I forced federal spending
downward, but this effort quickly brought me into a confrontation with some of the
leaders in my own party, to whom the phrase 'balanced budget' coming from a
Democratic President was almost blasphemous." Carter, *Keeping the Faith*, p. 76.

93. "The 1980 Democratic National Platform," p. 3.

94. Interview with Leon Panetta, Santa Cruz, California, October 10, 1981.

95. On this period, see Frederick F. Siegel, *Troubled Journey: From Pearl Harbor to
Ronald Reagan* (New York, 1984), and Thomas Byrne Edsall, *The New Politics of
Inequality* (New York, 1984).

96. Heller, *New Dimensions of Political Economy*, p. 125.

97. James L. Sundquist and David W. Davis, *Making Federalism Work* (Washington, D.C.,
1969), chap. 2.

98. The ACIR noted that the General Revenue Sharing program, "which affects almost
38,000 state and local units and was designed specifically to have the fewest possible
federal requirements on recipients," has the following restrictions: "a prohibition on
the use of funds for lobbying purposes, requirements for citizen participation, restrictions on debt retirement with revenue sharing funds, compliance with the prevailing
wage provisions for construction projects under the *Davis-Bacon Act*, requirements
with respect to wage rates for employees of recipient governments, protections against
discriminations by subcontractors, and restrictions against discrimination" in federally funded municipal services or the selection of facilities. There is a "very substantial federal presence in even this 'least intrusive' federal program, and it affects more
subnational governments than any other."*The Federal Role in the Federal System:
The Dynamics of Growth* (Washington, D.C.: Advisory Commission on Intergovernmental Relations, 1980), p. 87.

99. E. F. Schumacher, *Small Is Beautiful: Economics as if People Mattered* (New York,
1973).

100. Beer, "The Idea of the Nation," pp. 23, 29.

Chapter 7. Coming to Grips with a Symbol: Ronald Reagan and Unbalanced
Budgets

1. "Why Carter Wants a Balanced Budget," *San Francisco Examiner*, March 13, 1980.

2. *Public Papers of the Presidents of the United States: Ronald Reagan, 1982* (Washington, D.C.: GPO, 1983), 1:258.

3. Laurence I. Barrett, *Gambling with History* (New York, 1984), pp. 48–49. Barrett notes
that perhaps Reagan's favorite Jefferson quote is, "If we let the federal government tell
us when to sow and when to reap, we shall soon want for bread." Reagan also invoked
Jefferson when he defended the Screen Actors Guild before the House Un-American
Activities Committee. See Lou Cannon, *Reagan* (New York, 1982), p. 83.

4. *Public Papers of the Presidents of the United States: Ronald Reagan, 1982*, 1:457.

5. *Public Papers of the Presidents of the United States: Ronald Reagan, 1981* (Washington, D.C.: GPO, 1982), p. 657, and "From the Address by the Honorable Ronald
Reagan," *The Commonwealth* (San Francisco, Commonwealth Club) 64, 20 (May 19,
1980): 97.

6. *Public Papers of the Presidents of the United States: Ronald Reagan, 1981*, p. 683.

7. Ibid., p. 683.

8. *Public Papers of the Presidents of the United States: Ronald Reagan, 1982*, 1:301.
9. "From the Address by the Honorable Ronald Reagan," p. 97.
10. Herbert Stein, *Presidential Economics* (New York, 1984), chap. 7.
11. Author's transcript of the Carter-Reagan presidential debate held October 28, 1980, in Louisville, Kentucky.
12. Ibid.
13. "From the Address by the Honorable Ronald Reagan." See p. 97 for Reagan's intent to return the tax base to the states.
14. Richard A. Viguerie, *The New Right: We're Ready to Lead* (Falls Church, Va., 1980), pp. 180–81.
15. Author's transcript of the Carter-Reagan presidential debate held October 28, 1980, in Louisville, Kentucky.
16. "From the Address by the Honorable Ronald Reagan," p. 95.
17. Ibid., p. 96.
18. Barrett, *Gambling with History*, chap. 8.
19. Jack Kemp, *An American Renaissance: A Strategy for the 1980s* (New York, 1978), p. 103.
20. Ibid., p. 83.
21. Kemp's reluctance in 1980 to cut the social safety net, a term he helped popularize, was later matched by fellow supply-sider Arthur Laffer's reluctance to endorse the Reagan budget cuts in domestic spending. Said Laffer to a question about the cuts in January 1982, "First, . . . I didn't support a lot of these spending cuts that have gone through. In fact, that's why I am a professor . . . instead of with the administration. . . . But I don't support a lot of the welfare cuts." Laffer on William F. Buckley's "Firing Line," Program no. 493, January 7, 1982, p. 13.
22. William Greider, "The Education of David Stockman," *Atlantic Monthly* 248 (December 1981): 32.
23. "White House Knew Recession Coming," *San Francisco Chronicle*, June 10, 1982.
24. *Program for Economic Recovery* (Washington, D.C.: GPO, 1981), p. 47/25. Murray Weidenbaum kindly pointed out the significance of this table to the author in a conversation held in May 1984.
25. Roberts had this to say about Stockman and the deficits: "Stockman elevated a balanced budget into even more of an issue than he intended. It sent a signal that the administration placed such importance on a balanced budget that it would resort to producing one by hook or by crook. This confused some people about our priorities. The size of the budget deficit became the overriding measure of the administration's success or failure. . . . The economy had experienced deficits for the past two decades and would not have panicked over their continuation, especially if spending were brought under control and incentives restored." Paul Craig Roberts, *The Supply-Side Revolution: An Insider's Account of Policymaking in Washington* (Cambridge, Mass., 1984), pp. 97–98. In addition to the divisions among supply-siders, monetarists, and traditional budget-balancing conservative economists, divisions also existed within the supply-siders' camp. Roberts, for example, criticized Arthur Laffer for suggesting that the tax cuts' newly created revenues would balance the budget. Said Roberts, "None of the supply-siders within the administration were Lafferites promising that the tax-rate reductions would pay for themselves in higher revenues. . . . We assumed there would be a deficit but that it would be easier to finance because of a higher saving rate. We were trying to estimate the combination of revenue reflows, increases in private-sector saving, and reduction in the growth of federal spending that would eliminate the deficit as an *economic* problem." Ibid., pp. 95–96.
26. "Reagan Aides Hear Budget Attacked from Both Parties," *New York Times*, February 10, 1982.
27. Several descriptions of the FY 1982 budget battle exist, including Barbara Sinclair, *Majority Leadership in the U.S. House* (Baltimore, 1983), chap. 6, and the symposium "The Reagan Budget: Redistribution of Power and Responsibilities," in *PS* 14 (Fall 1981). Other references are cited in Appendix 2.

28. "Text of the President's Address Report on the State of the Nation's Economy," *New York Times*, February 6, 1981.

29. Ibid.

30. Ibid.

31. Ibid.

32. Interview with Norman Mineta, San Jose, California, August 22, 1981.

33. Interview with Leon Panetta, Santa Cruz, California, August 10, 1981.

34. See "GOP Does an About-Face on Deficit," [Oakland] *Eastbay Today*, December 9, 1981; "Reagan Aides Abandon GOP Rhetoric on Deficits," *Washington Post*, December 9, 1981; and "Reagan Aides Defend Deficit," *New York Times*, December 9, 1981.

35. Interview with William Niskanen, Washington, D.C., November 17, 1982.

36. Ibid.

37. Said Niskanen: "I think that there are two main reasons to be concerned about the deficit. One, is that it changes the time distribution of taxes. For a given flow of government services the effect of the deficit is to increase future tax payments relative to current tax payments. And that is part of the equity issue. . . . The other [reason] is that because it changes the time distribution of taxes, and because present voters and their representatives are probably not sufficiently concerned about the well-being of future voters, that it may very well lead to too-high government spending at the moment." Ibid.

38. See Niskanen's article in Brunner, ed., "Keynesian Policies, the Drift into Permanent Deficits and the Growth of Government: A Symposium," pp. 569–636.

39. "President's News Conference on Foreign and Domestic Matters," *New York Times*, December 18, 1981.

40. Ibid.

41. "'Busted' Budgets Confront Reagan," *U.S. News & World Report* (January 18, 1982): 48.

42. "Banks Keeping Loan Rates High to Protect Earnings, Regan Says," *New York Times*, February 16, 1983. In February 1982, Regan said, "we are confident that personal and business savings over the next few years will be adequate to finance . . . the projected deficits . . . and a very rapid increase in . . . [private] capital formation." "Statement by Secretary of the Treasury Donald T. Regan," *Treasury News*, February 8, 1982, p. 4.

43. "Playing It Loose at the Summit," *Time* (May 30, 1983): 15.

44. "Government Deficit Spending and Its Effects on Prices of Financial Assets," Office of the Secretary, Department of the Treasury, May 1983, p. 1. The report's assessment of the interest rate situation reflected the comments made by Treasury Undersecretary Beryl Sprinkel who commented in 1982: "Do large deficits at the present time lead to higher interest rates? . . . Historically they have not. For example, . . . a serious recession . . . ended in March of 1975. The deficit was larger as a percentage of GNP than our present deficit. In fact, credit demands rose as the economy rose. Inflation was going down then as now; interest rates declined through '75 and '76, and that's what I expect to happen as we get the money supply under control in the months ahead." "Why Are Interest Rates Rising?" *MacNeil-Lehrer Report*, February 5, 1982, Show no. 7160, Transcript no. 1660, pp. 3–4.

45. "Reagan Doesn't Know Which Aide Is Right on Deficits and Interest Rates," *San Francisco Examiner*, September 16, 1983.

46. "Regan Disowns Feldstein Report; Tells Senators to Throw It Away," *New York Times*, February 4, 1984.

47. "Reagan Invites Secret Talks with Soviets, Dismisses Deficits as Cause of Stock Slump," *Wall Street Journal*, February 16, 1984.

48. "Reagan Is Prodded for Deficit Action," *New York Times*, April 12, 1984.

49. "Transcript of Louisville Debate between Reagan and Mondale," *New York Times*, October 9, 1984.

50. "That Monster Deficit," *Time* (March 5, 1984): 61.

51. *Public Papers of the Presidents of the United States: Ronald Reagan*, 1982, 1:258.

52. Basic descriptions of New Federalism and an initial evaluation are found in Palmer

and Sawhill, eds., *The Reagan Revolution*, chap. 6, and Palmer and Sawhill, eds., *The Reagan Record*, chap. 7.

53. "O'Neill Tells Mayor They Are to Be Budget-Balance Fall Guys," *San Francisco Examiner*, January 28, 1982.

54. "State of the Union," *MacNeill-Lehrer Report*, January 27, 1982, Show no. 7153, Transcript no. 1653, p. 3.

55. "Transit in Trouble," *MacNeill-Lehrer Report*, March 24, 1982, Show no. 7193, Transcript no. 1693, p. 3.

56. "Tolerating Big Deficits," *New York Times*, January 29, 1982.

57. "Stockman Says Some States May Lose in 'New Federalism,'" *New York Times*, February 4, 1982. In addition to Stockman, Health and Human Services Secretary Richard Schweiker and Transportation Secretary Drew Lewis both publicly questioned the administrative complexity and financing of the swap. Schweiker, said an aide, "was concerned that the mechanics of this proposal and the various ramifications had not been explored in sufficient detail." "Cabinet Doubts on Reagan Plan," *San Francisco Chronicle*, February 9, 1982.

58. "Is a Balanced Budget Constitutional Amendment Necessary?" *San Francisco Examiner*, July 26, 1982.

59. "House, by 46 Votes, Rejects Proposal on a Budget Limit," *New York Times*, October 2, 1982.

60. "Congress, Frustrated by Complexities, Turns to the Quick Fix," *Washington Post*, July 25, 1982.

61. "Plan to Require Budget Balance Voted in Senate," *New York Times*, August 5, 1982.

62. "Balanced Budget Amendment," *San Francisco Examiner*, July 19, 1982, and "Balanced Budget Amendment Debate Commences in Senate," *Congressional Quarterly Weekly Report*, July 17, 1982, p. 1731.

63. "Leaders, Not Laws, Balance Budgets," *New York Times*, May 3, 1982.

64. "The Balanced Budget Amendment (I): Formula for a Depression," *Washington Post*, June 21, 1982.

65. *Congressional Record* (Washington, D.C.: GPO, February 5, 1985), p. S 1003.

66. "The Combined Effects of Major Changes in Federal Taxes and Spending Programs since 1981," Congressional Budget Office, April 1984, see esp. Tables 4 and 5.

67. "Effects of the Omnibus Budget Reconciliation Act of 1981 (OBRA) Welfare Changes and the Recession on Poverty," Subcommittee on Oversight and Subcommittee on Public Assistance and Unemployment Compensation of the Committee on Ways and Means, U.S. House of Representatives (Washington, D.C.: GPO, July 25, 1984).

68. "An Evaluation of the 1981 AFDC Changes: Initial Analysis" (Gaithersburg, Md.: U.S. General Accounting Office, April 2, 1984), Report no. GAO/PEMD-84-6.

69. Marilyn Moon and Isabel V. Sawhill, "Family Incomes: Gainers and Losers," in Palmer and Sawhill, *The Reagan Record*, esp. p. 330. Also worthwhile is John C. Weicher, ed., *Maintaining the Safety Net* (Washington, D.C., 1984).

70. Greider, "The Education of David Stockman," p. 72.

71. A Gallup Poll released in February 1981, after the FY 1982 budget proposal was distributed, found only 24 percent of respondents stating that President Reagan favored the rich, with 66 percent saying Reagan cared about Americans equally. "Public is 2–1 for Reagan's Budget Cuts," *San Francisco Examiner*, February 24, 1981. By the end of 1982, however, the polls repeatedly found that respondents believed Reagan's programs aided the wealthy. Furthermore, public opposition to domestic cuts increased. A *New York Times*/CBS News Poll conducted in May 1982 found that 61 percent of respondents opposed additional budget cuts in "programs for the poor" to balance the budget. "Budget-Stalled Politicians Fear the Voters' Wrath," *New York Times*, June 6, 1982. Nearly two years later a *Washington Post*/ABC News Poll identified a similar 2 to 1 ratio of respondents opposing new reductions in social spending to cut the deficit. "Tax Boosts Rejected in Poll on Deficit," *San Francisco Chronicle*, January 19, 1984.

72. *The Presidential Campaign 1976*, vol. 1, pt. 2: *Jimmy Carter*, p. 721.

73. Waite and Wakefield, "Federal Fiscal Programs," Table 2, p. 13. In the April 1982 edition of *Current Business,* the full-employment deficit estimate stood at $800 million for FY 1981. See p. 27.

74. Interview with Leon Panetta, August 10, 1981.

75. Interview with Norman Mineta, August 22, 1981.

76. "Budget Deficits," *MacNeill-Lehrer Report,* December 17, 1981, Show no. 7124, Transcript no. 1624, p. 5.

77. Dellums's comment was made in response to the author's question, at Congressman Dellums's constituency meeting, Berkeley, California, May 23, 1981.

78. Interview with Leon Panetta, August 10, 1981.

79. Ibid.

80. "Economy 'Dead in the Water'—Production Down Again," *San Francisco Chronicle,* April 16, 1982.

81. Congressman Wright was interviewed on "Meet the Press," November 7, 1982.

82. *Rebuilding the Road to Opportunity: A Democratic Direction for the 1980s,* Democratic Caucus, U.S. House of Representatives, September 1982, p. 19.

83. "Puzzle of the 'Structural Deficit' Penned by Reagan," *New York Times,* December 3, 1982.

84. See, for example, Walter Heller, "The Unavoidable Issue," *Wall Street Journal,* October 26, 1984.

85. The economic logic of the middle-expansion budget calculation is explained in Frank de Leeuw and Thomas M. Hollaway, "Cyclical Adjustment of the Federal Debt," *Survey of Current Business* (December 1983): 25–40. They write, "A budget based on a middle-expanson budget trend is not suitable for setting fiscal guidelines" (p. 29). The final publication of the full-employment budget data occurred in the August 1983 issue of *Survey of Current Business.*

86. "This Week with David Brinkley," February 26, 1984, no. 122, p. 9.

87. "Transcript of Mondale Address Accepting Party Nomination," *New York Times,* July 20, 1984.

88. "Excerpts from Platform the Democratic Convention Adopted," *New York Times,* July 19, 1984.

89. "Text of Reagan Speech Accepting Nomination for New Term," *New York Times,* August 24, 1984.

90. "Do Deficits Matter?" *Fortune* (March 5, 1984): 113.

91. "Playing for Time," *Time* (February 13, 1984): 11. Also see Herbert Rowen, "That Boring Deficit," *Washington Post,* February 2, 1984.

92. A *Newsweek* poll released on September 24 for example, found respondents agreeing 46 to 32 percent that Reagan would be better able to reduce the deficit than Mondale. "Bad News for Mondale," *Newsweek* (September 24, 1984): 28. A Gallup Poll produced the same results, with 39 percent favoring Reagan's ability to reduce the deficit, versus 35 percent for Mondale. "Big Reagan Lead on Economic Issues," *San Francisco Chronicle,* September 9, 1984. On the relative importance of the deficit issue, a Mervin Field "California Poll" found that as an issue rated by degree of concern, California respondents ranked the deficit as the tenth most important issue, tied with housing costs, but behind such issues as concern for toxic waste and problems of the elderly. "Crime, Schools Rank as Public Concerns; 'Toxics' Also an Issue," *San Jose Mercury News,* February 23, 1984. A *Newsweek* poll reported that respondents ranked the deficit issue seventh, behind the issues of inflation, protecting American jobs, education, and relations with the Soviet Union. "A *Newsweek* Poll," *Newsweek* (February 27, 1984): 44. Also see "Cutting the Deficit: Hard Choice," *National Journal* (August 4, 1984): 1495, which reported that respondents to surveys rejected the deficit as the most serious national problem.

93. "Poll Shows Many Choose Reagan Even if They Disagree with Him," *New York Times,* September 19, 1984.

94. Consider this progression of public opinion. A *New York Times/CBS News* Poll conducted during late May of 1982 found 55 percent of respondents willing to elimi-

nate the third year of the tax cut to reduce the deficit, versus 27 percent not willing. "Budget-Stalled Politicians Fear the Voters' Wrath," *New York Times*, June 6, 1982. Six months later, 62 percent of respondents to the same poll again favored eliminating the tax cut's third year. "The Federal Deficit," *New York Times*, January 25, 1983. By 1984, public opinion had changed. In November, according to a Gallup Poll, only 34 percent favored raising taxes to reduce the deficit versus 62 percent opposed. "Reagan Agenda Gets Mixed Review," *San Francisco Chronicle*, November 19, 1984. Nearly a year later, opinion remained the same, as only 25 percent of respondents to another Gallup Poll favored tax increases for that purpose, compared to 68 percent opposed. "Public Favors Budget Amendment," *San Francisco Chronicle*, September 9, 1985.

95. Daniel Patrick Moynihan, "Reagan's Inflate-the-Deficit Game," *New York Times*, July 21, 1985.
96. "Text of the President's State of the Union Message to Nation," *New York Times*, January 26, 1983.
97. "Federal Debt Said to Rekindle Resurgence of States' Powers," *San Francisco Examiner*, December 12, 1985.
98. David S. Broder, "Party Finds Unity, If Not Strength," *Los Angeles Times*, July 20, 1984.
99. Richard P. Nathan and Fred C. Doolittle, "The Untold Story of Reagan's 'New Federalism,'" *Public Interest* 75 (Fall 1984): 96–105. Also see George E. Peterson, "Federalism and the States: An Experiment in Decentralization," in Palmer and Sawhill, eds., *The Reagan Record*, pp. 217–59; "State Legislatures and Federal Grants: Developments in the Reagan Years," a symposium in *Public Budgeting and Finance* 4 (Summer 1984); "States Have Made Few Changes in Implementing the Alcohol, Drug Abuse, and Mental Health Services Block Grant" (Gaithersburg, Md.: U.S. General Accounting Office, June 6, 1984), Report no. GAO/HRD-84-52; "States Use Added Flexibility Offered by the Preventive Health and Health Services Block Grant" (Gaithersburg, Md.: U.S. General Accounting Office, May 8, 1984), Report no. GAO/HRD-84-41; "Maternal and Child Health Block Grant: Program Changes Emerging Under State Administration" (Gaithersburg, Md.: U.S. General Accounting Office, May 7, 1984), Report no. GAO/HRD-84-35; and "Block Grants Brought Funding Changes and Adjustments to Program Priorities" (Gaithersburg, Md.: U.S. General Accounting Office, February 11, 1985), Report no. GAO/HRD-84-33.
100. One brief review of state economic development activities is Mel Dubnick and Lynne Holt, "Industrial Policy and the States," *Publius* (Winter 1985): 113–29.
101. "Now What?" *New Republic* (November 26, 1984): 9.
102. "Required Reading: On Federalism," *New York Times*, January 7, 1986.

Appendix 1

1. Ratchford, *American State Debts*, p. 277.
2. A. James Heins, *Constitutional Restrictions against State Debt* (Madison, Wis., 1963), pp. 18, 81, 84–85.
3. Daniel C. Carson, "Bonds," *California Journal* (September 1984): 14–15.

Appendix 2

1. "Text of the President's Address Reporting on the State of the Nation's Economy," *New York Times*, February 6, 1981.
2. "Why Federal Spending Must Be Cut," *New York Times*, February 15, 1981.
3. "Proxmire Says Budget Cuts 'Too Feeble,'" *San Francisco Examiner*, February 11, 1981; and "Proxmire Wants Deeper Slashes in Budget," *San Francisco Chronicle*, February 16, 1981.
4. "Treasury Secretary Rejects Linking Tax Cuts to Budgetary Reductions," *New York Times*, February 4, 1981.
5. "Senate Votes Raise in U.S. Debt Ceiling," *New York Times*, February 7, 1981.

6. Steven Weisman, "Reaganomics and the President's Men," *New York Times Magazine*, October 24, 1982, pp. 83–85.
7. "Reception in Congress Is Generally Favorable," *Los Angeles Times*, February 19, 1981.
8. "Public is 2–1 for Reagan's Budget Cuts," *San Francisco Examiner*, February 24, 1981.
9. "Cool Reaction: Stocks, Dollars Slide," *San Francisco Examiner*, February 19, 1981.
10. "Despite Doubts, Byrd Plans Vote Favoring Budget," *New York Times*, April 3, 1981.
11. "Cut of $36.9 billion in Social Programs Is Voted by Senate," *New York Times*, April 4, 1981.
12. "Text of Statement on Economic Matters Adopted by House Democratic Caucus," *New York Times*, April 9, 1981.
13. Ibid.
14. "Transcript of Reagan Speech to House of Congress," *New York Times*, April 29, 1981.
15. "Facing Up to Budget Reality," *New York Times*, April 10, 1981.
16. Ibid.
17. *1981 Congressional Quarterly Almanac* (Washington, D.C.: Congressional Quarterly, 1982), p. 252.
18. For an interesting view of Senate Republican strategy, see James A. Miller and James D. Range, "Reconciling an Irreconcilable Budget: The New Politics of the Budgetary Process," *Harvard Journal on Legislation* 20 (1983): 4–30.
19. "Democrats in House Reunify to Fight on Budget Package," *New York Times*, June 18, 1981.
20. "Transcript of the President's News Conference on Foreign and Domestic Matters," *New York Times*, June 17, 1981.
21. A good description of the reconciliation fight is Steven S. Smith, "Budget Battles of 1981: The Role of Majority Party Leadership," in Allan Sindler, ed., *American Politics and Public Policy* (Washington, D.C.: Congressional Quarterly, 1984).
22. "Reagan's Wheeling and Dealing on Budget," *San Francisco Examiner*, June 26, 1981.
23. "Fed's Grip Will Tighten: Volcker," *San Francisco Examiner*, June 21, 1981.
24. "Reagan Says U.S. Will Adhere to Tough Monetary Policy," *Washington Post*, June 14, 1981.
25. "Republicans Warn Reagan that Cuts Would Be Beaten," *New York Times*, September 22, 1981.
26. "Baldridge Deviates from Reagan Position, Says Wider '82 Deficit Still Meets Pledge," *Wall Street Journal*, September 15, 1981.
27. "Time to Shape Up," *Wall Street Journal*, September 28, 1981.
28. "'Gypsy Moths' Poised to Fly against Reagan's New Cuts; Charge Pledges Were Broken," *Congressional Quarterly Weekly Reports*, October 10, 1981, p. 1951.
29. "House Hands Reagan Defeat on Budget Cuts," ibid., p. 1948.
30. "Balanced Budget Is 'Not Probable in '84,' Reagan Says," *New York Times*, November 1, 1981.
31. "Reagan Abandons Aim of Balancing the Budget by '84," *New York Times*, November 7, 1981.
32. Within the White House, the internal tensions that had been building since the earliest days of the Reagan administration became more intense and public. The basic division concerning fiscal policy involved those who wished to preserve the tax cut in the face of growing deficits, and the "traditionalist" or "pragmatists" who favored tax increases. By early November, newspapers carried such headlines as "Behind Bitter Feuds in the White House" to explain the conflict to their readers (*San Francisco Examiner & Chronicle*, November 8, 1981). But the *Atlantic* article on Stockman's position on the tax cuts was the most damning incident in the feud. (William Greider, "The Education of David Stockman," *Atlantic Monthly*, December 1981, pp. 27–54.) Supply-siders quickly responded to the story. Jude Wanniski said Stockman "slowly turned himself into an opponent." But Alan Reynolds declared Stockman's opposition was always evident: "He's always been a doubting Thomas. The minute he took office, he became a monomanical budget-balancer." Arthur Laffer said Stockman was "fin-

ished" and "he has lost his credibility" ("The Supply-Siders Respond," *New York Times*, November 15, 1981). In January, Laffer said the economy was "sicker than a dog" and "I put much of the blame on David Stockman. . . . This is the Stockman recession and the Stockman deficit. He was too concerned about budget deficits and watered down the tax cuts, which has slowed the economy." Laffer added the deficit "in and of itself is not a problem. It's a barometer of what's going on" ("Laffer Blames Bad Economy on Stockman," *San Francisco Chronicle*, January 11, 1982). In February, Paul Craig Roberts published an article in *Fortune* (February 22, 1982) called "The Stockman Recession: A Reaganite's Account," also laying to blame for the recession on Stockman.

33. On November 20, the day the first continuing resolution was to expire, the Senate adopted a resolution of $427 billion, extending to March 30, that called for a 4 percent reduction in domestic programs. Over the weekend the House-Senate Conference Committee struggled to create a new resolution acceptable to the president that could be approved before federal workers returned to their jobs on Monday. In the committee the Senate's delegates accepted the House's 2 percent cut in domestic programs, and a $427.9 billion resolution. According to the computers used by the House, this figure was close to the $4 billion in savings the president previously agreed to. But OMB's computers translated this budget authority into budget obligations to identify the deficit's new size, and found only $1.7 billion in outlay savings rather than $4 billion. The difference centered around the way the House's computer calculated entitlement spending, which OMB charged underestimated costs for food stamps and supplemental security programs. Reagan responded by using his first veto against the resolution. Congress quickly reacted to the November 23 veto by agreeing to another continuing resolution that simply extended the provisions of the first resolution.

34. " 'Pro Forma' Budget Resolution Reported," *Congressional Quarterly Weekly Report*, November 21, 1981, p. 2271.

35. "GOP Senators Assume Budget Leadership," *Congressional Quarterly Weekly Report*, November 14, 1981, p. 2217.

36. "President's News Conference on Foreign and Domestic Matters," *New York Times*, December 18, 1981.

37. Ibid.

38. "Voodoo Politics," *Wall Street Journal*, January 14, 1982.

39. "State of the Union: 'A New Beginning—But We Have Only Begun,' " *Los Angeles Times*, January 27, 1982.

40. "Budget Brings Attacks from Republicans and Democrats Alike in Congress," *New York Times*, February 7, 1982.

41. Ibid.

42. Ibid.

43. "G.O.P. Chiefs Warn Reagan on Budget; See Possible Shift," *New York Times*, February 12, 1982.

44. "Text of Reagan's Letter to Republican Members of Congress," *New York Times*, February 14, 1982.

45. "President Asks Critics of Budget for Alternatives," *New York Times*, February 10, 1982.

46. "Dole Seeks 2-Party Aid in Budget Cuts," *Los Angeles Times*, February 9, 1982.

47. Ibid.

48. Ibid.

49. "Business Leaders Object to Deficits in Reagan Budget," *New York Times*, March 4, 1982; "Cut Defense Budget, NAM Tells Reagan," *San Francisco Chronicle*, March 14, 1982; and "Reagan's Wall St. Support Slips," *San Francisco Chronicle*, March 18, 1982.

50. "President's News Conference on Foreign and Domestic Matters," *New York Times*, February 19, 1982.

51. "Rotten Economy Called Good Sign," *San Francisco Chronicle*, March 5, 1982.

52. "Excerpts from Volcker's Testimony," *New York Times*, February 11, 1982.

53. "President Terms Views of Business a Disappointment," *New York Times*, March 19, 1982.
54. "Reagan Defends Budget to Conservative Critics," *New York Times*, February 26, 1982.
55. "Senators Play Down Division on Budget; Prepare Other Plans," *New York Times*, March 4, 1982.
56. *Public Papers of the Presidents of the United States: Ronald Reagan, 1982*, 1:258.
57. "Budget Negotiations Fall Apart," *San Francisco Chronicle*, April 29, 1982.
58. The budget proposals (in billions of dollars) for the Reagan-O'Neill meeting were as follows:

	Republicans			Democrats		
	1983	1984	1985	1983	1984	1985
Revenue increases	25	35	50	30	50	65
Defense cuts	4	7	12	7	14	21
Entitlement cuts	6	8	11	3	4	5
Other domestic program cuts	6	11	18	3	7	13
Cost of living adjustment cuts	2	8	16	1	5	10
Adjusted deficit	105	83	38	104	70	30

Source: "The Summit That Failed," *Time* (May 10, 1982): 11.

59. The three budget resolutions defeated on May 27, 1982, incorporated the following numbers (in billions of dollars):

	Budget Committee	Republicans	Bipartisan
National security	224.40	225.30	221.85
Science, energy, resources	23.45	21.60	23.30
Agriculture	10.10	9.05	9.30
Housing, transportation, education, employment	58.80	57.15	58.85
Health and human services, veterans Other government	377.30	371.81	375.75
Interest	16.00	15.75	16.00
Offsetting receipts	115.00	112.80	112.55
Outlays	−44.50	−45.86	−46.80
Revenues	780.55	767.50	770.80
Deficit	676.70	665.90	675.75
	103.85	101.60	95.05

Source: "Competing House Budget Proposals," *New York Times*, May 23, 1982.

60. The two budget resolutions considered on June 10, 1982, in the House, plus the revised Reagan budget and the first resolution adopted in the Senate, incorporated the following numbers (in billions of dollars):

	Democrats	Republicans	Reagan	Senate
Military spending	212.3	214.0	223.2	215.3
Education	27.9	26.2	22.6	27.0
Income security	276.0	269.8	267.0	273.0
Health	80.9	77.8	78.1	77.7
Total outlays	784.2	765.2	785.5	784.3
Deficit	107.5	99.3	132.4	115.9

Source: "A Comparison of Various Budget Plans for the Fiscal Year," *New York Times*, June 10, 1982.

61. Mills and Palmer, *The Deficit Dilemma: Budget Policy in the Reagan Era* (Washington, D.C., 1984), Table 10, p. 25.
62. "Tax Bill Dumped on House Demos," *San Francisco Chronicle*, July 24, 1982.
63. William F. Buckley, Jr., in an article titled "Exit Reaganomics?" wrote: "The collapse of Reagonomics (as the event is accurately being described) is testimony to a failure of nerve and understanding. Sen. Robert Dole, R-Kan., the chairman of the Finance Committee, who mobilized all 11 Republican senators to vote for the highest single peacetime tax increase in U.S. history. . . . is suddenly being greeted as a hero—by the Democrats. And with good reason. . . . The philosophical basis of Reaganomics was in part that people overtaxed don't do as much. And in part that government does too much. Dole has capitulated on both fronts. . . . So along comes Dole with a 24-point tax increase, aimed primarily at depressing exactly those people and enterprises we need at this moment to energize." *San Francisco Examiner*, July 26, 1982.
64. "Reagan Aide Says Tax Cut Isn't Working," *San Francisco Chronicle*, August 16, 1982.
65. "Backing Off Economic Recovery," *New York Times*, August 17, 1982, and "Where Reaganomics Is Going Astray," *U.S. News & World Report* (August 23, 1982): 27.
66. "Stealth in the Night," *Wall Street Journal*, August 4, 1982.
67. "A No-Fingerprints Tax Bill," *Newsweek* (August 9, 1982): 16.
68. "Transcript of President's News Conference on Foreign and Domestic Matters," *New York Times*, August 14, 1982.
69. "Supply-Side's Sunk," *New York Times*, August 30, 1982.
70. "Congress Overrides Veto of Funding Bill," *Congressional Quarterly Weekly Report*, September 11, 1982, p. 2237.
71. "Will Reagan Change Course?" *Newsweek* (November 15, 1982): 34.
72. "The Emergence of Two Republican Parties," *Wall Street Journal*, January 4, 1983.
73. "Saving Reaganomics from Itself," *San Francisco Examiner*, November 29, 1982.
74. "The Midterm Crisis," *New York Times*, January 17, 1983.
75. "Power Slippage," *Providence Journal*, January 13, 1983.
76. Recessions and the Depression, 1929–82:

Business cycle peak	Cycle trough	Months Peak to trough	% Drop Industrial output	Peak Jobless rate
Aug. 1929	March 1933	43	53.4	24.9
May 1937	June 1938	13	32.4	20.0
Feb. 1945	Oct. 1945	8	38.3	4.3
Nov. 1948	Oct. 1949	11	9.9	7.9
July 1953	May 1954	10	10.0	6.1
Aug. 1957	April 1958	8	14.3	7.5
April 1960	Feb. 1961	10	7.2	7.1
Dec. 1969	Nov. 1970	11	8.1	6.1
Nov. 1973	March 1975	16	14.7	9.0
Jan. 1980	July 1980	6	8.7	7.8
July 1981	Nov. 1982	16	12.3	10.7

Source: "Economists Don't See Threats to Economy Portending Depression," *Wall Street Journal*, October 12, 1984. Also see "Ending Recession, Officially," *New York Times*, July 9, 1983.

77. "President Warned to Yield on Arms Because of Deficit," *New York Times*, January 5, 1983.
78. "3 Business Groups Urge Deeper Cuts in Defense," *San Francisco Chronicle*, January 19, 1983.
79. Ibid.
80. "The Federal Deficit," *New York Times*, January 25, 1983.

81. "Weinberger Urges Cut of $8 Billion in '84 Arms Budget," *New York Times*, January 11, 1983. Weinberger's list of selected reductions did not sit well with the Joint Chiefs of Staff, who objected to pay cuts and instead favored reduced weapons purchases. Said Air Force Chief of Staff General Charles Gabriel, "The part that bothers us most is the possibility of a pay cut." The chiefs also commented that Weinberger had not consulted with them where the cuts should take place. Added Gabriel, "I would have appreciated, as the other chiefs would have, having a part in that process." "Military Leaders would Rather Cut Arms, Not Salaries," *New York Times*, January 14, 1983.
82. "Shultz Role Reported Key to Reagan Shift on Taxes," *New York Times*, January 30, 1983.
83. "Text of the President's State of the Union Message to Nation," *New York Times*, January 26, 1983.
84. These figures (in billions of dollars) serve to compare the Carter and the Reagan military buildup, as represented in budget outlays. The first figure stands for the estimated spending for the fiscal year in which projections were made.

	1981	1982	1983	1984	1985	1986	1987	1988
Carter, Jan. 81	157.6	180.0	205.3	232.3	261.8	293.3	—	—
Reagan, Mar. 81	158.6	184.8	221.1	249.8	297.3	336.0	—	—
Reagan, Jan. 82	—	182.8	215.9	247.0	285.5	324.0	356.0	—
Reagan, Jan. 83	—	—	208.9	238.6	277.5	314.9	345.6	377.0

Source: "Military Spending Projections," *New York Times*, February 1, 1983.

85. "Text of the President's State of the Union Message to Nation," *New York Times*, January 26, 1983.
86. Ibid.
87. "Big Deficits Cut Urged by Group of U.S. Leaders," *New York Times*, January 20, 1983.
88. "Correspondence," *New Republic* (March 21, 1983): 4.
89. Ibid.
90. "Transcript of Statement by President on Budget," *New York Times*, March 19, 1983.
91. "Democratic Budget Is Adopted by House, 229–196," *New York Times*, March 24, 1983.
92. "GOP Finds Not Feeding Kids Is Very Dumb," *San Francisco Examiner*, February 23, 1983.
93. "Reagan Now Willing to Cut Defense Budget," *San Francisco Examiner*, April 5, 1983.
94. "$8 Billion Added to Reagan Budget by Senate Panel," *New York Times*, April 22, 1983.
95. "Senate Panel Votes Tax Rise into '84 Budget," *Wall Street Journal*, April 22, 1983.
96. "Debate on Budget Begins in Senate with G.O.P. Divided," *New York Times*, May 3, 1983.
97. "Road to the Budget Meanders through a Political Minefield," *New York Times*, May 15, 1983.
98. "Reagan Denounces Lawmakers Urging Increase in Taxes," *New York Times*, May 17, 1983.
99. Ibid.
100. "Reagan Scuttles Senate GOP Budget Compromise," *San Francisco Examiner*, May 18, 1983.
101. "Reagan Vows to Veto Senate's Big Budget," *San Francisco Examiner*, May 20, 1983.
102. "White House Criticizes Senate's 1984 Budget," *New York Times*, May 19, 1983.
103. Ibid.
104. "Reagan Blasts New Budget Plan," *San Francisco Examiner*, June 22, 1983.
105. The sense of compromise between the executive and the Congress over the budget was clearly evident in the appropriations passed through early October 1983. The presi-

dent had yet to veto any of the five bills sent to him. The following budget authority and budget outlay figures are in billions of dollars:

Bill		Reagan Jan. Request	June Result	Final Appropriation
Energy & water	BA	14.7	14.9	14.4
	BO	14.8	14.7	14.6
Housing, urban	BA	49.8	57.8	56.3
development	BO	58.0	58.2	58.6
Leg. branch	BA	1.5	1.5	1.5
	BO	1.5	1.5	1.5
Transportation	BA	10.9	10.9	10.9
	BO	25.0	25.4	25.4
Military const.	BA	8.7	7.3	7.1
	BO	7.3	7.1	7.1

Source: "New Realism Eases Budget Conflict," *New York Times*, October 2, 1983.

106. "House Democrats Shunning a Veto Battle with Reagan," *New York Times*, August 2, 1983.
107. Ibid.
108. Ibid.
109. "House Anti-Deficit Alliance Forms to Defeat O'Neill on Spending Bills," *Oakland Tribune*, November 9, 1983.
110. "Taking the Easy Way Out," *Time* (September 26, 1983): 17.
111. "On the Deficit, 'A World Turned Upside Down,'" *New York Times*, December 28, 1983.
112. "Reagan Doesn't Know Which Aide Is Right on Deficits and Interest Rates," *San Francisco Examiner*, September 16, 1983.
113. Ibid.
114. "Government Deficit Spending and Its Effects on Prices of Financial Assets," Office of the Secretary, Department of the Treasury, May 1983, p. 1.
115. "Feldstein Says Economic Growth Alone Won't Cut U.S. Deficit to Acceptable Level," *Wall Street Journal*, November 9, 1983. See also "Fuel for the $200 Billion Deficit," *San Francisco Examiner*, November 23, 1983.
116. "Text of Message from the President on the State of the Union," *New York Times*, January 26, 1984.
117. "Reagan Urged to Raise Taxes in 1985 Budget," *Washington Post*, January 5, 1984.
118. "Stockman Doubts Budget Can Be Slashed Much More, Cites White House 'Dreamers,'" *Wall Street Journal*, January 19, 1984.
119. Ibid.
120. Ibid.
121. "Democrats Wary of Reagan Call for Cooperation on Budget Cuts," *New York Times*, January 26, 1984.
122. "Democrats Want President to Move First on Budget Gap," *New York Times*, January 27, 1984.
123. "Reagan Plan: Share Blame," *New York Times*, Janaury 26, 1984.
124. "Fight to Cut Deficit Focuses on Defense," *Los Angeles Times*, February 2, 1984.
125. Ibid.
126. "Congress Study Sees Deficits Rise in Reagan Budget," *New York Times*, February 23, 1984.
127. "Feldstein Warns of Deficit Size by End of 1980s," *New York Times*, February 7, 1984.
128. "Reagan Aides Disagree on Plan to Cut Deficit," *San Francisco Chronicle*, February 3, 1984.
129. Ibid.

130. "Regan Disowns Feldstein Report: Tells Senators to Throw It Away," *New York Times*, February 4, 1984.
131. "Opening Meeting on Deficit Fails to Resolve Differences," *New York Times*, February 9, 1984.
132. "Congressional Panels Intent on Reducing Budget Deficit," *Congressional Quarterly Weekly Report*, February 25, 1984, p. 439.
133. "That Monster Deficit," *Time* (March 5, 1984): 60.
134. Ibid.
135. Ibid., p. 61.
136. *The 1984 Joint Economic Report*, Joint Economic Committee (Washington, D.C.: GPO, 1984), Report no. 98–362, p. 23.
137. Ibid., p. 22.
138. Ibid., p. 30.
139. "Reagan Gives Up on 2-Party Talks," *New York Times*, March 14, 1984.
140. "Reagan, GOP Offer Big Plan to Cut Deficit," *San Francisco Chronicle*, March 16, 1984.
141. "Raising the Ante on Reagan's Deficit Plan," *New York Times*, May 27, 1984.
142. Ibid.
143. "A Process in Decline," *New York Times*, August 6, 1984.
144. "Congress Approves Spending Bill and Works to Raise Debt Limit," *New York Times*, October 11, 1984.

Selected Bibliography

Adams, Henry. *History of the United States of America during the Administrations of Jefferson and Madison.* Chicago: University of Chicago Press, 1967.

Adams, Henry C. *Public Debts: An Essay in the Science of Finance.* New York: D. Appleton, 1887.

Anton, Thomas J. "Roles and Symbols in the Determination of State Expenditures." *Midwest Journal of Political Science* 11 (February 1967): 27–43.

Banning, Lance. *The Jeffersonian Persuasion: Evolution of a Party Ideology.* Ithaca: Cornell University Press, 1978.

Barrett, Laurence I. *Gambling with History: Reagan in the White House.* New York: Penguin Books, 1984.

Basler, Roy, ed. *The Collected Works of Abraham Lincoln. Vol. VIII.* New Brunswick, N.J.: Rutgers University Press, 1953.

Basset, John Spencer. *The Life of Andrew Jackson.* New York: Archon Books, 1967.

Baxter, R. Dudley. *National Debts.* London: Robert John Bush, 1871.

Beard, Charles. *An Economic Interpretation of the Constitution of the United States.* New York: Macmillan, 1960.

Beard, Charles, and Mary Beard. *The Rise of American Civilization: Vol. II, The Industrial Era.* New York: Macmillan, 1962.

Beer, Samuel H. "The Idea of the Nation." *New Republic* July 19, 26, 1982: 23–29.

Bell, Daniel. "Models and Reality in Economic Discourse." *The Crisis of Economic Theory.* Ed. Daniel Bell and Irving Kristol. New York: Basic Books, 1981, 46–80.

Binney, J. E. D. *British Public Finance and Administration, 1774–92.* London: Oxford University Press, 1958.

Black, Gilbert, ed. *Theodore Roosevelt, 1858–1919.* Dobbs Ferry, N.Y.: Oceana Publications, 1969.

Blau, Joseph, ed. *Social Theories of Jacksonian Democracy*. New York: Bobbs-Merrill, 1954.

Bolles, Albert S. *The Financial History of the United States, from 1774 to 1789: Embracing the Period of the American Revolution*. New York: D. Appleton, 1879.

———. *The Financial History of the United States, from 1789 to 1860*. New York: D. Appleton, 1883.

———. *The Financial History of the United States, from 1861 to 1885*. New York: D. Appleton, 1886.

Borden, Morton, ed. *The Antifederalist Papers*. East Lansing: Michigan State University Press, 1965.

Braybrooke, David, and Charles Lindblom. *A Strategy of Decision*. New York: Free Press, 1970.

Brooks, Stephen. "A Balanced Budget, 1972–1978: What Would Have Happened?" *D.R.I. Readings in Macroeconomics*. Ed. Allan R. Sanderson. New York: McGraw-Hill, 1981.

Brown, E. Francis. "The American Road to Fascism." *Current History* (July 1933): 392–98.

Brunner, Karl, ed. "Keynesian Policies, the Drift into Permanent Deficits and the Growth of Government: A Symposium." *Journal of Monetary Economics* 4 (1978): 567–636.

Brunner, Ronald D. "Book Review." *Political Psychology* 5 (1984): 109–10.

Buchanan, James M. *Public Principles of Public Debt*. Homewood, Ill.: Richard D. Irwin, 1958.

Buchanan, James M., and Richard E. Wagner. *Democracy in Deficit: The Political Legacy of Lord Keynes*. New York: Academic Press, 1977.

———. *Fiscal Responsibility in Constitutional Democracy*. Boston: Martinus Nijhoff Social Sciences Division, 1978.

Burkhead, Jesse. "The Balanced Budget." *American Economic Association Readings in Fiscal Policy*. Vol. III. Ed. Arthur Smithies and J. Keith Butters. New York: Richard D. Irwin, 1955.

Burner, David. *The Politics of Provincialism: The Democratic Party in Transition, 1918–1932*. New York: Norton, 1975.

Burns, James MacGregor. *Roosevelt: The Lion and the Fox*. New York: Harcourt, Brace, 1956.

Cagan, Phillip. *Persistent Inflation: Historical and Policy Essays*. New York: Columbia University Press, 1979.

Campbell, John Creighton. *Contemporary Japanese Budget Politics*. Berkeley: University of California Press, 1977.

Cannon, Lou. *Reagan*. New York: Perigee Books, 1982.

Carlson, Keith M., and Roger Spencer. "Crowding Out and Its Critics." *Federal Reserve Bank of St. Louis, Review* (December 1975): 1–17.

Carson, Daniel C. "Bonds." *California Journal* (September 1984): 14–15.

Carter, Jimmy. *Keeping Faith: Memoirs of a President*. New York: Bantam Books, 1982.

Castells, Manuel. *The Economic Crisis and American Society*. Princeton, N.J.: Princeton University Press, 1980.

Cates, William C. *Where is the Free Lunch?? The Voter's Guide to Government Economic Policy*. New York: Thomond Press, 1980.

Cawelti, John G. *Apostles of the Self-Made Man: Changing Concepts of Success in America.* Chicago: University of Chicago Press, 1965.

Cooke, Jacob E., ed. *The Reports of Alexander Hamilton.* New York: Harper Torchbooks, 1964.

Crallé, Richard K., ed. *Reports and Public Letters of John C. Calhoun. Vol. III.* New York: Russell & Russell, 1968.

Croly, Herbert. *The Promise of American Life.* Indianapolis: Bobbs-Merrill, 1975.

Dale, Edwin L. "When Will It Be Safe to Balance the Budget?" *American Fiscal and Monetary Policy.* Ed. Harold Wolozin. Chicago: Quadrangle Books, 1970, 105–12.

Dallek, Robert. *Franklin D. Roosevelt and American Foreign Policy, 1932–1945.* New York: Oxford University Press, 1979.

———. *Ronald Reagan: The Politics of Symbolism.* Cambridge: Harvard University Press, 1984.

de Leeuw, Frank, and Thomas M. Hollaway. "Cyclical Adjustment of the Federal Debt." *Survey of Current Business* (December 1983): 25–40.

Dewey, Davis Rich. *Financial History of the United States.* London: Longmans, Green, 1920.

Dickson, P. G. M. *The Financial Revolution in England: A Study in the Development of Public Credit, 1688–1756.* New York: St. Martin's Press, 1967.

Dorfman, Joseph. *The Economic Mind in American Civilization, 1601–1865. Vol. I.* New York: Viking Press, 1953.

Dubnick, Mel, and Lynne Holt. "Industrial Policy and the States." *Publius* (Winter 1985): 113–29.

Dwyer, Gerald P. "Inflation and Government Deficits." *Economic Inquiry* 20 (1982): 315–29.

Eckstein, Otto, and Christopher Probyn. "Do Budget Deficits Matter?" *Data Resources U.S. Review* (December 1981): 1.9–1.15.

Edelman, Murray. *Political Language: Words that Succeed and Policies that Fail.* New York: Academic Press, 1977.

———. *The Symbolic Uses of Politics.* Urbana: University of Illinois Press, 1980.

———. "Political Language and Political Reality," *PS* (Winter 1985): 10–19.

Edsall, Thomas Byrne. *The New Politics of Inequality.* New York: Norton, 1984.

Ehrbar, A. F. "Monetization of Deficits." *National Bureau of Economic Research Digest* (May 1983): 1–2.

Eisner, Robert, and Paul J. Pieper. "A New View of the Federal Debt and Budget Deficits." *American Economic Review* 74 (March 1984): 11–29.

Elliot, Jonathan, ed. *Debates on the Adoption of the Federal Constitution in the Convention Held at Philadelphia, in 1787; with a Diary of the Debates of the Congress of the Convention: as Reported by James Madison, a Member and Deputy from Virginia.* Philadelphia: J. B. Lippincott, 1845.

Evans, Roland Jr., and Robert D. Novak. *Nixon in the White House: The Frustration of Power.* New York: Random House, 1971.

The Federalist Papers: Alexander Hamilton, James Madison, and John Jay. New York: New American Library, 1961.

Ferguson, E. James. *The Power of the Purse.* Chapel Hill: University of North Carolina Press, 1961.

Fine, Sidney. *Laissez Faire and the General-Welfare State.* Ann Arbor: University of Michigan Press, 1964.

Fiorina, Morris P. *Congress, Keystone of the Washington Establishment.* New Haven: Yale University Press, 1979.

Fisher, Louis. *Presidential Spending Power.* Princeton, N.J.: Princeton University Press, 1975.

Foner, Eric. *Free Soil, Free Labor, Free Men.* Oxford: Oxford University Press, 1979.

Ford, Paul Leicester, ed. *The Works of Thomas Jefferson. Vol. VIII.* New York: D. Appleton, 1887.

Forsythe, Dall W. *Taxation and Political Change in the Young Nation, 1781–1833.* New York: Columbia University Press, 1977.

Franklin, Benjamin. *A Modest Enquiry into the Nature and Necessity of a Paper Currency. The Great Issues in American History.* Ed. Clarence L. Ver Steeg and Richard Hofstadter. New York: Vintage, 1969.

Friedman, Benjamin. "Crowding Out or Crowding In? Economic Consequences of Financing Government Deficits." *Brookings Papers on Economic Activities* 3 (1978): 593–654.

Friedman, Milton, and Anna Schwartz. *A Monetary History of the United States.* Princeton, N.J.: Princeton University Press, 1963.

Gallatin, Albert. *Views of the Public Debt, Receipts, & Expenditures of the United States.* Philadelphia: Mathew Carly, 1801.

Goodnow, Frank. *Politics and Administration.* New York: Russell & Russell, 1967.

Goodrich, Carter. *Government Promotion of American Canals and Railroads, 1800–1890.* New York: Columbia University Press, 1960.

Goodwyn, Lawrence. *The Populist Moment: A Short History of the Agrarian Revolt in America.* Oxford: Oxford University Press, 1978.

Gordon, Robert Aaron. *Economic Instability & Growth.* New York: Harper & Row, 1974.

Gordon, Robert J. *Macroeconomics.* Boston: Little, Brown, 1978.

———. "'Credibility' vs. 'Mainstream': Two Views of the Inflation Process" *Inflation: Prospects and Remedies.* Washington, D.C.: Center for National Policy, 1983.

Greene, T. H., and T. H. Grose, eds. *Essays: Moral, Political, and Literary by David Hume.* London: Longmans, Green, 1875.

Greer, T. H. "The Depression of 1819–1821." Ph.D. dissertation, University of California, Berkeley, 1938.

Greider, William. "The Education of David Stockman." *Atlantic Monthly* 248 (December 1981): 27–54.

Guess, George, and Kenneth Koford. "Inflation, Recession and the Federal Budget Deficit (or, Blaming Economic Problems on a Statistical Mirage)." *Policy Sciences* 17 (1984): 385–400.

Gutman, Herbert. "The Failure of the Movement by the Unemployed for Public Works in 1873." *Political Science Quarterly* 80 (1965): 254–76.

Hammond, Bray. *Banks and Politics in America from the Revolution to the Civil War.* Princeton, N.J.: Princeton University Press, 1957.

———. *Sovereignty and an Empty Purse, Banks and Politics in the Civil War.* Princeton, N.J.: Princeton University Press, 1970.

Hamovitch, William, ed. *The Federal Deficit: Fiscal Imprudence or Policy Weapon?* Boston: D.C. Heath, 1965.

Hartz, Louis. *The Liberal Tradition in America.* New York: Harcourt, Brace & World, 1955.

Heilbroner, Robert. "Reflections: The Deficit." *New Yorker* (July 30, 1984): 47–55.

Hein, Scott E. "Deficits and Inflation." Federal Reserve Bank of St. Louis *Review,* 63 (March 1981): 3–10.

Heins, A. James. *Constitutional Restrictions Against State Debt.* Madison: University of Wisconsin Press, 1963.

Heller, Walter W. *New Dimensions of Political Economy.* Cambridge: Harvard University Press, 1967.

Helton, Roy. "Must America Go Fascist? Debt Threatens Democracy." *Harper's Magazine* 179 (June 1939): 1–9.

Hicks, John D. *Republican Ascendancy, 1921–1933.* New York: Harper Torchbooks, 1963.

Higginbotham, Don. *The War of American Independence.* Bloomington: Indiana University Press, 1977.

Hofstadter, Richard. *The Age of Reform.* New York: Vintage, 1955.

Hoover, Herbert. *The Memoirs of Herbert Hoover: The Great Depression, 1929–1941.* New York: Macmillan, 1952.

Horrigan, Brian, and Aris Protopapadakis. "Federal Deficits: A Faulty Gauge of Government's Impact on Financial Markets." Federal Reserve Bank of Philadelphia *Business Review,* (March–April 1982): 3–15.

Howe, Daniel Walker. *The Political Culture of the American Whigs.* Chicago: The University of Chicago Press, 1979.

Ippolito, Dennis. *Congressional Spending Power.* Ithaca: Cornell University Press, 1981.

Josephson, Matthew. *The Politicos, 1865–1896.* New York: Harcourt, Brace & World, 1966.

Josephy, Alvin M., Jr. *On the Hill: A History of the American Congress.* New York: Simon and Schuster, 1979.

Kearny, John Watts. *Sketch of American Finances: 1789–1835.* New York: Knickerbocker Press, 1887.

Keller, Morton. *Affairs of State: Public Life in Late Nineteenth Century America.* Cambridge: Harvard University Press, 1977.

Kemp, Jack. *An American Renassiance: A Strategy for the 1980s.* New York: Harper & Row, 1978.

Kenyon, Cecelia, ed. *The Antifederalists.* New York: Bobbs-Merrill, 1966.

Keynes, John Maynard. *The General Theory of Employment, Interest, and Money.* New York: Harcourt Brace Jovanovich, 1964.

Kimmel, Lewis. *Federal Budget and Fiscal Policy, 1789–1958.* Washington, D.C.: Brookings Institution, 1959.

King, Donald Frederick. "From Redistributive to Hegemonic Logic: The Transformation of American Tax Politics, 1894–1963." *Politics & Society* 12 (1983): 1–52.

Koch, Adrienne, and William Peder, eds. *The Life and Selected Writings of Thomas Jefferson.* New York: Modern Library, 1944.

Kolko, Gabriel. *The Triumph of Conservatism.* New York: Free Press, 1963.

———. *Railroads and Regulations, 1877–1916.* New York: Norton, 1970.

Leibenstein, Harvey. "Microeconomics and X-Efficiency Theory." *The Crisis in Economic Theory.* Ed. Daniel Bell and Irving Kristol. New York: Basic Books, 1981, 97–110.

Letwin, William, ed. A Documentary History of American Economic Policy since 1789. New York: Norton, 1972.

———. Law and Economic Policy in America: The Evolution of the Sherman Antitrust Act. Chicago: University of Chicago Press, 1981.

Leuchtenburg, William E. Franklin D. Roosevelt and the New Deal, 1932–1940. New York: Harper & Row, 1963.

Levy, Leonard W., ed. Essays on the Making of the Constitution. New York: Oxford University Press, 1969.

Levy, Mickey. "Factors Affecting Monetary Policy in an Era of Inflation." Journal of Monetary Economics 8 (1981): 351–73.

Link, Arthur S. Woodrow Wilson and the Progressive Era. New York: Harper Torchbooks, 1963.

Lipson, Leslie. The Democratic Civilization. Oxford: Oxford University Press, 1964.

Lowi, Theodore. The End of Liberalism. New York: Norton, 1979.

Lustig, R. Jeffrey. Corporate Liberalism. Berkeley: University of California Press, 1982.

McConnell, Grant. The Decline of Agrarian Democracy. New York: Atheneum, 1977.

McCoy, Drew R. The Elusive Republic: Political Economy in Jeffersonian America. New York: Norton, 1980.

McFaul, John. The Politics of Jacksonian Finance. Ithaca: Cornell University Press, 1972.

McFeely, William S. Grant. New York: Norton, 1982.

McGrane, Reginald. Foreign Bondholders and American State Debts. New York: Macmillan, 1935.

MacLaury, Bruce K. "Which Way to a Balanced Budget?" Brookings, the Brookings Bulletin 16 (Summer 1979): 1–5.

Madison, James. The Journal of the Debates which Framed the Constitution of the United States: May–September, 1787. Ed. Gaillard Hunt. New York: Knickerbocker Press, 1908.

Main, Jackson Turner. The Antifederalists: Critics of the Constitution, 1781–1788. Chapel Hill: University of North Carolina Press, 1961.

———. Political Parties before the Constitution. New York: Norton, 1974.

Mandel, Ernest. Late Capitalism. London: NLB. Atlantic Highlands, N.J.: Humanities Press, 1975.

Marx, Leo. The Machine in the Garden. New York: Oxford University Press, 1964.

Meyer, Marvin. The Jacksonian Persuasion: Politics and Beliefs. Stanford, Calif.: Stanford University Press, 1957.

Miller, James A., and James D. Range. "Reconciling an Irreconcilable Budget: The New Politics of the Budgetary Process." Harvard Journal on Legistlation 20 (1983): 4–30.

Mills, Gregory B., and John L. Palmer. The Deficit Dilemma: Budget Policy in the Reagan Era. Washington, D.C.: Urban Institute Press, 1984.

Motley, Brian. "Real Interest Rates, Money and Government Deficits." Federal Reserve Bank of San Francisco Economic Review (Summer 1983): 31–43.

Nash, Gary B. The Urban Crucible: Social Change, Political Consciousness, and the Origins of the American Revolution. Cambridge: Harvard University Press, 1979. paper money + debt.

Nathan, Richard P., and Fred C. Doolittle. "The Untold Story of Reagan's 'New Federalism.'" *The Public Interest* 75 (Fall 1984): 96–105.

Niskanen, William A. "Deficits, Government Spending, and Inflation: What Is the Evidence." *Journal of Monetary Economics* 4 (1978): 591–602.

Nixon, Richard M. *Six Crises*. Garden City, N.Y.: Doubleday, 1962.

Noyes, Alexander Dana. *Forty Years of American Finance*. New York: G. P. Putnam's Sons, Knickerbocker Press, 1909.

Nugent, Walter T. K. *The Money Question during Reconstruction*. New York: Norton, 1967.

O'Connor, James. *The Fiscal Crisis of the State*. New York: St. Martin's Press, 1973.

Okun, Arthur M. *The Political Economy of Prosperity*. New York: Norton, 1970.

Ott, David J., and Attiat F. Ott. *Federal Budget Policy*. Washington, D.C.: Brookings Institution, 1977.

Padover, Saul K. *The Complete Jefferson*. New York: Duell, Sloan & Pearce, 1943.

Palmer, Bruce. *"Man over Money": The Southern Populist Critique of American Capitalism*. Chapel Hill: University of North Carolina Press, 1980.

Palmer, John L., and Isabel V. Sawhill. *The Reagan Record*. Cambridge: Ballinger, 1984.

———., eds. *The Reagan Experiment*. Washington, D.C.: Urban Institute Press, 1982.

Pancake, John S., ed. *Thomas Jefferson: Revolutionary Philosopher, A Selection of Writings*. Woodbury, N.Y.: Barron's, 1976.

Pastor, Robert A. *Congress and the Politics of U.S. Foreign Economic Policy*. Berkeley: University of California Press, 1980.

Patterson, Robert T. *Federal Debt Management Policies, 1865–1879*. Durham, N.C.: Duke University Press, 1954.

Peterson, Paul E. "The New Politics of Deficits." *The New Direction in American Politics*. Ed. John E. Chubb and Paul E. Peterson. Washington, D.C.: Brookings Institution, 1985, 365–397.

Phillips, Kevin. *Post-Conservative America: People, Politics, & Ideology in a Time of Crisis*. New York: Vintage Books, 1983.

Pierce, James L. "Interest Rates and Their Prospects in the Recovery." *Brookings Papers on Economic Activity* 1 (1975): 89–122.

Pitkin, Hanna Fenichel. *The Concept of Representation*. Berkeley: University of California Press, 1967.

Pocock, J. G. A. *The Machiavellian Moment: Florentine Political Thought and the Atlantic Republican Tradition*. Princeton, N.J.: Princeton University Press, 1975.

Pollack, Norman. *The Populist Response to Industrial America*. Cambridge: Harvard University Press, 1976.

Post, Gordon C., ed. *A Disquisition on Government and Selections from the Discourse, by John C. Calhoun*. New York: Bobbs-Merrill, 1953.

Rabushka, Alvin. *A Compelling Case for a Constitutional Amendment to Balance the Budget and Limit Taxes*. Washington, D.C.: Taxpayers Foundation, 1982.

Ratchford, B. U. *American State Debts*. Durham: Duke University Press, 1941.

Reagan, John H. *Memoirs: With Special Reference to Secession and the Civil War*. New York: Neale, 1906.

Remini, Robert V. *Andrew Jackson and the Bank War*. New York: Norton, 1967.

———. *Andrew Jackson and the Course of American Freedom, 1822–1832.* Vol. II. New York: Harper & Row, 1981.

Rezneck, Samuel. "Distress Relief, and the Discontent in the United States during the Depression of 1873–78." *Journal of Political Economy* 58 (1950): 494–512.

Roberts, Paul Craig. *The Supply-Side Revolution: An Insider's Account of Policymaking in Washington.* Cambridge: Harvard University Press, 1984.

Roley, V. Vance. "The Financing of Federal Deficits: An Analysis of Crowding Out." Federal Reserve Bank of Kansas City *Economic Review* (July–August 1981): 16–29.

Roosevelt, Elliot, ed. *F.D.R.: His Personal Letters, 1905–1928.* New York: Duell, Sloan and Pearce, 1948.

Roosevelt, Theodore. *An Autobiography.* New York: Charles Scribner's Sons, 1921.

Rose, Richard, and Guy Peters. *Can Government Go Bankrupt?* New York: Basic Books, 1978.

Rosenman, Samuel, ed. *The Public Papers of Franklin Delano Roosevelt.* Vol. I, *The Genius of the New Deal, 1928–1932.* New York: Random House, 1938.

Sampson, Anthony. *The Money Lenders: The People and Politics of the World Banking Crisis.* New York: Penguin Books, 1981.

Sapir, Edward. "Symbolism." *The Encyclopedia of the Social Sciences.* New York: Macmillan, 1934, 492–95.

Sargent, Thomas, J. "The Ends of Four Big Inflations." Working Paper 158, Federal Reserve Bank of Minneapolis, Revised May 1981.

———. "Stopping Moderate Inflation: The Methods of Poincaré and Thatcher." In *Inflation, Debt, and Indexation.* Ed. Rudiger Dornbusch and Mario Henrique Simonsen. Cambridge, Mass.: MIT Press, 1983, 54–96.

Schick, Allen. *Congress and Money.* Washington, D.C.: Urban Institute, 1980.

Schiesl, Martin J. *The Politics of Efficiency.* Berkeley: University of California Press, 1977.

Schlesinger, Arthur M., Jr. *The Age of Jackson.* Boston: Little, Brown, 1945.

———. *The Crisis of the Old Order, 1919–1933.* Boston: Houghton Mifflin, 1957.

Schultz, William J., and M. R. Caine. "Federalist Finance." *Hamilton and the National Debt.* Ed. George R. Taylor. Boston: D.C. Heath, 1950, 1–8.

Schumacher, E. F. *Small Is Beautiful: Economics as if People Mattered.* New York: Harper & Row, 1973.

Sears, David O., and Jack Citrin. *Tax Revolt: Something for Nothing in California.* Cambridge: Harvard University Press, 1982.

Seligman, Edwin R. A. *The Income Tax: A Study of the History, Theory, and Practice of Income Taxation at Home and Abroad.* New York: Macmillan, 1911.

Sharkey, Robert P. *Money, Class, and Party: An Economic Study of Civil War and Reconstruction.* Baltimore: The Johns Hopkins University Press, 1967.

Siegel, Frederick F. *Troubled Journey: From Pearl Harbor to Ronald Reagan.* New York: Hill and Wang, 1984.

Simon, Herbert. *Administrative Behavior.* New York: Free Press, 1967.

Sinclair, Barbara. *Majority Leadership in the U.S. House.* Baltimore: The Johns Hopkins University Press, 1983.

Skowronek, Stephen. *Building a New American State: The Expansion of National Administrative Capacities, 1877–1920.* Cambridge: Cambridge University Press, 1982.

Smith, Adam. *The Wealth of Nations.* London: Penguin Books, 1981.

Smith, Edward Conrad, ed. *The Constitution of the United States.* New York: Harper & Row, 1972.

Smith, Steven S. "Budget Battles of 1981: The Role of Majority Party Leadership." *American Politics and Public Policy.* Ed. Allan Sindler. Washington, D.C.: Congressional Quarterly, 1984, 43–78.

Solow, Robert M. "The Intelligent Citizen's Guide to Inflation." *Public Interest* 38 (1975): 30–66.

Stampp, Kenneth. *The Era of Reconstruction, 1865–1877.* New York: Vintage, 1965.

Stein, Herbert. *The Fiscal Revolution in America.* Chicago: University of Chicago Press, 1969.

———. "Balancing the Budget." *Contemporary Economic Problems, 1979.* Ed. W. Fellner. Washington, D.C.: American Enterprise Institute, 1979, 191–231.

———. *Presidential Economics.* New York: Simon & Schuster, 1984.

Stewart, Charles Haines III. "The Politics of Structural Reform: Reforming Budgetary Structure in the House, 1861–1921." Ph.D. dissertation, Stanford University, 1985.

Storing, Herbert. *What the Anti-Federalists Were For.* Chicago: University of Chicago Press, 1981.

Summers, Mark W. *Railroads, Reconstruction, and the Gospel of Prosperity.* Princeton, N.J.: Princeton University Press, 1984.

Sundquist, James L. *Politics and Policy: The Eisenhower, Kennedy, and Johnson Years.* Washington, D.C.: Brookings Institution, 1968.

———. *Dynamics of the Party System.* Washington, D.C.: Brookings Institution, 1973.

Sundquist, James L., and David W. Davis. *Making Federalism Work.* Washington, D.C.: Brookings Institution, 1969.

Taussig, F. W. *The History of the Tariff, 1860–1883.* New York: G. P. Putnam's Sons, 1885.

———. *The Tariff History of the United States.* New York: G. P. Putnam's Sons, 1923.

Taylor, George Rogers, ed. *Hamilton and the National Debt.* Boston: D. C. Heath, 1950.

Temin, Peter. *The Jacksonian Economy.* New York: Norton, 1969.

Thurow, Lester. *The Zero-Sum Society.* New York: Penguin Books, 1980.

Tobin, James. "A Keynesian View of the Budget Deficit." *California Management Review* 26 (Winter 1984): 7–14.

Van Deusen, Glyndon G. *The Jacksonian Era, 1828–1848.* New York: Harper & Row, 1959.

Viguerie, Richard A. *The New Right: We're Ready to Lead.* Falls Church, Va.: Viguerie Company, 1980.

Waite, Charles A., and Joseph C. Wakefield. "Federal Fiscal Programs." *Survey of Current Business* (February 1980): 12–17.

Wakefield, Joseph C. "Federal Budget Developments." *Survey of Current Business* (August 1983): 11–13.

Wander, William Thomas. "Patterns of Change in the Congressional Budget Process, 1865–1974." Paper, American Political Science Association, September, 6, 1981.

Warren, Charles. *The Making of the Constitution.* Boston: Little, Brown, 1928.

Webber, Carolyn C. "Development of Ideas about Balanced Budgets." *How to*

Limit Government Spending. Ed. Aaron Wildavsky. Berkeley: University of California Press, 1980.

Weicher, John C., ed. *Maintaining the Safety Net*. Washington, D.C.: American Enterprise Institute, 1984.

Weigley, Russell F. *The American Way of War*. Bloomington: Indiana University Press, 1975.

Weissman, Rudolph L., ed. *Economic Balance and a Balanced Budget: Public Papers of Marriner S. Eccles*. New York: Harper & Brothers, 1940.

Welter, Rush. *The Mind of America, 1820–1860*. New York: Columbia University Press, 1975.

West, Robert Craig. *Banking Reform and the Federal Reserve, 1863–1923*. Ithaca: Cornell University Press, 1977.

White, Leondard D. *The Federalists: A Study in Administrative History, 1789–1801*. New York: Free Press, 1965.

———. *The Jeffersonians: A Study in Administrative History, 1801–1829*. New York: Free Press, 1965.

———. *The Jacksonians: A Study in Administrative History, 1829–1861*. New York: Free Press, 1965.

Wildavsky, Aaron B. *How to Limit Government Spending*. Berkeley: University of California Press, 1980.

———. "Budgeting as Compromises among Social Orders." *The Federal Budget: Economics and Politics*. Ed. Michael J. Boskin and Aaron B. Wildavsky. San Francisco: Institute for Contemporary Studies, 1982, 21–38.

———. "The Budget as New Social Contract." *Journal of Contemporary Studies* 5 (Spring 1982): 3–19.

———. "The Once and Future School of Public Policy." *Public Interest* 79 (Spring 1985): 25–41.

Wilkeson, Samuel. *How Our National Debt May Be a National Blessing: The Debt is Public Wealth, Political Union, Protection of Industry, Secure Basis for National Currency, the Orphans' and Widows' Savings Fund*. Philadelphia: M'Lauglin Brothers, 1865.

Willes, Mark. " 'Rational Expectations' as a Counterrevolution." *The Crisis in Economic Theory*. Ed. Daniel Bell and Irving Kristol. New York: Basic Books, 1981, 81–96.

Wood, Gordon S. *The Creation of the American Republic, 1776–1787*. New York: Norton, 1969.

Young, James Sterling. *The Washington Community, 1800–1828*. New York: Harcourt, Brace & World, 1966.

Index

Library of Congress Cataloging-in-Publication Data
Savage, James D., 1951–
     Balanced budgets and American politics / James D. Savage. p.   cm.
     Bibliography: p.
     Includes index.
     ISBN 0–8014–2047–4
     1. Budget—United States—History.   2. Budget deficits—United
States—History.   3. Deficit financing—United States—History.
4. United States—Politics and government.   I. Title.
HJ2050.S28   1988
339.5'23'0973—dc19   87–25061